P9-DUU-270

*Arctic Ocean*

Barrow

**Arctic and Western Alaska**
Pages 218–235

**Eastern Interior Alaska**
Pages 180–201

ARCTIC AND WESTERN ALASKA

Fairbanks

Eagle

WESTERN INTERIOR ALASKA

EASTERN INTERIOR ALASKA

**Western Interior Alaska**
Pages 156–179

SOUTHWEST ALASKA

ANCHORAGE

Valdez

PRINCE WILLIAM SOUND

Seward

Dillingham

THE KENAI PENINSULA

Kodiak

*Gulf of Alaska*

Juneau

SOUTHEAST ALASKA

Ketchikan

**Southeast Alaska**
Pages 124–155

*Pacific Ocean*

# DK EYEWITNESS TRAVEL

# Alaska

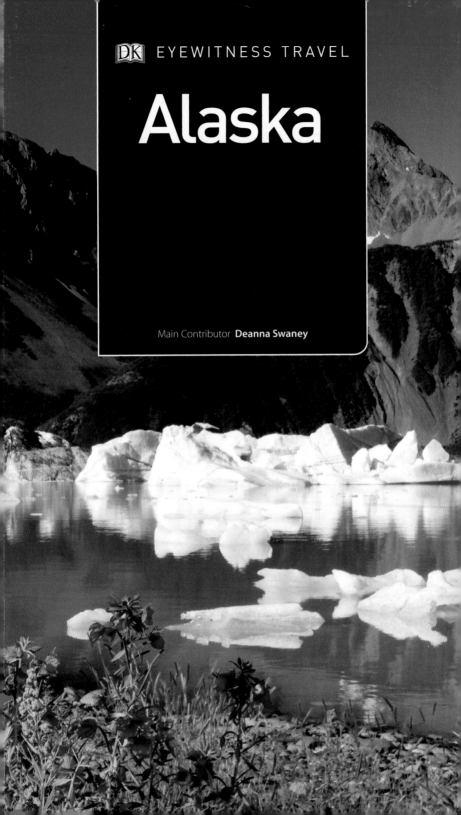

# DK EYEWITNESS TRAVEL

# Alaska

Main Contributor **Deanna Swaney**

**Managing Editor** Aruna Ghose
**Art Editor** Priyanka Thakur
**Project Editor** Ankita Awasthi
**Project Designer** Mathew Kurien
**Editor** Arundhti Bhanot
**Designer** Baishakhee Sengupta
**Senior Cartographer** Uma Bhattacharya
**Cartographer** Alok Pathak
**Senior Picture Researcher**
Taiyaba Khatoon
**Picture Researcher** Sumita Khatwani
**DTP Coordinator** Shailesh Sharma
**DTP Designers** Vinod Harish,
Azeem Siddiqui

**Contributors**
Deanna Swaney, Eric Amrine

**Photographers**
Nigel Hicks, Andrew Holligan

**Illustrators**
Arun Pottirayil, Madhav Raman,
T. Gautam Trivedi

Printed and bound in China

First American Edition, 2006
17 18 19 20 10 9 8 7 6 5 4 3 2 1

Published in the United States by
DK Publishing, 345 Hudson Street,
New York, New York 10014

**Reprinted with revisions 2008, 2010,
2012, 2015, 2017**

Copyright © 2006, 2017 Dorling Kindersley
Limited, London
A Penguin Random House Company

Published in the UK by Dorling Kindersley
Limited.

A catalog record for this book is available
from the Library of Congress.

ISSN 1542-1554
ISBN: 978-1-4654-6050-9

Floors are referred to throughout in
accordance with American usage;
ie the "first floor" is the ground level.

MIX
Paper from
responsible sources
FSC™ C018179
www.fsc.org

Alaskan totem pole detail

# Introducing Alaska

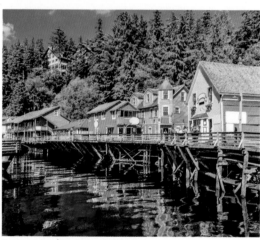

Creek Street's historic broadwalk in Ketchikan, Alaska

---

**The information in this
DK Eyewitness Travel Guide is checked regularly.**
Every effort has been made to ensure that this book is as up-to-date as possible
at the time of going to press. Some details, however, such as telephone numbers,
opening hours, prices, gallery hanging arrangements and travel information are
liable to change. The publishers cannot accept responsibility for any consequences
arising from the use of this book, nor for any material on third party websites, and
cannot guarantee that any website address in this book will be a suitable source of
travel information. We value the views and suggestions of our readers very highly.
Please write to: Publisher, DK Eyewitness Travel Guides, Dorling Kindersley,
80 Strand, London, WC2R 0RL, UK, or email: travelguides@dk.com.

---

◀ **Title page** Fireweed on the shore of Bear Glacier Lake, Kenai Fjords National Park  **Front cover image** Cabin on shore of Tangle
Lake, Alaska  **Back cover image** Ice and debris from a calving glacier dot scenic Glacier Bay in Alaska

# Contents

Downtown Anchorage, Alaska, and its reflection into Cook Inlet

The historical town of Kennicott in the Eastern Interior

# HOW TO USE THIS GUIDE

This guide helps you get the most from your visit to Alaska with expert recommendations and detailed practical information. The first section, *Introducing Alaska,* maps the state and sets it in its historical and cultural context. *Alaska Area by Area* focuses first on Alaska's largest city, Anchorage, then on the state's main regions, with all the major towns and important sights described and illustrated in rich detail. Restaurant and hotel recommendations and information about cruising the coastlines, hiking in the interior, and other outdoor activities can be found in *Travelers' Needs.* The *Survival Guide* contains practical tips on everything, from transport around the country to the Alaskan word for "Great!"

## Anchorage

The first section of *Alaska Area by Area* concentrates on the vibrant, culturally rich city of Anchorage and its municipality, from the sights and bustle of the historic center to places of interest in the wider city and the rural communities, historical attractions, and many areas of outstanding natural beauty in the surrounding landscape.

**Colored thumb tabs** continue through the extent of each section.

**1 Introduction** The city's geographical setting and economic life are described, as well as its historical development and features of interest to the visitor.

**A country map** shows the city's location in Alaska.

**2 City Map** For easy reference, the sights are numbered and located on a map. The main streets, bus stations and railway stations, parking areas, and civic buildings are also shown.

**Sights at a Glance** lists the city's sights by category, from historic buildings to hip neighborhoods, parks and outlying wilderness areas, museums, theaters, and other visitor attractions.

**3 Detailed Information** All the sights in the city are described individually. Addresses, telephone numbers, opening hours, admission charges, and information on how to get there are given for each sight. The key to symbols is shown on the back flap.

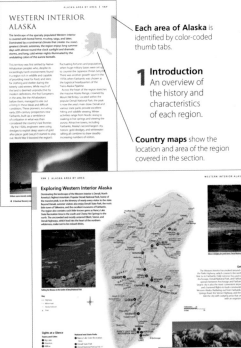

Each area of Alaska is identified by color-coded thumb tabs.

**1 Introduction**
An overview of the history and characteristics of each region.

**Country maps** show the location and area of the region covered in the section.

## Alaska Region by Region

In the chapters that follow the section on Anchorage, the state is divided into seven main regions. The map on the inside front cover shows these regional divisions. The most interesting places to visit are given on the Regional Map at the beginning of each chapter.

**2 Regional Map** This shows the main road network and gives an illustrated overview of the whole region. Interesting places to visit are numbered and there are useful tips on getting around.

**Practical information** at the start of each entry includes a map reference relating to the road map that appears on the inside back cover.

**3 Detailed Information** All the important towns and other places to visit are dealt with individually. They are listed in order, following the numbering given on the Regional Map. Each entry also contains practical information such as map references, addresses, telephone numbers, and opening times.

**Story boxes** explore some of the region's historical and cultural topics in detail.

**The Visitors' Checklist** provides a summary of the practical information you need to plan your visit.

**4 Alaska's Top Sights** These are given two or more full pages. All the important features of interest are highlighted.

**Expanded maps** and other illustrations make orientation easy.

# INTRODUCING ALASKA

# DISCOVERING ALASKA

The following tours have been created to take in a number of Alaska's highlights. In an area as vast and rugged as Alaska, some long-distance journeys are needed to reach more remote locations such as the Arctic; however, the itineraries are designed to keep travel time and distance realistic. To begin with, there are two three-day city tours, covering the most popular city, Anchorage, and its neighbor Seward. These tours can be taken on their own or combined to form a seven- or ten-day tour taking in the scenic Kenai Peninsula. The Kenai tour is followed by two seven-day itineraries encompassing the wildest and most scenic parts of the state: the far north and Arctic, and the Gold Rush Territory to the east. Pick, choose, and combine at your leisure.

**Aurora borealis**
A winter trip to Alaska can be made magical by the appearance of the aurora borealis, or Northern Lights.

0 kilometers      300

0 miles      300

Barrow

Prudhoe
Deadhors

Colville

Gates of the Arctic
National Park

Wise

Arctic Circle

Coldfoot
Koyukak River

Koyukuk

Arctic Circle Sign
Finger Mountain
Yukon River and
Trans-Alaska Pipeline

Yukon    Arctic Circle Trading Post

**Fairbanks**

See Kenai Peninsula
inset map

Anchorage

## A Week in the Far North and Arctic

- Experience the pristine wilderness of Alaska's far northern territory.

- Cross the line to get your official Arctic Circle Certificate.

- Visit a working oilfield, try your hand at panning for gold, and hear stories of survival in this harshest of climates.

- Watch a dog sled team train, and visit a Native village to meet with the elders.

- Brave the cold to catch the mesmerising Northern Lights across the sky.

**The Trans-Alaska Pipeline**
An astonishing feat of engineering, the pipeline crosses some of the most barren landscapes of North America, carrying the "black gold."

## A Week in Gold Rush Territory

- Tour the mighty Mendenhall Glacier, and hike along rainforest trails beside waterfalls and streams.

- Learn how thousands of prospectors staked their lives on dreams of gold.

- Ride the Alaska Marine Highway for the scenic cruise of a lifetime.

- Follow the prospecting trail on the White Pass railroad north to Canada's Yukon, site of the great Klondike Gold Rush.

- Visit Native galleries for high-quality arts and crafts.

- Learn about the extraordinary blending of Russian and American cultures in one of Alaska's most beautiful towns.

- Catch your own salmon or halibut; eat it fresh, or have it shipped home.

**The Yukon Route** A narrow-gauge railway follows the gold rush trail over the awesome White Pass summit.

### Key

— Far North and Arctic tour

— Gold Rush Territory tour

— Kenai Peninsula tour

## Outdoor Adventures in the Kenai Peninsula

- Take cruises and hikes to get close up to glaciers.

- Meet harbor seals, sea lions, and a giant octopus at the superb Alaska SeaLife Center.

- Make a helicopter trip to try your hand at dog-mushing.

- Practice your skills at fishing or sea-kayaking.

- Spot wildlife with the help of experienced guides on a river float trip.

- Browse local art galleries and see craftsmen at work; shop for unique souvenirs.

**Glacial majesty** Tour boats sail thrillingly close to the ice face, while everyone hopes to see the spectacle of the glacier calving.

## 3 Days in Anchorage

*Anchorage is a year-round destination with once-in-a-lifetime experiences. It's the most-visited city in Alaska.*

- **Arriving** Ted Stevens Anchorage International Airport is just 15 minutes' drive from downtown. Rent a car at the airport, or take the excellent bus or shuttle services into the city.
- **Getting around** Downtown Anchorage is easily explored on foot, but a car is convenient for further afield.

### Day 1
**Morning** A few days in the state's largest city gives you enough time to enjoy the main sights. Spend your first morning visiting the **Anchorage Museum** (see pp72–3) to get grounded in the city's history and its connection to Native American tribes, gold miners, and modern pioneers. Stop for a leisurely lunch downtown in the area along 5th and 6th Streets, where brewpubs, fine restaurants and casual cafés cluster.

**Afternoon** Lace up your boots for a hike or rent a bike to enjoy the **Tony Knowles Coastal Trail** (see pp78–9), a gentle, paved trail that winds 11 miles (18 km) from downtown through pristine forests and streams. End the day with a drink at one of the pubs overlooking **Lake Hood** (see p79).

### Day 2
**Morning** Take a city trolley tour to get an overview of the city, or book a flightseeing tour for a bird's-eye view of the entire city and the top of Denali. If visiting on a summer weekend stop in at the **Anchorage Market** (see p74) and have lunch in the Eat Local section, with Alaska-grown produce, seafood, and meats. Or, in winter, shop where the locals do at the **5th Avenue Mall** (see p93), with major national stores and shops showcasing Alaskan products.

**Afternoon** Take a shuttle bus or drive to the excellent **Alaska Zoo** (see p80) to see and learn more about the state's wildlife, including grizzly bears and mighty moose. Another option is a salmon-fishing cruise, where you're guaranteed to land a delicious fish, prepared at the dock ready for eating or shipping back home. End the day with live theater or music at the **Center for Performing Arts** (see p94).

### Day 3
**Morning** Pay a visit to the **Alaska Native Heritage Center** (see pp76–7), a famous educational and cultural center that celebrates the arts and traditions of the state's 11 major native cultural groups. Be sure to visit the six full-sized Native dwellings built on the shores of Lake Tiulana. Watch Native artists demonstrating their work.

**Afternoon** Take a small-boat cruise from Whittier through Prince William Sound, during which you'll glide past hundreds of glaciers, very likely spot black bears on the shore, and view myriad species of seabirds.

## 3 Days in Seward

*Located on the southern coast, Seward is home to one of Alaska's oldest communities and is surrounded by spectacular scenery.*

- **Arriving** Seward is a short flight from Anchorage, but the 120-mile (190-km) drive from Anchorage south to Seward is magnificent, taking you along the dramatic coastline of Turnagain Arm.
- **Moving on** Drive back to Anchorage, or to Cooper Landing to extend the trip. Or, fly back to Anchorage from Kenai Municipal Airport.

### Day 1
**Morning** After your trip from Anchorage, head for one of the many casual restaurants on the **waterfront** (see p102) for an early lunch of freshly caught salmon or other fish. Stretch your legs with a stroll around the downtown historic district to visit some of the quaint shops and art galleries.

**Afternoon** Book a helicopter for a flight to a dog camp at the top of one of the nearby glaciers. Glide across the snow and glacial ice with a team of working dogs, play with husky puppies, and hear trail stories from your Alaskan musher. Dine at your hotel.

### Day 2
Take a day-cruise into **Kenai Fjords National Park** (see pp106–7), where you'll view wildlife, see tidewater glaciers; and enjoy a sumptuous buffet ashore at Fox Island, in the private Fox Island Lodge. National Park rangers give a presentation on the area's wildlife, which includes many different types of whales, seals, sea lions, otters, and porpoises.

The Tony Knowles Coastal Trail, popular with walkers, joggers, and cyclists

For practical information on getting around Alaska's cities see pp280–91

The icy tongue of Exit Glacier, spilling down from the Harding icefield west of Seward

## Day 3

**Morning** Take a hike around **Exit Glacier** (see p103) for some of the best, most expansive views of this mammoth icefield. Alternately, visit the birds, marine mammals, and other residents at the **Alaska SeaLife Center** (see pp104–5), Alaska's only public aquarium and a world-class marine research and wildlife rescue center.

**Afternoon** Back to Anchorage, or drive on to Cooper Landing; see Day 3 of the Kenai Peninsula tour (below).

## Outdoor Adventures in the Kenai Peninsula

- **Duration** 7 days
- **Airports** Ted Stevens Anchorage International Airport, Kenai Municipal Airport
- **Transport** Renting a car allows you to stop as often as you like to view the scenery and wildlife. Tour buses also offer frequent trips and options.

## Days 1 and 2: Seward
Arriving from Anchorage, select two days from the 3-day Seward tour (see facing page and above).

## Day 3: Cooper Landing
Make your way to **Cooper Landing** (see p100), at the confluence of Kenai Lake and the Kenai River, and fuel up with lunch at your hotel when you arrive. Spend the afternoon with expert guides on a float trip through the turquoise waters of the Upper Kenai River, passing through scenic wilderness and viewing wildlife. Dinner in Cooper Landing, perhaps at a roadhouse overlooking the river.

## Day 4: Homer
Pack a lunch and make tracks for **Homer** (see pp112–13) along the Sterling Highway, with sweeping views of Cook Inlet, mountains, and volcanoes. Visit the Alaska Islands and Oceans Visitor Center (and pick up a Hiking Trails Map) as you come into town. Take an afternoon stroll along the **Homer Spit** (see p113), a long narrow finger of land jutting into Kachemak Bay, pausing at the shops, galleries and pubs to enjoy the life of this artisan community. Select one of the restaurants for dinner.

## Day 5: Homer
Three excellent options for an all-day excursion all involve fun on Kachemak Bay: a boat cruise to fish for halibut, with lunch provided on board; a boat cruise to **Halibut Cove** (see p113), with lunch and dinner provided; or sea-kayaking along coast, with lunch provided.

## Days 6: Homer
Visit the **Pratt Museum** (see p112), which specializes in early homesteading, Native Alaskan traditions, and local art, or the contemporary **Bunnell Strett Arts Center** (see p112), then lunch nearby. Afterwards, take a water taxi to **Kachemak Bay State Park** (see p113) and enjoy an easy 3.5 mile (6 km) hike on the Grewingk Lake Glacier Trail, above the forest to the foot of a glacier. Dinner at your hotel.

## Day 7: Homer back to Anchorage
Breakfast in town (and pack a box lunch) before making a leisurely return journey to Anchorage, stopping along the spectacular **Turnagain Arm** (see pp84–5). As you approach the city lights, see nesting birds from the boardwalks on Potter Marsh, before heading back to Anchorage for a pleasant dinner.

The Harrington Cabin, reconstructing life on a 1940s homestead, at Homer's Pratt Museum

## A Week in the Far North and Arctic

- **Airports** Ted Stevens Anchorage International Airport is the departure point for an early morning flight to Fairbanks, your base for venturing into the Arctic.

- **Transport** In Fairbanks, several tour companies offer tours along the famous Dalton Highway, the only highway in the US to cross the mighty Yukon River and to connect the highway system to the Arctic Ocean.

### Day 1: Arctic Circle

Arrive in **Fairbanks** *(see pp174-8)* and join a tour north toward Prudhoe Bay. Stop at the Arctic Circle Trading Post on the Elliott Highway before turning onto Alaska's great wilderness road, the **Dalton Highway** *(see pp222–3)*. View the mighty **Yukon River** *(see pp174–8)* and the **Trans-Alaska Pipeline** *(see pp174–8)*, then cross the Arctic Circle to get your official Arctic Circle Certificate. Overnight at the Yukon Crossing or Coldfoot.

### Day 2: Coldfoot

In summer, take a scenic float down the Middle Fork of the Koyukak River, stopping along the shore for a barbecue lunch.

The remote Dalton Highway, stretching across northern Alaska

If it's winter, book a dog sled adventure or take a bus trip to a viewing station for a chance to glimpse the aurora borealis, or Northern Lights. Be prepared, though – this is officially the coldest place in North America.

### Day 3: Coldfoot to Prudhoe Bay

Continue along the Dalton Highway to **Prudhoe Bay** *(see p224)*, with spectacular views into Gates of the Arctic National Park and the Arctic National Wildlife Refuge. After crossing the precipitous **Atigun Pass** *(see p223)*, scan the vast Arctic tundra for caribou, musk oxen, wolves, bears, and peregrines. End the day with a buffet dinner in Deadhorse.

### Day 4: Prudhoe Bay

Visit the oilfields, with lunch at a restaurant that caters to the rough-and-ready oilfield workers. Get a taste of the real north by dipping your toe in the frigid waters of the Arctic Ocean. Overnight in Deadhorse.

### Day 5: Wiseman

Return south toward Coldfoot, stopping en route to stroll through the historic gold-mining village of **Wiseman** *(see p224)*, the only community that is occupied year-round along the Dalton Highway and not dedicated to oilfield enterprises.

### Day 6: Finger Mountain

Head back down the Dalton Highway for a hike at **Finger Mountain** *(see p222)*. Admire the tundra wildflowers and grand views, then return to Fairbanks for a hearty dinner at a restaurant along the Chena River.

### Day 7: Fairbanks

Enjoy a **Riverboat Discovery** *(see p175)* cruise and learn about life at an Athabaskan Indian village. Take a vintage train to pan for gold at **Gold Dredge No. 8** *(see p178)*. Visit the **University of Alaska Museum of the North** *(see p175)*, one of Alaska's top 10 attractions. Alternatively, fly to **Barrow** *(see pp226–7)* for a glimpse of Native culture and an excursion to the northernmost point in the US.

Arctic winters in Alaska offer the chance to see the mesmerising, rippling spectacle of the aurora borealis

For practical information on traveling around Alaska see pp280–91

Native arts and artifacts on display at the Alaska State Museum

## A Week in Gold Rush Territory

- **Getting there** Juneau has an international airport, or, from Anchorage, take a tour bus, plane, or train.

- **Transport** The itinerary is planned around internal flights, ferries, and guided day trips and tours.

### Day 1: Juneau

Make your first port of call from **Juneau** (see pp142–3) the **Mendenhall Glacier** (see p45), calling into the Visitor Center for an interpretive talk then hiking through the rainforest. You'll pass by waterfalls and streams, with views of the base of the glacier itself. Have a light lunch and spend the remaining daylight hours strolling and shopping for Native art and limited-edition local designer goods in the Mendenhall Valley shopping districts or downtown on South Franklin Street.

### Day 2: Juneau

Visit the expanded **Alaska State Museum** (see p142) for a broad overview of Native art and culture, as well as state history. The **Last Chance Mining Museum** (see p143) celebrates the city's mining history. Have a lunch of fresh seafood in one of the downtown restaurants just a few blocks from the docks. In the afternoon, ride the **Mount Roberts Tramway** (see p143) from almost sea level to 1,800 ft (550 m) up Mount Roberts, for a wide-angle view of downtown and the Gastineau Channel.

### Day 3: Ketchikan

Take the short flight to **Ketchikan** (see pp128–9) in time for a lunch of fresh fish by the cruise ship docks, or a brew at the Arctic Bar, a local favorite for almost 80 years. Explore the arty district around Mission, Main, Front, and Creek Streets, perhaps picking up some original art and finding somewhere for dinner.

### Day 4: Ketchikan to Skagway

Take the **Alaska Marine Highway** (see pp290–91) to Skagway; grab a recliner in the lounge or the heated solarium, and watch the stunning scenery drift past, catch up on a book, or chat to your fellow passengers. It's a 22-hour trip; if that's an adventure too far, travel by air instead (you'll probably need to transfer in Juneau).

### Day 5: Skagway

In **Skagway** (see pp150–51) it's hard to escape the town's Gold Rush history, so dive right in. Top attraction is the scenic, sometimes hair-raising Summit Tour on the narrow-gauge **White Pass and Yukon Route Railroad** (see pp153), following the trail of the prospectors.

### Day 6: Sitka

Take a small plane from Skagway to **Sitka** (see pp140–41) to explore this Baranof Island city, the 19th-century hub of Russian-American culture. Tour the city's historic buildings and learn about the Tlingit people at **Sitka National Historical Park** (see p141). Stay overnight; Sitka has some excellent hotels and restaurants.

### Day 7: Sitka to Juneau

With its access to the open ocean as well as inland waters, Sitka offers small, inexpensive fishing opportunities. Take a trip with a local charter captain and wait for the tug of a fish on your line. Return by air to Juneau for dinner on the waterfront.

Creek Street has a notorious past as Ketchikan's former red-light district (see p128)

# Putting Alaska on the Map

Flanked by the Arctic and Pacific Oceans, separated
from Russia by the Bering Strait, and bordered by
Canada in the east, Alaska lies across the Arctic Circle.
Covering over 586,400 sq miles (1.5 million sq km)
and with just 735,000 people, it is the largest and least
densely populated US state. Almost half of all Alaskans
live in Anchorage, while the rest are concentrated
around Fairbanks, Southeast Alaska, the Mat-Su Valley,
and the Kenai Peninsula. The spectacular landscape,
dotted with national parks, is dominated by glaciers,
rugged mountain ranges, island chains, broad
river valleys, and wide coastal plains.

Barrow
Wainwright
Point Lay
Umiat
Colville
Point Hope
Kivalina
Anaktuvuk Pass
Noatak
Kotzebue · Kiana · Ambler · Wise
Cold
Arctic Circle
Shishmaref · Bettles
A L A S K
Wales · Deering
Teller · Kougarok
Koyukuk · Huslia
Council · Tanana
Koyukuk · Manley
Gambell · Shaktoolik · Galena · Ruby · Sp
Savoonga · Nome · Unalakleet · Poorman
Stebbins
*Bering Sea*
Kotlik · Ophir
Sheldon · Anvik · McGrath
Point · Holy Cross · Iditarod
Hoope · y · Stony River · Ta
Newtok · Aniak · Sleetmute · Anch
Mekoryuk · Bethel · Kashegelok
Kwigillingok · Kenai
Kipnuk · Soldotn
Quinhagak · Ninilchik
Aleknagik · Iliamna
Platinum · Togiak · Kakhonak
Dillingham · Naknek
Egegik · King Salmon
Pilot Point · Port Lions · Kodi
Port Heiden · Akhiok · Old Harbo
Port Moller · Chignik
Cold Bay · King · Sand
St. Paul · Cove · Point
*Pribilof* St. George
*Islands*
Unalaska/Dutch · Akutan
Harbor

Point Lay
Kougarok
RUSSIA
Arctic Circle

*Koyukuk*
*Yukon*
*Kuskokwim*
*Yukon*
*Alaska Peninsula*

## Key
━━ Alaska highway
━━ Highway
┈┈ Minor road
─── Railroad
━━ International border

0 kilometers        200
0 miles                    200

*Aleutian  Islands*

*P a c i f i c
O c e a n*

**For keys to symbols** *see back flap*

*Arctic Ocean*

*Beaufort Sea*

e Bay
Kaktovik
dhorse

**North America**

ALASKA

CANADA

*Pacific Ocean*

UNITED STATES OF AMERICA

MEXICO

Inuvik

Arctic Village

dalar

: Yukon

*Yukon*

Circle

ood

Central

Chena Hot Springs

Fairbanks

6

Eagle

Delta Junction

Chicken

Paxson

Tok

Northway

Glennallen

Chitina

McCarthy

Valdez

ittier

Cordova

Yakutat

Arctic Circle

Norman Wells

*Great Bear Lake*

CANADA

Dawson City

Whitehorse

Watson Lake

Fort Nelson

Haines Junction

Skagway

Haines

Gustavus

Juneau

*Gulf of Alaska*

Sitka

Petersburg

Wrangell

Hyder

Craig

Ketchikan

Hydaburg

Prince Rupert

Prince George

*Haida Gwaii*

tian Islands

0 km        300

0 miles        300

Islands

*Buldir Island*

Kiska Island

*Semisopochnoi Island*

*Great Sitkin Island*

*Atka Island*

*Seguam Island*

*Umnak Island*

Unalaska/Dutch Harbor

*at Islands*

Amchitka Island

Amlia Island

*Adak Island*

*Aniukta Island*

*Fox Islands*

*Andreanof Islands*

# A PORTRAIT OF ALASKA

Dominated by thundering glaciers, vast forests, wild rivers, and island-studded seas and fjords, Alaska is undoubtedly one of America's most scenic states. The magnificence of the land, wildlife-viewing opportunities, an almost unmatched range of outdoor activities, and the chance to explore the state's Russian and Native heritage, all combine to draw visitors to Alaska.

Detached from the rest of the country by Canada's Yukon Territory and British Columbia, Alaska is the largest state in the US. While its monumental size can at times seem overwhelming, no one could fail to appreciate the grandeur of the land.

Evidence of Alaska's Native heritage abounds in towns and villages, where many indigenous groups keep their age-old traditions alive. Museums across the state are filled with Native artifacts and ceremonial objects, but the best place for an overview of these diverse cultures is the Alaska Native Heritage Center in Anchorage.

Remnants of Alaska's Russian past are also still in evidence. In the 18th century,

Russian Orthodox clergy followed Russian trappers to Alaska and converted many locals to the Orthodox faith. Several large communities have at least one Russian Orthodox church, and the cities of Kodiak, Sitka, and Unalaska retain especially strong Russian influences.

The state offers an incredible variety of outdoor activities, including white-water rafting and wildlife viewing in the summer, and skiing and dog sledding in the winter. It is also one of the top cruise destinations in the world, with spectacular trips in the Gulf of Alaska and through the quiet channels of the Inside Passage.

Traditional crosses and domes of St. Innocent Russian Orthodox Cathedral in Anchorage

◀ Carved and painted totem pole, characteristic of many Alaskan Native cultures

Serene landscape of the Chugach National Forest along the Seward Highway

## The Land and Ecology

Alaska's wilderness landscapes and diverse wildlife have long provided both resources and inspiration for those fortunate enough to experience them. The impact of humans reaches back many thousands of years to when the first Native peoples are said to have arrived via the Bering land bridge. Roaming across the landscape in search of resources, these semi-nomadic hunter-gatherers lived largely in harmony with the environment.

When the Russians arrived in the 18th century, however, their interest in sea otter and seal pelts sparked drastic declines in populations of those marine mammals, which have only recently begun to return in large numbers. The Russians were followed by Gold Rush prospectors, who trailed the Interior rivers in search of gold. Large-scale dredging along these watercourses left mountains of tailings, or mining residue, that remain as unsightly scars across the landscape.

After the discovery of oil on the North Slope in the 1970s, the Trans-Alaska Pipeline was built amid widespread concern that it would alter the ecology along its corridor. As a result of extensive environmental impact studies, the pipeline was designed to allow caribou to migrate freely beneath it or over it, and drilling companies were required to follow strict drilling and cleanup guidelines.

Today, Alaska has the largest population of bears, moose, wolves, and bald eagles in the US, and also supports species, such as musk ox and caribou, that are found in no other US state. The prolific wildlife is due not only to Alaska's relative remoteness, but also to the fact that it has more protected or semi-protected habitat than any other state.

However, Alaska faces several prominent ecological issues, from the possibility that an enormous gold mine will be developed on the Bristol Bay Watershed to the aerial hunting of wolves. Global warming also ignites

Caribou on the autumn tundra, Denali National Park

passions. Scientists report that human-created greenhouse gases, especially in Arctic regions, have caused rapid changes. Alaska faces dramatic changes as rising sea levels erode coastal villages, glaciers continue to recede, ocean acidification threatens fish and crab populations, and insect infestations and forest fires become more devastating. Polar bears and walruses also face a bleak future as the sea ice melts.

## The Economy

Historically, Alaska's economy revolved around timber, fishing, and mining, but that changed in the 1960s when oil was discovered at Prudhoe Bay. Even with the closure of most sawmills, commercial fishing and seafood processing remain viable industries. The most prominent export is salmon, and Alaska provides one of the world's last wild stocks of salmon. However, competition with cheaper farmed salmon from Chile, Norway, Scotland, and other places led to declines in the market in the 1990s. Since then, prices have rebounded as consumers have come to appreciate the advantages of wild Alaskan salmon over farmed fish. On the mining front, the zinc mine near Kotzebue and a large gold mine near Fairbanks are also proving profitable.

Alaska Pipeline with the backdrop of the Alaska Range

In addition, both tourism and government agencies provide major sources of employment.

## Government and Politics

In general, Alaskan politics are far more conservative than most other US states. Due to its small population of around 735,000, Alaska is represented in the US Congress by the usual two senators but only one representative. It also has a state governor and lieutenant governor, and a bicameral legislature. Unlike other states, Alaska has no county governments, but is instead organized into boroughs and municipalities.

Cruise ship *Carnival Spirit* docked at the marina in Seward

Yup'ik dancer performing at the Anchorage Native Heritage Center

Alaska's position as the crossroads between North America and Asia makes it a militarily strategic site for the US. During World War II, the Aleutian Islands were attacked by Japanese forces and even today, Alaska is considered a first line of defense against potential troubles from the west. Anchorage and Fairbanks have army and air force bases, and there are military installations across the state.

Politically, the most sensitive issues involve resource exploitation. One very vocal group of mostly younger people view the land as a wilderness to be preserved, while others who arrived in the earlier, more rough-and-ready days can be opportunists who see vast wealth to exploit. Conflicts between these two groups frequently escalate into national debate.

## People and Society

On the whole, Alaskans are friendly and genuinely welcome visitors with great pride in their home state. While typically American in most respects, Alaskans are usually younger and live a somewhat more rugged life. Beyond the major cities, most people are accustomed to the remoteness, extreme cold, and high retail prices. Alaska has more hunting licenses per capita and more subsistence hunters living off the land than any other state. More Alaskans own snow-machines (the local term for snowmobiles) and all-terrain vehicles than other Americans, and about one in 50 residents is a private pilot.

All but about 30 percent of today's Alaskans are transplanted from elsewhere and are in the state by choice. Many have come for economic opportunities or with the military, but a majority

Colorful buildings in downtown Juneau in Southeast Alaska

have moved here because of a perceived sense of individual freedom that is becoming increasingly rare in most of the Lower 48 (the contiguous US states).

Demographically, about 15 percent of Alaskans are of Native heritage, while the rest are mainly of European descent. Over 18 percent of the population is African-American, Hispanic, Asian, or Pacific Islander, and minority numbers are increasing, especially in Anchorage. Most of the Native population lives in rural Alaska off the road system, while other minorities live primarily in Juneau, Anchorage, Fairbanks, and other large towns. Significant numbers of Asians, mainly Koreans and Filipinos, work as temporary laborers on fishing boats and in canneries along the Gulf of Alaska, and every summer, the cruising and tourist industry employs hundreds of seasonal workers.

Most Alaskans tend to hole up during the cold, dark months of winter, preferring to work on indoor projects and plan for the summer, although this hibernation is usually broken up by forays into the outdoors to ski, ice-fish, buzz around on snowmachines, or go mushing (dog sledding). In the

Kayaking in glacial waters in Southeast Alaska

endless daylight of summer, however, Alaskans go into overdrive, packing in as many activities as possible before the season winds down, the days shorten and winter returns. While summer visitors would be forgiven for assuming that all Alaskans are hyperactive, there is so much to see and do that it is almost impossible not to join them in their infectious round-the-clock summer spirit.

Fly fishing in the clear blue waters of the Kenai River

# Alaska's Native Cultures

Alaska's Native peoples have long enjoyed rich cultures based upon deep spiritual values derived from their relationship to the plants, animals, and climate of their natural environments. There is no single "Native" culture or way of life, as each group has its own traditions and arts that were initially linked to the environment they lived in and the available resources *(see pp26–7)*. While few Natives now strictly follow traditional ways, many have a renewed interest in preserving their heritage, both through material arts and the revival of Native languages. Evidence of this resurgence is seen in Native villages and cultural centers, where visitors can meet Native Alaskans and explore their traditions, art, and crafts.

Summer visitors to Kotzebue participating in a blanket toss

**Traditional housing** included Aleut semi-subterranean shelters, such as this *ulax* replica at the Alaska Native Heritage Center *(see pp76–7)*.

**The raven** is honored in the colorful stylized motif that graces the front of this clan house.

**The colors** used were significant. Red represented valor, blue stood for the sea and sky, and white signified space and peace.

## Clan Houses

*These community dwellings, such as this Tlingit Raven clan house in Totem Bight State Historical Park (see p129), housed up to 50 people in one large room. Each family had its own space, but shared a single fireplace and stored its belongings beneath the planked flooring.*

**Doorways** were small to conserve heat, and those passing through needed to stoop down to enter.

**Whaling** is an annual springtime event for Inupiat and St. Lawrence Island Yup'ik peoples, who set out in traditional sealskin boats called *umiaks* as soon as ice conditions permit. The skins need to be changed every other year to remain watertight.

**Igloos** (structures constructed of blocks of ice) were historically built by Inuit hunters and mountain climbers as temporary shelters. The word itself simply means "house."

**Dancing**, as in this Inupiat performance, is usually accompanied by chanting and drumming and is used to celebrate festive events and ceremonial rituals.

**Drumming** and drum-making, using caribou hide or sealskin, are spiritually rooted Inupiat traditions. Here, a Kotzebue elder beats a drum while chanting in the Inupiat language.

**The main house pole** shows Duk-toothl, a legendary man of the Raven clan, who wears a weasel skin hat.

**Totem pole raisings** are festive events for the Tlingit, Haida, and Tsimshian peoples of Southeast Alaska. Historically, such events were commemorated by potlatches, or gifting feasts. Here, Tsimshian celebrants lift a pole into place at a gathering of three clans in Metlakatla.

**Soapstone carving** is prominent among the Inupiat and Yup'ik, who use soft black soapstone to create figurines of hunters, dancers, and animals. They also make scrimshaw, intricate designs carved on ivory or whalebone.

**Each eye** of the raven in this design has been expanded to depict a complete face.

**Athabaskan beaded boots** are traditionally worn by women for dancing on festive occasions. The designs are usually intricate and demonstrate great skill.

**Aleut baskets**, such as this one at the Anchorage Museum of History and Art, are tightly woven of Aleutian Island grasses.

**Tlingit masks** feature human-like visages, depicting interaction between humans and supernatural beings, or animals, that represent individual clans, such as Beaver or Wolf.

## Native Art and Crafts

*Every Native group celebrates its cultural heritage in arts and crafts that utilize locally available media. Thus, the Inupiat used walrus ivory for scrimshaw, while Aleuts are skilled at basket-weaving. Historically, all Native art either had a practical or ceremonial use. Today, while much of the art still serves traditional purposes, works are also sold in shops across Alaska. They may also be purchased directly from the artists.*

# Native Peoples of Alaska

Some anthropologists believe that the first Native peoples migrated to Alaska 30,000 to 12,000 years ago during the Ice Age that lowered sea levels and created a land bridge across the Bering Strait. These hunter-gatherers, ancestors of modern-day Indian peoples, were followed by the Inuit and Aleut peoples, who arrived by boat starting around 8,000 years ago, after the disappearance of the land bridge. There are, however, other theories that dispute this. Today, about 15 percent of Alaska's population claims Native descent. The Inuit or Eskimo include the Inupiat, Alutiiq, Aleut, Yup'ik, while the Indians include the Tsimshian, Athabaskan, Eyak, Tlingit, and Haida. While the term "Eskimo" ("eaters of raw meat" in Athabaskan) is generally not considered offensive in Alaska, Native Alaskans usually refer to themselves as members of a particular group, or collectively as Natives.

**Key**

- Athabaskan
- Tlingit
- Haida
- Tsimshian
- Inupiat
- Yup'ik
- Aleut and Alutiiq

Athabaskan family with pelts from the winter catch

## Athabaskan

Historically, the Athabaskans occupied the vast taiga forests of the Interior, which are characterized by a harsh climate. Largely a hunting and gathering society, the Athabaskans spent summers in riverside tent camps, collecting and drying fish and game for the cold season. In winter, they lived in houses made of sod and wood. Their clothing was made primarily of caribou or moose hide, colorfully decorated with porcupine quills and, after the arrival of the Europeans, with traded goods such as beads. Modern Athabaskans live mainly in the Interior, many in Fairbanks, where they enjoy an urban lifestyle but also make efforts to demonstrate their traditional ways to visitors.

## Tlingit

Alaska's Tlingit (pronounced KLINK-it), a Northwest Coast culture, have long inhabited Southeast Alaska. Historically, the Tlingit were a seafaring people, and their traders traveled as far as present-day Washington State in huge ocean-going canoes hewn from single cedar logs. Traditional Tlingit society had no central government, but each village had a stratified society that included high-ranking families, commoners, and slaves captured from neighboring tribes. Like the Haida, Tsimshian, and other Northwest Coast cultures, the Tlingit carved totem poles (see p129) to commemorate the culture unique to their respective clans. Pole-raisings and memorial ceremonies were accompanied by grand feasts called potlatches. Currently, the art of totem carving is re-emerging across Southeast Alaska, and other Tlingit arts are enjoying widespread popularity.

Tlingit dancer dressed in traditional style

Haida man in a bark hat and button cloak

## Haida

The Haida share many cultural traditions with the Tlingit, including clan structures and totem pole carving. Expert sailors, they were known for their decorative ceremonial canoes. They traditionally depended on salmon and sea mammals for their subsistence. In the late 19th century, as many as 10,000 Haida lived in far southern Alaska, but by the 1890s, their numbers had been decimated by diseases brought in by Western explorers. Today, the Alaskan Haida population is about 2,000, but many more claim partial Haida descent. While they are now centered on Hydaburg on Prince of Wales Island, people of Haida descent live across southern Alaska.

## Tsimshian

Alaska's Tsimshian are descendants of 823 people who left Canada with Anglican missionary, Father Duncan, after local authorities denied their land claims. Settling in an abandoned Tlingit settlement on Annette Island, which they named Metlakatla after their village in British Columbia, they set up a model Protestant Christian community of white houses and well-appointed churches. The Tsimshian were the only Alaskan Native group that rejected the Alaska Native Claims Settlement Act of 1971 (see p60). As a result, they are the only Native group to retain sovereignty over their land, with Annette Island being Alaska's only official Indian Reservation.

Tsimshian drummers at a ceremony

## Inupiat

Inupiat men returning with a caribou caught in Kobuk Valley National Park

The Inupiat (plural Inupiaq) mainly occupy areas along the Arctic Ocean coast and on the North Slope. Prior to European contact and influence, distinct Inupiat groups of extended families occupied home territories between Norton Sound on the Bering Strait and the Canadian border. Some groups were settled, but others traveled great distances to cooperatively hunt seals, whales, caribou, and other game animals. The Inupiat had no chiefs, but each family was headed by an *umialik*, who managed food and other family needs. Women were responsible for gathering plants and berries, skinning animals, drying *muktuk* (whale blubber), meat, and fish, and preparing food. While conflicts existed between groups, peaceful interaction did occur, especially during trade fairs at the end of each hunting season, which drew participants from as far away as Siberia. While some Inupiat today work for Native corporations or government agencies, many rural residents still make a livelihood from subsistence hunting, fishing, and gathering.

## Yup'ik

The Yup'ik traditionally lived on the broad, marshy plains of the Yukon-Kuskokwim Delta, as well as on the Bering Sea coast and parts of the Seward Peninsula. Due to the milder and more vegetated environment, the Yup'ik made more use of wood, vegetables, and land animals than the Inupiat. With summer hunting camps, they also had permanent villages, where men lived in *qasgiqs*, or communal houses, and women and children in sod dwellings called *enet*. Lacking the resources Europeans wanted, the Yup'ik first encountered Westerners much later than the Aleut, Alutiiq, and Inupiat. In recent years, many Yup'ik have moved to towns, especially Bethel, but some still practice subsistence hunting or spend the summers working in family fish camps.

Yup'ik family beneath an *umiak*, a traditional skin boat

## Aleut (Unangax̂) and Alutiiq (Sugpiaq)

Alutiiq woman in a beaded headdress

Both the Aleut and Alutiiq live in Southwest Alaska, the former in the Aleutian Islands and the latter from Prince William Sound to Kodiak Island and the Alaska Peninsula. The difference in their languages, however, suggests that they have entirely separate origins. Despite Southwest Alaska's stormy climate, both groups had a maritime hunting culture, using *baidarkas* (skin boats) to chase seals, otters, and whales. Early Russian otter hunters often killed or enslaved them and also introduced foreign diseases. The Russian Orthodox clergy that followed converted large numbers to the church, which remains a strong spiritual force for both groups. During World War II, entire villages were transferred to evacuation centers in Southeast Alaska to keep them from being taken prisoner by the Japanese. Aleut people often prefer the name Unangax̂ and Alutiiq call themselves Sugpiaq.

# Volcanoes and Earthquakes

Alaska lies on the geologically active Pacific Ring of Fire, where tectonic shifts can result in earthquakes and volcanic eruptions. One of the earth's tectonic plates is sliding under another, causing major geological changes. The entire southern Alaskan region is geologically dynamic; it is the site of about 8 percent of all the world's earthquakes and boasts dozens of active volcanoes. The second strongest earthquake in recorded history struck Southcentral Alaska in 1964, and in 1912, Novarupta exploded in what was the second most powerful volcanic eruption ever recorded.

**Locator map**

━ Aleutian Megathrust

— Subduction zone

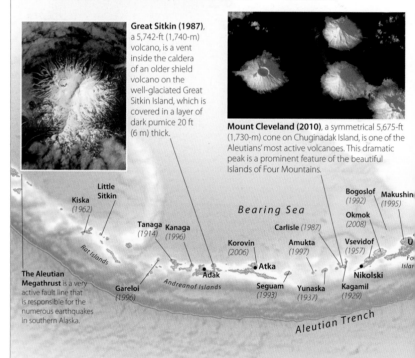

**Great Sitkin (1987)**, a 5,742-ft (1,740-m) volcano, is a vent inside the caldera of an older shield volcano on the well-glaciated Great Sitkin Island, which is covered in a layer of dark pumice 20 ft (6 m) thick.

**Mount Cleveland (2010)**, a symmetrical 5,675-ft (1,730-m) cone on Chuginadak Island, is one of the Aleutians' most active volcanoes. This dramatic peak is a prominent feature of the beautiful Islands of Four Mountains.

*Bearing Sea*

**Little Sitkin**

**Kiska** *(1962)*

**Tanaga** *(1914)* **Kanaga** *(1996)*

*Rat Islands*

**Korovin** *(2006)*

**Carlisle** *(1987)*

**Bogoslof** *(1992)* **Makushin** *(1995)*

**Okmok** *(2008)*

**Amukta** *(1997)*

**Vsevidof** *(1957)*

**U**

Fo
Islar

**The Aleutian Megathrust** is a very active fault line that is responsible for the numerous earthquakes in southern Alaska.

**Gareloi** *(1996)*

*Andreanof Islands*

**Adak**

● **Atka**

**Seguam** *(1993)*

**Yunaska** *(1937)*

**Kagamil** *(1929)*

**Nikolski**

*Aleutian Trench*

## Tectonic Activity

The distinctive chain of islands and peaks that makes up the Aleutian Islands is the result of plate tectonics – the movement of the interlocking plates of the earth's crust that ride on the molten material (magma) in the mantle. At the subduction zone, the oceanic Pacific plate is being forced under the continental North American plate, creating the Aleutian Trench. North of this zone, fractures in the continental plate allow magma from below to migrate upward. When the pressure increases, the magma bursts through the crust in dramatic volcanic activity.

North American (continental) plate

Volcanic zone

Aleutian Trench

Pacific (oceanic) plate

Model of a subduction zone and trench

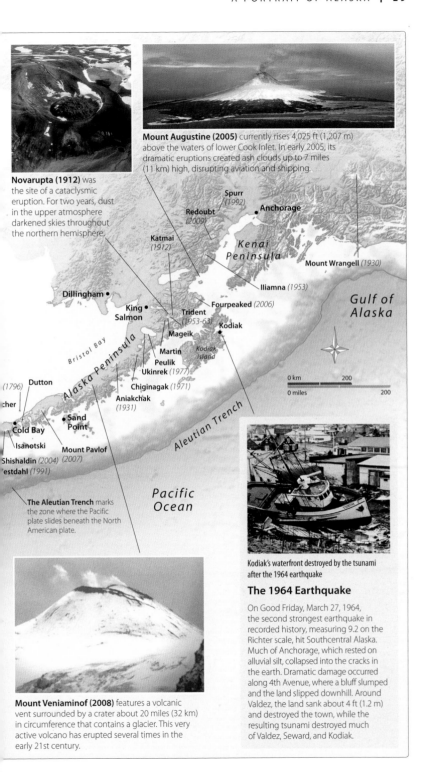

**Novarupta (1912)** was the site of a cataclysmic eruption. For two years, dust in the upper atmosphere darkened skies throughout the northern hemisphere.

**Mount Augustine (2005)** currently rises 4,025 ft (1,207 m) above the waters of lower Cook Inlet. In early 2005, its dramatic eruptions created ash clouds up to 7 miles (11 km) high, disrupting aviation and shipping.

Spurr *(1992)*

Redoubt *(2009)*

Anchorage

Katmai *(1912)*

*Kenai Peninsula*

Mount Wrangell *(1930)*

Iliamna *(1953)*

Dillingham ●

Fourpeaked *(2006)*

*Gulf of Alaska*

King ●
Salmon

Trident *(1953-63)*

Mageik

Kodiak

Martin

*Kodiak Island*

*Bristol Bay*

Peulik

Ukinrek *(1977)*

*Alaska Peninsula*

Chiginagak *(1971)*

Aniakchak *(1931)*

0 km          200
0 miles          200

*(1796)* Dutton

cher

● Sand Point

● Cold Bay

Isanotski

Mount Pavlof

Shishaldin *(2004)* *(2007)*

estdahl *(1991)*

*Aleutian Trench*

**The Aleutian Trench** marks the zone where the Pacific plate slides beneath the North American plate.

*Pacific Ocean*

Kodiak's waterfront destroyed by the tsunami after the 1964 earthquake

### The 1964 Earthquake

On Good Friday, March 27, 1964, the second strongest earthquake in recorded history, measuring 9.2 on the Richter scale, hit Southcentral Alaska. Much of Anchorage, which rested on alluvial silt, collapsed into the cracks in the earth. Dramatic damage occurred along 4th Avenue, where a bluff slumped and the land slipped downhill. Around Valdez, the land sank about 4 ft (1.2 m) and destroyed the town, while the resulting tsunami destroyed much of Valdez, Seward, and Kodiak.

**Mount Veniaminof (2008)** features a volcanic vent surrounded by a crater about 20 miles (32 km) in circumference that contains a glacier. This very active volcano has erupted several times in the early 21st century.

# Alaska's Glaciers

Much of Alaska's spectacular landscape has been shaped by 5,000 major and countless minor glaciers that scraped downhill from icefields in the coastal mountains, gouging out steep-sided valleys. As glaciers melted, valleys that were below sea level were filled by seawater to create long, narrow fjords. Although glaciers continue to reshape the landscape, most of these rivers of ice – the earth's largest reservoir of freshwater – are currently receding, and scientific research suggests that human-caused warming of the planet may be the primary reason.

**Crevasses** develop when stresses on the flowing ice cause large cracks in glaciers. The largest crevasses are found on steep sections of rapidly flowing ice.

**Outlet Glaciers**, such as Mendenhall Glacier near Juneau, spill down steeply from icefields, creating ravines that serve as outlets for the icefield. They often flow into lakes created by the glacier's terminal moraine, a ridge of debris at the foot of the glacier.

## Glacial Changes

*As glaciers flow downhill, friction against the rock melts the bottom ice, forming a "slide" so the glacier can surge ahead. Increasing air temperatures can cause melting at glacier faces, but can also cause surging, as higher temperatures mean more snowfall, and therefore, pressure, on parent icefields. Tidewater glaciers flowing into warming seas tend to recede due to higher water temperatures.*

**Lateral moraines** are strips of ground rock on the edges of glaciers.

**Bergy bits** are large chunks of glacier ice or small icebergs, rising up to 13 ft (4 m) out of the water.

## Alaska's Prominent Glaciers

**Key**

① Aialik *(see p107)*
② Exit *(see p103)*
③ Portage *(see p85)*
④ Eklutna *(see p83)*
⑤ Matanuska *(see p184)*
⑥ Columbia *(see p119)*
⑦ Worthington *(see p121)*
⑧ Childs *(see p123)*
⑨ Bering *(see p41)*
⑩ Kennicott *(see p193)*
⑪ Malaspina *(see p155)*
⑫ Hubbard *(see p31)*
⑬ Margerie *(see p146)*
⑭ Mendenhall *(see p145)*

Alaska
Canada
Alaska
Canada
Gulf of Alaska
Pacific Ocean

0 km    200
0 miles    200

**Valley Glaciers** are created when the weight of an icecap is great enough to make its edges flow downhill, creating rivers of ice that grind away underlying rock to form valleys. Valley glaciers are subdivided into outlet, tidewater, and piedmont glaciers.

**Hanging glaciers** in high mountain valleys may eventually become tributaries of a main valley glacier.

**Medial moraines** are wide, dark strips of debris and ground rock in the middle of valley or tidewater glaciers.

**Icefields**, including the Juneau, Harding, and Bagley Icefields, are formed between high mountains when snow compresses into ice under the weight of additional snowfall. Liquid water beneath glaciers and shallow portions of icefields is revealed in deep wells called *moulins*, French for "mills." Peaks rising from icefields are called *nunataks*.

**Growler ice** is a small chunk of floating ice that releases trapped air as it melts, making a growling noise.

**Fjords**, such as Prince William Sound's College Fjord, are narrow submarine valleys flanked by steep, glacier-carved walls that may erode into gentler slopes over time.

## Hubbard Glacier

Located near the town of Yukutat, Hubbard Glacier is North America's largest tidewater glacier, and one of the only advancing glaciers in Alaska. In 1986, it rammed across the mouth of Russell Fjord in just a few days, turning the fjord into a lake and trapping marine life on the wrong side of the ice wall. While the fjord has since reopened, the glacier still occasionally surges and may eventually seal off the fjord.

# Landscape and Wildlife

With its range of landforms and wild country, Alaska naturally supports a wealth of wildlife, not only in the mountains and forests, but also on the barren tundra, in the surrounding seas, and even in the cities and towns. In fact, Anchorage has a healthy moose population, and bears are occasionally sighted in city parks. Perhaps the most reliable wildlife viewing venue is Denali National Park. Visitors to the park's interior are typically treated to sightings of grizzlies, moose, caribou, Dall sheep, and a host of birds and smaller animals. A wealth of marine mammals – sea lions, sea otters, seals, and whales – abound in the Gulf of Alaska, Bering Sea, and the Arctic Ocean. Sightings are practically guaranteed on Inside Passage cruises, and on day cruises and ferry trips in Southeast Alaska, Prince William Sound, and the Kenai Fjords.

**Orcas** are often seen in the Gulf of Alaska and its sheltered bays, where visitors can also spot other marine mammals such as seals and otters.

### Temperate Rainforest

The islands of the eastern Gulf Coast and Southeast Alaska form the world's largest expanse of temperate rainforest *(see p131)*. Conifers such as Western hemlock and Sitka spruce dominate, but there is also muskeg or spongy bog, composed of sphagnum moss, peat, and ground cover.

### Taiga and Boreal Forest

The boreal forest *(see p161)*, which covers most of the Alaskan mainland, ranges from mixed birch to black and white spruce woodland. Low-lying, poorly drained areas are typified by taiga, characterized by bog dominated by spindly black spruce.

**Black bears** are the most common and widely distributed of North America's three species of bears *(see p111)*. At about 5 ft (2 m) in length, they are the smallest. They range in color from black to almost white.

**Lynx** are officially the only wild cats native to Alaska. They are distinguished by long tufts on each ear, while their unusually large paws act as snowshoes in very deep snow and aid in winter hunting.

**Sitka black-tailed deer** are native to the Southeast, whose old-growth forests provide optimal foraging and habitat.

**Moose**, the largest member of the deer family, can weigh up to 1,500 lb (675 kg). Besides pondweed, they feed on willow, birch, and aspen twigs.

## Rocky Coastlines

In many places along the coast of the Gulf of Alaska and the Bering Sea, the land rises from the sea in rocky beaches and high cliffs that are frequently pummeled by storms and pounding waves. The seas, rich in plankton and fish, support both nesting birds and marine mammals, such as sea otters, seals, sea lions, and walruses. Below the high-tide line, seaweed beds and tide pools provide a habitat for mollusks and soft-bodied creatures such as octopuses and jellyfish.

**Northern fur seals** haul out on the Pribilof Islands to breed and bear pups. About 700,000 of them – half of the world's popula-tion – have been known to gather here every summer. In the past decade, however, the numbers have declined sharply.

**Walruses**, with their distinctive coarse whiskers and ivory tusks, are seen mainly on rocky Bering Sea beaches, where males break their journey northward to their breeding grounds around the Arctic Ocean.

## High Mountains and Icefields

The alpine areas of Alaska are found in the high mountain ranges that arc along the southern coast of the state and in the peripheral ranges crossing the Interior and Arctic regions. The southern ranges are capped by extensive icefields that give rise to the valley glaciers that carve intermontane valleys and fjords.

## Arctic Tundra

Most of Arctic and Western Alaska is covered with Arctic tundra *(see p225)*, which ranges from rolling expanses covered by low shrubs and miniature grasses to spongy tussocks and vast open plains. Despite the harsh climate, the shallow soils support a diversity of plant life including flowers, berries, and lichen.

**Dall sheep** inhabit alpine meadows and steep slopes, fleeing to rocky crags to escape pursuers. These herbivores are rarely found below the timberline.

**Musk oxen**, hunted to extinction in Alaska, were reintroduced from Greenland in the 1930s. *Qiviut*, their soft, warm underhair, is spun into fiber.

**Caribou** in Alaska number about a million individuals. Herds of up to 400,000 migrate annually between summer and winter ranges that can be up to 250 miles (400 km) apart.

**Hoary marmots** burrow on alpine slopes and use high-pitched whistles as alarm signals. These rodents hibernate for seven months.

# Birds of Alaska

From tiny hummingbirds to enormous trumpeter swans, Alaska's bird life is varied and prolific, with 437 identified species and over 60 incidental visitors. Bald eagles can be spotted in old-growth timber, while sandpipers and peeps scurry around at the water's edge. Countless migratory birds summer in Alaska, and loons, snow geese, and herons can be seen at lakes and ponds across the state. On the remote Pribilofs, red-legged kittiwakes, puffins, crested auklets, and many others nest on the storm-battered sea cliffs.

**Bird-watching** is popular on coastal cruises, such as this tour at Glacier Bay.

### Cliff-nesters

*Many Alaskan seabirds nest on sea cliffs to protect their nests and hatchlings from predators. The best places to see nesting gannets, fulmars, petrels, cormorants, puffins, kittiwakes, and other cliff-nesting birds include Glacier Bay, Kenai Fjords National Park, and the Pribilof Islands.*

**Thick-billed murres** inhabit large cliff colonies, but do not build nests, instead laying their eggs on bare rock.

**Glaucous gulls**, among the world's largest gulls, live on the Pribilof Islands *(see pp216–17)* and on the western and northern coasts, from the Yukon-Kuskokwim Delta to Canada's northern regions. The similar, but smaller, glaucous-winged gull breeds along Alaska's southern coasts.

**Black-billed magpies** have a lustrous green iridescence on their wings and tails. They can be seen in open country, but need birch, cotton-woods, or shrubs for nesting.

### Winter Birds

*Most nesting and migratory birds in Alaska go south in winter, but Steller's jays, magpies, ravens, and ptarmigan are year-round residents. The availability of food in towns has changed the migratory patterns of ducks and geese and it is often possible to see them in mid-winter in the Southeast. Chickadees, nuthatches, and other small birds that winter in Alaska can also be seen around bird-feeders in the south.*

**The raven** has long been revered by indigenous peoples as the creator of the world and bringer of daylight. These intelligent corvids especially like to raid urban garbage bags.

**The willow ptarmigan**, the official state bird, is seen all year round. Its plumage, brilliant white in winter, becomes a mottled brown in summer to blend in with the forest floor.

## Freshwater birds

*During the spring and summer mating season, Alaska's lakes and muskeg attract ducks, snow geese, trumpeter and tundra swans, blue herons, loons, and several species of grebes. Sandhill cranes, which perform an elaborate mating dance, can be most easily seen in Creamer's Field in Fairbanks (see p174).*

**Horned puffins** are excellent swimmers, spending the winters offshore and nesting in rock clefts in the summer.

**Arctic terns**, frequently observed swooping over lakes throughout Alaska, migrate 25,000 miles (40,000 km) each year between their Arctic breeding grounds and their wintering grounds in Antarctica. Usually smaller than gulls, they will attack anything – even a human – that approaches their chicks.

**Red-legged kittiwakes**, found in the Pribilof Islands, build cliff nests made of mud, grass, and kelp.

**The red-throated loon**, much rarer than the iconic common loon, is one of Alaska's five loon species. Their haunting calls are signature sounds of the North American wilderness.

**Trumpeter swans**, with wingspans of up to 7 ft (2 m), are the world's largest waterbirds. Surprisingly efficient flyers, they migrate at altitudes up to 10,000 ft (3,000 m) at speeds of up to 60 mph (100 kph). They are most readily seen in their nesting grounds on the Copper River Delta *(see p123)*.

**Snowy owls** are perhaps the most spectacular summer birds on the Arctic coast. Diving from the sky with outstretched talons, these birds can drive away even an advancing caribou.

## Raptors

*Alaska is home to a variety of raptors, not the least of which is the US national bird, the magnificent bald eagle. Denali National Park (see pp166–9) and other parts of the Interior also have a healthy population of golden eagles. Other common raptors include merlins, red-tailed hawks, harriers, ospreys, peregrines, and numerous species of owl.*

**Bald eagles**, although established across the Lower 48, are found in their greatest numbers in Alaska. From October to December, thousands of eagles gather along the Chilkat River, but they can also be readily spotted almost anywhere in southern Alaska from late spring to early fall.

# Russian Culture in Alaska

While modern Alaska is tied ideologically to mainstream USA and traditionally to its own Native cultures, there are also remnants of 18th- and 19th-century Russian colonization. The distinctive crosses and onion-domed spires of Orthodox churches across Alaska attest to the fact that the colonizers were not just concerned with trade, but also brought with them their religious convictions, converting many Native Alaskans to their faith. Today, most Southwest Alaska villages still have a Russian Orthodox majority population.

**Russian Big Diomede** (right) and the US island of Little Diomede (left) lie in the Bering Strait.

**Icons** include All Saints of Alaska: Innocent, Herman, Jakov, Juvenali, and Peter the Aleut.

**A Russian priest** and settlers gather with Native Tlingit people in traditional dress in this photograph taken in Sitka circa 1900.

**Deacon doors** in this chapel have icons of St. Stephen (left) and St. Lawrence (right).

**Alexander Baranov** (1747–1819) is honored with this statue in Sitka, where he once lived. Attracted to Alaska by the fur trade, he became the manager of the Russian-American Company in 1790 and the first Colonial Governor of Russian America in 1799.

## Old Believers

In 1652, Patriarch Nikon of Moscow ordered reforms to traditional Orthodoxy and excommunicated any dissidents. Many of the dispossessed, calling themselves Old Believers, fled to Siberia to escape persecution. In 1945, to escape the Soviet system, many migrated to Brazil and eventually to the USA. In the late 1960s, one group established several villages around Nikolaevsk, which are modern Alaska's only Russian settlements. Currently, about 2,000 Old Believers, who still speak Old Russian, live largely by fishing and farming.

Old Believer women working in the fields near Nikolaevsk

**The analogian** displays icons for worshipers, who may not approach the iconostasis.

**The New Archangel Dancers** of Sitka perform Russian folk songs and dances to promote Alaska's Russian heritage.

**The Holy Assumption of the Virgin Mary Russian Orthodox Church**, in Kenai, was completed in 1895. A distinctive crown-shaped cupola marks this National Historic Landmark.

**The Russian Bishop's House** is the oldest intact Russian building in Sitka. Built in 1842 by the Russian American Company as the Bishop's residence, it also functioned as an orphanage, school, and seminary.

**The iconostasis** separates the church from the altar and symbolizes separation between the human world and the Divine. Only men may pass this wall.

**The altar**, behind the iconostasis, is where the priest celebrates the Holy Liturgy.

**St. Nicholas Russian Orthodox Church** (1893) was founded for Juneau's mostly Tlingit Orthodox community.

## Orthodox Interiors

*The interiors of Russian Orthodox churches are simple in layout, but are lavishly decorated with rich colors and beautiful, vibrant icons, as seen here in the chapel at St. Herman's Theological Seminary in Kodiak. In most Orthodox churches there are no pews, as worshipers are expected to stand in deference to Christ's suffering.*

**St. Michael's Russian Orthodox Cathedral**, in Sitka, was begun in 1844 when the original cornerstone was laid by Bishop Veniaminov. Destroyed by fire in 1966, the church was rebuilt and reconsecrated by 1976.

**Spirit houses** grace the churchyard behind St. Nicholas Russian Orthodox Church in the tiny Athabaskan village of Eklutna. Each of these structures is a gravesite and is decorated according to individual family traditions.

# Cruising the Inside Passage

First time and repeat passengers fill cruise ships every year to sail the Inside Passage and experience some of the most breathtaking vistas this sliver of Alaska can offer. The Inside Passage is usually remote, remarkable, and ultimately rewarding in rain or shine. Majestic tidewater glaciers, gouged-out valleys, and impenetrable forests compete for views of whales, bears, and eagles. Along with bustling ports of call, cruising here makes perfect sense. Cruise ships call on quaint fishing outposts, hidden coves, and small cities that dot the coastline – many in places inaccessible except by boat or floatplane.

**Tracy Arm** twists into the mainland from Stephens Passage and rewards with a blanket of icebergs, created by the calving Sawyer Glaciers.

**Locator**

— Area of main map

**Skagway**, a slice of Gold Rush mining history, nestles at the end of narrow Taiya Inlet.

⑦ Skagway

⑥ Haines

**Haines** sits in a gorgeous location on the Chilkat Peninsula, below the Fairweather Range.

Juneau ⑤

• Gustavus

*To the Gulf Route (see pp40–41)*

**Hoonah** is a quietly fascinating Tlingit settlement along Icy Strait where humpback whales are frequently sighted.

Sitka

**Juneau**, the nation's smallest state capital, boasts a vibrant tourist economy that caters to cruise ship passengers.

**Glacier Bay** *(see pp146–7)* is almost entirely water-access only. Cruise ships easily bring their passengers within camera range of some of the park's 12 spectacular tidewater glaciers.

## PORTS OF CALL

**Sitka's** mix of Russian and Tlingit culture makes it a fascinating port of call and its protected location within a verdant valley is stunning. Most sights are within walking distance of the docks.

**Petersburg** lies at the north end of the Wrangell Narrows, a barely navigable passage lined with dense forests, hunting and fishing lodges, and homes for rugged vacationers. The town retains its strong Norwegian influence and remains less explored than Ketchikan or Juneau.

### Planning a Cruise

**Cruises** either sail a round trip through the Inside Passage from a port to the south (often Seattle or Vancouver), or cruise one way, adding on the Gulf Route and starting or ending at Anchorage. **Consider splashing out** on a cabin with a balcony, or at least a porthole, for great views. **Take** memory cards, and batteries for your camera. **For more information** on booking and planning see pp256–63.

0 km                50

0 miles               50

**Wrangell** is a laid-back town at the mouth of the Sitkine River. The totems at Chief Shakes Island are a highlight.

**Misty Fiords National Monument** *(see p130)* is on the itinerary of many smaller ships, which conduct slow tours of its placid waters. This protected area is a wonderland of bottomless fjords and granite escarpments laced with waterfalls.

**Key**

–– Suggested route

Kake

③ Petersburg

② Wrangell

Kuiu Island

Ketchikan ①

Prince of Wales Island

Prince Rupert, Canada

**Frederick Sound** is the widest body of water in the Inside Passage and serves as a nutrient-rich feeding ground for Pacific Ocean humpback whales. They rise above the water with jaws gaping during feeding.

**Ketchikan** welcomes more than 900,000 cruise ship visitors every season. Many visitors head to Tlingit presentations at Saxman village and Totem Bight.

# Cruising the Gulf Route

Vast seascapes and endless mountain ranges are the great attraction of a Gulf of Alaska cruise. The shoreline has relatively few conventional or convenient cruise destinations; instead of ports, the wilderness of several national parks, forests, and wildlife refuges commands attention. Mammoth calving glaciers, such as the Hubbard, are top of the itinerary on all cruise lines and many passengers tack on a multi-day trip north from Seward to Denali *(see pp166–9)*. Most ships transit the Gulf's wild expanse between Whittier or Seward and Juneau during the night; however, there may still be enough light between May and late July for whale-watching.

**College Fjord** *(see p119)* snakes towards the pinnacles of the Chugach Range, dazzling at every turn. The dense network of tidewater glaciers were named for Ivy League schools.

**Whittier** has become an important port of call, as it is so close to Anchorage and on Passage Canal, an inlet just off beautiful Prince William Sound.

**Locator**

— Area of main map

**Seward** is the beginning or end point for some cruises sailing the Gulf of Alaska. Nestled between mountains and the sea, this attractive city has plenty of charm.

### PORTS OF CALL

① **Cordova** *see p122*
② **Valdez** *see pp120–21*
③ **Whittier** *see p118*
④ **Seward** *see pp102–5*

**Prince William Sound's** fragile environment has made a partial recovery since 1989's disastrous Exxon Valdez oil spill *(see p121)*. Wildlife sightings are practically guaranteed.

**Valdez**, a coastal port between the two flanks of the vast Chugach National Forest, is notable for being at the end of the famed Trans-Alaska Pipeline. Large cruise ships do not stop here.

## Planning a Cruise

**Cruises through** the Gulf of Alaska are usually part of a one-way trip from either Vancouver or Seattle to Anchorage and also include the Inside Passage.

**Ships** dock in Seward or Whittier and passengers travel to or from Anchorage via train or bus.

**A tour to Denali** will take at least three nights; the train trip is spectacular (see pp286–7).

**For more information** on booking and planning see pp256–63.

**Hubbard Glacier** (see p31), Alaska's longest tidewater glacier, stretches across 6 miles (10 km) of Yakutat Bay's headwaters. Massive columns of ancient ice tumble from the glacier's face with the sound of thunder followed by a dull splash.

**Key**

— — Suggested route

**Malaspina Glacier**, at 1,500 square miles (3,890 sq km), is the largest piedmont glacier in North America. It was named for the 18th-century Spanish explorer, Alejandro Malaspina.

① **Cordova**

• *Alaganik*

**Cape Yakataga**

*Kayak Island*

**Icy Bay** was formed within the last century when four tidewater glaciers retreated. Its icy waters provide spectacularly isolated sea kayaking.

**Bering Glacier** dramatically surges forward up to 328 ft (100 m) per day about every 20 years, sometimes filling the lake at its foot with calving icebergs.

**Yakutat** (see p155), a tiny Tlingit town on the route to Hubbard Glacier, boasts one of the most dramatic coastal locations on the continent.

*To the Inside Passage (see pp38–9)*

**Cordova**, inaccessible by road or rail, is an occasional port of call for small ships. Originally the terminus of the Copper River and Northwestern Railway (see p187), which served the copper mines at Kennicott, today it is a pleasant fishing town.

# Dog Sledding

The Native peoples of Alaska's northern regions have long relied on dog sleds as essential survival tools in the winter, using them while hunting, trading, or moving camp. As other people moved to Alaska, dog sleds continued to play an important role, delivering medicine, food, and mail. While the practical use of dog sleds has now been replaced by snowmachines, dog sledding, locally called "mushing," is popular as a recreational activity and is the official state sport.

Historical image of Alaskan mail carriers delivering mail via dog sled

**Alaskans** traditionally made sleds of wood, bone, sinew, and rawhide, but modern sleds are made of wood, steel, plastics, Kevlar, and aluminum. Here, Inupiat elder Don Smith works on a sled in his workshop in Kiana, near Kotzebue.

**Dog sleds** are built on wooden or aluminum runners, with an area in the front to carry freight, passengers, or tired or injured dogs.

**Wheel dogs**, at the very back, help in steering the sled.

**Mushers** either stand on the runners of the sled or jog behind or alongside.

## The Sled Team

*For mushers, dog sledding is as much an art form as a sport. In the harsh winter wilderness, the close interplay of human and dog is symbiotic: for the musher, the dog team is a faithful lifeline in an exposed environment, while for the dogs, the musher is a trusted companion who supplies sustenance. The dogs are directed not by reins, but by the musher's spoken commands to the lead dogs, who guide the others accordingly.*

## Sled Dogs

*Malamutes, Siberians, Samoyeds, and other purebred huskies are popularly associated with dog sledding, but are rarely used as sled dogs. Most mushers prefer mixed-breed dogs that are bred for speed and endurance.*

**Dog team transport**, when the dogs are not running, is in mobile kennels mounted on the back of pick-up trucks.

**Wind-resistant kennels** provide shelter for sled dogs at home. On the trail, they sleep outdoors on hay, eating meat and fish for energy and warmth. Bred for Alaskan winters, they perform best at about -29° C (-20° F).

**Denali Park Rangers** use sleds to patrol the park in winter, but summer visitors can watch demonstrations of dog sleds adapted for use on trails.

## Alaska's Dog Sled Races

*Dog sled races feature in winter festivals all over Alaska, but the best-known mushing event is the famed Iditarod. Other popular races include the Yukon Quest, Glennallen's Copper Basin 300, which is a qualifier for the Iditarod, and the World Championship Sled Dog Races. Racers come from all over the world to serve apprenticeships with established mushers and learn how to care for the dogs and cope with the elements.*

**Lead dogs**, in the front, follow the musher's commands.

**Team dogs** follow the swing dogs and provide a steady pulling action.

**Swing dogs** back up the lead dogs and assist in steering.

**The Yukon Quest** is one of Alaska's major dog sled races. The 1,000-mile (1,600-km) race follows a Gold Rush and historic mail delivery route between Whitehorse, Canada, and Fairbanks, Alaska.

**The World Championship Sled Dog Races** take place on a short track around Anchorage during the Anchorage Fur Rendezvous. This weekend event focuses more on speed and strategy than on endurance, which is the main factor in long-distance mushing.

## The Last Great Race on Earth

Dog sled team pulling out of the Iditarod starting line

Historically, the Athabaskans called their hunting grounds Haiditarod, "the distant place." In 1910, the derivation Iditarod was given to the rough trail between Seward and Nome. In 1925, dog teams transported life-saving diphtheria serum to epidemic-stricken Nome along a portion of this trail. To commemorate this feat, a dog sled race between Anchorage and Nome was initiated in 1973 by legendary musher Joe Redington, affectionately known as the "Father of the Iditarod." Held in early March, this annual event begins with a ceremonial start in Anchorage and restarts the next day from Willow. Each year, the race follows one of two alternating courses. The leaders usually complete the 1,100-mile (1,760-km) run in about nine days.

# Sportfishing in Alaska

Sportfishing is Alaska's most popular sport, and Alaskans fish regularly while outsiders often make it their main reason to visit the state. Some visit in the hopes of shipping home a crate of frozen fish, but for most the real attraction is the opportunity to spend some solitary time outdoors. However, anglers in the best fishing areas may find themselves up against hordes of competing fishermen. Remote sites and wilderness lodges offer more serene experiences. Those whose chief objective is to catch fish will find lakes and streams so prolific that success is practically guaranteed, even when several anglers are competing.

**Catch-and-release fishing** is a popular pastime that also maintains breeding stocks.

**Dipnetting** is a favored way of catching Copper River red salmon and the small and greasy hooligan (eulachon) in Turnagain Arm *(see pp84–5)*. Only Alaska residents are permitted to use dipnets.

### Fly Fishing

*Fly fishing, which involves the use of a long, light rod, an artificial fly made of fur, feathers, or yarn, and a heavy line that helps to place the fly accurately, is used primarily to catch salmon and trout in smaller lakes, rivers, and streams. The most rewarding fly fishing is found in wilderness waterways accessed by bush plane.*

### Special Fishing Tours

*Anglers in Alaska can choose from a range of sportfishing packages, which typically include transportation, tackle, food, and accommodation. Tours range from deep-sea fishing charters to superb fishing adventures at remote lodges that are approachable only by floatplane.*

**Charter fishing tours** involve chartering a boat with a guide for half a day or a full day. Sportfishing vessels can travel far from shore to find the best sportfishing grounds for enthusiastic anglers looking for a good catch.

**Fly-in fishing**, a quintessential Alaskan experience, involves a floatplane flight to a remote lake for some quiet angling.

**Combat fishing** is common in Kenai Peninsula rivers when the salmon are running. Competing anglers stand elbow-to-elbow, trying to land one of the thousands of fish going upstream.

### Tips for Anglers

**Fishing licenses:** non-residents pay $20 per day, $35 for 3 days, $55 for a week, $80 for 2 weeks, and $145 for a year. Licenses can be bought at tackle or grocery stores across Alaska, or purchased in advance at **W** adfg.alaska.gov
**Best fishing sites:** the Kenai River, Bristol Bay, Homer Spit, Seward, and Kodiak offer the best salmon fishing. Halibut are found along the Kenai Peninsula, Kodiak Island, and Southeast Alaska. Lakes and streams across Alaska have great trout fishing.

**Waterproof waders** made of a synthetic rubber are essential gear for anglers in Alaska.

**Deep-sea fishing** for the huge halibut known as "barn doors" is especially popular around Homer and Deep Creek on the Kenai Peninsula.

## Alaskan Sportfish

*Alaska offers keen anglers excellent fishing opportunities, and a wide variety of game fish are available in the state's waterways and along the coasts. Salmon is the most popular catch, but halibut, trout, and grayling are also highly prized.*

**King (chinook) salmon**, the largest of all Pacific salmon, are relatively common in Bristol Bay and the Kenai River.

**Arctic grayling**, a game fish, is found in clear, cold streams in the Interior between April and September.

**Halibut**, which occasionally weigh over 300 lb (135 kg), are found in the Gulf of Alaska, especially around Homer.

**Red (sockeye) salmon** run from May to mid-August in Southwest, Southcentral, and Western Alaska.

**Rainbow trout**, found in rivers from Southeast Alaska to the Kuskokwim Delta, are best fished in spring and fall.

**Arctic char** are found in clear, fresh waters in Interior and Southern Alaska between May and September.

# ALASKA THROUGH THE YEAR

Alaskans are festive types and nearly every town and village has evolved its own celebrations. Events that are not music- or sports-related typically focus on a local commodity, historic or ethnic event, some sort of novelty, or a natural phenomenon, such as events based around the midnight sun or sea ice. The atmosphere ranges from the elegant formality of the Sitka Summer Music Festival to uninhibited revelry at the Salmonfest. Summer festivals are often boisterous, round-the-clock affairs, while winter events give people the opportunity to get out of the house during the darkest days of the year. On Alaska Day and the Fourth of July, the entire state joins in the festivities, usually with displays of fireworks, but some communities often stage large celebrations that draw people from across the state.

Bird's-eye view of the rides at the Alaska State Fair

## Spring

In the spring, as the days grow longer, the ice is starting to break up, the birds are beginning to return, and Alaskans are gearing up for summer activity. Some communities try to get a jump on the excitement by staging early festivities, but the weather can be unpredictable, with snow possible in April and May.

### April

**Alaska Folk Festival** *(mid-Apr)*, Juneau. This weeklong festival features the hottest folk and bluegrass performers from around Alaska and the Northwest. Participants can also attend free dance work-shops at the festival.
**Alyeska Spring Carnival** *(3rd week)*, Girdwood. This popular spring festival is the ski resort's finale for the season, with a freestyle competition, kids' games, and the Slush Cup, where skiers and snowboarders attempt to cross an icy pond at full speed. Most end up very wet and cold.

### May

**Copper River Delta Shorebird Festival** *(1st week)*, Cordova. The return of shorebirds to the Copper River Delta is marked with three days of bird-related activities, including talks and the Great Cordova Birder's Challenge.
**Kachemak Bay Shorebird Festival** *(1st full weekend)*, Homer. Birding trips, music, kayaking, and bird-oriented activities honoring 100,000 shorebirds on the beaches of Kachemak Bay.
**Little Norway Festival** *(weekend nearest May 17)*, Petersburg. A vibrant celebration of the town's Norwegian roots, including a traditional *bunader* dress competition, parade, and Norwegian delicacies.
**Great Alaska Craftbeer and Homebrew Festival** *(3rd weekend)*, Haines. This competition between home- and microbrewers is an excellent opportunity to taste some unusual beers.
**Crab Festival** *(Memorial Day weekend)*, Kodiak. The end of the crab season is marked with music, festivities, and races, including one in which teams wearing heavy survival suits swim out to boats in the harbor.

## Summer

Summer is understandably the favorite season of most Alaskans, and communities organize an explosion of festivities designed for both locals and tourists. Attendees can plan on partying late into the midnight brightness.

### June

**Sitka Summer Music Festival** *(three weeks in Jun)*, Sitka. This popular event attracts international classical musicians every summer. Book chamber music performances in advance.
**Copper River Wild Salmon Festival** *(2nd week)*, Cordova. This event commemorates the famous Copper River reds with a dance, a salmon banquet, and

Musicians performing at the Sitka Summer Music Festival

a marathon race along the Copper River Highway.

**Midnight Sun Festival** *(Jun 21)*, Fairbanks. The festival features live music, a classic auto show, and the Alaska Goldpanners Midnight Sun Baseball Game, played by natural light at midnight.

**Nalukataq** *(late Jun)*, Barrow. An early summer festival that celebrates the end, and hopefully the successes, of the spring whaling season with Inuit games, a feast, and a blanket toss.

**Alaska Highland Games** *(last weekend)*, Palmer. Visitors can see the hammer toss, stone and caber throws, eat haggis, and listen to bagpipe music.

## July

**Independence Day** *(Jul 4)*, across Alaska. While there are statewide celebrations, Seward has the biggest event with its Mount Marathon Race. Seldovia and Skagway are also popular venues.

**Girdwood Forest Fair** *(1st weekend)*, Girdwood. This very popular festival takes place about an hour south of Anchorage in the resort town of Girdwood. Food and craft booths cover the grounds, and partygoers dance to bands on two stages. Campsites are available.

Athlete participating in the high kick event, World Eskimo-Indian Olympics in Fairbanks

**World Eskimo-Indian Olympics** *(mid-Jul)*, Fairbanks. This Native event includes an array of traditional games, including the kneel jump, toe kick, blanket toss, ear pull, and greased pole walk.

**Alaska Bearpaw Festival** *(mid-Jul)*, Eagle River near Anchorage. On offer are bear-oriented events, including a parade, a teddy bear picnic, Miss Bear Paw Pageant, and a 300-yard (270-m) dash called Running with the Bears.

**Fairbanks Golden Days** *(3rd week)*. An air show and a host of citywide activities are part of this event, which ends with a grand parade featuring a junk truck and a "hoosegow" (jail) wagon.

**Deltana Fair** *(last weekend)*, Delta Junction. A carnival, rodeo, and outhouse and mud bog races are on offer at this agricultural fair.

**Arctic Thunder** *(last weekend)*, Anchorage. Featuring ear-splitting maneuvers by the Air Force Thunderbirds, this is an unmissable summer event at the Joint Base Elmendorf-Richardson (JBER).

**Southeast Alaska State Fair** *(4th week)*, Haines. This fair features a farmers' market, a lumberjack show, pig races, a dog show, and live music.

## August

**Salmonfest** *(1st weekend)*, Ninilchik. Originally called 'Salmonstock', this Woodstock-style campout, with non-stop partying, bills itself as 'Three Days of Fish, Love, and Music'. Music styles range from rock and folk to blues and indie. There is also a daily children's program.

**Blueberry Arts Festival** *(1st weekend)*, Ketchikan. The humble blueberry is honored with pie-eating contests, art exhibitions, folk music, food stalls, and even a slug race.

**Seward Silver Salmon Derby** *(mid-Aug)*, Seward. Alaska's most famous salmon derby offers a $10,000 grand prize and a total purse of $100,000.

Crowds at the Fourth of July parade in downtown Seward

Bald eagles crowding cottonwood trees in the fall, Haines

## Fall

As tourists and seasonal workers leave, birch trees turn yellow, the air fills with the scent of woodsmoke, and over half the state's population ends up at the Alaska State Fair. With winter approaching, the frenetic activity of summer begins to wind down, with one last burst of excitement on Alaska Day.

### September
**Alaska State Fair** *(Aug–Sep)*, Palmer. This extremely popular 11-day event attracts visitors from all over the state with agricultural exhibits (including gargantuan vegetables), livestock auctions, art, food and retail booths, rides, music and theater performances, lumberjack shows, and other daily events.
**Kodiak State Fair and Rodeo** *(1st weekend)*, Kodiak. Stock-car racing, a rodeo, and live music are the highlights of this small fair.
**Labor Day** *(1st Mon)*, across Alaska. Although this is celebrated statewide, Nome hosts the quirkiest events, including a Rubber Duck Race and a Bathtub Race.
**Klondike Trail of '98 International Road Relay** *(early Sep)*, Skagway to Whitehorse. This demanding relay attracts up to 150 teams of 10 runners each, who race along the 110-mile (176-km) Klondike Highway between Skagway and Whitehorse, Canada, following the 1890s Gold Rush trail.

### October
**Alaska Day** *(Oct 18)*, across Alaska. Celebrated statewide, this day marks Russia's handing over of Alaska to the US in 1867. Sitka has one of the largest festivals, featuring wonderful Russian costumes and dances, a parade, and a re-enactment of the flag-raising ceremony.

### November
**Alaska Bald Eagle Festival** *(2nd week)*, Haines. Live music, photography workshops, and lectures fête the phenomenal return of the bald eagles to the Chilkat Valley in the fall.
**Carrs/Safeway Great Alaska Shoot-Out** *(Thanksgiving weekend)*, Anchorage. The University of Alaska Anchorage hosts top basketball teams in one of the largest pre-season tournaments in the US.

## Winter

In early winter, Christmas preparations dominate, and Alaska's snow and cold provide a quintessential holiday atmosphere. After New Year, those who haven't migrated to warmer climes participate in winter festivities, including ice-sculpture contests, indoor sports, dog sled races, and ski events.

Taking an icy dip in the Polar Bear Jump-Off, Seward

## December

**Wilderness Woman**
*(1st weekend)*, Talkeetna. Pitting women against each other in order to gain the favor of Talkeetna's single men, this competition includes snowmachine driving, wood chopping, and providing a sandwich and beer to a bachelor watching TV. It winds up with a Bachelor Auction.

**Colony Christmas** *(2nd weekend)*, Palmer. Old-fashioned Christmas festival echoing the Matanuska Valley Colony of the 1940s with reindeer sleigh rides, fireworks, caroling, and food.

World Ice Art Championship, Fairbanks

## January

**Russian Orthodox Christmas** *(Jan 7)*, across Alaska. Russian Orthodox communities mark Christmas with both solemn commemorations and joyous celebration. Traditions include "starring," in which carolers carry a decorated star from house to house singing religious carols called *koyadki*.

**Polar Bear Jump-Off** *(3rd weekend)*, Seward. People jump into icy Resurrection Bay dressed up in costumes.

## February

**Iceworm Festival** *(1st weekend)*, Cordova. Iceworms, small, thin worms that actually do inhabit glacial ice, are the inspiration for this wacky winter event. A 150-ft (45-m) long iceworm is paraded through the streets, and there is a carnival, dress-up competition, talent show, and the crowning of Miss Iceworm.

**Yukon Quest International Sled Dog Race** *(early Feb)*, Whitehorse to Fairbanks or vice versa. The race follows a route along the Yukon river and over the wild mountains between Fairbanks and Whitehorse.

**Anchorage Fur Rendezvous** *(Feb–Mar)*, Anchorage. Originally meant to bring fur trappers and buyers together, "Fur Rondy"

features a snow sculpture competition, the World Championship Sled Dog Races, and a run with the reindeer.

**Nenana Ice Classic** *(Feb–Apr)*, Nenana. Bets are laid on the exact minute that the ice breaks up on the Nenana River, with all correct entries splitting the purse.

## March

**Iditarod Trail Sled Dog Race** *(early Mar)*, Anchorage to Nome. This classic race is ceremonially flagged off from Anchorage and restarts in Willow the next day, arriving in Nome nine days later.

**World Ice Art Championship** *(early Mar)*, Fairbanks. Huge blocks of ice are sculpted into artistic forms. Dozens of teams, including participants from China, Japan, and Russia, take part in this impressive contest.

**Bering Sea Ice Golf Classic** *(at the end of the Iditarod race)*, Nome. Golf on the frozen Bering Sea, with orange golf balls and painted greens.

**Pillar Mountain Golf Classic** *(late Mar)*, Kodiak. A one-hole, par 70 golf game played up the slopes of 1,400-ft (424-m) Pillar Mountain, with the aim of hitting the ball into a bucket at the summit.

Team starting off in the Iditarod Trail Sled Dog Race

# The Climate of Alaska

Alaska's wide range of climates can be divided into six major zones. The Southeast experiences mild winters and cool, rainy summers. Shielded from the Gulf of Alaska by mountains, the region around Cook Inlet has longer, colder winters and shorter, warmer summers than elsewhere around the Gulf. The Aleutians have year-round stormy, blustery weather. The coldest winter temperatures are found in the Interior, where -40° C (-40° F) or lower is not uncommon, although the summer more than compensates with sunny days up to 32° C (90° F). Arctic winters are not as cold as those in the Interior, but snow can linger until July. The alpine climate is dictated by terrain and altitude.

### Climate Zones

- Arctic (cold dry): Short, cool summer and long, cold winter.
- Interior (cold to hot): Extremely cold winters and warm summers.
- Southcentral (cold to warm): Variable winter, warm summer.
- Alpine (variable): Weather depends on terrain and altitude.
- Bering Sea (mild and stormy): Year-round blustery conditions.
- Southeast Maritime (cool wet): Cool rainy summer, mild winter.

**BARROW**

| month | Apr | Jul | Oct | Jan |
|---|---|---|---|---|
| °C/F (max) | -14/6 | 8/46 | -7/20 | -13/8 |
| °C/F (min) | -22/-8 | 1/34 | -12/10 | -29/-20 |
| hrs | 16 | 24 | 9 | 0 |
| in | 0.2 | 0.9 | 0.5 | 0.2 |

**DUTCH HARBOR**

| month | Apr | Jul | Oct | Jan |
|---|---|---|---|---|
| °C/F (max) | 3/38 | 13/55 | 7/44 | 1/34 |
| °C/F (min) | -2/28 | 8/46 | 2/35 | -4/24 |
| hrs | 14 | 16 | 11 | 8 |
| in | 2.0 | 2.4 | 4.2 | 2.8 |

Average daily maximum temperature

Average daily minimum temperature

Daily hours of sunshine mid-month

Average monthly rainfall

*Arctic Ocean*

Barrow

*Chukchi Sea*

Nome

*St. Lawrence Island*

*Norton Sound*

A L

*Bering Sea*

*Nunivak Island*

*Bristol Bay*

Cold Bay

Dutch Harbor

*Aleutian Islands*

*Pacific Ocean*

| 0 kilometers | 200 |
|---|---|
| 0 miles | 200 |

## FAIRBANKS

| | **23**/73 | | |
|---|---|---|---|
| °C/F | **11**/52 | | |
| **6**/42 | | **0**/32 | |
| **-7**/20 | | **-8**/17 | **-18**/-2 |
| | | | **-28**/-19 |

| | | | |
|---|---|---|---|
| ☀ | **15** hrs | **20** hrs | **10** hrs | **5** hrs |
| ☂ | **0.2** in | **1.8** in | **0.8** in | **0.6** in |
| month | **Apr** | **Jul** | **Oct** | **Jan** |

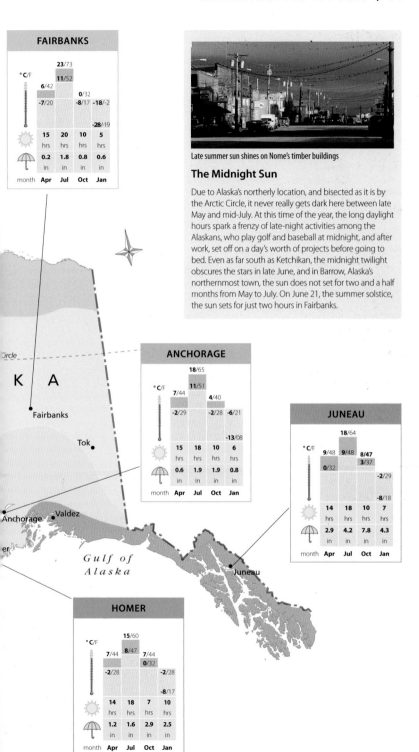

Late summer sun shines on Nome's timber buildings

### The Midnight Sun

Due to Alaska's northerly location, and bisected as it is by the Arctic Circle, it never really gets dark here between late May and mid-July. At this time of the year, the long daylight hours spark a frenzy of late-night activities among the Alaskans, who play golf and baseball at midnight, and after work, set off on a day's worth of projects before going to bed. Even as far south as Ketchikan, the midnight twilight obscures the stars in late June, and in Barrow, Alaska's northernmost town, the sun does not set for two and a half months from May to July. On June 21, the summer solstice, the sun sets for just two hours in Fairbanks.

## ANCHORAGE

| | **18**/65 | | |
|---|---|---|---|
| °C/F | **11**/51 | | |
| **7**/44 | | **4**/40 | |
| **-2**/29 | | **-2**/28 | **-6**/21 |
| | | | **-13**/08 |

| | | | |
|---|---|---|---|
| ☀ | **15** hrs | **18** hrs | **10** hrs | **6** hrs |
| ☂ | **0.6** in | **1.9** in | **1.9** in | **0.8** in |
| month | **Apr** | **Jul** | **Oct** | **Jan** |

## JUNEAU

| | **18**/64 | | |
|---|---|---|---|
| °C/F | **9**/48 | **8**/47 | |
| **9**/48 | | **3**/37 | |
| **0**/32 | | | **-2**/29 |
| | | | **-8**/18 |

| | | | |
|---|---|---|---|
| ☀ | **14** hrs | **18** hrs | **10** hrs | **7** hrs |
| ☂ | **2.9** in | **4.2** in | **7.8** in | **4.3** in |
| month | **Apr** | **Jul** | **Oct** | **Jan** |

K A

Circle

Fairbanks

Tok

Anchorage • Valdez

*Gulf of Alaska*

Juneau

## HOMER

| | **15**/60 | | |
|---|---|---|---|
| °C/F | **8**/47 | | |
| **7**/44 | | **7**/44 | |
| **-2**/28 | | **0**/32 | **-2**/28 |
| | | | **-8**/17 |

| | | | |
|---|---|---|---|
| ☀ | **14** hrs | **18** hrs | **7** hrs | **10** hrs |
| ☂ | **1.2** in | **1.6** in | **2.9** in | **2.5** in |
| month | **Apr** | **Jul** | **Oct** | **Jan** |

# THE HISTORY OF ALASKA

Known to the Aleut peoples as Alaxsxaq, "The Great Land," Alaska has been defined by cycles of prosperity and stagnation. Russian traders in the 18th century were followed by Gold Rush prospectors in the 1890s who struggled north with dreams of fantastic wealth. The discovery of North Slope oil in the 1960s led to a new boom that not only drew people to Alaska and rejuvenated its economy, but continues to affect the state and its fortunes today.

During the Pleistocene era, between 1.8 million and 11,000 years ago, the growth of continental ice sheets caused sea levels to drop temporarily and expose shallow sea floors. The sea floor between Asia and North America formed a land bridge known as Beringia. This relatively dry and ice-free area provided access across open tundra to Alaska. As a result, the Alaskan Interior became a migration corridor from Central Asia to other parts of the North American continent. This led some anthropologists to believe that Alaska was the point of entry for some of the first people to set foot on the continent.

However, timelines differ between researchers. Some believe that the first groups of hunter-gatherers arrived from Siberia as recently as 12,000 years ago, but other evidence suggests that the first migration may have taken place as early as 30,000 to 25,000 years ago. Despite such discrepancies, it is generally thought that this early migration brought the ancestors of the modern Athabaskan, Tlingit, Haida, and Tsimshian peoples, who are still resident across Alaska. By about 15,000 years ago, most of the continental ice covering Alaska had melted, closing off the Bering land bridge but opening up migration routes deeper into the continent. Although opinions vary, modern scientific thought suggests that most contemporary Native groups across the Americas are descended from these Central Asian migrants.

It is estimated that the first Inuit peoples arrived in western Alaska by *umiak* (skin boat) after the ice had melted. Some researchers date this to 8,000 years ago, while others claim it was as recent as 4,500 years ago. These hunters, familiar with Arctic coastal conditions, followed a maritime hunting culture along the Bering Sea and Arctic Ocean coasts. Over the next few thousand years, they spread farther southeast to the Cook Inlet region and east through northern Canada as far as Greenland. The Aleut settled in Southwest Alaska, as evidenced by the remains of their ancient *barabaras* or *ulax* (semi-subterranean sod dwellings).

*Inuit stone harpoon blade*

| 30,000 BC | 20,000 BC | 10,000 BC | AD 1 | AD 1000 |
|---|---|---|---|---|

**30,000–12,000 BC** First settlers cross the Bering land bridge to Alaska

**10,000 BC–AD 1000** At least 5,000 sites of human habitation across Alaska

**1000–1700** First Inuit settlers arrive in upper Cook Inlet region

**23,000–7,500 BC** Wisconsin Ice Age and migrations east and south

**8,000–4,500 BC** Inuit and Aleut migration to Alaska from Asia by *umiak* (skin boat)

**2,500–1,500 BC** Inuit migrations into Canada and as far as Greenland

**1700** Denaʻina Athabaskans begin settling around upper Cook Inlet

◀ Painting depicting the signing of the Alaska Treaty of Cession, March 30, 1867

Color engraving dated between 1820 and 1840 depicting Alaska during Captain Cook's 1778 voyage

## European Explorers and the Russian Era

It is possible that the first European to sight Alaska was the Spaniard Bartolomeo de Fonte, who is said to have sailed up the Inside Passage in 1640. Semyon Dezhnev, the first Russian in the region, saw the Bering Strait in 1648 and reported that a "great land" existed to the east. He was followed in 1728 by Vitus Bering, a Dane sailing for Tsar Peter the Great. Sailing through the Bering Strait, he claimed the land for the Russian Empire. In 1741, Bering set out on another voyage, with Alexei Chirikov as the commander of the second vessel. Chirikov landed on Prince of Wales Island in Southeast Alaska, paving the way for the eventual establishment of Russian America. Bering did not survive the journey, but his crew returned with sea otter pelts. Their success inspired many hunters and traders, known as *promyshleniki*, who headed for Alaska, exploiting not only the land's natural wealth, but also the labor of the Aleuts.

By 1772, a Russian settlement at Unalaska was harvesting the prized sea otter pelts throughout the Aleutians. Two years later, Spanish captain Juan Perez reported a Russian presence on Prince of Wales Island. In 1778, on his third and final voyage, British captain James Cook sailed the *Resolution* up the Southeast Alaskan coast and through Cook Inlet to the site of present-day Anchorage in his unsuccessful attempt to find the Northwest Passage to Europe.

To discourage British interest in the region, merchant and head of the Russian-American Company, Grigory Shelikov, established the first permanent Russian community at Three Saints Bay on Kodiak Island in 1784. Eight years later, he was granted a fur monopoly by Tsarina Catherine II. Over the next decade, both George Vancouver, who had been one of Cook's lieutenants, and Alejandro Malaspina of Spain, explored the Southeast and the Gulf of Alaska for their respective countries. Despite their efforts, Russian influence

**1725** Bering explores the area east of the Russian mainland

*Vitus Bering*

**1733** On Bering's second expedition, Georg Wilhelm Steller conducts nature studies in Alaska

**1764** Clashes between Russians and Aleuts

**1781** Grigory Shelikov establishes Russian-American fur trading company

**1720**     **1740**     **1760**     **1780**

**1728** Bering sails through Bering Strait, but does not land in Alaska

**1741** Alexei Chirikov reaches Prince of Wales Island; Bering dies on Bering Island in the Komandorski Islands

**1772** Russian settlement established at Unalaska

**1784** Shelikov sets up a town on Kodiak Island

in the region continued to expand, and at one stage the colony extended as far south as Fort Bragg in northern California.

Under the directorship of former sales representative Alexander Baranov, the Russian-American Company was granted a trade monopoly by Tsar Paul I in 1799. He was also authorized to make Sitka the seat of colonial government. Just two years later, the Russian fort at Sitka was attacked and destroyed by Tlingit protesting their forced allegiance to the tsar. Despite the defeat, the Russians returned in 1804 and Sitka was rebuilt as a veritable stockade. In 1824, Russia, Britain, and the United States signed a treaty forming the boundaries of Russian America and British Canada roughly along Alaska's current boundaries.

William H Seward, US Secretary of State

### The Sale of Alaska

By the 1830s, the Russian population of Sitka had grown to around 1,300, with Baranov emerging as the most powerful man in the North Pacific region. At the same time, overhunting of sea otters and fur seals caused a sharp decline in the profitability of the fur trade, which was replaced by fishing, shipbuilding, and lumbering. Realizing that American traders and Britain's Hudson Bay Company already had interests in Alaska, Russia began to lose enthusiasm for its distant and increasingly unproductive colony. In 1859, Tsar Alexander II authorized his agent, Baron Edward de Stoeckl, to negotiate the sale of Alaska to the United States.

Initially, Congress was reluctant to consider the purchase, especially during the 1861–65 Civil War. In 1866, California fur companies expressed interest in the Russian-American Company but it was not until 1867 that Secretary of State William H Seward championed the cause of purchasing Russian interests in North America. President Andrew Johnson and the US Congress agreed to buy Alaska for the paltry sum of $7.2 million or – as is frequently noted – about 2 cents an acre. At Sitka on October 18, 1867, ownership was officially transferred and the US flag was raised. Despite the low price, the American public generally thought Alaska was a waste of money, and dubbed the new acquisition "Seward's Folly," "Seward's Icebox," "Walrussia," and "Uncle Sam's Attic."

Hand-colored woodcut depicting Sitka in 1869

**1799** Tsar Paul I grants trade monopoly to Russian-American Company; Baranov sets up Russian fort and political capital at Sitka

*1867 political cartoon on the purchase of Alaska*

**1848** New England whalers begin commercial whaling in Alaskan waters

**1867** US Secretary of State William H Seward purchases Alaska for $7.2 million

| 1800 | 1820 | 1840 | 1860 |
|---|---|---|---|

**1791** George Vancouver of Britain and Alejandro Malaspina of Spain explore Southeast Alaska

**1840** Russian Orthodox diocese established for Alaska

**1859** Russian attaché Edward de Stoeckl is granted authority to negotiate the sale of Alaska to the US

**1861** American Civil War begins

# The Gold Rush

In the decade after the US purchase of Alaska, there was very little interest in the new acquisition, but this changed in 1880 when gold was found at the site of present-day Juneau. Little had come of earlier strikes on the Kenai Peninsula and in the Stikine Valley, but the Juneau find sparked off a fresh wave of interest. With the discovery of gold in the Klondike and in the beach sands of Nome in the late 1890s, a frenzied Gold Rush began. By the time it ended around 1905, interest in Alaska had waned again, but a small number of adventurous homesteaders continued to venture north in search of opportunity.

**Key**

☐ Gold Rush Territory 1867–1905

--- Key routes to gold mining areas

**Transport and communication routes** were set up as a result of the Klondike Gold Rush. Telegraph lines were laid and the White Pass and Yukon Route Railroad was built in 1898 to link Skagway with the Klondike, opening up the Interior to the outside world.

**Gold pans** were used to separate river gravel and alluvial gold.

**Streams** carried the gravel that contained gold.

**Steamships** were used by people who had the means to sail up the Yukon River to the gold-fields. Others took the All-American Route from Valdez across Valdez Glacier and up the Copper River system to the Yukon River.

**"Grubstakes"** were carried by all prospectors on the Chilkoot Trail, who hauled load after load of supplies over the steep pass. Fearing that unprepared miners would face starvation, Canadian officials required each man to carry a year's worth of supplies and food.

**Women travelers** such as Edith Van Buren *(left)* and Mary Hitchcock ushered in a new phase of Klondike history – while prospectors struggled to reach the goldfields, they sailed up the Yukon into Dawson as tourists in 1898.

**Capturing the popular imagination**, the Gold Rush was well represented in prose, poetry, and movies. Charlie Chaplin's *The Gold Rush* (1925), with the Tramp as a gold prospector in the Klondike, portrayed the harsh conditions faced by the prospectors.

**Tents** served as home to prospectors in the northern wilderness, and tent cities sprang up around major discoveries.

**Gold Rush literature** includes the works of Robert Service *(see pp200–201)*. Known as the "Bard of the Yukon," Service immortalized this era with his poetry, which includes "The Spell of the Yukon," "The Cremation of Sam McGee," and "The Call of the Wild," which are popular even today.

## Gold Panning

*In the river valleys of Interior Alaska and the Klondike, prospectors staked claims and set up operations to extract placer gold, particles of gold found in alluvial or glacial deposits concentrated in wilderness streams. Early prospectors used little more than shovels and gold pans, while others set up simple water-powered dredges.*

**Gold Rush mining tools** were usually basic, and included sluice boxes, gold pans, pickaxes, and shovels. Modern placer miners use gasoline dredges to process the gravel.

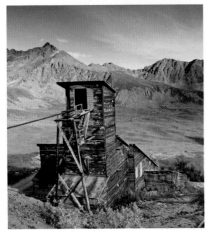

**After the Gold Rush**, most prospectors returned home penniless, having squandered their riches on frontier vices. By the 1920s, seams began to play out, and although the World War II ban on gold mining was lifted in 1946, postwar inflation made mining unprofitable. Operations such as Independence Mine *(see pp90–91)* began closing down, leaving derelict mines and dredges strewn across Alaska.

Timber structures under construction on Main Street in Anchorage in 1915

## The Gold Rush

After the purchase of Alaska, few Americans had any interest in their new acquisition. However, the discovery of gold near Juneau in 1880 and subsequently in the Canadian Klondike focused outside attention on Alaska and led to a Gold Rush that lasted for nearly two decades. By the time the Gold Rush era ended around 1905, most Americans had lost interest in Alaska, but a small, steady stream of hardy men continued to head north in search of land to homestead. In 1900, the capital was moved from Sitka to Juneau, and by 1906, Alaska had a non-voting member in Congress; it gained official Territorial status barely six years after that.

## Developing the New Territory

In the years leading up to World War II, an increasing population and interest in timber resources and seafood transformed the new territory from a useless outpost to a viable part of the USA. In the 1920s, Alaskan Natives, along with other Native Americans, were granted voting rights and then US citizenship. The Alaska Railroad between Seward and Fairbanks was completed in 1923, rejuvenating the city of Anchorage, which had sprung up in 1914 as a railway construction camp and service center for miners from the Kenai Peninsula.

During the Great Depression of the mid-1930s, President Franklin D Roosevelt's New Deal established the Matanuska Valley Colony at Palmer. Some 200 farming families, mostly from the Midwest states of Minnesota and Wisconsin, were resettled here to try their hand at farming and raising dairy cattle. Although the project enjoyed only limited success, the area remains Alaska's most productive farming region.

Workers marching back to camp during the construction of the Alaska Highway, 1942

**1872** Gold discovered around Sitka

**1880** Joe Juneau and Richard Harris unearth gold near present-day Juneau

**1884** US Congress passes Organic Act, providing education to all residents of Alaska

**1891** First oil claims staked in Cook Inlet

**1896** Gold discovered in the Klondike in Canada

Gold panning in Nome

**1900** Alaska's capital moved from Sitka to Juneau

**1902** Gold found near Fairbanks

**1912** Novarupta erupts; Alaska becomes a US Territory

**1914** Tent city of Anchorage founded as a construction camp for the Alaska Railroad

1880    1890    1900    1910

## The War Years

When Japan attacked Pearl Harbor on December 7, 1941, the American government realized the vulnerability of Alaska's position in the North Pacific, with Anchorage as close to Tokyo as it is to Washington, DC. Fears of invasion were well-founded and the Japanese launched an air attack on the Aleutians on June 3, 1942. Four days later, they captured Attu Island, taking the locals

US troops carrying a wounded soldier on Attu Island in 1943

prisoner. The US government was quick to retaliate. Hundreds of other islanders were evacuated to Southeast Alaska, troops and about 70 US Navy ships were dispatched to the Aleutians, and military bases were established at Akutan, Amchitka, and Adak. The islands were successfully recaptured by August 1943.

During this period, a large portion of the state's current highway system was developed. The greatest project was the 1,440-mile (2,304-km) Alaska Highway, which connected Alaska to the rest of the US by road (see pp290–91). This phenomenal feat involved punching a route through trackless territory, felling trees, and bridging wild rivers. Despite incredible hardships, the project was completed in eight months and 12 days, and the road was opened on October 25, 1942.

## Statehood

In 1942, Anchorage had a population of just 7,724, but the development brought about by the war caused that number to

increase to 43,314 by 1945. Several other towns grew almost as dramatically. At this point, it was clear that Alaska had matured and was on the road to eventual statehood. In 1955, Alaskans elected delegates to a constitutional convention, which would draft a constitution for the new state. The resulting document was adopted the following year, and in 1958 President Dwight D Eisenhower signed the Statehood Bill that made Alaska the 49th state of the US on January 3, 1959.

Mile 0 marker of the Alaska Highway in the town of Dawson Creek, Canada

**1923** Completion of the Alaska Railroad

Alaska State flag and US flag

**1942** Japanese invade the Aleutian Islands; Alaska Highway completed

**1955** Alaskans elect delegates to a constitutional convention

**1956** Voters adopt the new Alaskan constitution

1920      1930      1940      1950      1960

**1924** Congress extends citizenship to Native Americans

**1935** Matanuska Valley Project brings families from the US Midwest to farm in Alaska

**1943** US forces finally repel the Japanese from the Aleutians

**1959** Alaska becomes a state on January 3

**1922** Native voting rights established

Anchorage's 4th Avenue, a day after the massive 1964 Good Friday earthquake

## The Oil Boom

In 1957, oil was discovered in Cook Inlet and by the mid-1960s, platform installations were producing 200,000 barrels of oil per day. However, a major setback occurred on March 27, 1964, when one of the 20th century's strongest earthquakes – 9.2 on the Richter scale – rocked Southcentral Alaska, causing widespread destruction. Due to the low population density, loss of life was minimal and property damage

was limited to $500 million. Despite this tragedy, Alaska continued to grow. In 1968, the Atlantic-Richfield Company (ARCO) drilled an exploratory well at Prudhoe Bay on the Arctic coast and discovered an estimated 9.6 billion barrels of recoverable oil reserves on state-controlled land. Alaska sold oil leases worth $900 million, and six years later, the Alyeska Corporation began construction of the Trans-Alaska Pipeline and the black gold rush was on. Thousands of workers flooded into Alaska for well-paying pipeline jobs and 39 months and $8 billion later, the oil began to flow. In 1982, the resulting oil revenues were used to establish a state savings account, the Alaska Permanent Fund. Its future is uncertain due to falling oil prices, but for now, it still pays annual dividends to state residents.

## ANCSA and ANILCA

In 1971, Congress passed the then controversial Alaska Native Claims Settlement Act (ANCSA), which attempted to compensate Alaska Natives for the loss of

Endicott Oil Production Island at Prudhoe Bay on Alaska's North Slope

**1968** The first oil is pumped at Prudhoe Bay

**1971** ANCSA (Alaska Native Claims Settlement Act) passed

**1980** ANILCA (Alaska National Interest Lands Conservation Act) passed

**1985** Alaska purchases Alaska Railroad from federal government

| 1965 | 1970 | 1975 | 1980 | 1985 | 1990 |

**1964** Good Friday earthquake seriously damages Anchorage, Valdez, Seward, and Kodiak

**1969** North Slope oil leases sold for $900 million

**1976** Willow selected as the new capital site

**1977** Trans-Alaska Pipeline completed

**1989** *Exxon Valdez* hits Bligh Reef and spills oil into Prince William Sound

Workers cleaning oil-covered rocks after the *Exxon Valdez* spill

their lands. The Act transferred 68,750 sq miles (178,000 sq km) of land to 12 newly established and potentially profit-making Native Corporations, which roughly coincided with tribal and sub-tribal boundaries. Alaska Natives were made shareholders in their respective corporations and were given substantial control over the assets. This arrangement effectively avoided the Reservation system used in the Lower 48 and nullified any claims to Native sovereignty.

In 1980, President Jimmy Carter signed the Alaska National Interest Lands Conservation Act (ANILCA), which set aside 162,500 sq miles (420,870 sq km) as protected wilderness. As a result, a host of national parks were created, including Wrangell-St. Elias, Kenai Fjords, Gates of the Arctic, and Katmai. Unfortunately, interpretation of other facets of ANILCA have since created rifts between urban residents and rural Alaska Natives, who do not consider their homeland to be "wilderness." Many of them feel that they should have priority access to the land for subsistence purposes. City and town dwellers, however, who are constitutionally entitled to the same access to fish, water, and wildlife, also want to be permitted to exercise their rights. After more than three decades, the dispute continues.

The 1989 *Exxon Valdez* oil spill (see p121) in Valdez Arm cost the company billions of dollars and damaged both the delicate ecology of Prince William Sound and the public opinion of Alaska's oil industry. Although Alaska faces the dual challenges of falling oil prices and decreasing production, fossil fuels continue to finance state government and supply a diminishing portion of US markets. Debates about opening the remote Arctic National Wildlife Refuge to oil drilling and building natural gas pipelines currently enjoy considerably less fervor than in the heyday. Fortunately, a diversifying economy has lessened Alaska's reliance on primary natural resources in favor of tourism and service industries.

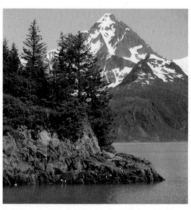

Aialik Bay in Kenai Fjords National Park, which was created in 1980 under ANILCA

| | **2004** 10,000 sq miles (26,300 sq km) of Alaska burn in the worst wildfire season since statehood | | **2007** Climate scientists call global warming "unequivocal" and point to dramatic changes in the Arctic that threaten Alaska's wildest places | **2014** A bill is signed declaring the state's 20 indigenous languages as official languages | |
|---|---|---|---|---|---|
| Japanese freighter aground and spills fuel at Unalaska | | | | | |
| **1995** | **2000** | **2005** | **2010** | **2015** | **2020** |
| **1994** Due to high cost projections, voters reverse capital move initiative; Juneau remains the capital | | **2006** Mount Augustine erupts, with pyroclastic flows and plumes of ash | **2010** Alaska population reaches 710,000<br><br>**2009** Eruption of Mount Redoubt spreads ash over southcentral Alaska | | |

# ALASKA
# AREA BY AREA

# Alaska at a Glance

Thanks to its plate tectonics and glaciation, Alaska has a magnificent array of landforms. In the Southeast, forested hills and ice-covered peaks rise above deep, winding fjords. Farther north, rugged mountains and rivers fringe the highways. Beyond the main routes, Alaska offers a wealth of variations on the wilderness theme, including temperate rainforests, Arctic tundra, volcanic islands, and boreal forests. Wildlife is plentiful and adventure activities abound, ranging from Nordic skiing to whitewater rafting. Anchorage, Fairbanks, and Juneau provide urban counterpoints to Alaska's wild expanses, offering excellent museums, restaurants, hotels, and shopping opportunities.

**Barrow** *(see pp226–7)*, well above the Arctic Circle, is the northernmost settlement in the US.

**Denali National Park** *(see pp166–9)* is Alaska's top visitor attraction. Its name comes from the 20,320-ft (6,194-m) mountain formerly called Mount McKinley, but now officially known by its Native name, Denali, an Athabaskan word meaning "The Great One." The park is home to moose, Dall sheep, caribou, and grizzlies.

• Barrow

ARCTIC AND WESTERN ALAS(
(See pp218–35)

• Kotzebue

• Nome

SOUTHWEST
ALASKA
*(see pp202–17)*

• Bethel

THE K
PENIN
*(See pp?*

Kod

**The Aleutians** *(see pp212–15)* are a long chain of stormy volcanic islands.

Unalaska • *Islands*

*Aleutian*

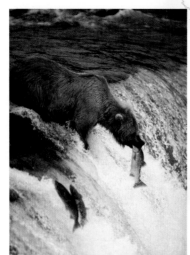

**Katmai National Park** *(see pp210–11)* takes in a vast wilderness of icy lakes, volcanic landscapes, and a wild sea coast. The McNeil and Brooks Rivers have bountiful salmon runs that attract brown bears.

◄ Glacial blue pools seen from a flightseeing trip over forested wetland south of Anchorage

**Kenai Fjords National Park** *(see pp106–7)*, near Seward, draws kayakers and day cruisers with its rugged coastlines, high peaks, icefields, and glaciers. The seas here, rich in crustaceans, fish, and plankton, host a wide variety of marine mammals.

**Kennicott** *(see pp188–9)* in Wrangell-St. Elias National Park, was the processing site for the area's prolific copper mines. The remaining ghost town is now the park's most popular destination.

EASTERN
INTERIOR
ALASKA
*(See pp180–201)*

WESTERN
INTERIOR
ALASKA
*(See pp156–79)*

ANCHORAGE
*(See pp66–95)*

PRINCE
WILLIAM SOUND
*(See pp114–23)*

Juneau

SOUTHEAST
ALASKA
*(See pp124–55)*

Ketchikan

**Columbia Glacier** *(see p119)*, west of Valdez, spills down from the Chugach Mountains to calve icebergs into Prince William Sound, whose waters are a favorite of kayakers and anglers.

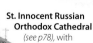

**St. Innocent Russian Orthodox Cathedral** *(see p78)*, with distinctive onion domes, dominates Russian Orthodox activity in Anchorage.

**The Beaver Clan House** *(see p129)*, in Saxman Totem Park near Ketchikan, provides visitors with a feel for Alaska's intriguing Native cultures.

# ANCHORAGE

Spread across an alluvial plain between the lofty Chugach Range and the waters of Cook Inlet, Anchorage is Alaska's largest city. In less than a century since its founding in 1914, this former tent city has grown into the economic, commercial, and transport hub of the state. With excellent museums, theaters, parks, and shops, Anchorage is not only the perfect urban foil for Alaska's wilderness, but an ideal jumping-off point for adventures farther afield.

The original tent city on the shores of Ship Creek was a service camp for the Alaska Railroad. An early sale of lots led to the growth of downtown Anchorage on the nearby bluffs, while the banks of Ship Creek developed into the town's port, shipping, and industrial district.

The massive Good Friday earthquake of 1964 destroyed parts of Anchorage, but construction of the Trans-Alaska Pipeline in the 1970s completely changed the profile of the city. A large share of oil revenue came to Anchorage, leading to an explosion of growth. The downtown area was revitalized with new sports arenas, civic centers, and performing arts venues, and outlying suburbs were integrated into the urban area. Today, the municipality of Anchorage, with a population of over 300,000 people, includes not only the city proper, but also the Joint Base Elmendorf-Richardson (JBER), several villages along Turnagain Arm, and a string of suburbs, including Eagle River and Chugiak, along Knik Arm. It also takes in the vast swathe of Chugach State Park, which brings the "real Alaska" right to the city's back door. To the north, the growing Matanuska-Susitna (Mat-Su) Borough provides space and a more outdoorsy lifestyle than is possible in Anchorage proper.

All year round, travelers will find numerous good hotels and excellent restaurants. In the summer, however, downtown Anchorage comes into its own, bustling with visitors from across the world who stop off to see the sights and prepare for adventures in the more remote parts of the state.

Native Alaskans performing traditional dances at the Alaska Native Heritage Center

◀ *Crystal Lattice*, a contemporary sculpture by Robert Pfitzenmeier, Anchorage Museum

# Exploring Anchorage

The historic downtown area and the older neighborhoods of Smuggler's Cove and Turnagain form the core of Anchorage. The main sights of interest – including the Alaska Public Lands Information Center, Anchorage Museum, and Town Square – are centered around this core, within walking distance of one another. Avenues in this central area run east-west and are numbered. Streets run north-south and are lettered from A Street westward and named alphabetically for Alaskan towns from Barrow Street eastward.

**Beyond Anchorage**

## Sights at a Glance

### Areas of Natural Beauty
⓫ Ship Creek Salmon Viewing Platform
⓬ Tony Knowles Coastal Trail
⓮ Lake Hood and Lake Spenard
⓳ Hilltop Ski Area
㉖ Bodenburg Butte
㉚ Hatcher Pass

### Parks and Theme Parks
❼ Resolution Park
⓱ H2Oasis
⓲ Alaska Zoo
⓴ *Chugach State Park pp82–3*
㉑ Alaska Botanical Garden
㉓ Eklutna Historical Park
㉕ Reindeer Farm
㉗ Musk Ox Farm
㉙ *Independence Mine State Historical Park pp90–91*

### Museums and Theaters
❶ *Anchorage Museum pp72–3*
❷ FOAST Law Enforcement Museum
❻ 4th Avenue Theater
❾ *Alaska Native Heritage Center pp76–7*
⓭ Alaska Aviation Heritage Museum

### Buildings, Neighborhoods, and Towns
❸ Anchorage Market & Festival
❹ Log Cabin Visitor Information Center
❺ Alaska Public Lands Information Center
❽ Oscar Anderson House
❿ St. Innocent Russian Orthodox Cathedral
⓯ Spenard
⓰ Alaska Wild Berry Products
㉔ Palmer
㉘ Wasilla

### Tour
㉒ *Turnagain Arm Tour pp84–5*

Signpost reflecting the city's self-proclaimed status as an air crossroads

*For hotels and restaurants in this area see p242 and pp250–51*

## Getting Around

The main sights, concentrated in downtown Anchorage, are best explored on foot. While People Mover buses connect the Dimond Center, Downtown, and Muldoon Transit Centers with most parts of town, the most convenient way to explore farther afield is by car. The Seward Highway is the main north-south corridor, while the main east-west route is the Glenn Highway. Anchorage International Airport, 4 miles (6 km) southwest of the city center, handles domestic and international flights and is served by taxis and buses. Alaska Railroad operates a year-round service between Anchorage and Fairbanks and summer trains to Seward and Whittier.

### Greater Anchorage

**Key**

Area of the main map

**Key**

Place of interest

# Street-by-Street: Downtown Anchorage

Although Anchorage began as a tented construction camp on the shores of Ship Creek, the 1915 sale of lots shifted its center to the site of present-day downtown Anchorage. After almost a century of growth and development, along with restoration work after the massive 1964 earthquake, downtown Anchorage today features a mix of historic buildings and modern high-rises interspersed with small private homes. Containing an open-air weekend market, a variety of shops, and most of the city's main sights, as well as a lovely town square and pleasant ornamentation including public artwork and flower baskets hanging from lampposts, this compact area is a joy to explore on foot.

Anchorage's busy 4th Avenue filled with visitors and locals

**❺ Alaska Public Lands Information Center**
The Center has details on Alaska's millions of acres of wild places, including Denali and 14 other national parks.

**❻ 4th Avenue Theater**
The Art Deco-style 4th Avenue Theater, which was built in 1947, survived the Good Friday earthquake of 1964.

**❸ The Anchorage Market and Festival** Alaskan arts and crafts, snacks, and fresh produce are on sale here.

**❹ Log Cabin Visitor Information Center**
This picturesque downtown log building has an oft-photographed sign showing the distance to other cities around the globe.

**★ Town Square**
With over 9,000 plants, this is a popular lunch and concert spot. In the winter, it boasts an ice rink and hosts the New Year's fireworks display.

For hotels and restaurants in this area see p242 and pp250–51

**The Wyland Whale Mural**
Created freehand by Robert Wyland in 1994, the mural depicting a family of bowhead whales is painted on a wall east of the Town Square.

**Locator Map**
*See Street Map pp68–9, D4, D5 & E5*

**❷ FOAST Law Enforcement Museum**
Founded in 1991, one of the most prominent exhibits in the museum is a sparkling, fully restored 1952 Hudson Hornet patrol car.

A STREET
C STREET
ENUE
6TH AVENUE
7TH AVENUE

**Key**
— Suggested route

0 meters        100
0 yards         100

**❶ ★ Anchorage Museum**
One of the state's premier museums, this houses excellent collections of historical artifacts, as well as traditional Native and modern Alaskan art.

**Balto's Statue**
This champion sled dog's bronze statue stands outside the turreted Wendler Building.

## Baseball in Alaska

Each summer, top baseball players from major American colleges come to Alaska to play on six semi-pro teams. Two teams, the Anchorage Bucs and the Anchorage Glacier Pilots, play at Mulcahy Stadium at E. 16th and Cordova. This is a great chance to watch the players of tomorrow – many Bucs and Glacier Pilots have gone on to play in the majors, including Reggie Jackson, Dave Winfield, Mark McGuire, Randy Johnson, Kurt Suzuki, J D Drew, Rick Aguilera, and Jered Weaver. Other Alaska Baseball League teams are in Fairbanks, Palmer, and Kenai.

# ❶ Anchorage Museum

Covering 170,000 square feet, including 2 acres (1 ha) of landscaped public space, Alaska's largest museum reopened in 2009 following a $106-million expansion. The museum houses exhibits on Alaskan history, science, and Native culture, along with some of the state's finest art. The Imaginarium Discovery Center is a highlight, as are the planetarium and artifacts from Alaskan Native cultures. Additionally, the museum hosts approximately 20 visiting exhibits annually from around the world.

The slick, modern facade of the Anchorage Museum

**The Smithsonian Arctic Studies Center** houses a remarkable collection of Native artifacts on loan from the Smithsonian.

Fourth floor

Third floor

**★ Mount McKinley by Sydney Laurence**
Considered one of Alaska's most popular painters, Sydney Laurence (1865–1940) is perhaps best known for his series of paintings of Denali (formerly known as Mount McKinley), including this iconic depiction of the mountain in enigmatic Alaskan light. Several of Laurence's atmospheric landscapes are on display at the museum.

## Gallery Guide

*The Imaginarium Discovery Center covers much of the first floor, which also houses the Alaska Resource Center (open for public research) and the Art of the North gallery, which features a broad scope of Alaskan and Circumpolar North art through the ages. The second-level galleries exhibit native and contemporary art, and explore 10,000 years of Alaskan history. Changing exhibits are displayed on level three, which also gives access to the fourth floor gallery and expansive views of the Chugach Mountains.*

Main entrance

First floor

**Key**

- The Alaska History Gallery
- Imaginarium Discovery Center
- Special exhibits
- Art of the North
- Arctic Studies Center
- Conoco Phillips Gallery
- Alaska Resource Center
- Planetarium
- Non-exhibition space

Vintage Hudson Hornet patrol car, FOAST Law Enforcement Museum

## ❷ FOAST Law Enforcement Museum

245 W 5th Ave. Map E4. **Tel** 279-5050. 🚌 to Downtown Transit Center. **Open** 10am–4pm Mon–Fri, noon–4pm Sat. 🅰 🏠
W alaskatroopermuseum.com

Founded with a handful of officers in 1941 as the Alaska State Highway Patrol, Alaska's law enforcement agency also served as the Territorial Police and the State Police before being named the Alaska State Troopers in 1967. The Fraternal Order of the Alaska State Troopers (FOAST) established the museum in 1991.

In the early days, the Troopers protected half a million square miles (1,295,000 sq km) of territory using the fairly basic technology of the time. One display exhibits a typical 1940s law enforcement office, where sealskin boots, snowshoes, a clunky period radio, typewriter, and telephone illustrate the wide range of duties a trooper was expected to fulfill.

The most popular exhibit is the shiny 1952 Hudson Hornet patrol car, one of the fastest vehicles of its era, now lovingly restored. Other displays showcase memorabilia from the days of the US Marshals, including a poster offering a $1,000 reward for Alaska's first serial killer, Edward Krause, who killed ten people between 1912 and 1915. Another intriguing device is the Harger Drunkometer, a confounding forerunner of the modern breathalyzer.

Second floor

**Prospector's Cabin**
A diorama in the Alaska Gallery shows a log cabin with a prospector weighing gold using a small balance scale.

**Yup'ik Ceremonial Mask**
This traditional Yup'ik mask, made of wood, feathers, and pigment, was created in the Kuskokwim Delta circa 1900. Masks represented characters and experiences in performances and stories.

★ **Imaginarium Discovery Center**
This kid-friendly science space has many hands-on attractions, such as a floor that responds to human movement.

The picturesque Log Cabin Visitor Information Center

## ❸ Anchorage Market & Festival

3rd Ave at E St. **Map** D4. **Tel** 272-5634. 🚌 to Downtown Transit Center. **Open** mid-May–mid-Sep: 10am–6pm Sat & Sun. ♿

A favorite of both locals and tourists, this weekend market attracts hundreds of people on summer weekends to a large downtown parking lot across from the Hilton Hotel. The event combines a farmers' market, craft booths, food, and entertainment. You'll find more than 300 vendors selling made-in-Alaska pottery, nature photography, clothing, home-made jams and birch syrup, Alaskan keepsakes, nesting dolls, colorful flowers, and an array of fresh Mat-Su Valley produce. There are plenty of fast food stalls too, selling a range of tasty snacks from pizza slices and Kachemak Bay oysters to sweet funnel cakes. The market is open rain or shine.

## ❹ Log Cabin Visitor Information Center

546 W 4th Ave. **Map** D4. **Tel** 257-2363. 🚌 to Downtown Transit Center. **Open** mid-May–mid-Sep: 8am–7pm daily; mid-Sep–mid-May: 9am–4pm daily. **Closed** public hols. ♿
🔲 anchorage.net

Operated by the Anchorage Convention and Visitors Bureau, this helpful center is in the heart of downtown Anchorage. The flower-bedecked, sod-roofed log cabin is a favorite

spot for photos, and outside there are equally picturesque signposts showing the distance in miles to many international cities. The main visitor center fills a second building. Here you'll find visitor brochures, free guides to nearby parks, and other publications, plus helpful staff to answer travel questions.

## ❺ Alaska Public Lands Information Center

605 W 4th Ave. **Map** D4. **Tel** 644-3661, (866) 869-6887. 🚌 to Downtown Transit Center. **Open** last Mon May (Memorial Day)–first Mon Sep (Labor Day): 9am–5pm daily; remainder of the year: 10am–5pm Tue–Fri. **Closed** public hols.
🔲 alaskacenters.gov

The Federal government manages more than 60 percent of Alaska lands, including

Classic neon sign of Anchorage's 4th Avenue Theater

15 national parks, the nation's 2 largest national forests, 16 national wildlife refuges, and millions of acres of other public lands. This information center, which is housed within the old Federal Building, has displays on Alaska's wildlife and natural areas, a plethora of books and other publications, and an auditorium for nature videos and talks.

If you're looking for advice on anything from buses into Denali or bush flights into the Arctic National Wildlife Refuge, this is a great place to ask experienced staff. Daily historical walks are also offered. It is located across the street from the Log Cabin Visitor Information Center. There are also branches in Fairbanks, Tok, and Ketchikan.

## ❻ 4th Avenue Theater

630 W 4th Ave. **Map** D4. 🚌 to Downtown Transit Center. **Closed** to the public.

Designed in 1941 in classic Art Deco style by B Marcus Priteca, the old 4th Avenue Theater, also known as the Lathrop Building, is the quintessential Anchorage landmark. Construction began in 1941 at the cost of one million US dollars, and the building opened to the public with the film *The Al Jolson Story*. With 960 seats spread over its main floor and the balcony, the 4th Avenue Theater served as the city's only movie house for over four decades. Remarkably, the theater survived the enormously destructive 1964 Good Friday earthquake *(see p29),* which leveled other buildings along 4th Avenue. A restoration project in the mid-1980s revived its opulent Italian marble and walnut wood interiors, which are adorned with impressive bronze relief murals depicting scenes from Alaskan history. Though currently closed, there are plans to redevelop the building; however, the theater's historic significance means that this has met with opposition.

## Urban Wildlife in Anchorage

While Anchorage may not be representative of the Alaskan wilderness, it is home to an array of wild denizens. Along with a host of birds and squirrels, moose are resident across the city. All year round, lone bulls and mothers with calves may be seen raiding gardens, snarling at traffic, and causing serious accidents that

Urban moose climbing up the front steps of an Anchorage house

often do more damage to the car than to the moose. In addition, both brown and black bears inhabit city parks and have been known to harass joggers and cyclists on city trails, while red foxes may be observed prowling the sidewalks.

The Captain Cook Monument, a life-size bronze statue in Resolution Park

## ❼ Resolution Park

320 L St. **Map** B4. 🚌 to Downtown Transit Center. **Open** 24 hrs daily. ♿

Named after Captain Cook's flagship, Resolution Park offers visitors one of the best views in Anchorage, taking in Cook Inlet and both Mount Susitna (a magnificent low mountain to the northwest, also known as The Sleeping Lady) and spectacular Denali on a clear day. The active volcanoes south of Denali, Mount Spurr and Redoubt, are also visible.

The centerpiece of this small park is the **Captain Cook Monument**, commemorating the 200th anniversary of James Cook's exploration of Alaska. An 18th-century British naval officer and explorer with a natural talent for physics and

mathematics, Cook led several expeditions around the world. In 1776, on his third voyage in HMS *Resolution*, he sailed north along the continent's west coast in search of the Northwest Passage (a navigable link between the Atlantic and Pacific Oceans), and passed the present-day site of Anchorage, giving his name to Cook Inlet. Derek Freeborn's life-sized bronze statue, based on the one in Whitby, UK, from where Cook first set sail, was donated to Anchorage during the US Bicentennial celebrations in 1976.

Just one block east, in front of the Carr-Gottstein Building, is Josef Princiotta's fabulous 1973 bronze sculpture, **The Last Blue Whale**. Adding a wonderful sense of perspective is a small beleaguered boat on the ripples of water near the tail of the gigantic whale.

## ❾ Oscar Anderson House

420 M St. **Map** B4. **Tel** 274-2336. 🚌 to Downtown Transit Center. **Open** Jun–Aug: noon–4pm Tue–Sun. 🚫 📷 ♿

This historic home was built in 1915 by Oscar Anderson, a Swede who is said to have been the 18th resident of the original tent city of Anchorage. While still living on the beach after his arrival in town, Anderson established the Ship Creek Meat Company and the Evan Jones Fuel Company. Due to a shortage of building materials, his house, the first permanent wood-frame structure in town, had only one and a half stories and measured just 800 sq ft (72 sq m). Anderson lived here until his death in 1974, and two years later, it was deeded to the City of Anchorage by his widow.

The building has since been meticulously restored to reflect the period in which it was built, and is listed on the National Register of Historic Places. Various exhibits reveal the history of the city, and many of Anderson's original belongings are on display, including a working 1909 player piano. A Swedish Christmas open house is held here in traditional style each December. Next to the house, **Elderberry Park** offers great views of Knik Arm and the chance to spot beluga whales.

Oscar Anderson House, Anchorage's oldest wood-frame building

# ❾ Alaska Native Heritage Center

Situated in a lovely wooded corner of Anchorage, the Alaska Native Heritage Center uses exhibits, workshops, and outdoor displays to preserve and perpetuate Native Alaskan culture. One of Anchorage's most popular attractions, this educational and cultural institution gives visitors the opportunity to experience a range of diverse Native traditions at a single site. Among the center's highlights are five Native "villages," which are based on broad tribal groupings that draw upon cultural similarities or geographic proximity. Native Alaskans throughout the site interpret aspects of their cultures.

*Raven the Creator*, by John Hoover, at the Welcome House

**Southeast Alaska Natives Village Site**
Revealing the cultures of the Tsimshian, Eyak, Tlingit, and Haida peoples of Southeast Alaska, this site consists of a simple, undecorated clan house and a carving shed where Native artists work on totem poles.

## KEY

① **Village Circle**

② **Raven the Creator**

③ **Talking Circle**

④ **The Aleut (Unangax̂) and Alutiiq (Sugpiaq) Village Site** occupies a *ciqlluaq* (also called a *barabara* or *ulax*), a traditional semi-subterranean sod-covered home.

⑤ **The Inupiat and St. Lawrence Yup'ik Village Site** is housed in a *qargi*, a community house usually made from sod blocks laid over whalebone frames.

⑥ **The Yup'ik and Cup'ik Village Site** features a circular *qasgiq*, or men's house. Here, visitors can watch Native Alaskans in traditional clothing interpret the Yup'ik way of life.

⑦ **Lake Tiulana** forms a natural centerpiece for the village tour.

★ **Welcome House**
The first stop for visitors, the Welcome House contains the Hall of Cultures, with craft displays and historical exhibits, and the Gathering Place, where Native dancers, storytellers, and drummers perform.

*For hotels and restaurants in this area see p242 and pp250–51*

## Exploring the Center

*The center sprawls across 26 acres (10 ha) of land not far from down-town Anchorage. A trail winds around a large central lake, leading past five Native villages and a Village Circle and Talking Circle where Native games are often demonstrated. The center also presents workshops, films, storytelling, and numerous other cultural programs. To fully explore the site will take at least half a day.*

### VISITORS' CHECKLIST

**Practical Information**
Muldoon Rd North, exit
from Glenn Hwy. **Map** F1.
**Tel** 330-8000, (800) 315-6608.
**Open** early May–early Sep:
9am–5pm daily; open for special
events early Sep–early May.
🅿 discounted rates for seniors
and children up to 16, free for
kids under 6. ♿ 🖥 📷
Ⓦ **alaskanative.net**

**Transport**
🚌 Free shuttle from Anchorage
Museum and from some hotels.

**★ Athabaskan Village Site**
This site consists of a large earth-floored log cabin that served as a traditional Athabaskan home. Here, Athabaskan docents explain the use of the home's various rooms and demonstrate traditional tools and implements.

## The Welcome House

Beyond the information desk and gift shop in the entrance area is the circular Gathering Place, an arena for traditional performances. Beyond the Crossroads foyer are the theater and the Hall of Cultures, with exhibits and stands where Native artisans create and sell their work. There is also a large research library.

Exit to the village sites

Main entrance

Library exit

The unique Welcome House entrance ushers visitors into the center

**Key**
- ☐ Crossroads
- ☐ Theater
- ☐ Hall of Cultures
- ☐ Library
- ☐ Gathering Place
- ☐ Non-exhibition space

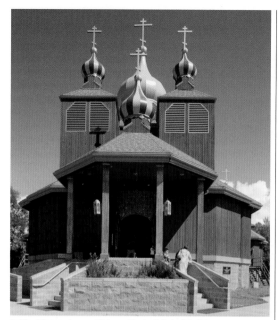

Traditional domes and crosses of St. Innocent Russian Orthodox Cathedral

### ⑩ St. Innocent Russian Orthodox Cathedral

401 Turpin St. **Map** F1. **Tel** 333-9723. 🚌 8. **Open** only for services. ♿ 🚫 ✝ 6pm Sat, 9am Sun, 6pm Thu. 🆆 sicanc.org

The heart of Russian Orthodox activity in the Anchorage area, this beautiful cathedral was named in honor of the erudite 18th-century bishop Ioan Veniaminov. Arriving in Unalaska in the early 1820s, he built churches and schools, developed a written version of the Aleut language, and produced an Aleut Bible, for which he was canonized in 1977 as St. Innocent. Due largely to the efforts of such missionaries, Alaska is today the leading diocese of the Russian Orthodox Church in the Western Hemisphere.

The most striking features of St. Innocent are its 12 blue onion domes. As with most Orthodox places of worship, the cathedral is full of beautifully colored icons, paintings, and religious artifacts. Although the cathedral is usually closed to the public, its opulent interior

can be seen during services, on feast days, or during other significant events of the Russian Orthodox calendar.

### ⑪ Ship Creek Salmon Viewing Platform

North side of Ship Creek footbridge, off Whitney Ave. **Map** E3. **Open** 24 hrs. Derby tickets: available at the cabin next to Comfort Inn on the south bank of Ship Creek.

Flowing between downtown and the Port of Anchorage, Ship Creek is a mecca for urban fishermen. Each year, the nearby salmon hatchery releases up

to 250,000 king salmon smolt, which swim downstream into Cook Inlet, spending seven years at sea before returning to spawn. To the north of the bridge across Ship Creek, a viewing platform gives visitors the opportunity to observe the salmon crowding their way upstream and jumping at the weir.

In the summer, anglers in hip-waders descend to the riverbanks in hopes of reeling in one of the 5,000 fish that are caught here each year. To fish here requires an Alaska fishing license, which is available in local shops. Fishing derbies may yield up to $10,000 for lucky anglers who catch specially tagged fish.

### ⑫ Tony Knowles Coastal Trail

Western end of 2nd Ave. **Map** B4. 🚌 7A. ♿

The most popular biking and jogging trail in Anchorage, the Tony Knowles Coastal Trail passes the attractive Elderberry Park on the downtown waterfront and follows the coastline south to Kincaid Park. One of the highlights along the 11 mile (17 km) trail is Westchester Lagoon, where walkers can observe waterfowl or cross over to the gravel beaches of Knik Arm. On clear days, there are great views across Cook Inlet to the volcano, Mount Spurr. Midway along the route, Earthquake Park has exhibits on the devastating 1964 Good Friday earthquake, which created the

Cyclists pedaling down Anchorage's scenic Tony Knowles Coastal Trail

1928 Stearman on display, Alaska Aviation Heritage Museum

dramatic bluff visible here. At the southern end of the trail, the 2 sq miles (5.7 sq km) Kincaid Park, a forested glacial moraine area, offers excellent summer hiking and a network of Nordic ski trails in the winter. The park also has the city's largest population of moose.

## ⓲ Alaska Aviation Heritage Museum

4721 Aircraft Dr. **Map** E1. **Tel** 248-5325. 🚌 7A. **Open** mid-May–mid-Sep: 9am–5pm daily; mid-Sep–mid-May: 9am–5pm Wed–Sun. 🚐 🚻 📷
ⓦ alaskaairmuseum.org

Located on the shores of Lake Hood, the Alaska Aviation Heritage Museum is a must-see for anyone interested in the lives and achievements of traditional bush pilots and their planes. There is detailed coverage of the state's World War II history, including the Japanese invasion, along with collections of artifacts, photographs, aviators' clothing, and newspaper accounts of highlights in Alaskan aviation.

The museum also preserves an extensive collection of historic aircraft, including: a 1928 Stearman bush plane that was among the first to land on Denali in 1932; one of only two remaining 1928 Hamilton Metalplanes; Merle "Mudhole" Smith's 1929 Cordova Airways TravelAir; a 1929 Loening seaplane first flown to Alaska Territory in 1946 by former governor Jay Hammond; and a 1931 Fairchild Pilgrim aircraft. A 100-seat theater is available for viewing a library of film footage about Alaska's early pilots.

Floatplane taking off from the Lake Hood and Lake Spenard complex

### Bush Flying in Alaska

Visitors who wish to fly into a remote lodge or enjoy a wilderness fishing trip are likely to employ an Alaskan bush pilot. These legendary aviators fly across untracked country, land on lakes and gravel bars, and defy natural conditions that most conventional pilots prefer to avoid. About 1 in 50 Alaskans has a pilot's license, and the state supports over 290 charter companies. Careful preparations are essential as drop-offs and pickups are prescheduled and can be disrupted by bad weather or unforeseen circumstances.

## ⓮ Lake Hood and Lake Spenard

Lakeshore Drive. **Map** E1. 🚌 7A. **Open** 24 hrs. 🚻

Keeping Anchorage in touch with the Alaska that exists beyond its urban boundaries, this is the largest and busiest floatplane base in the US. It handles up to 800 takeoffs and landings per day and anyone chartering a bush flight into a remote area will probably depart from here. The best viewpoint to watch the flights is behind the Department of Transportation building. A lakeside park features a roped-off swimming area.

Anchorage's Lake Hood and Lake Spenard floatplane base

## ⓯ Spenard

**Map** E1. 🚌 7.

Anchorage's funky Spenard district was once a separate town, connected to downtown by the winding Spenard Road. Visitors to the neighborhood may come across a scattering of less-than-reputable businesses, throwbacks to Spenard's grittier days.

Despite its past and its somewhat unsavory reputation, Spenard is rapidly becoming a fashionable neighborhood. The derelict buildings and trailer parks are giving way to houses, health food eateries, second-hand shops, motels, and atmospheric bars and clubs. The corner of Spenard and Northern Lights has a REI store (see p93), along with a Kaladi Brothers coffee shop and one of Alaska's finest bookstores, Title Wave Books.

Village buildings at Anchorage's popular Alaska Wild Berry Products

## ⑯ Alaska Wild Berry Products

5225 Juneau St. **Map** F2. **Tel** 562-8858.
🚌 60. **Open** Jan– May: 10am–8pm
Mon–Sat, noon–6pm Sun; Jun–Aug:
10am–9pm daily; Sep–Oct:10am–
8pm Mon–Thu, 10am–9pm Fri & Sat,
11am–8pm Sun; Nov–Dec: 10am–
9pm Mon–Sat, 11am–8pm Sun.
**Closed** Thanksgiving, Christmas,
and New Year's Day. 🎴 🚻 🖉 🏠
🇼 alaskawildberryproducts.com

Located on the banks of the
scenic Campbell Creek, Alaska
Wild Berry Products is a popular
tourist attraction. It boasts
the world's largest chocolate
waterfall, a 20 ft (6 m) cascade
of melted chocolate, which
conjures up images of Roald
Dahl's *Charlie and the Chocolate
Factory*. Through observation
windows, visitors can watch as
the company's jams and sweets
are made.
   A stroll around the Wild Berry
Park and Village leads to a trail
and reindeer enclosures. The
attached Sourdough Mining
Company serves traditional
Alaskan fare and holds gold
panning demonstrations.
Visitors staying downtown
can call for a free pickup. There's
another outlet in Wasilla *(see p89)*.

## ⑰ H2Oasis

1520 O'Malley Rd. **Map** F2. **Tel** 522-
4420. 🚌 2. **Open** late May–late Aug:
10am–8pm Mon–Sat, 11am–7pm
Sun; late Aug–late May: 3–8pm Mon,
Wed, & Fri, 10am–8pm Sat & Sun. 🏊
🚻 🖥 Riverwalk: **Open** 7–10am Mon,
Wed, & Fri. 🇼 h2oasiswaterpark.com

Alaska's only indoor water park,
H2Oasis has activities for all ages.
The Lazy River encircling the

park offers tubing opportunities
as well as a **Riverwalk**, a fitness
walk in slow running water,
three times a week. A Wave
Pool provides body surfing at
a balmy 27° C (80° F) – even
in winter. The
Pirate Ship fea-
tures slides for
children. Visitors
can barrel down
a 500-ft (150-m)
water coaster on
an inflatable raft, or body-slide
down the tamer enclosed water
tube. Adult swimmers can later
relax in a whirlpool spa.

Sign at Alaska Zoo, south
of Anchorage

## ⑱ Alaska Zoo

4731 O'Malley Rd. **Map** F2. **Tel** 346-
2133. 🚌 shuttle from downtown.
**Open** Mar, Apr, Oct: 10am–5pm daily;
May & Sep: 9am–6pm daily; Jun–Aug:
9am–9pm daily; Nov–Feb: 10am–4pm
daily. 🎴 🚻 🖥 🇼 alaskazoo.org

In 1966, the Crown Zellerbach
Pulp Company staged a contest,
offering either $3,000 or a baby
elephant as the grand prize. To
the company's surprise, the
Anchorage grocer who won
chose the baby elephant.
Eventually, Annabelle the Asian
elephant was donated to local
horse rancher Mrs. Seawell, who
decided that the community
needed a public zoo. The Alaska
Children's Zoo opened in 1969,
developing slowly into what is
today the sprawling Alaska Zoo.
   Although Annabelle is no
longer alive, visitors can see
a host of Alaskan and exotic
animals. There are enclosures
for moose, reindeer, and Dall
sheep. Waterfowl ponds provide
a habitat for tundra and trumpeter swans. There are snow
leopards and
Siberian tigers, as
well as a brown
bear, polar
bears, Bactrian
camels, and even
a yak. Children
will enjoy the petting zoo.

## ⑲ Hilltop Ski Area

Upper Abbot Rd. **Map** F2. **Tel** 346-
2167. **Open** winter: 3–8pm Mon–Thu,
3–9pm Fri, 9am–9pm Sat, 9am–5pm
Sun. 🎿 🚻 disabled adaptive skiing
programs available. 🖥 🖉 🏠
🇼 hilltopskiarea.org

New skiers and those without
the time or money to head
for the larger Alyeska Resort in
Girdwood will appreciate the
30-acre (12-ha) Hilltop Ski Area,
Anchorage proper's only ski

Families enjoying the tropical environs of H2Oasis

Cemetery of the Eklutna Historical Park with its brightly painted "spirit house" graves

resort. Here, the longest run (2,090 ft/637 m) offers a gradient that drops a gentle 295 ft (90 m). There are numerous other runs of varying difficulty. Access to the ski slopes is provided by a rope tow and a chairlift. In the adjacent Hillside Park, Nordic skiers will find 22 miles (32 km) of groomed cross-country trails.

## ⓴ Chugach State Park

*See pp82–3.*

## ㉑ Alaska Botanical Garden

4601 Campbell Airstrip Rd. **Map** F2. **Tel** 770-3692. 🚌 1, 75. **Open** daylight hours daily, year-round. 🅿️ 📷 Jun–Aug: 1pm daily. ♿ limited access. 🏛️ 🌐 alaskabg.org

Amid the beautiful birch and spruce forests of Far North Bicentennial Park nestles the 110-acre (44-ha) Alaska Botanical Garden. Opened in 1993, the area features a formal herb garden, two perennial gardens, an alpine rock garden, and a wildflower path dotted with erratic boulders left behind by glaciers. Boreal flora is showcased with more than 1,100 perennials and 150 native species of hardy flowering plants, shrubs, and other northern vegetation *(see p161)*. The 1-mile (2-km) long interpretive Lowenfels Family

Nature Trail follows the north fork of Campbell Creek, which is home to a summer run of king salmon. The trail offers views of the Chugach Range and reveals the geological history of the Anchorage Bowl. In the summer, the area is ideal for photography and bird-watching, and during the winter, the various trails serve as Nordic ski routes. As moose and bears inhabit the area, dogs are not allowed.

Blue poppies, Alaska Botanical Garden

## ㉒ Turnagain Arm Tour

*See pp84–5.*

## ㉓ Eklutna Historical Park

Mile 26, Glenn Hwy. **Map** B2. **Tel** 688-6026. 🚌 Anchorage–Mat-Su. **Open** mid-May–mid-Sep: 10am–5pm Mon–Sat. 📷 ♿ 🎁 9–10:30am Sun. 🏛️ 🌐 eklutnahistoricalpark.org

Forming the centerpiece of the tiny village of Eklutna, the Eklutna Historical Park was established to preserve and portray the heritage of the Athabaskan people. Founded in 1650, it is the oldest continually inhabited village in the Anchorage area. With the coming of Russian missionaries in the early 19th century, most of the locals converted to Russian

Orthodoxy, as evidenced by the onion-domed St. Nicholas church. The adjacent cemetery has over 100 graves covered with colorful "spirit houses," decorated according to individual family traditions. Early 20th-century implements used here and Athabaskan beadwork and snowshoes can be seen at the Heritage House museum.

A 3-mile (5-km) return walk, over the Glenn Highway and through birch forests, leads to scenic **Thunderbird Falls**. During the winter, this 200-ft-(60-m-) high cascade becomes a spectacular icefall.

Hiking in the lush landscape below Thunderbird Falls near Eklutna

# ⑳ Chugach State Park

Encompassing almost 770 sq miles (2,000 sq km), Chugach State Park is America's third largest state park, and one of the most accessible from an urban area. This fabulously scenic glaciated region, situated right in Anchorage's backyard, includes icefields, glaciers, high peaks, forests, and mountain lakes, all within hiking distance of the city. While no roads cross the park, there are several hiking trails through spectacular scenery, as well as plenty of opportunities to view wildlife, including moose, black and brown bears, Dall sheep, mountain goats, marmots, and a host of smaller animals. Birdlife is profuse, especially along the park's many rivers, and close-up views of salmon are available from a platform near the Eagle River Nature Center.

Hikers passing through meadows on Crow Pass Crossing

**Symphony Lake**
Cold, clear Symphony Lake, along the South Fork of the Eagle River, lies in a deep valley between the glaciated peaks of the Harmony Mountains.

**Key**

═══ Highway

═══ Minor road

▪ ▪ Trail

━━━ Alaska Railroad

▪ ▪ Park boundary

△ Peak

Fort Richardson

Anchorage

Powerline Pass Trail

Flattop Mountain
3,510 ft

Powerline Pass

Rabbit Lake

Indian Cr Trail

Bird Cree Tra

Bird

Bird

**★ Flattop Mountain**
Alaska's most climbed mountain, the 3,510 ft (1,070 m) Flattop makes a popular outing for visitors who can manage the steep 1,310 ft (393 m), two-hour-long ascent.

## Exploring the Park

*From the Eagle River Nature Center, the easy half-mile (1 km) Rodak Nature Trail and 3 mile (5 km) Albert Loop Trail lead to grand views of the Eagle River Valley. A popular day hike is the 6 mile (10 km) return hike to Echo Bend on the Old Iditarod Trail, which connects Eagle River with Girdwood.*

*For hotels and restaurants in this area see p242 and pp250–51*

★ **Eklutna Lake**
The glacial blue waters of Eklutna Lake sparkle in the sun. The camp-ground at the lake offers pleasant picnic and camping spots, while the lakeshore trail provides access to challenging alpine hikes up Twin Peaks and Bold Ridge.

## VISITORS' CHECKLIST

**Practical Information**
Eastern part of the Municipality of Anchorage. **Map** F2. ℹ Potter Section House, Mile 115, Seward Hwy. 🏕 🏔 🌐 **dnr.alaska.gov/ parks/units/chugach**
Eagle River Nature Center: Mile 12, Eagle River Road. **Tel** 694-2108. **Open** May–Sep: 10am–5pm Wed–Sun; Oct–Apr: 10am–5pm Fri–Sun. 🅿 only for trailhead parking. ♿ 🌐 **ernc.org**

**Transport**
**Taxi** from Anchorage and Eagle River; by trail from Anchorage, Eagle River, Peters Creek, and Girdwood.

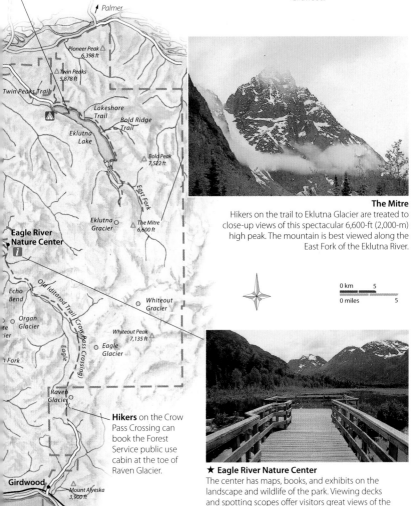

**The Mitre**
Hikers on the trail to Eklutna Glacier are treated to close-up views of this spectacular 6,600-ft (2,000-m) high peak. The mountain is best viewed along the East Fork of the Eklutna River.

**Hikers** on the Crow Pass Crossing can book the Forest Service public use cabin at the toe of Raven Glacier.

★ **Eagle River Nature Center**
The center has maps, books, and exhibits on the landscape and wildlife of the park. Viewing decks and spotting scopes offer visitors great views of the river valley and the surrounding peaks.

**For keys to symbols** *see back flap*

# ㉒ Turnagain Arm Tour

The curious name of the 50-mile (80-km) long fjord known as Turnagain Arm was bestowed by explorer Captain James Cook in 1778. He was forced to "turn again" after discovering that it was impossible to navigate a sea route between Cook Inlet and the fabled Northwest Passage. Today, a drive along the Arm's shore makes a rewarding day trip from Anchorage. A lovely stretch of the 120-mile (200-km) Seward Highway, which connects Anchorage and Seward (*see pp102–3*), following the fjord's north shore through Chugach State Park and Chugach National Forest, offering spectacular views of the Kenai Mountains across the water.

Driving along the scenic Seward Highway next to Turnagain Arm

① **Anchorage Coastal Wildlife Refuge**
Just south of Anchorage at Mile 117, a series of boardwalks provide views across Potter Marsh, frequented in the summer by nesting ducks, geese, swans, and other waterfowl.

**Key**

- ▬▬▬ Tour
- ▬▬▬ Main road
- ▭▭▭ Minor road
- ▪ ▪ ▪ Trail
- ──── Alaska Railroad
- ⋮⋮⋮ Road-rail tunnel
- △ Peak

② **Beluga Point**
At Beluga Point (Mile 110) visitors can observe Turnagain Arm empty and refill twice daily in a wall of water known as the Bore Tide, which ranges from 2 to 6 ft (60 cm–2 m), occasionally topping a dramatic 8 ft (2.5 m).

*(Map labels: Anchorage, SEWARD HIGHWAY, ALASKA RAILROAD, ① , ② , Cook Inlet, Bird, Turnaga..., Hope, Sunrise, Chugach, National, Resurrection Creek)*

## Beluga Whales

The distinctive whale known as the beluga (*Delphinapterus leucas*) is one of several beaked whales that inhabit the Arctic, North Atlantic, and North Pacific Oceans. The name beluga, meaning "the white one," was given by Russian explorers, who probably first observed them in the Bering Sea. These mammals are 13 to 15 ft (4 to 4.5 m) in length and weigh about 2,500 to 3,500 lbs (1,100 to 1,600 kg). In the summer, pods migrate into Turnagain Arm to feed and may be observed from the shore, although the Cook Inlet population has been declining dramatically in recent years, alarming scientists.

Beluga whale breaking the surface

### ③ Girdwood and Alyeska Resort
The village of Girdwood, 40 miles (65 km) from Anchorage, revolves around Alyeska, Alaska's most popular ski resort. Summer visitors can ride the gondola to the top of Mount Alyeska for sweeping views over the fjord and surrounding mountains.

### ④ Crow Creek Trail
From Crow Creek Road, a 4-mile (6-km) trail climbs past Gold Rush relics to Crow Pass, which has fine views of Raven Glacier, then continues through Chugach State Park to the Eagle River Nature Center.

### Tips for Drivers
**Starting point:** 12 miles (19 km) S of downtown Anchorage.
**Length:** 50 miles (80 km).
**Stopping-off points:** The McHugh Creek Wayside at Mile 112 offers pleasant picnic spots. Potter Section House at Mile 115 houses the Chugach State Park Headquarters. Bird Point Wayside at Mile 97 has lovely views of the surrounding forests and peaks.
**Campgrounds:** Bird Creek at Mile 101 offers good, basic sites.

### ⑤ The "Drowned Forest"
At the head of the fjord, the highway passes through a ghostly "drowned forest" of bleached dead trees, created after the 1964 earthquake (see p29) caused the land to slump 4 ft (1.2 m), allowing salt seawater to rush in.

### ⑥ Alaska Wildlife Conservation Center
This center houses and cares for displaced animals, including bears and wood bison, in a wonderful natural setting, presenting great photo opportunities. It also focuses on public education and conservation of Alaskan wildlife.

0 km          5
0 miles          5

### ⑦ Begich-Boggs Visitors' Center
Built on a terminal moraine left by the receding Portage Glacier beside Portage Lake, the center has exhibits on Alaskan glaciers. The film *Voices from the Ice* is screened hourly and describes the dynamics of valley glaciers.

### ⑧ Portage Glacier
One of Alaska's most visited glaciers, Portage Glacier extends into Portage Lake and is best viewed on cruises from the visitors' center. A level 2-mile (3-km) loop track leads to the foot of nearby Byron Glacier.

Alaska Railroad train travelling along Turnagain Arm between Anchorage and Seward ▶

Hay bales on a Mat-Su Valley farm near Palmer

## ❷❹ Palmer

42 miles (70 km) NE of Anchorage.
**Map** C1. 🚞 6,000. ✈ from
Anchorage. ℹ 723 S Valley Way,
745-2880. 🛒 Fri. 🎪 Alaska State Fair
(Aug–Sep), Colony Christmas (Dec).
W **palmerchamber.org**

Historically best known as a
farming community, the town
of Palmer nestles beneath
Matanuska Peak and the
Talkeetna Range along
the glacial Matanuska River.
Founded as a social experiment
in 1935 as part of President
Franklin D Roosevelt's New
Deal, it was settled by 200
Midwestern families *(see p58)*.
Each family in the newly established Matanuska Colony was
given 40 acres (16 ha) of land
for vegetable farming, growing
hay, and raising dairy cattle.
Today, while farming is still
important, Palmer's outskirts
are rapidly turning into bed-
room suburbs for Anchorage,

due mainly to the city's
dwindling land and high costs.
The surrounding Matanuska
and Susitna Valleys, popularly
abbreviated to Mat-
Su, are now among
the fastest-growing
regions of Alaska.
Well worth visiting
is the **Colony House
Museum**, which
reflects one of the five
basic farmhouse styles
available to the Colony
farmers. Inside, their story
is told with old newspaper
articles, period furnishings,
and artifacts.
For 12 days in August and
September, Palmer hosts the
**Alaska State Fair** *(see p48)*,
the state's biggest annual
event, drawing nearly half of
Alaska's population. The fair
features the valley's famous
giant vegetables, as well as
other agricultural displays,
crafts, livestock, food and

retail booths, live music, a
rodeo, Native dancing and
blanket tossing, and a range
of competitions.

**Ⓜ Colony House Museum**
316 E Elmwood Ave, Palmer.
**Tel** 745-1935. **Open** Jun–Aug:
10am–4pm Tue–Sat. 📷

## ❷❺ Reindeer Farm

5561 S. Bodenburg Loop Rd.
Palmer, AK 99645. **Map** C2.
**Tel** 745-4000. **Open** May–mid-Sep:
10am–6pm daily. 📷 📷 ♿
W **reindeerfarm.com**

Located in one of the original
Colony farmhouses on the flat
farmlands off the
Old Glenn Highway,
the Reindeer Farm
lets visitors see
reindeer close-up.
Children are invited
to hand-feed and pet
the animals, and meet
an elk, a moose, and
a black-tailed deer.
Those inclined to
outdoor activities can join
a horseback trail ride.

Reindeer at the farm
near Palmer

## ❷❻ Bodenburg Butte

Adjacent to the Reindeer Farm at Mile
11.5, Old Glenn Hwy. **Map** C2.

Rising out of the farmlands
on the Knik River flats south
of Palmer, the 900 ft- (270m-)
high Bodenburg Butte is one
of the Matanuska Valley's most
prominent landmarks. It was
created when Knik Glacier rode
over a small knob of resistant
bedrock, leaving a glacier-
scraped dome known as a
*roche moutonnée*. Once used
for military training, it is now a
popular picnic and hiking spot
with a windy summit from where
parasailers can launch out over
the flats. The steep trail leading
to the summit starts opposite the
Reindeer Farm and soon passes
from the stands of birch at the
base into open grassy ridges
and rocky bluffs near the top.
The two-hour-long round trek
is worth it for the views from
the summit, which take in the
Palmer area and Knik Glacier.

---

### Green Giants

Alaskans are rightfully proud of the produce grown in the
Matanuska Valley. The growing season may be short, but thanks
to the long summer days, vegetables continue to grow around
the clock, resulting in enormous carrots, turnips, zucchini, and
other produce. At the annual Alaska State
Fair, awards are given for the largest vegetable of each variety. The record-winning
rutabaga (swede) was 75 lb (34 kg), while
the largest pumpkin weighed in at a
whopping 942 lb (428 kg). The most
popular annual competition is for the
cabbage – the world-record holder,
grown in Wasilla in 2009, tipped the scales
at 127 lb (38 kg), winning the $2,000 grand
prize. Local farmers and gardeners are still
trying to break that record.

Gargantuan cabbage from
the Mat-Su

Abandoned snow-covered Mat-Su Valley barn near Bodenburg Butte

## ㉗ Musk Ox Farm

8 miles (13 km) N of Palmer at 12850 E Archie Rd, Mile 50, Glenn Hwy. **Map** C1. **Tel** 745-4151. **Open** May–Sep: 10am–6pm daily; Oct–Apr: by appt. 📷 📹 📷 **W** muskoxfarm.org

The Musk Ox Farm is home to the only domestic herd of musk oxen in the world. Hunted to extinction in Alaska in the 19th century, they were reintroduced from Greenland in the 1930s. Musk oxen now inhabit Nunivak Island, the Seward Peninsula, and the North Slope of Alaska.

Anthropologist John Teal started the farm in Fairbanks in 1964. Now located in Palmer, the farm gathers *qiviut*, the fine underwool of the musk ox, and distributes it to Native women. They spin and knit the *qiviut* into soft, warm garments using patterns and motifs unique to their villages. The farm is open to the public and runs short tours.

## ㉘ Wasilla

45 miles (72 km) N of Anchorage. **Map** B1. 🚂 5,500. 🚍 from Anchorage. ℹ️ Mat-Su Convention and Visitors Bureau, Tel 746-5000. **W** cityofwasilla.com

Home to former governor Sarah Palin, Wasilla is a long strip of unfocused development along the Parks Highway. The town was founded in 1917 and began to grow when the Parks Highway was completed in the 1970s, eventually becoming the commercial center of the Mat-Su Borough. Although not the prettiest Alaskan town, Wasilla does have several worthwhile attractions. Most of these sights are clustered north of the railroad station, off the highway at the Old Wasilla Townsite Park. The park includes historic homes, the original Wasilla School, an old barn and blacksmith shop, a reconstructed bathhouse, and the Dorothy Page Museum, named for the woman who founded the Iditarod Trail Sled Dog Race (*see p43*) with musher Joe Redington.

The **Museum of Alaska Transportation and Industry**, formerly the Air Progress Museum of Anchorage, was renamed and shifted to Palmer after a fire. When it outgrew that site in 1992, it moved to its present home west of Wasilla. In addition to a large gallery and exhibit hall, the museum has an outdoor collection that includes *umiaks* (skin boats), railway memorabilia, and vintage steam engines, aircraft, and vehicles.

Situated near the former Iditarod restart site, the **Knik Museum and Musher's Hall of Fame** is located in an old roadhouse. Visitors can see objects from the now-defunct town of Knik, as well as Iditarod exhibits such as race trophies, charcoal drawings of past winners, and a presentation on famous Alaskan mushers.

### 🏛 Museum of Alaska Transport and Industry
5 miles (8 km) W of Wasilla at 3800 W. Museum Drive. **Tel** 376-1211. **Open** May–Sep: 10am–5pm daily. 📷 **W** museumofalaska.org

### 🏛 Knik Museum and Musher's Hall of Fame
Mile 13.9, Knik Rd. **Tel** 376-2005. **Open** Jun–Aug: noon–6pm daily. 📷

Bull musk oxen facing off on a snowy plain

# ㉙ Independence Mine State Historical Park

Most people associate gold mining in Alaska with the placer gold *(see p57)* diggings in the Klondike. However, starting in 1906, a gold-bearing quartz lode was being tapped in the Talkeetna Mountains. Two mines were established in the scenic mountain valley of the Little Susitna River, the Alaska Free Gold Mine on Skyscraper Mountain and the Independence Mine on Granite Mountain. In 1938, the two were merged into the Alaska-Pacific Consolidated Mining Company. Although the mines were producing large amounts of gold, the activity was deemed non-essential during World War II, and after the war, government restrictions on private ownership of gold spelled the end of the mine. The site was designated a State Historical Park in the late 1970s.

Mine buildings scattered across Fishhook Valley

★ **Bunk Houses**
Three of the larger buildings at Independence Mine served as bunk houses. One was built in 1939 and functioned as a supply warehouse, engineering office, and school. A small, well-appointed building nearby had self-contained housing units for top mine officials.

## Key

① **The New Bunk House** was built in 1940 to accommodate 50 people. It also contained rooms used for classes and for screening films.

② **The Manager's House** was constructed in 1939 to house the mine manager's family and guests. Today, the distinctive building serves as the park's Visitor Center and administrative headquarters.

③ **The New Mess Hall**, constructed in 1941, had a well-equipped kitchen, bakery, butchery, scullery, and a dining hall that seated 160 people.

④ **The Administrative Building** was used as an office, storeroom, and bunk house during an attempt to reopen the mine in 1946.

⑤ **Mechanical and repair shops** housed plumbing, carpentry, and electrical operations.

⑥ **The Assay Office** now houses the site museum.

⑦ **An ore conveyor** brought ore into the mill where it was sorted and crushed to extract the gold.

⑧ **The Hard Rock Trail** leads to a park overlook near the Water Tunnel Portal.

## Exploring the Mine

*To fully explore the park's historic buildings and ruins will take two to three hours. The Main Trail is an easy, level route that begins at the Manager's House and loops past the Mess Hall, Administrative Building, and Bunk Houses, with a short detour to the Museum (Assay Office). The more challenging 20-minute Hard Rock Trail climbs the tundra-covered hillside to an overlook near the Water Tunnel Portal and Mine Shops. Guided tours of the mine last between 60 and 90 minutes.*

Hatcher Pass Road winding through the
Independence Mine area

# ⚅ Hatcher Pass

21 miles (34 km) N of Palmer at Mile
19 of the Hatcher Pass Road. **Map** B1.
**Taxi** from Anchorage, Willow, &
Palmer. The pass is usually closed from
September to May; check in advance.

Beyond Independence Mine,
the Hatcher Pass Road climbs
up onto the "tail" of the
Talkeetna Range that reaches
westward toward Willow and
makes a wonderful driving or
biking route. The road is paved
only as far as the Independence
Mine turn-off and Hatcher Pass
Lodge at Mile 17. Shortly after,
at Mile 19, it crosses 3,886-ft
(1,166-m) Hatcher Pass, one of
Alaska's highest road passes,
before twisting for another
31 miles (50 km) to Willow.

Just beyond the pass, the
road passes through the
Summit Lake State Recreation
Site. The lake itself is a small
alpine tarn in a glacial cirque,
or steep-walled basin, and is
accessed by a trail around its
perimeter and along the bluff
overlooking it. The inspiring
views take in the Susitna Valley,
Willow Creek, and the Alaska
Range in the distance.

In the summer, Hatcher Pass
is an excellent paragliding
venue, and a number of hiking
trails, including the popular
Gold Mint Trail, take off into
the peaks and valleys. In the
winter, the attraction is the
network of Nordic skiing and
snowmachining trails that
lead into the wilds of the
Talkeetna Mountains.

★ **Mill Complex**
The 1937 mill complex, uphill from the mine
offices, includes a welding shed, ore sorting
plant, machine shop, and blacksmith. An
aerial tramway carried supplies up the hill
and returned laden with ore.

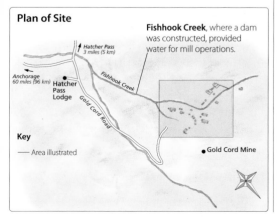

## Plan of Site

**Fishhook Creek**, where a dam
was constructed, provided
water for mill operations.

Hatcher Pass
3 miles (5 km)

Anchorage
60 miles (96 km)

Hatcher
Pass
Lodge

Fishhook Creek

Gold Cord Road

Gold Cord Mine

**Key**

— Area illustrated

# SHOPPING IN ANCHORAGE

Anchorage is arguably the best place in Alaska to pick up gifts and souvenirs that are unique to the state. Throughout downtown, numerous small shops sell inexpensive gifts and mementos, while a range of higher-quality shops and art galleries offer Alaskan art and photography, furs, local foods, Native arts and crafts, and antiques. Mainstream shopping ranges from warehouse-like box stores, such as Fred Meyer outlets, to large shopping malls and the more upmarket Nordstrom store. Due to its position as a jumping-off point for adventure activities, the city is also an excellent place to pick up outdoor supplies, and several local outlets sell camping, hiking, cycling, boating, hunting, and fishing gear to help prepare for outdoor adventures.

Soapstone carvings on display at Anchorage's Weekend Market

## Markets and Fairs

Every Saturday and Sunday, between mid-May and mid-September, the **Anchorage Market and Festival** *(see p74)* fills the parking lot downtown at 3rd Avenue and E Street, selling Alaskan crafts, souvenirs, freshly cooked food, and clothing. From June to August, at the Northway Mall grounds in East Anchorage, the **Wednesday Market** sells similar items from 11am to 5pm. The **Center Market** inside the Sears Mall offers gourmet and farm foods every Wednesday and Saturday year-round. The ultimate informal shopping experience is undoubtedly the annual **Alaska State Fair** *(see p48)* in Palmer.

## Alaskan Arts and Antiques

One of the best ways to find unusual Alaskan photography, art, and original creations is to attend the First Friday openings of art galleries. The **Iditarod** **Trail Store** sells official Last Great Race patches, dog booties, posters, and other memorabilia. A legacy of the Gold Rush, Alaskan gold makes excellent jewelry, souvenirs, and investment items. The **Alaska Mint** sells Alaskan gold and silver coins and medallions. The gift shop at the **Anchorage Museum** has a fine selection of works by Alaskan artists, including traditional pieces. In the summer, local artists have their wares on display in the atrium. In addition, fine art galleries are dotted throughout downtown Anchorage.

## Native Arts and Crafts

Alaska's most unique product is clothing made of *qiviut*, the fine underwool of the musk ox, sold at the **Oomingmak Musk Ox Producers' Co-operative**. *Ulus*, rounded knives used by Native women, are also popular. Most gift shops sell them but the **Ulu Factory** has the largest selection of authentic knives. Other gifts include baskets made of grass, bark, and baleen (also called whalebone), beaded purses and belts, and fine scrimshaw art on ivory and bone. The **Alaska Native Medical Center Craft Shop** sells high quality Native objects from all over Alaska. At the **Alaska Native Heritage Center** *(see pp76–7)*, visitors can watch artists at work and purchase gifts from the on-site shop. **One People Gifts** is a cooperative shop selling authentic Native arts and crafts.

While shopping for Native art, especially soapstone carvings, it is best to be careful, as items mass-produced abroad are occasionally sold as Native art. The state-run Silver Hand program guarantees that products tagged with the Silver Hand label were made by Native Alaskans using Alaskan materials. However, the program is not universal, and plenty of legitimate crafts do not carry the label.

Pottery and wood-crafted ducks for sale in an Anchorage shop

## Alaskan Foods

**10th and M Seafoods** sells smoked fish and freshly caught salmon, and will also smoke, freeze, and package visitors' own catch of fish or game for the trip home. **Alaska Sausage and Seafood** will turn hunters' moose, caribou, or deer into sausage products, and sells smoked salmon and reindeer sausage. **Alaska Wild Berry Products** *(see p80)* is the best place for Alaskan berries made into jam and sweets. Exotic seafood is available at the three **New Sagaya's Markets**, the city's prominent Oriental groceries.

## Department Stores

The main shopping malls in Anchorage are occupied by department stores of varying price and quality. The most down-to-earth choice is the **Dimond Center**, which features Gap and Old Navy for clothing and Best Buy for electronics.

The midtown **Sears Mall** has a large Sears Department Store, which sells clothing and appliances, while the downtown **5th Avenue Mall** is best known for its Nordstrom store. There are also a large number of box stores, massive outlets that sell just about everything at discounted prices. The most pleasant of these are the **Fred Meyer** stores, which also have a grocer, bakery, and deli. The cheapest places are the membership warehouses **Costco** and **Sam's Club**, which sell quality items in bulk.

## Sporting Goods

Due to its outdoor orientation, Anchorage is an excellent place to stock up on gear before heading out into the wilderness on a camping, hiking, backpacking, fishing, hunting, whitewater rafting, or kayaking trip. One of the most popular stores in town is **REI** (Recreational Equipment Incorporated), a membership retailer that mainly stocks equipment, clothing, and lightweight gear for non-motorized sports. **Alaska Mountaineering and Hiking**, a similar outlet nearby, sells gear from a range of manufacturers and is aimed primarily at rock climbers and mountaineers. For keen hunters, anglers, and campers, there are no better outfitters than the mind-boggling **Cabela's** and **Sportsman's Warehouse**, both of which offer everything from camouflage clothing, winter gear, footwear, and salmon smokers to hunting hides, rifles, pontoon boats, and skinning knives.

Visitors who are in town in the cold season and want to try out some winter sports can drop by **Play It Again Sports** and pick up warm clothing, as well as used and new skiing, skating, snowshoeing, and hockey equipment at discounted prices.

# DIRECTORY

## Markets and Fairs

**Anchorage Market and Festival**
3rd Ave & E St. **Map** D4. **Tel** 272-5634.
w anchoragemarkets.com

**The Center Market**
The Mall at Sears, 600 N. Lights Blvd. **Map** E1. w thecentermarket.com

**Wednesday Market**
Northway Mall. **Map** F1. **Tel** 272-5634. w anchoragemarkets.com

## Arts, Crafts, and Antiques

**Alaska Mint**
429 W 4th Ave. **Map** D4. **Tel** 278-8414.
w alaskamint.com

**Alaska Native Medical Center Craft Shop**
4315 Diplomacy Dr. **Map** F1. **Tel** 729-1122.
w anthc.org

**Iditarod Trail Store**
5th Avenue Mall, 320 W 5th Ave. **Map** E5. **Tel** 276-2350. w iditarod.com

**One People Gifts**
425 D St. **Map** D4. **Tel** 274-4063.

**Oomingmak Musk Ox Producers' Co-operative**
604 H St. **Map** C5. **Tel** 272-9225. w qiviut.com

**Ulu Factory**
211 W Ship Creek Ave. **Map** E3. **Tel** 276-3119. w theulufactory.com

## Alaskan Foods

**10th and M Seafoods**
1020 M St. **Map** E1. **Tel** 272-3474, 800-770-2722. w 10thandmseafoods.com

**Alaska Sausage and Seafood**
2914 Arctic Blvd. **Map** E1. **Tel** 562-3636.
w alaskasausage.com

**New Sagaya's Markets**
3700 Old Seward Hwy. **Map** F1. **Tel** 561-5173.
900 W 13th Ave. **Map** E1. **Tel** 561-5173. 2525 Blueberry Road. **Map** E1. **Tel** 563-0220. w newsagaya.com

## Department Stores

**5th Avenue Mall**
320 W 5th Ave. **Map** E5.

**Costco**
330 W Dimond Blvd. **Map** E2. **Tel** 344-6436. 4125 Debarr Road. **Map** F2. **Tel** 269-9510. w costco.com

**Dimond Center**
Dimond Blvd & Old Seward. **Map** F2. **Tel** 344-2581.
w dimondcenter.com

**Fred Meyer**
7701 Debarr Rd. **Map** F1. **Tel** 269-1700.
w fredmeyer.com

**Sam's Club**
8801 Old Seward Hwy. **Map** F2. **Tel** 522-2333. w samsclub.com

**Sears Mall**
Benson & Seward Hwy. **Map** E1. **Tel** 264-6695.
w mallatsears.com

## Sporting Goods

**Alaska Mountaineering and Hiking**
2633 Spenard Rd. **Map** E1. **Tel** 272-1811.
w alaskamountaineering.com

**Cabela's**
155 W 104th Ave. **Map** F2. **Tel** 341-3400.

**Play It Again Sports**
2636 Spenard Rd. **Map** E1. **Tel** 278-7529.
w playitagainsportsanchorage.com

**REI**
1200 W Northern Lights Blvd. **Map** E1. **Tel** 272-4565. w rei.com

**Sportsman's Warehouse**
8681 Old Seward Hwy. **Map** F2. **Tel** 644-1400.
w sportsmanswarehouse.com

# ENTERTAINMENT IN ANCHORAGE

While Anchorage may be better known as a launch pad to the wilderness, it nonetheless offers a range of entertainment that is more vibrant than any other Alaskan city. The seemingly endless daylight hours of summer are ideal for outdoor activities, while in autumn and winter, indoor pursuits such as concerts, theater, opera, and ballet are available. The Alaska Center for the Performing Arts, in downtown Anchorage, is renowned for its cultural events, while the Sullivan Arena hosts rock concerts and sporting events. The city also has numerous cinemas, bars, and nightclubs, many of which offer live entertainment and excellent locally produced brews.

## Information and Tickets

Published every Thursday, the *Anchorage Press* is the best source of information on art exhibitions, concerts, festivals, and sports. This free weekly paper is distributed to businesses across the city. The **Anchorage Convention and Visitors' Bureau** also keeps abreast of upcoming events. Tickets for most programs can be easily bought at the Alaska Center for the Performing Arts or obtained directly from the various venues. Alternatively, **Ticketmaster** outlets can be found at Fred Meyer stores around the city.

## Theater and Concerts

Major theater and musical productions are staged at the Atwood Concert Hall, the Discovery Theater, and the Sydney Laurence Theater, all located in the **Alaska Center for the Performing Arts**. The

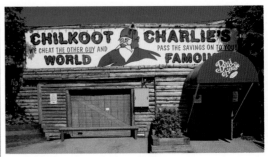
The log cabin theme at Chilkoot Charlie's in Anchorage

**Anchorage Opera**, the **Alaska Dance Theatre**, the **Anchorage Symphony Orchestra**, and the **Anchorage Concert Association** perform at the center. The **Sullivan Arena** hosts pop and rock concerts, while plays and small classical music shows are held at the Wendy Williamson Auditorium, the Arts Theater, and the Arts Recital Hall at the **University of Alaska Anchorage**.

## Cinema

While there are no real art film venues in Anchorage, several multiplex cinemas such as **Regal Tikahtnu Stadium Cinemas** and **Century 16 Cinemas** screen popular first-run films. Showing inexpensive second-run movies, the **Bear Tooth Theatre Pub** also offers some excellent microbrewery beer and good food in a bar-and-restaurant environment. For extensive film reviews, there is the *Anchorage Press*, while cinema listings are outlined in the city's main newspaper, the *Alaska Dispatch News*.

## Cultural Presentations

The large open theater at the **Alaska Native Heritage Center** (*see pp76–7*) plays host to a range of Native arts, theater, dance, and sports demonstrations. The **Anchorage Museum** (*see pp72–3*) often features visiting art exhibitions. On the first Friday of every month, galleries across Anchorage hold art openings, usually attended by showcased artists. During the winter, the downtown **Dena'ina Civic and Convention Center** hosts a variety of cultural events as well.

## Clubs and Bars

Anchorage enjoys a vibrant nightlife, with a good variety of clubbing and drinking venues on offer. For rock, pop, and sheer mayhem, the hotspot is **Chilkoot Charlie's**, popularly nicknamed "Koot's." Downtown, head to **Humpy's Great Alaskan Alehouse** (*see p250*) for live music, a packed dance floor, microbrews on draught, and tasty pub grub. **Cyrano's Off Center Playhouse** showcases live performances by Cyrano's Theatre Company. For

Traditional dance performance at the Alaska Native Heritage Center

Anchorage Glacier Pilots playing the Bucs at Mulcahy Stadium

basketball team hosts the **Great Alaska Shootout** in late November, and the **Alaska Aces** hockey team play at the Sullivan Arena in winter. The **World Championship Sled Dog Races** are held in February, while the **Iditarod Trail Sled Dog Race** is flagged off in early March.

fans of the amber fluid, the **Glacier Brewhouse,** the **Moose's Tooth** pub-cum-pizzeria (sister joint to the Bear Tooth Theatre Pub) and the **Snow Goose** (see p250 for all three venues) can between them serve up a limitless selection of microbrewery beers. The most popular LBGT bar and entertainment center is **Mad Myrna's**.

## Sports

Although Anchorage has no major league baseball or NHL hockey team, it takes pride in sport. During the summer, the Alaska Minor Baseball League's **Anchorage Glacier Pilots** and **Anchorage Bucs** play in town. The **University of Alaska Anchorage (UAA) Seawolves**

## Children

With an array of children's activities on offer, Anchorage promises to be a fun experience for the family. The Children's Gallery at the **Anchorage Museum** (see pp72–3) caters specifically to youngsters with its extraordinary **Imaginarium Discovery Center,** home to a host of fun activities. The **Alaska Zoo** (see p80) offers a wonderful day out for kids.

---

# DIRECTORY

## Information and Tickets

**Anchorage Convention and Visitors' Bureau**
546 W 4th Ave. **Map** D4.
**Tel** 274-3531.
w anchorage.net

**Anchorage Press**
540 E 5th Ave. **Map** E5/F5.
**Tel** 561-7737.
w anchoragepress.com

**Ticketmaster**
w ticketmaster.com

## Theater and Concerts

**Alaska Center for the Performing Arts**
621 W 6th Ave. **Map** D5.
**Tel** 263-2900.
w myalaskacenter.com

**Alaska Dance Theatre**
550 E 33rd Ave. **Map** F1.
**Tel** 277-9591.
w alaskadancetheatre.org

**Anchorage Concert Association**
430 W 7th Ave, No. 200.
**Map** D5. **Tel** 272-1471.
w anchorageconcerts.org

**Anchorage Opera**
1507 Spar Ave.
**Map** E4. **Tel** 279-2557.
w anchorageopera.org

**Anchorage Symphony Orchestra**
400 D St No. 230.
**Map** D4. **Tel** 274-8668.
w anchoragesymphony.org

**Sullivan Arena**
1600 Gambell St.
**Map** F1. **Tel** 279-0618
(Box Office).
w sullivanarena.com

**University of Alaska Anchorage**
Department of Theatre and Dance, 3211 Providence Dr.
**Map** F1. **Tel** 786-4849 (Box Office). w theatre.uaa.alaska.edu

## Cinema

**Bear Tooth Theatre Pub**
1230 W 27th Ave.
**Map** E1. **Tel** 276-4200.
w beartooththeatre.net

**Century 16 Cinemas**
301 E 36th Ave. **Map** F1.
**Tel** 770-2602.

**Regal Tikahtnu Stadium Cinemas**
1102 N Muldoon Rd.
**Map** F1. **Tel** (844) 462-7342.

## Cultural Presentations

**Dena'ina Civic and Convention Center**
600 W 7th Ave. **Map** D5.
**Tel** 263-2850.
w anchorageconventioncenters.com

## Clubs and Bars

**Chilkoot Charlie's**
2435 Spenard Road.
**Map** E1. **Tel** 272-1010.
w koots.com

**Cyrano's Off Center Playhouse**
413 D St. **Map** D4. **Tel** 274-2599. w cyranos.org

**Mad Myrna's**
530 E 5th Ave. **Map** F1.
**Tel** 276-9762.

## Sports

**Alaska Aces**
724 E 15th Ave, Suite C.
**Map** E1. **Tel** 258-2237.
w alaskaaces.com

**Anchorage Bucs**
**Tel** 561-2827.
w anchoragebucs.com

**Anchorage Glacier Pilots**
207 E Northern Lights Blvd No. 105. **Map** E1.
**Tel** 274-3627.
w glacierpilots.com

**Great Alaska Shootout**
3211 Providence Dr.
**Map** F1. **Tel** 786-1250.
w goseawolves.com

**Iditarod Trail Sled Dog Race**
2100 S.Knik-Goosebay Road, Wasilla.
**Map** B1. **Tel** 376-5155.
w iditarod.com

**University of Alaska Anchorage (UAA) Seawolves**
3211 Providence Dr.
**Map** F1. **Tel** 786-1250.
w goseawolves.com

**World Championship Sled Dog Races**
400 D St No. 110. **Map** D4.
**Tel** 274-1177.
w furrondy.net

# THE KENAI PENINSULA

Frequently referred to as Alaska's Playground for the range of outdoor activities it offers, the Kenai Peninsula is a microcosm of the state. Its eastern half has forested slopes and icefields, and a coast cut by deep fjords and dramatic valleys that usher glacier ice into the sea. The west is gentler, with muskeg bog, rolling, lake-studded lowlands full of wildlife, and seas that brim with marine life.

Situated on the northern shore of the Gulf of Alaska, the peninsula derives its name from the Kenaitze people of the Dena'ina Athabaskans, who moved here from the interior regions of Alaska. With the coming of the Russians in the late 18th century and the establishment of the towns of Ninilchik and Kenai, Native culture gradually began to give way to Russian influences, as the peninsula became the main focus of Russian activity in Alaska.

After the US purchased Alaska in 1867, the area remained a backwater until the discovery of gold near Hope in the 1890s. Since then, Seward has gained importance as a center for transportation and shipping, Homer thrives on its fisheries, and the economy around Kenai and Soldotna is driven mainly by sport-fishing and waning oil and gas extraction in Cook Inlet. The entire peninsula has also benefitted from tourism. Its proximity to Anchorage and its diverse landscape has helped make the region one of the most populated, best connected, and most visited in the state. With its relatively dense road network, the Alaska Railroad, the Marine Highway, and the cruise ship port at Seward, the peninsula is an easily accessible destination for most independent travelers and those on package tours.

The area offers stunning drives that wind through the Chugach National Forest. Kenai Fjords National Park and many state parks offer campsites, beaches, and miles of hiking trails. In the summer, outdoors enthusiasts bound for activity-packed weekends crowd onto the scenic Seward Highway, while anglers gravitate toward the Kenai River, or opt for deep-sea fishing in Kachemak Bay. For those interested in soaking up Russian ambience and history, the towns of Ninilchik, Nikolaevsk, and Seldovia make good stopping-off points.

Rolling fields and verdant mountains of the Kenai Peninsula

◀ Fresh catch of halibut and other fish displayed on the dock at Seward

# Exploring the Kenai Peninsula

The varied landscape of the Kenai Peninsula takes in everything from fjords and glaciers to forests and muskeg. Kenai Fjords National Park contains the Harding Icefield, one of the largest in the US. The peninsula also features three very distinctive urban areas – practical Seward, the bustling, commercial Kenai-Soldotna region, and free-spirited Homer. These towns boast some excellent attractions, including Seward's Alaska SeaLife Center and Homer's Oceans and Islands Visitors' Center, as well as good places to stock up on supplies for outdoor activities. For the adventurous, the Kenai River is ideal for rafting and fishing, while the Resurrection Pass Trail is Alaska's most popular multi-day hiking route.

Visitors at the tour offices and gift shops along the Homer Spit

## Sights at a Glance

**Towns and Cities**
1. Hope
2. Moose Pass
3. Cooper Landing
6. *Seward pp102–5*
8. Sterling
9. Soldotna
10. Kenai
13. Clam Gulch
14. Ninilchik
15. Anchor Point
16. Nikolaevsk
17. *Homer pp112–3*

**National and State Parks**
7. *Kenai Fjords National Park pp106–7*
11. Captain Cook State Recreation Area
12. Kenai National Wildlife Refuge

**Area of Natural Beauty**
4. *Kenai River*

**Tour**
5. *Resurrection Pass Trail p101*

## Getting Around

It is easiest to explore the region with an organized tour or by car. The Seward Highway links the Kenai Peninsula to Anchorage, while the Sterling Highway runs along the peninsula's west coast. In the summer, Homer Stage Line buses connect Anchorage and Homer on weekdays, while daily Park Connection Motorcoach buses run between Seward and Denali National Park. Also in the summer, there is a daily Alaska Railroad service from Seward, and the Marine Highway ferry *Tustumena* calls at Homer and Seldovia. Homer and Kenai are served by year-round scheduled flights from Anchorage.

*For hotels and restaurants in this area see pp242–3 and pp251–2*

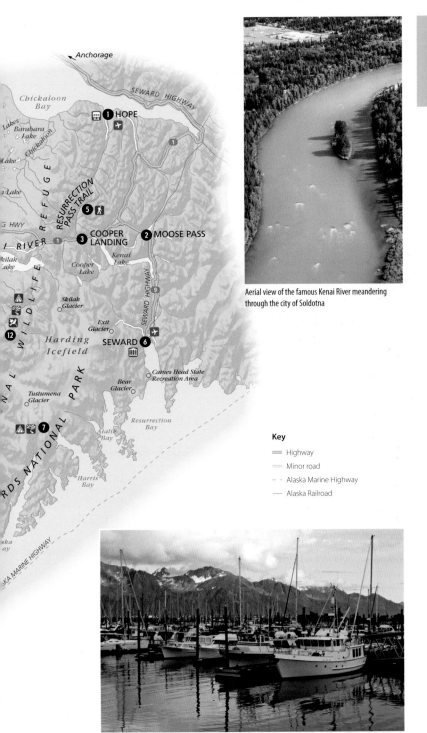

Aerial view of the famous Kenai River meandering through the city of Soldotna

Charter vessels and fishing boats at a pier in Seward

**Key**

━━━ Highway

┅┅┅ Minor road

– – Alaska Marine Highway

──── Alaska Railroad

Lakeside views from the quaint vilage of Hope

# ❶ Hope

88 miles (141 km) S of Anchorage.
**Transport map** B3. 🚐 190. ✈
⛷ Wagon Trail Run (3rd weekend in Jul). 🅦 hopealaska.info

The historic gold-mining town of Hope nestles at the mouth of Resurrection Creek on the southern shore of Turnagain Arm *(see pp84–5)*. Named after Percy Hope, a 17-year-old prospector, Hope's heyday was in the late 1890s, when it was a rollicking Gold Rush town. By the end of the decade, however, many of the town's inhabitants had pulled up stakes and headed for the Klondike goldfields.

Today, despite its proximity to Anchorage and the Seward Highway, Hope remains a quiet place. Most visitors stroll around town and visit the 1902 log social hall and the old 1896 general store, now home to the Seaview Café and Bar. Recreational opportunities here include camping at Porcupine Campground, rafting on Six-Mile Creek, and hiking the Gull Rock Trail. More energetic hikers can try the **Resurrection Pass Trail**, which passes both historic and modern-day gold diggings.

# ❷ Moose Pass

98 miles (158 km) S of Anchorage.
**Transport map** B3. 🚐 220.
🚌 Anchorage–Seward. **Tel** 288-3101 (Trail Lake Lodge). ⛷ Moose Pass Solstice Festival (weekend nearest June 21). 🅦 moosepassalaska.com

Moose Pass village began life in 1912 as a construction camp on the Alaska Railroad. The area was named in 1903, after, it is said, a moose blocked the

passage of a mail-carrying dog team. To the west of the Seward Highway stands a landmark waterwheel, constructed in 1976 by the Estes Brothers who still run a grocery located in the adjacent 1928 building. Moose Pass sits on the south side of Trail Lake, and a local air taxi provides flightseeing trips.

North of Moose Pass, a salmon hatchery next to North Trail Lake is the starting point of the 21-mile (35-km) **Johnson Pass Trail**. Following the lakeshore, the trail climbs over its namesake before descending to Granite Creek at Mile 62.9 of the Seward Highway.

# ❸ Cooper Landing

98 miles (158 km) S of Anchorage.
**Transport map** B3. 🚐 290.
🚌 Anchorage–Homer. **Tel** 595-8888. ℹ️ Mile 48, Sterling Hwy.
🅦 cooperlandingchamber.com

Named after Joseph Cooper, who was the first to discover gold in the area in 1894,

Cooper Landing was one of the few places in Alaska that continued producing gold into the 20th century. The town sprawls along the Sterling Highway in a string of eateries, lodges, gift shops, and fishing fitters. At the **K'Beq Kenaitze Footprints Heritage Site**, Dena'ina Natives share their traditions through interpretive walks featuring archeological sites. Local artists make and sell Dena'ina arts and crafts.

# ❹ Kenai River

**Transport map** A3. 🚌 Anchorage–Homer. 🛶

Originating between high peaks above the glacier-blue Kenai Lake, the Kenai River rushes westward from Cooper Landing, where whitewater rafting, kayaking, and canoeing are on offer. The Kenai then passes the mouth of the Russian River before flowing out of the mountains and onto the flats around Skilak Lake.

Among the world's most productive salmon streams, the lower Kenai is the original combat fishing river, with fierce competition among anglers for fishing space. People flock to the river on summer weekends, temporarily making the Sterling Highway one of Alaska's busiest roads. Continuing west from its Skilak Lake outlet, the river flows past innumerable public campsites and private cabins to its mouth at Kenai.

A freezing Kenai River flowing past Cooper Landing

# ❺ Resurrection Pass Trail

The 38 mile (61 km) Resurrection Pass Trail on the Kenai Peninsula is Alaska's most popular multi-day hiking route. Beginning at the Kenai River along the Sterling Highway, it climbs through spruce forest and past Juneau Creek Falls into the subalpine zone. The trail crosses the 2,600 ft (780 m) Resurrection Pass before descending along Resurrection Creek to the trailhead near the gold mining village of Hope. An alternative is to hike the 10 mile (16 km) Devil's Pass Trail from Mile 39.5 on the Seward Highway, and then take the Resurrection Pass Trail to either Hope or the Sterling Highway.

## Tips for Walkers

**Starting point:** Kenai River at the Sterling Highway. Due to the net altitude loss, it is best to hike the trail from south to north.
**Length:** the 38 mile (61 km) trail can take between two and six days to cover.
**Accommodation:** there are several forest service public use cabins along the trail. It is essential to pre-book (see p241).

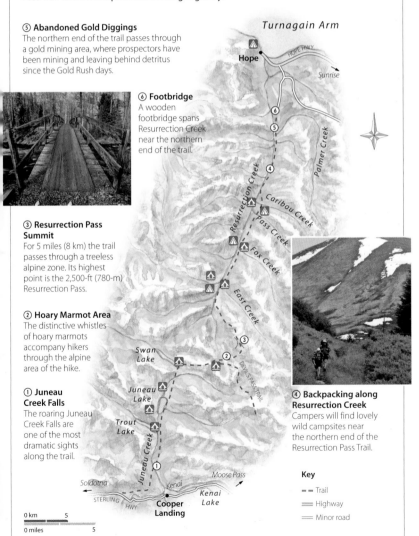

### ⑤ Abandoned Gold Diggings
The northern end of the trail passes through a gold mining area, where prospectors have been mining and leaving behind detritus since the Gold Rush days.

### ⑥ Footbridge
A wooden footbridge spans Resurrection Creek near the northern end of the trail.

### ③ Resurrection Pass Summit
For 5 miles (8 km) the trail passes through a treeless alpine zone. Its highest point is the 2,500-ft (780-m) Resurrection Pass.

### ② Hoary Marmot Area
The distinctive whistles of hoary marmots accompany hikers through the alpine area of the hike.

### ① Juneau Creek Falls
The roaring Juneau Creek Falls are one of the most dramatic sights along the trail.

### ④ Backpacking along Resurrection Creek
Campers will find lovely wild campsites near the northern end of the Resurrection Pass Trail.

**Turnagain Arm**

Hope
HOPE HWY
Sunrise
Palmer Creek
Resurrection Creek
Caribou Creek
Pass Creek
Fox Creek
East Creek
DEVIL PASS TRAIL
Swan Lake
Juneau Lake
Trout Lake
Juneau Creek
Moose Pass
Soldotna
STERLING HWY
Cooper Landing
Kenai
Kenai Lake

### Key
- - Trail
═══ Highway
── Minor road

0 km — 5
0 miles — 5

For keys to symbols see back flap

# ❻ Seward

Considered to have one of Alaska's most scenic locations, Seward is also known for its saltwater salmon fishing, its rollicking Independence Day celebrations, and its access to Kenai Fjords National Park *(see pp106–7)*. Although the Russians set up a shipyard here in 1793, the town was founded in 1903 by John Ballaine, who decided that its deepwater port would be an ideal location for a railhead. The railway came to fruition in 1923 and Seward thrived, but the 1964 earthquake destroyed most of the town. However, Seward was rebuilt, and to mark its revitalisation, its newspaper was named the *Phoenix Log*.

Ship's anchor on display at Seward's waterfront

### 🚌 Benny Benson Memorial
♿

Located next to the lagoon just to the west of the Seward Highway stands a memorial honoring Benny Benson and his contribution to Alaska. Carved on Alaska stone by artist Damon Capurro, the memorial is engraved with the words of the Alaska flag song by Marie Drake and Elinor Dusenbury.

In 1926, George Parks, the governor of Alaska, asked schoolchildren to submit ideas for a state flag with essays explaining their design. Of the 142 entries submitted, the judges' unanimous choice was that of Benny Benson, a 13-year-old Alutiiq boy who lived at Seward's Jesse Lee Orphanage. Benson's essay explained that the flag's blue field represented the Alaska sky as well as the forget-me-not, the state flower. The North Star stood for the future State of Alaska, the most northerly in the Union, while the Great Bear constellation symbolized strength. Alaska's flag is now generally regarded as the most beautiful of all the US state flags *(see p59)*.

### 🎣 Seward Waterfront
♿ 🚻 🅿 📷

Situated a short distance away from the small boat harbor and downtown Seward, the waterfront lies within easy reach of the port, rail depot, and airport. For most of the year, row upon row of yachts, pleasure craft, and fishing boats peacefully bob in the waters beneath the snow-covered peaks across the bay.

In the summer, however, the waterfront transforms into a bustling tourist complex. Here, the town's thousands of visitors and cruise ship passengers can organize tours and fishing trips, join Kenai Fjords cruises, plan outdoor activities, and shop for gifts in a growing number of souvenir shops. At the southern end, the shops give way to an often packed tent and RV campground that stretches along the shore for almost 2 miles (3 km).

### 🏛 Kenai Fjords National Park Information Center

1212 4th Ave. **Tel** 422-0500. **Open** late May–early Sep: 9am–7pm daily; early May–mid-Sep: 9am–5pm daily. ♿ 📷
**W** nps.gov/kefj

The handsome building that houses the Kenai Fjords National Park Information Center sits on the Seward waterfront. It features several exhibits detailing aspects of the glaciation that created the park's spectacular landscapes, as well as the wildlife and prolific birdlife that inhabits it *(see pp106–7)*. A free video runs intermittently, outlining natural history and park landscapes, including remote sites that few visitors are able to reach.

### 🏛 Seward Community Library and Museum

6th & Adams. **Tel** 224-3902.
**Open** mid-May–mid-Sep: 10am–5pm Tue–Sat, 1–5pm Sun; mid-Sep–mid-May: noon–5pm Fri & Sat, by appt Tue–Thu. 📷 summer only. ♿ 📷

Located on the first floor of the town's library, the Seward Museum offers a glimpse of the

Kenai Fjords National Park Information Center on the Seward Waterfront

Visitors exploring the magnificent Exit Glacier

### Exit Glacier
8 miles (13 km) W of Seward on Exit
Glacier/Herman Leirer Rd. 422-
0500. limited. nps.gov/kefj

The impressive Exit Glacier,
2,500 ft (762 m) high and
3 miles (5 km) long, is the only
part of Kenai Fjords National
Park that is accessible by road.
Pouring down from Harding
Icefield, it is the most readily
accessible walk-up glacier
in Alaska. From the seasonal
visitors' center at the end of
the road, a short wheelchair-
accessible trail leads to a hiking
route across the rocky terminal
moraines to the glacier face. The
energetic can hike the steep
4-mile (6-km) Harding Icefield
Trail up the western flank of
Exit Glacier to the vast Harding
Icefield. Camping is not permitted on the trail, but there
is a public use cabin and free
campground nearby.

history of the Resurrection Bay
area, from pre-Russian contact
to the 1964 Good Friday earthquake. As well as the permanent
exhibition, rotating temporary
displays focus on interesting
aspects of social history, such
as a collection of items from the
Brown & Hawkins store, in business here from 1904 to 2013.

### Alaska SeaLife Center
See pp104–5.

### Caines Head State Recreation Area
water taxi from Seward.
alaskastateparks.org

During World War II, the US
Army built Fort McGilvray on
the rocky headland known as

Caines Head, as well as a
dock at North Beach and
a garrison at South Beach.
The area still has ammunition
storage bunkers and gun
emplacements used to guard
the port and Resurrection
Bay when Alaska's Aleutian
Islands were attacked by
Japanese forces.

The shale-covered beaches
are ideal for anglers, and sea
kayakers will enjoy paddling
here. Hiking is also possible,
but the 3-mile (5-km) walk
from Tonsina Point is possible
only at low tide, so hikers on
the return trip will probably
need to camp overnight. Note
that the remains of the South
Beach garrison are unstable.

## Sights at a Glance
① Benny Benson Memorial
② Seward Waterfront
③ Kenai Fjords National Park
Information Center
④ Seward Community Library
and Museum
⑤ Alaska SeaLife Center

0 meters 800
0 yards 800

# Seward: Alaska SeaLife Center

On the lovely Resurrection Bay waterfront in Seward, the Alaska SeaLife Center integrates museum exhibits, aquarium displays, and hands-on experiences to provide an educational introduction to the maritime world of Alaska's southern coasts. Initially conceived as a coldwater marine research and rehabilitation facility to study and protect sealife and provide public education – especially in the aftermath of the 1989 *Exxon Valdez* oil spill *(see p121)* – the center was opened in May 1998 and has since grown into one of Alaska's best-loved attractions. Highlights include several innovative tours and a series of spectacular tanks with underwater viewing windows that allow visitors to look at a variety of creatures in naturalistic habitats.

Facade of the extensive Alaska SeaLife Center in Seward

**The Resurrection Bay Overlook** provides an opportunity to view harbor seals, sea otters, whales, and birds in their natural habitat.

**The Harbor Seal Habitat** resembles a rocky coastline where seals can be seen in great numbers.

★ **Windows to the Sea**
Visitors enjoy close-up views of fish, harbor seals, octopuses, and several affable Steller sea lions.

★ **Denizens of the Deep**
Among several hands-on Encounter Tours is the Octopus Encounter, where participants meet a giant Pacific octopus, and there is also the chance to join a harbor seal training session.

## Gallery Guide

*Windows to the Sea on the first floor provides underwater views of Alaskan sealife. The second floor has a host of exhibits, including the Discovery Pool and the Seabird Habitat, showcasing various aspects of the marine world.*

Entrance

**★ Discovery Touch Pool**
The pool offers a hands-on experience of Alaska's underwater world. Children can enjoy touching such creatures as sea cucumbers, starfish, anemones, and sea urchins, as well as underwater plant life.

**The Research Deck Overlook** provides a view of the animals involved in rehabilitation or research projects.

Discovery Classroom

Second floor

Steller Sea Lion Habitat

**The research and rehabilitation facilities** are designed to combine scientific study, wildlife rehabilitation, and public education.

First floor

**Key**

- ⬜ Windows to the Sea
- ⬜ Aquariums
- ⬜ Rocky Coast Gallery
- ⬜ Salmon Stream
- ⬜ The Resurrection Bay Overlook
- ⬜ Research Facilities
- ⬜ A Closer Look
- ⬜ Non-exhibition space

**★ Seabird Habitat**
A large aviary on the second floor encloses cliffs housing a selection of the bird species that inhabit the islets in the Gulf of Alaska. Diving seabirds are visible in the tank in the Windows to the Sea exhibit below.

**Bering Sea Gallery**
This gallery contains a series of images and illustrative displays about Alaska's marine ecosystem. Attractive cutouts and interactive kiosks explain various facets of the state's sealife and address rehabilitation concerns.

# ❼ Kenai Fjords National Park

Covering 950 sq miles (2,460 sq km), Kenai Fjords National Park takes in some of Alaska's finest and most accessible coastal scenery, glacial landscapes, and diverse marine wildlife. The crown of the park is the Harding Icefield. This vast expanse of ice, interrupted only by an occasional *nunatak (see p31)*, feeds the glaciers that flow down from the heights to form the park's deep valleys and fjords. The seas, rich in fish, crustaceans, shellfish, and plankton, also provide a habitat for a range of readily observed birds and marine mammals, including sea otters, Dall porpoises, Steller sea lions, and several whale species.

**Locator Map**
  ▨ Kenai Fjords National Park

**Calving Glaciers**
Tidewater glaciers such as Holgate Glacier regularly calve icebergs into the fjords in the park. Kayakers must watch out for large waves generated by falling house-sized chunks.

0 km     5
0 miles     5

**Key**
▬▬ Highway
▬▬ Minor road
▬ ▬ Park boundary

*Hardir Icefiel*

Northwestern Glacier

Holgate Glacier

*Harri*

*Northwestern Fjord*

McCarty Glacier

*Har Ba*

*McCarty Fjord*

*Gulf of Alas*

**Whale-Watching**
Summer visitors often spot sounding or breaching whales in these waters, which serve as summer feeding grounds for humpbacks and migratory routes each spring and fall for gray whales. Minke whales and pods of porpoises are also seen in the summer.

**★ Harding Icefield**
The 70-mile- (113-km-) long and 30-mile- (48-km-) wide Harding Icefield stretches across the Kenai Mountains and creates all of Kenai Fjord's glaciers. Hikers can access it via a steep trail from Exit Glacier. The icefield also draws experienced backcountry skiers keen to explore its farthest reaches.

**The Kenai Fjords National Park Information Center** *(see p102)* in Seward issues backcountry permits and provides information.

**★ Fjord Cruises in Aialik Bay**
This 20-mile- (32-km-) long fjord is the most popular destination for day cruises. Visitors are usually guaranteed a dynamic show as huge chunks of ice calve off the towering face of Aialik Glacier.

## Exploring the Park
*Kenai Fjords' only road ends at the Exit Glacier parking lot, where an easy half-mile (1-km) trail leads to good views of the glacier face. A challenging 6-mile (10-km) return trail goes up to Harding Icefield. To see the park's wildlife and calving glaciers, visitors can join a half- or full-day fjords cruise with Seward-based operators (see p267). Several local companies also offer guided multi-day kayak trips into the park.*

**★ Steller Sea Lion Rookery**
On the lonely, rocky outcrops of the Chiswell Islands, passengers on day cruises can approach one of Alaska's most prominent Steller sea lion rookeries. The islands also have impressive bird cliffs with nesting puffins and kittiwakes.

For keys to symbols *see back flap*

## ❽ Sterling

134 miles (215 km) SW of Anchorage. **Transport map** A3. 🚹 5,000. 🚌 Anchorage–Homer.

The name of the game in the 5 mile (8 km) strip known as Sterling is fish. Nearly all the businesses along the Sterling Highway cater to the anglers who flock to the town when the salmon are running. This community is also home to numerous private recreational cabins on the banks of the Kenai river.

Anyone who has ever wanted to try their hand at landing a monster salmon will find plenty of equipment and advice in Sterling, as well as along the highway between here, Soldotna, Kenai, and Homer. The area's most worthwhile site is **Skilak Lake**, which features lovely wild lakeside campsites and hiking trails. In the winter, the area's many frozen lakes, including Seven Lakes and Hidden Lake, make a pretty sight, but in the summer, the congestion around this area can be frustrating.

## ❾ Soldotna

148 miles (238 km) SW of Anchorage. **Transport map** A3. 🚹 4,000. 🛫 🚌 Anchorage–Homer. 🛈 44790 Sterling Hwy; 262-9814. 🛒 Farmer's Market, 10am–2pm Saturdays in summer. 🌐 **soldotnachamber.com**

As the primary commercial and service center of the Kenai Peninsula, Soldotna features

Log cabin at the Soldotna Historical Society Museum

Holy Assumption of the Virgin Mary Russian Orthodox Church, Kenai

fast-food franchises, stores, and visitor accommodation options. Founded in the 1940s as a retail hub at the junction of the Sterling and Kenai Spur Highways, it was incorporated only in 1967. While the area experienced steady growth, unbridled sprawl, and congestion in the late 20th century, much of the surrounding land remains protected under federal management.

Five sites around town – the Soldotna Visitors' Center, Rotary Park, Soldotna Creek Park, and the Centennial and Swiftwater Campgrounds – have set up "Fishwalks" along the Kenai River. These boardwalks, designed to protect the fragile riverbank, allow public access to the river for fishing and salmon-viewing.

On Centennial Park Road, the **Soldotna Historical Society Museum** features a collection of homesteaders' cabins from the 1940s. It also has a Territorial log school, Native artifacts, and a collection of stuffed wildlife.

## ❿ Kenai

11 miles (18 km) NW of Soldotna. **Transport map** A3. 🚹 7,000. 🛫 🚌 Anchorage–Homer. 🛈 11471 Kenai Spur Hwy; 283-1991. 🎉 Kenai River Festival (2nd weekend in Jun). 🌐 **visitkenai.com**

The Kenai Peninsula's largest city, Kenai also ranks as one of Alaska's best-preserved historic communities. In 1791, Russian fur traders came in contact with the region's Dena'ina Athabaskan people and established St. Nicholas Redoubt, the second permanent Russian settlement in Alaska. In 1869, two years after the purchase of Alaska, the US Army built Fort Kenay to provide a military presence in the Cook Inlet region. Extensive oil exploration began in the 1950s, and the Tesoro Alaska refinery at Nikiski is now a major economic player.

Visitors can stroll around the historic Old Town near the beach, which has the 1881 Parish Rectory House, the 1906

Historic buildings at the old salmon cannery complex at Kenai Landing, Kenai

St. Nicholas Chapel, a replica of Fort Kenay, and the onion-domed **Holy Assumption of the Virgin Mary Russian Orthodox Church**. Founded in 1846, the church's present building was constructed between 1894 and 1895. The interior is decorated with Russian artifacts, some from the early 19th century.

In spring, the salt marsh at **Kenai Flats State Recreation Site**, across the Warren Ames Bridge over the Kenai River, attracts large flocks of Siberian snow geese. With interpretive panels, picnic tables, a board-walk, and viewing scope, it will delight birders. A little farther west, on Cannery Road, a salmon cannery compound dating from 1922 has been converted into Kenai Landing. The ware-house has been dismantled, but recent renovations include the historic administration building.

## ⑪ Captain Cook State Recreation Area

25 miles (40 km) N of Kenai at Mile 36, Kenai Spur Hwy. **Transport map** A3. 262-5581. dnr.alaska.gov/parks/units/captcook.htm

Located on the shores of Cook Inlet, the Captain Cook State Recreation Area is named after British explorer Captain James Cook, who explored the area in 1778. One of Alaska's quieter parks, its forests, lakes, streams, and beaches offer picnic sites, hiking routes, and camping at the large Discovery Campground, as well as swimming, canoeing, and fishing in Stormy Lake. Wildlife, including moose, bears, loons, and sandhill cranes, can be spotted in the park. The beach is popular with agate hunters, but visitors should avoid the dangerous mudflats just offshore.

Along the dead-end road to the recreation area, visitors can pick up supplies and look around the oil town of **Nikiski**, 9 miles (14 km) to the south. Formerly known as North Kenai, this town began as a homesteading area in the 1940s and grew with the discovery of oil in Cook Inlet. At the end of Nikiski Beach Road, fine views open up across Nikishka Bay and the Cook Inlet oil drilling platforms, and beyond to the active volcano Mount Spurr. The large domed Nikiski pool, funded by the oil companies, boasts a hot tub and a winding 136 ft (41 m) water slide that is very popular with residents and visitors.

## ⑫ Kenai National Wildlife Refuge

**Transport map** A4. Anchorage–Homer. Ski Hill Rd, 43655 Kalifornsky Beach Rd, Soldotna; 262-7021. kenai.fws.gov

The Alaska National Interest Lands Conservation Act of 1980 (see p61) changed the name of the Kenai National Moose Range to the Kenai National Wildlife Refuge, and expanded it to its current area of almost 3,125 sq miles (8,094 sq km). The refuge covers high peaks, glaciers, muskeg, and lake-studded bog. This landscape provides habitat for a range of wildlife, from mountain goats, Dall sheep,

Kenai National Wildlife Refuge sign

and bears to moose, caribou, and wolves. The refuge is also home to lynx, coyotes, and waterfowl such as trumpeter swans and migratory birds.

Access to the refuge's wild southern part can be challenging, but the northern areas feature several public campgrounds, 200 miles (322 km) of hiking trails, and two world-class canoe routes. The 80 mile (128 km) **Swanson River Canoe Route** links over 40 lakes with the Swanson River, ending in the Captain Cook State Recreation Area. The 60 mile (96 km) **Swan Lakes Loop** is a system of 32 lakes, accessible from the Swanson River and Swan Lake Roads. Equipment can be hired and tours organized in nearby towns.

Lakes and forests at the Kenai National Wildlife Refuge

## ⓭ Clam Gulch

23 miles (37 km) S of Soldotna.
**Transport map** A3. 🚂 180.
🚌 Anchorage–Homer.

As its name might suggest, the highlight at Clam Gulch is clamming. The village itself is small, consisting of a few houses and some services, but beneath the sands of the beautiful Cook Inlet coast lie some of the world's most productive razor clam beds. At low tide, this is the best place in Alaska to dig for these delicious treats.

Diggers will need rubber boots, a clam shovel, bucket, and an Alaska fishing license *(see p45)*. The daily limit per person is 60 clams. The clams are usually about 6 inches (15 cm) beneath the surface. A small dimple in the sand indicates the presence of a clam, but it is best to dig to the side to avoid breaking its shell. Clams will attempt to flee by burrowing into the sand, so diggers may well have to give chase. It is best to carry the clams in a bucket of saltwater, adding a bit of corn meal to let them clean themselves before they are cooked.

## ⓮ Ninilchik

40 miles (65 km) S of Soldotna.
**Transport map** A4. 🚂 880.
🚌 Anchorage–Homer. ℹ️ 567-3571. 🎵 Salmonfest Music Festival, first weekend Aug.
🌐 **ninilchikchamber.com**

This traditional Russian-era Native village, whose name means "peaceful riverside place," is centered around the 1901 **Transfiguration of Our Lord Church**. The photogenic onion-domed church sits beside a rambling Russian Orthodox cemetery and offers fine views across the inlet. While the church is open for Sunday services, it is closed to the public on other days.

The Ninilchik River, a short walk to the north of the Visitors' Center, and Deep Creek, to the south, are world-class salmon fishing streams. Deep-sea charters provide access to offshore halibut and salmon. When the king salmon are running upstream (usually the first two weeks of June), the Deep Creek State Recreation Area Campground and the Ninilchik River Campground fill up and spill over into surrounding private sites and RV parks. Anglers will probably enjoy the scene, while others may prefer quieter areas.

Anchor Point sign highlighting its location on the highway system

## ⓯ Anchor Point

61 miles (98 km) S of Soldotna.
**Transport map** A4. 🚂 1,900.
🚌 Anchorage–Homer. ℹ️ Sterling Hwy, opposite Anchor River Inn; 235-2600. 🌐 **anchorpointchamber.org**

Named after an anchor that the British explorer Captain James Cook lost on his voyage up Cook Inlet, the Anchor Point community was established by homesteaders in 1949. The major attraction at this westernmost point on the contiguous US Highway system is the Anchor River, with its abundant supply of king and silver salmon, and rainbow, Dolly Varden, and steelhead trout. The seas around the area are rich in saltwater salmon and halibut.

Anglers usually stay at the Anchor River State Recreation Area at Anchor Point. Those who prefer a quieter campsite can opt for the beautiful (and angler-free) Stariski State Recreation Area north of Anchor Point. The park is perched on a bluff with views across Cook Inlet to the volcanoes beyond.

## ⓰ Nikolaevsk

64 miles (103 km) S of Soldotna.
**Transport map** A4. 🚂 320.

Settled in 1960, Nikolaevsk village is home to the Old Believers, a sect of Russian Orthodoxy that broke away from the mother church and settled in Siberia after the 17th-century religious reforms *(see pp36–7)*. Those who wound up in Alaska established Nikolaevsk and several surrounding villages.

Visitors arriving along the 9-mile (14-km) drive from Anchor Point might feel as if they have passed through a time warp. With distinctive architecture and demeanor, the villagers' lifestyle has only been lightly touched by the 21st century. One exception is an enterprising local woman who runs the Samovar Café and a gallery of costumes and artwork.

There is a lovely Russian Orthodox Church which is worth a look, but its interior is closed to the public.

The traditional Transfiguration of Our Lord Church, Ninilchik

# The Bears of Alaska

Most visitors to Alaska want to see bears, and nearly everyone does. One often hears, "When you're in Alaska, you're never far from a bear," and while that does not hold true for the Aleutian Islands, the rest of the state is prime bear habitat. Alaska is home to three species of bears – black, brown, and polar. Alaskan brown bears are further divided into two kinds, the smaller grizzlies of the Interior and the enormous brown bears of Southwest Alaska. They are not a true subspecies, however, and the size variations are due only to differences in their diet. Active in summer, many bears become dormant in winter, retreating to dens and living on fat reserves. Cubs are often born during dormancy. Bears can be aggressive, particularly when protecting cubs or competing with each other during the breeding season.

**Brown bears**, numbering about 40,000 in Alaska, are resident from the Southeast to the Arctic. The smaller grizzlies eat more vegetation, whereas Kodiaks *(see p207)*, which can measure up to 12 ft (4 m) tall when standing on their hind legs, eat a high-protein fish diet.

**Black bears**, which measure an average of 5 ft (1.5 m) in length, are the smallest Alaskan bears. These predominantly vegetarian bears are found everywhere in Alaska except the Arctic tundra and the Aleutian Islands.

## Bear Safety

- Store food in a bear-proof container, and cook away from tents. Never eat or keep snacks in your tent.

**YOU ARE IN BEAR TERRITORY**
Do Not Leave Food Unattended
Unattended items subject to
Impound and $50 Fine
11 AAC 12.230)

Bear safety sign

- In a bear encounter, do not run, as that may elicit a chase response.
- In a defensive attack, curl up in a ball with knees tucked into the stomach, arms wrapped around the face, and hands laced behind the back of the neck.
- In an aggressive attack, fight back with as much strength as possible. Poke at the bear's eyes and nose, punch it in the face, and try to hit it with a hiking pole or stick.
- Polar bears are the only species that stalk humans, and in an aggressive attack, a firearm will provide the only reasonable protection.

**Polar bears**, which inhabit the Arctic Ocean coastline, subsist mainly on marine mammals. Swimming across open water, they spend most of their lives roaming the ice floes in search of seals, but come ashore in the fall to breed *(see p227)*.

| Bear | Identification | Best Times to See | Best Places to See |
|---|---|---|---|
| Black *(Ursus americanus)* | Black or cinnamon coat; pointed muzzle | Spring, summer, and fall | Anan Creek Wildlife Observatory |
| Brown *(Ursus arctos)* | Dark brown to blond coat; prominent shoulder hump | Summer to fall | Denali National Park and Katmai National Park |
| Polar *(Ursus maritimus)* | Creamy coat; longer neck than other bears | Spring and fall | Barrow and Kaktovik |

Ramp to the small boat harbor on Homer Spit

## ⑰ Homer

84 miles (135 km) S of Soldotna.
**Transport map** A4. 🚠 5,000. ✈
🚌 ⛴ 🛈 201 Sterling Highway,
235-7740. 🐦 Kachemak Bay
Shorebird Festival (2nd weekend
in May). 🆆 **homeralaska.org**

Founded in 1895 and named
for Homer Pennock, a New
York con man who spent a
few months in the area, Homer
sells itself as the "end of the
road." It is a refuge for visitors,
artists, and anglers, as well as
some modern-day Pennocks.
In 1886, Homer got its first
post office, and in the late
1890s, a coal-shipping
settlement occupied the tip
of Homer Spit that runs into
Kachemak Bay. However, the
village was abandoned in
1902 when the coal seams
became unviable.The handful
of residents who remained in
town turned to farming and
fishing. From 1910 onwards,
Homer expanded from a
fishing village into a pleasant
small town.

Homer continues to attract
outsiders, causing rapid development of its bluffs and foot-
hills. For visitors, the town
means bird-watching, halibut
fishing, shopping for local
arts, and visits to the nearby
Kachemak Bay State Park.
Homer also boasts the world-
class Alaska Islands and Oceans
Visitors' Center and several
interesting museums.

### 🏛 Pratt Museum
3779 Bartlett St. **Tel** 235-8635.
**Open** mid-May–mid-Sep: 10am–
6pm daily; mid-Sep–Dec & Feb–
mid-May: noon–5pm Tue–Sun. 🅿
📷 ♿ botanical garden only. 📷
🆆 **prattmuseum.org**

Homer's natural history
museum covers the geology,
flora, fauna, and oceanography
of the peninsula, as well as
homesteader and Native
cultures. The Kachemak Bay
exhibit uses photographs,
videos, and interactive computer
programs to provide a sense of
the place. Detailed coverage
of the 1964 earthquake and the
1989 *Exxon Valdez* oil spill *(see
p121)* is displayed downstairs.
Trails through the botanical
gardens outside the main
building lead past 150 identified
species of local plants. The
Harrington Cabin displays
artifacts from Homer's 1940s
homesteading era.

Engaging exhibits inside Homer's
Pratt Museum

### 🏛 Bunnell Street Arts Center
106 W Bunnell Ave. **Tel** 235-2662.
**Open** 11am–5pm Mon–Fri, noon–
4pm Sat. ♿ ✉ 📷 🆆 **bunnell
arts.org**

Drawn by its scenic location,
several artists made Homer
their home, and as a result,
sundry street fairs, workshops,
and galleries sprang up. One
of the most renowned is the
Bunnell Street Arts Center,
which was founded by an
artists' group in 1989. Housed
in the 1937 Old Inlet Trading
Post building, which was once
a commercial hub for homesteaders, the gallery now showcases contemporary fine art.

### 🏛 Alaska Islands and
Ocean Visitors' Center
95 Sterling Hwy. **Tel** 235-6961.
**Open** late May–early Sep: 9am–5pm
daily; winter: noon–5pm Tue–Sat. ♿
📷 🆆 **islandsandocean.org**

This highly worthwhile stop
is probably the finest center
of its kind in Alaska. A wealth
of original exhibits, including a
replica of a Bering Sea seabird
rookery and a recording of
conservationist and researcher
Olaus Murie dictating his
journal, detail the natural
history of the Alaska Maritime
National Wildlife Refuge and
the Kachemak Bay Research
Reserve. Visitors can also hike
along a boardwalk to Beluga
Slough's tidal marshes or watch
an award-winning film on the
Aleutian Islands.

### 🌿 Carl E. Wynn Nature Center

E Skyline Dr. **Tel** 235-5266.
**Open** mid-Jun–early Sep: 10am–6pm
daily. 🅿️ 🚻 ♿ limited. 📷
🌐 **akcoastalstudies.org**

This center is set amid spruce forests and meadows on the bluffs overlooking Homer. Formerly the homestead of naturalist Carl E Wynn, it was donated to the Center for Alaskan Coastal Studies in 1990. Visitors can enjoy bird-watching, stroll amid wildflowers, or explore the variety of vegetation from upland coastal forests to boreal forests. The center also offers guided walks highlighting local wildlife and shrubs.

Wildflowers at the Carl E. Wynn Nature Center outside Homer

### 🌿 Homer Spit

🚤 🍽️ 🏨 ⛺

Thought to be a remnant of an ancient glacial moraine, Homer Spit has been spared from the ravages of the sea by reclamation and rock walls. This is Homer's main tourist district, taking in the small boat harbor, the ferry terminal, a hotel, myriad eateries, and a host of fishing charter companies. The **Salty Dawg Saloon**, with its distinctive lighthouse tower, is listed as a maritime landmark. Around 1900, it served as the headquarters for the Cook Inlet Coal Fields Company. Today, this atmospheric drinking den is unmissable.

The Spit is also a camping venue with communities of RVs and tents strung along the northern shore.

Rocky Island off Kachemak Bay State Park

### Seldovia

20 nautical miles (32 km) S of Homer.
🏔️ 260. ✈️ charter floatplane from Homer. ⛴️ from Homer. 🎉 July 4 parade and canoe jousting.
🌐 **seldoviachamber.org**

Seldovia was inhabited by Dena'ina people as early as the 16th century. Russians settled here around 1800, naming the place Zaliv Seldevoe (Herring Bay). In the early 20th century, the area's flourishing herring trade increased the town's population to about 2,000, but the boom was shortlived.

Today, Seldovia is a small fishing village with an active Native association. Visitors can stroll along the waterfront boardwalk, explore the Village Tribe Museum and Visitors' Center, and visit the 1891 St. Nicholas Russian Orthodox Church, which crowns a hill overlooking the harbor.

Salty Dawg Saloon lighthouse, Homer Spit

### 🚢 Kachemak Bay State Park

8 nautical miles (12 km) across the bay from Homer. **Tel** 262-5581.
⛴️ from Homer. 🏔️ 🏕️
🌐 **alaskastateparks.org**

Alaska's first state park and one of the largest coastal state parks in the US, the Kachemak Bay State Park and the adjoining Kachemak Bay State Wilderness Park take in 625 sq miles (1,619 sq km) of islands, forests, glaciers, beaches, and rocky coastlines. This critical habitat area supports several species of marine life, including whales and sea otters, land mammals such as coyotes and black bears, and birds that include eagles and puffins. About 80 miles (130 km) of hiking trails lace the waterfront area of the park, across the bay from Homer. Trails from primitive beach campsites lead to ridges and remote coastlines.

### Halibut Cove

12 miles (19 km) SE of Homer.
🏔️ 75. ⛴️ from Homer.
🌐 **halibutcove.com**

Halibut Cove happily receives short-term visitors, but is keen to avoid the unbridled growth of Homer. This scenic little cove makes an excellent launch point for hikes into the adjacent Kachemak Bay State Park. There is also a restaurant and several lodges, as well as a number of artists' galleries. The most renowned of these is the Cove Gallery of the late Diana Tillion, who used octopus ink for her works. Access is by local water taxi, but day tours that include dinner in Halibut Cove are also available.

# PRINCE WILLIAM SOUND

The northernmost extent of the Gulf of Alaska, Prince William Sound is a large bay studded with forested islands. Lying to the east of the Kenai Range and south of the heavily glaciated Chugach Range, the massive sound is roughly twice the size of Massachusetts, with convoluted coasts lined with large tidewater glaciers and sheltered waters that harbor a rich variety of wildlife.

Home to the Eyak, Dena'ina, and other Native peoples, the Prince William Sound area was first explored in 1778 by the British captain James Cook and by the Spanish explorer Don Salvador Fidalgo in 1790, both of whom were searching for the elusive Northwest Passage. The first serious scientific study of the area was conducted in June 1899 by the Harriman Expedition, which included eminent scientists and artists. Much of their vast collection of specimens, illustrations, and photographs is now at the Smithsonian Institution in Washington, DC.

In the early decades of the 20th century, the area's economy received a boost when the town of Cordova became the railhead for the Copper River and Northwestern Railway. In the 1970s, Valdez, by virtue of being the northernmost ice-free port in North America, was chosen as the site of the marine terminal for the Trans-Alaska Pipeline. Since then, oil tankers have shared the shipping lanes with Marine Highway ferries, fishing boats, kayakers, and, more recently, cruise ships calling into the port of Whittier.

Despite the environmental damage suffered in the 1989 *Exxon Valdez* oil spill, most of the sound has come back, at least on the surface. Although herring fisheries have never recovered, marine life is again prolific and wildlife watching cruises can be very rewarding. Bird-watchers will enjoy the kittiwake colonies near Whittier and the migratory birds of the Copper River Delta. Kayaking among the ice floes in the bay is another popular activity, as is hiking around the glaciers.

Fisherman's Memorial overlooking Cordova's boat harbor

◀ Meltwater cascading down forested slopes near Whittier, Prince William Sound

# Exploring Prince William Sound

Alaska's greatest concentration of tidewater glaciers form the highlight of Prince William Sound. Three main towns, prosperous Valdez, cozy Cordova, and tiny Whittier, flank the sound. They serve as bases for popular cruises that visit Blackstone Bay, College Fjord, and the massive Columbia Glacier, and offer opportunities to view seals, whales, and sea otters. East of Cordova, the arresting beauty of the Copper River Road makes for a wonderful drive through the bird-watching area of Alaganik Slough and the Copper River Delta to the Childs Glacier and famed Million Dollar Bridge.

Remnants of the winter snow on the Copper River Highway near Cordova

Private yachts and boats crowding Whittier's Small Boat Harbor

## Sights at a Glance

**Towns and Cities**
① Whittier
⑤ Valdez
⑥ Cordova

**Areas of Natural Beauty**
② Blackstone Bay
③ College Fjord
④ Columbia Glacier
⑦ Copper River Highway

## Getting Around

Scheduled flights operate between Anchorage, Valdez, and Cordova. In the summer, Alaska Marine Highway ferries run on most days between Whittier, Valdez, and Cordova. Private vehicles can get to Valdez on the Richardson Highway. A toll tunnel from the Seward Highway provides access to Whittier. While there's no outside road access to Cordova, it's worth taking a vehicle on the ferry in order to drive the Copper River Highway. Perhaps the best way to see the sound, however, is on an organized cruise from Whittier or Valdez.

*For hotels and restaurants in this area see p243 and p253*

Marshland at Alaganik Slough near Cordova, Prince William Sound

0 km 25
0 miles 25

Glennallen

Tonsina Glacier
Valdez Glacier
Worthington Glacier
RICHARDSON HIGHWAY
Ticket

**5 VALDEZ**

Keystone Canyon
Tasnuna

Meteorite Mt
6,566 ft

Cordova Peak
7,730 ft

Bremner

Copper

Childs Glacier
Million Dollar Bridge
Van Cleve Lake
Mount Tom White
10,637 ft
Miles Glacier

Port Gravina

Sheridan Glacier
Martin River Glacier

**CORDOVA 6**
**10 COPPER RIVER HIGHWAY 7 COPPER RIVER HIGHWAY**

Hawkins Island

Kushtaka Lake

Alaganik Slough
Martin Lake
Bering Lake

Bering Glacier

**Key**

〓 Highway
⋯ Minor road
— Alaska Railroad
– – Alaska Marine Highway
– – Anton Anderson Memorial Tunnel
△ Peak

Ice floes in the bay near Columbia Glacier, Prince William Sound

**For keys to symbols** *see back flap*

Pleasure boats docked at Whittier, at the western edge of Prince William Sound

# ❶ Whittier

59 miles (95 km) SE of Anchorage.
**Transport map** E4. 🚐 220.
🚂 from Anchorage via Portage.
🚢 from Valdez and Cordova.
**W** whittieralaska.gov
Anton Anderson Memorial Tunnel:
**Open** 15 mins hourly in each
direction. **W** tunnel.alaska.gov

Whittier's name came from
the adjacent Whittier Glacier,
named after the American
poet John Greenleaf Whittier.
Founded in 1943, when the US
Army used this ice-free port to
build an Alaska base, the town
was made accessible by the
3-mile (5-km) Anton Anderson
road-rail toll tunnel, which
connects Turnagain Arm
with Passage Canal, an arm
of Prince William Sound.

Despite its spectacular
setting, surrounded as it is by
glaciers and thundering waterfalls, Whittier is probably one
of Alaska's oddest towns. The
army, not especially concerned
with aesthetics, housed their
personnel in Soviet-style high-
rise apartment buildings. After

the army left in 1960, the few
hundred residents who stayed
behind continued to live in
two towers, one of which, the
14-story Begich Towers, has
now been converted into con-
dominiums. The town's other
occupied building is the less
obtrusive Whittier Manor. Most
residents are accustomed to
unflattering remarks about
these buildings, and even
seem proud of the undeniably
quirky architecture.

One of Whittier's main
attractions is a large colony
of black-legged kittiwakes in
the cliffs across Passage Arm,
which can be viewed on sea
kayaking trips. Lovers of the
outdoors will also enjoy the
26 Glacier Cruise run by
**Phillips Cruises and Tours**.
The cruise boats travel deep
into Barry Arm and College
Fjord, offering visitors close-up
views of wildlife and glaciers.

**Phillips Cruises and Tours**
Cliffside Marina. **Tel** 276-8023, (800)
544-0529. Cruises depart May–Sep
12:30pm daily. **W** phillipscruises.com

# ❷ Blackstone Bay

**Transport map** E4. 🚢 from Whittier.

One of Alaska's most dramatic
sights, the 18-mile- (29-km-)
long Blackstone Bay lies at the
foot of three calving tidewater
glaciers – Blackstone, Beloit,
and Northland. These choke
the upper portion of this
spectacular fjord with growler
ice, bergy bits, and small
icebergs (see pp30–31).

From the unofficial campsite
at the southern end of Willard
Island, campers have a front-
row view of nature's intriguing
displays, as well as a minor
lesson in physics. As chunks
calve off the glaciers, three
types of waves appear. First,
light waves make the calving
visible to observers. Several
seconds later, a sound wave
arrives, carrying the thunder-
like crack of the breaking ice.
Finally, after a minute or so,
the waves created by the
big splash roll onto the shore.

Most visitors to Blackstone
Bay arrive on day cruises from
Whittier, but it is also popular
as a venue for ocean kayaking
(see 266–7). Kayakers typically
take two days to reach Willard
Island in the middle of the
fjord. Although it can be an
enjoyable experience to paddle
around between the bergs,
visitors should be careful not
to approach the glacier faces
or be caught on an incoming
tide. Pieces of ice, pushed
by the forceful current, can
crush a kayak.

Sea kayakers gliding past Blackstone Glacier, Blackstone Bay

# ❸ College Fjord

**Transport map** E4. 🚢 tour from Whittier. 📷

The College Fjord arm of Prince William Sound and the neighboring Harriman Fjord include an impressive concentration of easily accessible tidewater glaciers, as well as myriad valley glaciers and hanging glaciers (see pp30–31).

In 1899, New York railroad magnate Edward Harriman launched a scientific expedition along the Alaskan coast, including College Fjord, where he named the glaciers after the Ivy League colleges attended by the scientists on board his ship, the *George W. Elder*. As one travels into the fjord, the glaciers on the left are named for women's colleges and those on the right for men's schools. Chunks as large as a house often calve from the massive 300-ft- (90-m-) high glacier faces.

# ❹ Columbia Glacier

**Transport map** E3. 🚢 tour boats from Valdez. 📷

During the 1980s, 40-mile- (64-km-) long, 2,000-ft- (600-m-) thick Columbia Glacier was a highlight on the Alaska Marine Highway route between Whittier and Valdez. Ferries would typically stop amid the

Black-legged kittiwakes perching on a small ice floe

## Kittiwakes

The towering cliffs across Passage Arm from Whittier are home to a colony of thousands of black-legged kittiwakes (*Rissa tridactyla*). During the summer nesting season they can be seen wheeling around the precarious cliff faces where they nest, breed, and hatch their chicks. With a relatively rapid wingbeat, kittiwakes are highly maneuverable and able to land on narrow cliff ledges even in strong winds. In the winter, these pelagic gulls spend most of their time on the open ocean, feeding on small fish and plankton.

groups or rafts of sea otters and icebergs laden with harbor seals, and blast their horns with the hope that the vibrations would cause the glacier to calve.

However, in the early 1980s, Columbia Glacier began to surge at a pace as great as 115 ft (35 m) per day, calving icebergs into Prince William Sound much faster than snow compression on the ice field could replace it. It is thought that the melting ice created a cushion of water beneath the main ice sheet, allowing the glacier to progress without

being impeded by the friction of ice against rock. It calved so much ice that it choked the waters between its 3-mile (5-km) wide face and its terminal moraine with large icebergs that froze together. As a result, the glacier face has receded about 13 miles (21 km) since 1982 and can no longer be reached by ferry, although there are hopes that this may stabilize. Currently, this active glacier is most readily accessed on day cruises (check out www. stephenscruises.com) and private tour boats from Valdez.

Cruisers aboard a tour boat approaching Columbia Glacier, Prince William Sound

Display of a trapper's cabin, Valdez Museum

# ❺ Valdez

304 miles (487 km) E of Anchorage.
**Transport map** E4. 🚗 4,000. ✈
🚢 from Whittier, Cordova.
ℹ️ 309 Fairbanks Dr, 835-2984.
🌐 valdezalaska.org

The most important town of the Prince William Sound region, Valdez was named after the bay Port Valdez, which in turn, was named by Spanish explorer Don Salvador Fidalgo after Spanish naval officer Antonio Valdes y Basan in 1790. The town was founded in 1897 about 4 miles (6 km) east of its current location as a jumping-off point for prospectors heading to the Klondike goldfields.

With the discovery of copper in the Wrangell Mountains, Cordova became the terminus of the Copper River and Northwestern Railway (see p187) and Valdez slid into decline. In the early 20th century, however, Valdez became the terminus

for a wagon road to connect the nearby Fort Liscum with Fort Egbert on the Yukon River. After the 1964 earthquake utterly destroyed Old Valdez, the town was rebuilt at its present location.

As the northernmost ice-free port in North America, it was chosen to be the terminus of the Trans-Alaska Pipeline (see p186), which brought prosperity to the town during its construction.

Modern Valdez enjoys a lovely setting between the mountains and the sea. Day trips and organized cruises to north-eastern Prince William Sound provide good wildlife viewing, including sightings of whales, seals, sea otters, and birds around Columbia Glacier.

Pipeline Workers' Monument

## 🏛 Valdez Museum
217 Egan Dr. **Tel** 835-2764.
**Open** summer (Memorial Day to Labor Day): 9am–5pm daily; winter: noon–5pm Tue–Sun. 🎦 ♿ 📷
Remembering Old Valdez: 436 S Hazelet Dr. **Tel** 835-5407. **Open** summer only, 9am–5pm daily. 🎦
♿ 📷 🌐 valdezmuseum.org

This excellent museum, which takes at least two hours to explore fully, reveals the history of Valdez and Prince William Sound, as well as the Alaskan oil industry. The museum's most well-known display is probably the 1886 hand-pumped Ahrens steam fire engine, lovingly

polished and tended. A replica of the Pipeline Workers' Monument, dedicated to the men who built the pipeline, is among the displays. There are photographs depicting the 1964 earthquake and Valdez's rebirth as an oil town, as well as Native artifacts and mockups of an old miner's cabin, a period photography studio, and a historic 1880s bar. The *Exxon Valdez* spill gets rather minimal coverage.

The **Remembering Old Valdez** exhibit, housed in an old warehouse nearby, contains a 1:20 scale model of Old Valdez as it appeared before the 1964 earthquake. It also has historic vehicles and a high-tech exhibit on earthquakes. A visit to the actual site of Old Valdez, east of town, gives a vivid idea of the devastation that occurred there.

## 🏛 Whitney Museum
303 Lowe St. **Tel** 834-1690. **Open** May–mid-Sep: 9am–7pm daily. 🎦
♿ 🌐 mjwhitneymuseum.org

For more than half a century, philanthropists Maxine and Jesse Whitney traveled around the villages of Alaska, buying art and other items directly from artists and craftsmen. In the 1980s, they donated their collection to the Prince William Sound Community College. This museum is thought to have the world's largest private collection of Native Alaskan art, artifacts, and stuffed wildlife. It houses some of the finest examples of Inuit scrimshaw, as well as a ship and an aircraft carved entirely of ivory. One room is filled with nothing but baskets, another is dedicated to historic Gold Rush exhibits, and yet another to fascinating rocks and minerals.

There is also an extensive collection of Native dolls, garments, weapons, masks, and household implements. In addition, the museum contains larger exhibits such as an old Inuit kayak with whale baleen stays, a lovely Russian prayer rug, and a sofa made of moose horn.

Ahrens steam fire engine occupying pride of place in Valdez Museum

Hiking the challenging trail up to the face of Worthington Glacier

### Keystone Canyon

Mile 12.8–Mile 15.9 on the Richardson Highway.

This canyon was named after the Keystone State (Pennsylvania) by Captain William Ralph Abercrombie, following a failed 1884 expedition to sail up the Copper River to the Yukon. Keystone Canyon contains both the Richardson Highway, one of Alaska's most scenic highways and buried stretches of the Alaska Pipeline.

East of Valdez, at Mile 13, two great waterfalls spill down the slopes into the slate-gray Lowe River. A paved turnout provides access to **Horsetail Falls**, north of the highway. A bit farther along, the lovely **Bridal Veil Falls** tumble down into a deep, rainbow-flanked pool. Farther east, the highway climbs out

of the canyon into an alpine landscape beneath the ice-sculpted spires of the eastern reaches of the Chugach Range.

### Worthington Glacier

Mile 28.7 on the Richardson Highway . 🏕 🚠 ⓦ **dnr.alaska.gov/parks/aspunits**

The Worthington Glacier, protected in the Worthington Glacier State Recreation Site, flows steeply down the icy peak of the 6,130-ft- (1,840-m-) high Girls Mountain in a series of

fingers that extend to within 430 yards (400 m) of the road. Visitors can admire the scene from below or follow the challenging Ridge Trail up the glacier's lateral moraine and right to its face. There is an information desk and a small shop, which also provides shelter.

The Blueberry Lake State Recreation Site, 4 miles (7 km) south of the glacier, makes a great stop. North of the campground is **Thompson Pass**, Alaska's snowiest spot.

Spectacular cascade of Horsetail Falls, Keystone Canyon

### Exxon Valdez Oil Spill

On March 23, 1989, the tanker *Exxon Valdez*, under the command of Captain Joseph Hazelwood, was forced to change course to avoid an iceberg near the mouth of Columbia Bay. The ship struck Bligh Reef and started leaking oil. As much as 11 million gallons (42 million liters) of oil spilled into the sound. Clean-up crews were slow to respond, and although dispersants were eventually applied, the weather was too calm for them to be effective. Even a week later, only a few skimmer vessels had been deployed. The oil contaminated 1,500 miles (2,400 km) of

Cleaning an oil-covered bird after the oil spill

coastline, killing fish, whales, seals, sea otters, and birds. Nearly 10,000 workers were employed to count dead wildlife and clean up the sound and surrounding areas, often wiping the black sludge off rocks by hand. The effort cost Exxon $1.25 billion. In 1991, the State of Alaska and the federal government reached an out-of-court settlement, requiring Exxon to pay $1 billion in restitution. In 1994, a class-action suit awarded $5.2 billion in damages but Exxon appealed and a much smaller settlement of $507m was granted in 2009.

## ❻ Cordova

50 miles (80 km) SE of Valdez.
**Transport map** E4. 🚠 2,200. ✈
🚢 Valdez, Whittier. ℹ 404 1st St,
424-7260. 🎭 Iceworm Festival (1st
weekend in Feb), Copper River Delta
Shorebird Festival (1st week of May),
Copper River Wild Salmon Festival
(late July). 🆆 **cityofcordova.net**

Smaller than nearby Valdez, rainy
little Cordova offers a slice of
the independent, self-sufficent
character of "old Alaska" that has
faded in more accessible places
along the road system. There is
a quiet charm in wandering its
steets or strolling past the fish
canneries. This scenic town is
linked to the outside world only
by plane or the ferries of the
Marine Highway.

Initially a Gold Rush town,
Cordova became the Copper
River and Northwestern Railway
railhead, linking the copper
mines at Kennicott *(see pp188–9)*
with the coast.

Fisherman's
Memorial

The railroad
functioned
until the mines
closed down in
1938. Although
Cordova was
badly damaged
by the 1964
earthquake, it
bounced back
as a fishing
town and is
known for its
Copper River reds,
prized salmon that are shipped
fresh to restaurants both inside
and outside Alaska.

### 🏛 Cordova Historical Museum

622 1st St. **Tel** 424-6665. **Open** late
May–early Sep: 10am–5pm Tue–Sat.
🐾 ♿ 🅿 🆆 **cordovamuseum.org**
This small museum, housed in
the Centennial Building, features
several interesting exhibits. In
addition to works by Alaskan
artists, including painter Sydney
Laurence (who spent some time
in Cordova around 1900), the
museum houses an old skin-
covered canoe and a collection
of antique photographs. One
exhibit explains the effects
of the 1964 earthquake and
another showcases Cordova's

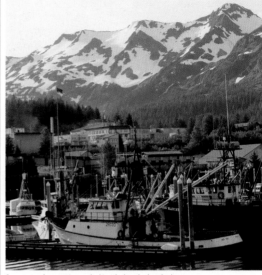

Snow-capped mountains overlooking the boat harbor, Cordova

Iceworm Festival *(see p49)*, held
in February to relieve the stress
of wintertime cabin fever. There
is a thoughtful display on the
Copper River and Northwestern
Railway, along with examples of
copper jewelry and implements.
A video showcases high points
in the town's history.

### 🏛 Prince William Sound Science Center

300 Breakwater Ave, Cordova Harbor.
**Tel** 424-5800. **Open** 8:30am–5:30pm
Mon–Fri. ♿ 🆆 **pwssc.org**
Founded immediately after the
1989 oil spill, this scientific base
at Cordova harbor's entrance
is home to teams of research
scientists studying the Prince
William Sound ecosystem.
The center offers a fine view
from the deck over-
looking the water.
The researchers
here can answer
questions and
provide insights
into the long-
term effects of the
*Exxon Valdez* oil
spill on the sound
and its ecology.
The center also
offers numerous
educational programs. These
include holding field trips and
science projects for families and

Logo, Prince William Sound
Science Center

adults, informative scientific
seminars in isolated communities around Prince William
Sound, and summer camps
for local schoolchildren.

### 🏛 Ilanka Cultural Center

110 Nicholoff Way. **Tel** 424-7903.
**Open** summer: 10am–5pm Mon–Fri;
winter: 10am–5pm Tue–Fri. 🐾
donations accepted. ♿ 🅿
🆆 nveyak.com/ilanka-cultural-
center

Situated opposite the
Fisherman's Memorial on
Nicholoff Way, the Ilanka
Cultural Center was founded to
preserve the culture of the Eyak
tribe, and in fact the last Native
speaker of the Eyak language
died in 2008. The Eyak people's
stories are told in an interesting
collection of artifacts
and photographs.
Other exhibits
include a complete
orca skeleton and
a contemporary
subsistence totem
pole. The work of
carver Mike Webber,
the pole is intended
to reflect the foods,
clothing, and dance
regalia of the tribe.
The center also provides studio
space for Eyak artisans to
produce their work.

# ❼ Copper River Highway

**Transport map** E4. 🏔 Childs Glacier.
Forest Service: 612 2nd St, Cordova;
424-7661. **W** fs.usda.gov/chugach

There is little to prepare visitors for the arresting beauty of the 48-mile (77-km) drive along the Copper River Highway between Cordova and the end of the road at the **Million Dollar Bridge**. Along the way, a number of short hiking trails and roadside views, as well as abundant wildlife and a few obligatory sights, will easily fill up a full day.

The gravel road, which is always open for visitors, and usually free of snow by late April, follows the roadbed of the historic Copper River and Northwestern Railway. At Mile 4, a marker provides information on its construction and history. At Mile 5.7, the road passes the Forest Service's **Eyak River Trail**, a 2-mile (3-km) hike, which includes a long boardwalk over muskeg. The variety of birdlife found here makes it a favorite walking trail of birders.

About 7 miles (11 km) north along a side road from Mile 13.7, a short walk leads onto the terminal moraine of **Sheridan Glacier**, with fine views of its blue ice. The steep 3-mile (5-km) Sheridan Ridge Trail climbs to a good view. After another 4 miles (6 km) along the highway, a rugged side route leads south to **Alaganik Slough**, which has a picnic site and a 990-ft (300-m) elevated boardwalk over a

Million Dollar Bridge across the Copper River near Cordova

wetland. Vast watery views are on offer, replete with colorful wildflowers such as irises. Every summer, thousands of waterfowl, including 7 percent of the world's trumpeter swans, descend on this spot to nest, and countless shorebirds screech overhead.

Beginning around Mile 25 for 10 miles (16 km), the view from the road takes in more water than land as the route crosses the **Copper River Delta** over a series of bridges and causeways.

Once across the river, the road passes through birch and cottonwood forests to its end at the Million Dollar Bridge. This impressive structure, a part of the Copper River and Northwestern Railway, actually cost a million dollars to build in 1910. It had to be constructed in the winter to avoid the summer advance of the adjacent **Childs**

Wild iris at Alaganik Slough

and **Miles Glaciers**. The northernmost span collapsed in the 1964 earthquake and it took nearly 40 years of makeshift repairs to reopen it to traffic. The road, however, ends barely a mile or so farther on. Views from the bridge take in both Childs Glacier and the expansive Miles Glaciers, which has receded over a mile (2 km) since the bridge was built.

There is a small five-site campground at Childs Glacier, offering excellent views of the glacier face across the roiling gray Copper River. Campers here are treated to an all-night symphony of thunder-like booms and cracks as the glacier calves. Signs dotted around the area warn visitors that about once a year, the calving of large chunks into the water generates waves of up to 40 ft (12 m) that have been known to wash across the campground.

Childs Glacier near Million Dollar Bridge along the Copper River Highway

# SOUTHEAST ALASKA

Nature prevails throughout the Panhandle, a narrow 400-mile (640-km) strip of islands and coastline that reaches southeastward from the Alaskan mainland. The spectacular scenery of Southeast Alaska, from the threaded passageways of the Alexander Archipelago to the rugged Coast Mountains, combines with its easy accessibility to make it one of Alaska's most visited regions.

For the Tlingit, Haida, and Tsimshian peoples who have inhabited this area for thousands of years, Southeast Alaska has provided not only beauty, but also bounty – seas full of fish, wildlife to hunt, and a wealth of enormous trees to provide wood for homes and boats. When the first Russians arrived, the Native peoples fought to defend their homeland, but were ultimately forced to accept the inevitable political, economic, and lifestyle changes that were introduced by the newcomers.

Fortunately, many of the traditional ways of the Native peoples have been preserved, not only in museums, but in villages with significant indigenous populations. Several towns, especially Wrangell and Sitka, have grown around Russian forts, while the discovery of gold was the impetus for the creation of Juneau

and Skagway. In 1900, the discovery of gold near Juneau along with its strategic location along the Klondike route led to its becoming the capital of Alaska, taking over from Sitka. Other towns, such as Ketchikan and Petersburg, grew around fisheries, canneries, and timber mills.

Today, Southeast Alaska is the favored venue for most Alaska cruises *(see pp38–9)*, and the region sees large numbers of visitors each summer. With local economies increasingly dependent upon tourism, ports such as Ketchikan, Skagway, and Sitka cater to cruise ship passengers with a variety of day tours and shopping opportunities. A limited number of ships are also permitted to enter Glacier Bay National Park, a UNESCO World Heritage Site, with its renowned whale-watching and glacier viewing opportunities.

Tour boat passengers admiring a glacier in Glacier Bay National Park and Preserve

◀ St. Michael's Russian Orthodox Cathedral in Sitka

# Exploring Southeast Alaska

The Southeast, often the first part of the state seen by visitors traveling north, is archetypal Alaska. The main towns – bustling Ketchikan, beautiful Sitka, friendly little Wrangell, and Juneau, the capital – enjoy spectacular settings along narrow ocean channels next to rainforested slopes and glaciated peaks. The Tongass National Forest covers almost the entire region, including lush Prince of Wales Island and Misty Fiords National Monument. Anan Creek Wildlife Observatory and Admiralty Island National Monument offer excellent bear viewing, while Glacier Bay National Park and the Juneau Icefield provide awe-inspiring vistas.

Totem pole topped by a bald eagle at Saxman Totem Park near Ketchikan

Creek Street above Ketchikan Creek, Ketchikan

## Getting Around

The best way to get around Southeast Alaska is by plane, both on the scheduled flights that connect Skagway, Juneau, Sitka, Wrangell, Petersburg, and Ketchikan, and the floatplanes that fly to remote homesteads and lodges. The Alaska Marine Highway is a lifeline, with ferries connecting most towns. Other companies provide access to Prince of Wales Island and Glacier Bay National Park. Although Haines, Skagway, and Hyder are linked to the Canadian highway system, the lack of continuous roads within the region means that cars are not very helpful in getting around, except along the limited highways around individual towns.

*For hotels and restaurants in this area see pp243–4 and pp253–54*

## Sights at a Glance

**Towns, Cities, and Islands**

**National and State Parks**

**Areas of Natural Beauty**

**Tours**

Aerial view of the spectacular Glacier Bay National Park

**Key**

━━━ Highway

════ Minor road

– – – Alaska Marine Highway

▬▬▬ International border

△ Peak

0 km           50

0 miles        50

HAINES CUT-OFF TOUR ⑱ ⑰ GOLD RUSH ROUTES

⑯ SKAGWAY

⑮ HAINES

GLACIER BAY NATIONAL PARK ND PRESERVE

⑭

Gustavus

*Spencer*

Elfin Cove

Hoonah

*bi Island*

Pelican

⑪ TENAKEE SPRINGS

Angoon

*Kruzof Is*

⑩ SITKA

*Baranof Island*

Port Alexander

*Cape Ommaney*

*Christian Sound*

*Coronation Is*

*Noyes Is*

Klawock

Craig

*Baker Is*

Hydaburg

*Dall Is*

*Juneau Icefield*

*Saint Therese Shrine*

*Mendenhall Glacier*

Douglas ⑬ JUNEAU

⑫

*Chichagof Island*

*Icy Strait*

ADMIRALTY ISLAND NATIONAL MONUMENT

*Chatham Strait*

*Frederick Sound*

Kake

*Kupreanof Island*

⑧ PETERSBURG

⑨ MITKOF HWY

WRANGELL ⑥

*Tongass National Forest*

Point Baker

*Wrangell Island*

⑦ ANAN CREEK WILDLIFE OBSERVATORY

*Mt Willibert* △ 6,759 ft

*Coffman Cove*

*Cleveland Peninsula*

Meyers Chuck

PRINCE OF WALES ISLAND

Hollis

*Revillagigedo Island*

⑤

KETCHIKAN ①

Saxman

③

② METLAKATLA

Kasaan

④ HYDER

MISTY FIORDS NATIONAL MONUMENT

*Coast Mountains*

*Alexander Archipelago*

**For additional map symbols** *see back flap*

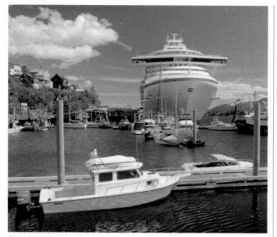
Cruise ship anchored at Ketchikan, a popular stop on cruise routes

# ❶ Ketchikan

235 miles (378 km) S of Juneau.
**Transport map** F5. ✈ 8,000. ⛴
🚢 Bellingham–Skagway. ℹ 50 Front
St and Cruise Ship berths, 225-6166,
(800) 770-3300. 🎭 Blueberry Arts
Festival (1st weekend in Aug).
Ⓦ visit-ketchikan.com

Situated on the southwestern
end of Revillagigedo Island,
Ketchikan likes to call itself
Alaska's First City, because it is
the first Alaskan city that visitors
see when arriving on a cruise
ship or ferry.

Originally a Tlingit fish camp
called Kitschk-Hin (meaning
"thundering eagle wings creek"),
the town's growth started in 1885
when Irishman Mike Martin
staked a claim near Ketchikan
Creek and set up a fish cannery.
By the 1930s, the town's dozen
canneries had earned it the title
Salmon Capital of the World.
Its other big economic resource,
the Ketchikan Pulp Company's
paper mill at Ward Cove,
operated for over 40 years
until it shut down in 1997.

Despite that major loss,
Ketchikan bounced back.
Today, Alaska's sixth largest city
thrives as a major stop for cruise
ships and as a regional service
center. Built on pilings, the city
center lies along the waterfront,
while older neighborhoods
climb the slopes of nearby
hills accessible by steep
streets and wooden staircases.

## 🏛 Great Alaskan Lumberjack Show

420 Spruce Mill Way. **Tel** 225-9050.
🚌 Ketchikan city bus. **Open** May–
Sep: four shows daily when cruise
ships are in port. 🅿 ♿ 🏪
Ⓦ alaskanlumberjackshow.com

Held in an amphitheater on
the site of the old Ketchikan
Spruce Mill, this lively show
displays hand-sawing, tree-
climbing, and log-rolling. It
is all done in a spirit of fun,
and the actors and lumberjack
competitors are so engaging
that much of the audience
seems happy to participate.
The original 1898 mill was
the world's largest spruce
mill and provided work for
lumberjacks who prepared
timber to be used during the
Gold Rush, for building aircraft
during World War II, and for
local canneries. The mill finally
closed in 1993.

## 🏛 Southeast Alaska Discovery Center

50 Main St. **Tel** 228-6220. 🚌
Ketchikan city bus. **Open** May–
Sep: 8am–5pm daily; Oct–Apr:
10am–3pm Mon–Fri. ♿ ⛴ 🏪
Ⓦ alaskacenters.gov/ketchikan.
cfm

Both a museum and a visitors'
center for the 26,000-sq mile
(68,000-sq km) Tongass National
Forest, the lush temperate
rainforest which covers the
region, the Southeast Alaska
Discovery Center is a mine of
information. Totem poles from
the region's three main Native
cultures, Tlingit, Haida, and
Tsimshian are displayed, and the
historical, cultural, natural, and
economic story of Southeast
Alaska is told through exhibits.
Other displays feature traditional
Tlingit salmon-drying, forest
ecosystems, and local fishing
techniques such as purse sein-
ing, gillnetting, and trawling.

Silver salmon sculptures at the Southeast
Alaska Discovery Center

## 🏛 Creek Street

🚌 Ketchikan city bus. 🅿 🚻 🏪
**Dolly's House Open** May–Sep: 8am–
5pm daily when cruise ships are in port.
🅿 Ⓦ creekstreetketchikan.com

A pedestrian boardwalk built
on pilings over Ketchikan Creek,
Creek Street was the town's red-
light district for half a century.

Dolly's House built on the pilings of Creek Street

In the early 1900s, well-heeled newcomers to the north side of town decided to clean up the neighborhood by banishing the "working girls" to the south side. Creek Street was soon notorious for its bars and bordellos, and it was here that Frenchie, Black Mary, and Dolly Arthur plied their trade.

Most of their houses have been turned into shops and eateries, but **Dolly's House** is now a museum. Visitors learn interesting facts about those bawdy days, such as how Creek Street's construction lent itself to surreptitious trap-door deliveries of alcohol after it was banned by the 1917 Bone Dry Law.

The street is a perfect spot to watch spawning salmon swim upstream. Visitors can also take the funicular from the end of the street up to the Cape Fox Lodge or follow the Married Man's Trail, once used by men hoping for a clandestine Creek Street encounter.

### 🏛 Saxman Totem Park

2 miles (4 km) S of Ketchikan at Mile 2.5, S Tongass Hwy. **Tel** 225-4846. 🚌 Ketchikan city bus. **Open** daily, tours in summer. 🎫 👢 📷 🌐 alaska.org/detail/saxman-totem-park

Founded in 1894, the Native village of Saxman today has the finest display of totem poles in Southeast Alaska. The village was settled by Tlingit from the villages of Tongass and Cape Fox at the southern tip of Alaska, who were persuaded to move here by Presbyterian missionaries. Begun in the late 1930s as a Civilian Conservation Corps (CCC) project, Saxman Totem Park has grown into a popular attraction. In addition to the renovated poles brought from surrounding villages, there is the colorful Beaver Clan House and the Frog Wall, which features dozens of frog faces. A large carving shed houses the workshops of Alaska's best totem carvers.

### 🏛 Totem Bight State Historical Park

10 miles (16 km) N of Ketchikan. ℹ 9883 North Tongass Hwy, 247-8574. 🚌 Ketchikan city bus. 👢 📷 🌐 dnr.alaska.gov/parks/units/totembgh.htm

As Europeans established permanent settlements in Southeast Alaska, many Natives joined them, and their traditional villages fell into ruins. In 1938, the CCC launched a project to restore old totem poles that lay rotting in abandoned villages. Native carvers were hired to re-create the damaged poles, which were placed in a forested site near the Tongass Narrows, and by 1942, 15 poles and a clan house had been completed. In 1970, Totem Bight was designated a State Historical Park. Today, a walkway between the totems leads to the water and a replica clan house that once would have held 30 to 50 people.

Totems along a forest walkway, Totem Bight State Historical Park

Detail of a totem pole at Saxman Totem Park near Ketchikan

### Totem Poles

Alaska's Tlingit, Haida, and Tsimshian peoples carve at least six types of totem poles to support buildings, tell stories, and honor people or special events. Never meant to be objects of veneration, poles were cultural symbols, carved of western red cedar with designs that included stylized clan totems, such as Raven, Beaver, Frog, Bear, Wolf, and Killer Whale, and painted in symbolic colors. Due to the iron tools gained by trade with Europeans, the mid-19th century saw an especially prolific carving period. This ended with the arrival of missionaries in the late 19th century, who discouraged pole raisings and potlatches, the gifting feasts that accompanied them. Pole carving was revived in the 1930s by the CCC, which launched a project to restore old poles and commission locals to carve new ones. Today, master carvers still create poles and pass on the craft to apprentices.

Metlakatla's boat harbor on Annette Island

## ❷ Metlakatla

18 miles (29 km) SW of Ketchikan.
**Transport map** F5. ⬛ 1,400.
✈ Ketchikan. ⛴ from Ketchikan.
ℹ 886-8687. ⓦ **metlakatla.com**

Located on Annette Island
southwest of Ketchikan,
Metlakatla was founded in 1887
by Scottish clergyman Father
Duncan. After falling out with
the church in Old Metlakatla,
Canada, he fled to
Annette Island
with over 800
of his Tsimshian
followers *(see
p27)*. In 1891,
the US Congress
gave them
possession of the
island. Because
the Tsimshian rejected ANCSA
in the early 1970s *(see p60)*, they
retained their sovereignty, and
Annette Island is now Alaska's
only Indian reservation, with
an economy dependent on
fishing and the timber industry.
Metlakatla's main appeal
lies in its quiet, small-town
atmosphere. The **Duncan**

Sign, Annette
Island Reserve

**Cottage Museum** contains
Father Duncan's educational
and medical materials, musical
instruments, and a phonograph
built by Thomas Edison himself.
The **Le Sha'as Tsimshian** clan
house is worth a visit to watch
dance performances and totem
carvers at work. There's also a
pleasant, short hike up Yellow Hill
for great Inside Passage views.

## ❸ Misty Fiords National Monument

22 miles (35 km) E of Ketchikan.
**Transport map** F5. ✈ charter
floatplane from Ketchikan.
ⓦ **fs.usda.gov/tongass**

Misty Fiords is a hidden gem, not
only because it is little-known
outside Southeast Alaska, but
also because it's often hidden
in rain behind a bank of clouds.
Characterized by wild fjords,
alpine lakes, roaring water-falls,
rainforests, snowy peaks, and
soaring 3,000-ft (915-m) granite
cliffs, the site was first identified

in the 1793 journals of Captain
George Vancouver, one of
Captain Cook's lieutenants.
The profuse wildlife includes
bears, deer, mountain goats,
bald eagles, and whales.
Many travelers opt for boat
and floatplane tours, such as the
boat-in, fly-out tour organized
by **Allen Marine Tours**.

**Allen Marine Tours**
5 Salmon Landing #215, Ketchikan.
**Tel** 225-8100, (877) 686-8100.
ⓦ allenmarinetours.com

## ❹ Hyder

2 miles (4 km) W of Stewart, BC
(Canada), 75 miles (120 km) E of
Ketchikan. **Transport map** F5. ⬛ 90.
✈ Stewart. 🚌 Stewart–Terrace.
ℹ 222 5th Ave, Stewart, BC, (888)
366-5999. 🎪 International Stewart
and Hyder Rodeo (2nd week in Jun),
International Days (1st weekend in Jul).

Isolated from the rest of Alaska
by a roadless range of mountains, Hyder sits on the US
border at the end of Canada
Route 37A. Despite the fact
that it works on Canadian time,
has a Canadian phone code,
and sends its children to
Canadian schools, it enjoys
a very Alaskan atmosphere.
For visitors, the town is an
attraction in itself, with its historic buildings and more bars
per capita than any town in
Alaska. The scenic but rough
25-mile- (40-km-) long **Granduc
Road** heads north from Hyder,
following the Salmon River past
old gold mines to a grand view
of Salmon Glacier. The area also
has a large number of brown
bears, and salmon crowd the
streams in summer.

The atmospheric Misty Fiords National Monument

# Alaska's Temperate Rainforests

Characterized by lush, rain-soaked mosses, lichens, shrubs, and ferns sheltering beneath enormous coniferous trees, the forests of Southeast Alaska make up the northern extent of the world's largest temperate rainforest. Much cooler than their tropical counterparts, temperate rainforests have climatic conditions that are marked by average summer temperatures of less than 16° C (61° F), a cool dormant season, and at least 55 inches (140 cm) of precipitation per year. At the southern end of the Panhandle, the rainfall can exceed 200 inches (508 cm) per year, but moving north, it decreases to around 60 inches (150 cm) near Juneau. The most prominent trees in Alaska's rainforest are the Sitka spruce and western hemlock, followed by mountain hemlock, yellow cedar, and western red cedar. Rarer conifers include mountain juniper, subalpine and silver fir, and Pacific yew.

**Rainforest trees** typically live from 200 to 1,000 years. When they fall, they decompose into a rich organic material that nourishes vegetation.

**Ferns** prefer moist conditions with low levels of light and thrive under the temperate rainforest cover.

## Flora and Fauna

*Alaska's temperate rainforest includes a canopy composed of tall coniferous trees, while smaller shade-loving trees and shrubs make up the understory. On the damp, shady forest floor grow ferns and large-leafed plants. Fauna species include river otters, pine martens, and boreal toads.*

**Devil's Club**, a spiny plant, dominates the floor of the rainforest where little sunlight filters through.

**The Tongass National Forest**, the world's largest temperate rainforest, covers the Southeast Alaskan mainland and over 1,000 islands, and includes Wrangell Narrows, a narrow waterway between Mitkof and Kupreanof Islands.

**Sitka black-tailed deer**, endemic to the region, feed on the native hemlock, berries, and lichens.

**Epiphytic mosses and lichens** draw nutrients and moisture directly from the air, using the host trees just for support.

**Porcupines**, second in size to beavers among Alaskan rodents, are nocturnal animals.

# ❺ Prince of Wales Island

Named for the son of King George III by Captain George Vancouver in 1793, Prince of Wales Island lies mostly within the Tongass National Forest. The third largest island in the US after Hawaii and Kodiak, it is home to both the Haida and Tlingit peoples, as well as a number of outsiders attracted by its beauty and solitude. It is laced with 1,400 miles (2,240 km) of old logging roads, half of which are passable by cars. One of the most interesting activities here is simply to drive through the forests and muskeg of the interior. Access to the island is either by ferry from Ketchikan or Wrangell, or by floatplane.

Densely forested islets off Prince of Wales Island

## Craig

90 miles (145 km) W of Ketchikan.
🏔 1,200. ✈ charter floatplane. ⛴ to Hollis. ℹ USFS, 900 9th St, 826-3271.
ⓦ **princeofwalescoc.org/communitiesb/craig**

The largest town on the island, Craig is also its only community without a Native majority. It was named for Craig Millar who, with the help of local Haida, set up the first saltery on Fish Egg Island in 1907, followed by a sawmill and a salmon cannery. Due to poor salmon runs, fishing declined in the 1950s, but in 1972, the Head Sawmill, north of Craig, boosted the town's faltering economy. Today, Craig is the island's service center, with a bank, hotel, gas station, and several restaurants.

## Klawock

5 miles (8 km) N of Craig. 🏔 750.
✈ ⛴ to Hollis. ℹ 6488 Klawock–Hollis Hwy, 755-2626. ⓦ **princeof walescoc.org**

Named for the first Tlingit settler, Kloo-wah, the village of Klawock was originally a summer fishing camp. A trading post and saltery were set up here in 1868, and a

decade later, it became the site of Alaska's first salmon cannery. Today, the town boasts a hatchery on the shores of Klawock Lake, a sawmill, a log-sorting yard, and a dock for loading timber. In keeping with the timber theme, electricity is provided by a wood-fired generator.

**Klawock Totem Park**, next to the town library, has about 20 restored poles from Tuxekan, a Tlingit winter village to the north. Across the Hollis-Craig highway from the Chamber of Commerce is the Gaan Ax Adi Clan House, with a carving shed where visitors may sometimes see new totems being carved. The airport, the only one on the island, has an unattended 6,000-ft (1,800-m) paved runway with pilot-controlled lighting – remarkable given its location.

**Key**

=== Minor road

0 km        30
0 miles              30

Tlingit totem poles in the village of Klawock

Students paddling a traditional Haida canoe that they have carved

## Hydaburg

45 miles (72 km) SE of Craig. 380.
charter floatplane.

As rural Alaskan towns go, the little Haida village of Hydaburg is as picturesque as it gets. Although the town was not founded until 1912, when the three villages of Sukkwan, Howkan and Klinkwan combined, Haida peoples have occupied the area since the 18th century, when they migrated from British Columbia. Today, the town has the largest Haida population in Alaska.

Hydaburg's Totem Park is well worth a visit. Its collection of restored totems, with their unique emphasis on pastel colors, stands apart from others in the region.

## Thorne Bay

39 miles (63 km) NE of Craig. 480.
floatplane from Ketchikan.

Nestled between rolling hills and the sea, Thorne Bay was named in honor of Frank Manley Thorn, superintendent of the US Coast and Geodetic Survey in the 1880s. During its heyday in the mid-20th century, Thorne Bay was North America's largest logging camp, but the mill closed in the 1990s and the economy now depends on fishing.

A popular visitor attraction here is the **Honker River Canoe Route**, which begins at Coffman Cove Road and winds through a chain of lakes down to Thorne Bay. The area also has several campsites, forest service cabins, hiking trails, and picnic areas.

## Kasaan

49 miles E of Craig. 55. charter floatplane.

Deriving its name from the Tlingit word for "pretty town," Kasaan does indeed have a lovely setting between forested mountains and the sea. It was founded in 1892 when mining and fishing jobs attracted the Haida here from the now-abandoned Old Kasaan. Today, most Kasaan residents depend on their harvests of deer, fish, shrimp, and crab.

In the 1930s, the Haida Chief Sonihat built the Whale clan house, and the various totems around the village were transferred to the same site, forming the **Kasaan Totem Park**. A 15-minute trail through beach-side woods leads to the park, where the decaying poles and clan house, almost swallowed by the undergrowth and unspoilt by commercial trappings, lend an authentic air to the picturesque scene.

## El Capitan Cave

Mile 50, N Prince of Wales Rd. **Tel** 828-3304. **Open** mid-May–early Sep: Mon–Sat. mandatory, at 9am, noon, & 3pm: book 2 days in advance.

Sited northwest of Whale Pass, El Capitan Cave is the largest and longest of the limestone caves dotted around the karst region of northern Prince of Wales Island. In these caves, paleontologists have uncovered human remains dating back about 9,500 years, the oldest found in the region. A 12,300-year-old brown bear skeleton was discovered in El Capitan Cave, while a more remote cave yielded a 45,000-year-old bear skeleton.

Over 2 miles (3 km) of passageways in El Capitan Cave have been surveyed. Guided tours using helmets and headlamps are offered. Reservations must be made two days in advance, but rare walk-ins are allowed. Young children under 7 years are not allowed in the cave. The tour begins with a steep climb up 367 steps, and a fair degree of physical fitness is required.

## Forestry in Southeast Alaska

Since the late 19th century, forestry and forest products have been an economic factor in the Tongass National Forest, and from the 1940s to 1990s, they were the mainstay of Alaska's economy. The prime western hemlock and Sitka spruce of Southeast Alaska were exported, while lower quality timber was reduced to pulp for the paper industry. In the 1990s, economic and environmental pressures combined with decreasing harvest limits caused the closure of the Sitka and Ketchikan mills. Today the industry plays only a minor role in Alaska's economy.

Worker adjusting truckload of logs for delivery

Wrangell's harbor against the backdrop of the Coast Mountains

# ❻ Wrangell

80 miles (128 km) N of Ketchikan.
**Transport map** F5. ✈ 2,400. 🚢
from Ketchikan. 🚢 from Ketchikan,
Petersburg, or Juneau. ℹ Nolan
Center, 296 Campbell Drive, 874-
2829/800-367-9745. ⛰ 🎣 Stikine
River Birding Festival (early May).
Ⓦ **wrangellalaska.org**

Founded as Redoubt St. Dionysius
in 1833 by the Russians, the
original fort on this site was
intended to protect Russian fur
trading interests from the British
and Spanish. The local Tlingit,
under Chief Shakes V, recognized the economic benefits of
cooperation with the Russians
and joined them at the redoubt
in 1834. In the same year, combined Tlingit and Russian forces
managed to repel the British
forces led by Peter Skeen Odgen,
who had attempted to establish
a fur trading post. In 1868,
following Alaska's transfer to the
US, the Americans established
a military fort that they named
after the head of the Russian-
American Company, Baron
Ferdinand von Wrangel.

Today, Wrangell is a friendly
little town, attracting a few
adventurous visitors and a
handful of small cruise ships
in the summer. The real draw
is the Stikine River, just outside
town, as well as Anan Creek
and outlying parts of Wrangell
Island, both popular for wildlife
viewing. From the town, forest

roads lead to free campgrounds,
the best of which are at Nemo
Point, 14 miles (22 km) south,
offering wonderful high altitude
views over Zimovia Strait.

## 🏛 Wrangell Museum

Nolan Center, 296
Campbell Drive. **Tel** 874-
3770. **Open** May–Sep:
10am–5pm Mon–Sat;
Oct–Apr: noon–5pm
Tue–Sat. 🅿 ♿ 📷

Housed in the same
building as the town's
visitor information
office and convention
center, the Wrangell
Museum contains a
wonderful collection
of artifacts. The large entryway
features the original 17th-
century houseposts of the
Frog Clan from the Tlingit Tribal

Tlingit housepost,
Wrangell Museum

House on Chief Shakes Island.
Electronic lighting on the
ceiling of the lobby simulates
the undulations of the aurora
borealis. Museum displays
begin with the natural history
of the region and proceed
chronologically
through exhibits on
Native culture, the fur
trade, military history,
the Stikine Gold Rush,
fishing, and forestry.
The museum is also
a repository for
thousands of historic
images and numerous
audio and video
records, which are
available for viewing.

## 🏛 Chief Shakes Island

Shakes St.
Accessible by a wooden walkway
across an arm of the harbor, Chief
Shakes Island is a park and a
repository for Tlingit totems
dating from 1840 to 1940.
Opened in 1940 and restored
in 2013, the large replica **Tlingit
Tribal House**, a National Historic
Site, was named Ck! Udatc
Hit ("House of Many Faces") in
reference to the human visages
in its design. Inside are replica
houseposts of the Frog Clan, and
dotted around the park are
several distinctive totems. The
peaceful park overlooks the
picturesque harbor, and on
sunny days, its green lawns
provide a perfect place to relax.

Totem pole and Tlingit Tribal House on
Chief Shakes Island

◀ The beautiful town of Sitka, on the west coast of Baranof Island

### ⬚ Petroglyph Beach State Historic Site

Half a mile (1 km) N of Wrangell at Grave St. **Open** 24 hrs. ♿ limited.

Archeologists believe that an ancient culture already occupied the Wrangell area before the modern-day Tlingit arrived. Evidence suggests that these early groups were here around 10,000 years ago, at the end of the last Ice Age, and that they established subsequent settlements 5,000 and 3,000 years ago. It is thought that these early people made some of the 40 petroglyphs that adorn the rocks of the beach. However, the artwork reveals little information about their culture, except that the simplest spiral and sun designs match petrogylphs found as far away as South America. The petroglyphs of wolves, bears, and orcas found on the same beach were probably carved by the Tlingit. Most of the petroglyphs, carved on boulders scattered along several hundred feet of beach, have been eroded over time by the sea. A visitors' platform provides access to the beach, where the state has reproduced the most interesting petroglyphs to allow visitors to make rubbings of the carvings without damaging the originals.

**Petroglyph of a fish on a boulder**

### 🏞 Stikine River

🚢 tour boats. 🎣 🏔 🛶

The glacier-fed Stikine River is the biggest draw for visitors to Wrangell. Originating in the mountains of British Columbia, the 360-mile (576-km) river flows through 30 miles (48 km) of the Stikine-LeConte Wilderness on the Alaskan mainland to its mouth across the narrows near Wrangell.

Several companies organize jetboat tours, which head upstream through spectacular mountain scenery and past waterfalls and the iceberg choked face of Shakes Glacier. There is a delightful lunch spot here, overlooking the glacier. There are also good

Kayaking in the blue waters of the Stikine River

opportunities to see harbor seals, black bears, spawning salmon, and the world's largest summer concentration of bald eagles. A popular destination is **Chief Shakes Hot Springs**, where open-air hot tubs offer soaking in a wild setting.

### 🏌 Muskeg Meadows Golf Course

Mile 0.5, Ishiyama Dr. **Tel** 874-4653. or phone for pickup from town. **Open** Apr–Nov: 9am–6pm. 🏌 💻 📷 �🅦 **wrangellalaskagolf.com**

The non-profit Wrangell Golf Club was established in 1993 to carve a nine-hole, par 36 course from the muskeg bog for which it was named. From 1995 to 1998, volunteers cleared trees, laid wood pulp to create the fairways, planted grass, and installed the greens, resulting in a beautiful course set amid spruce and cedar rainforest. This is the world's only golf course with a 'Raven Rule', which states that if a raven steals a golf ball, it can be replaced without penalty, provided the golfer has a witness.

### ❼ Anan Creek Wildlife Observatory

31 miles (50 km) S of Wrangell. **Transport map** F5. **Tel** 874-2323. 🚁 by floatplane. 🚢 tour boat. **Open** year-round. 🏌 🏔 book in advance. Permits: required Jul 5–Aug 25, book at ⓦ **fs.usda.gov/tongass**

Located on the Cleveland Peninsula, Anan Creek is the site

of one of Alaska's greatest pink salmon runs. The fish are slowed by a waterfall half a mile (1 km) inland, which attracts large numbers of hungry brown and black bears. Adjacent to the falls, a wildlife observatory, which is actually a large viewing platform, allows visitors close-up views of the feeding bears. During the salmon run, sea otters, harbor seals, and bald eagles can also be spotted along the shore near the mouth of Anan Creek.

While wildlife is usually visible all summer, permits are needed to visit the observatory in July and August. Only 60 permits are issued for each day. Four permits are also available for those staying at the nearby Anan Bay public use cabin – the only accommodation available in the area. However, local tour operators pre-book permits and make them available to visitors on their tours.

Black bear feeding with cub at the rapidly flowing Anan Creek

Houses built on pilings above Hammer Slough in Petersburg

# ❽ Petersburg

32 miles (51 km) N of Ketchikan.
**Transport map** F5. 🏔 3,000. ✈
from Ketchikan, Wrangell & Juneau.
🚢 from Ketchikan, Sitka, Wrangell, &
Juneau. 🛈 1st & Fram St, 772-4636.
🎭 Little Norway Festival (weekend
nearest May 17). 🌐 **petersburg.org**

Named for Norwegian settler
Peter Buschmann, Petersburg
nestles on sheltered Mitkof
Island beside a calm sea.
Buschmann, who arrived to
homestead in the area in 1890,
initiated the development of
the town. By 1900, realizing
that glacier ice could be used
to preserve fish, he set up the
Icy Strait Packing Company
cannery. By the 1920s, jobs
created by the town's businesses had attracted over 600
people. Petersburg now has
crab, shrimp, salmon, and
herring fisheries, as well as
Alaska's largest halibut fleet.
Petersburg enjoys spectacular

mountain views that include
the precipitous Devil's Thumb,
towering at 9,077 ft (2,767 m)
and straddling the Canadian
border about 40 miles (64 km)
away. The major attractions
for visitors are the beautiful
hinterlands of Mitkof Island and
neighboring Kupreanof Island,
which offer superb hiking,
camping, fishing, boating,
and kayaking.

## 🏛 Sing Lee Alley

Built on pilings above
Hammer Slough,
this picturesque
boardwalk is one of
Petersburg's oldest
historic streets. At
No. 23, the distinctive
Sons of Norway Hall,
built by Norwegian
immigrants in 1912,
has graceful decorative scroll
paintings called *rosemaling* on
its facade. The adjacent Bojer
Wikan Fishermen's Memorial

Park features a statue of Bojer
Wikan, a local fisherman lost
at sea. The replica Viking ship
*Valhalla*, used in the Little
Norway Festival, is kept here.
The street also has a pleasant
café and bookshop.

Bojer Wikan statue,
Sing Lee Alley

## 🏛 Clausen Memorial Museum

203 Fram St. **Tel** 772-3598.
**Open** May–early Sep: 10am–
5pm Mon–Sat. **Closed** public
holidays. 🅿 📷 🌐 **clausen
museum.com**

The compact Clausen
Memorial Museum
showcases the history
and culture of the
Petersburg and
Kupreanof Island area.
Besides a replica of a
1970s-era fish packer's
office, it features a fish
trap, a collection of old nautical
and fishing gear, and a Tlingit
dugout canoe. The most
popular exhibit, however,
representing every angler's
dream, is the 125-lb (56-kg)
stuffed king salmon.

# ❾ Mitkof Highway

**Transport map** F5. 🛈 12 N Nordic
Dr, 772-3871. 🏔 🌐 **fs.fed.us/r10/
tongass/districts/petersburg**

The scenic Mitkof Highway
follows the coastline from
Petersburg to the southern end
of Mitkof Island. At Mile 14.5,
a lovely boardwalk trail crosses

Sons of Norway Hall with the Viking ship *Valhalla*, Sing Lee Alley

*For hotels and restaurants in this area see pp243–4 and pp253–4*

the muskeg to access some picnic spots and the salmon run at **Blind River Rapids**. Wintering trumpeter swans can be seen from mid-October to December at the Swan Observatory at Mile 16. Not far ahead, at Mile 18, the Crystal Lake Hatchery and Blind Slough Recreation Area offer scenic picnic sites.

The beautiful **Man Made Hole** at Mile 20 was once a quarry that has filled with water to form a lake. A gentle trail winds around its perimeter on boardwalks and gravel. At Mile 22, the pretty Ohmer Creek Campground offers visitors free camping at the island's only public campsite.

## ⑩ Sitka

*See pp140–41.*

Brightly painted houses at Tenakee Springs flanking the calm inlet

## ⑪ Tenakee Springs

48 miles (78 km) N of Sitka. **Transport map** E5. 🚌 130. 🚢 Sitka–Juneau. ℹ 736-2207. Bathhouse: at ferry dock. **Open** men: 2–6pm & 10pm–9am daily; women: 9am–2pm & 6–10pm daily. 🌐 tenakeespringsak.com

Situated on the eastern shores of Chichagof Island, the village of Tenakee Springs takes its name from the Tlingit Tinaghu, meaning "Copper Shield Bay," after three prized copper shields that were lost in a storm in Tenakee Inlet.

Historically, the town's main attraction was the 42° C (108° F) hot spring, which made the area bearable in all seasons. In 1895, a **Bathhouse** was built to enclose the spring, and Snyder's

Mud flats and forests on Admiralty Island

Mercantile, launched in 1899, still runs as a general store.

Today, the picturesque village stretches along a single street, which is limited to pedestrian traffic. The nearby Native village of Hoonah, accessible by ferry, has the Icy Strait Point zipline, over 1 mile (1.6 km) long, which is a popular attraction on some cruise ship routes.

## ⑫ Admiralty Island National Monument

43 miles (70 km) NE of Sitka. **Transport map** F5. ✈ charter float-plane from Juneau. 🚢 Sitka–Angoon; tour boat Juneau–Pack Creek. ℹ 586-8800. 🅿 📷 ⚠ 🚻 Permits required to visit Pack Creek Jun–mid-Sep.

Called Kootznoowoo (meaning "Fortress of Bears") by the Tlingit people, Admiralty Island National Monument sprawls across 1,492 sq miles (3,865 sq km). Lying within the

Tongass National Forest, almost 98 percent of this lush rainforest is a designated wilderness area. The main site of interest for wildlife enthusiasts is **Pack Creek** in the Stan Price State Wildlife Sanctuary at the island's northeast corner. This area is home to the world's densest population of brown bears. Sitka black-tailed deer can be seen along the shore, and Mitchell, Hood, Chaik, and Whitewater Bays contain porpoises, seals, and sea lions. Summer access to the tidal estuary and bear-viewing tower is by permit only; permits can be booked online at www.recreation.gov.

The sole settlement on the island is **Angoon**, a small Native village accessible via the Marine Highway. Kayakers and canoeists will enjoy the **Cross-Island Canoe Route**, which connects Angoon with Mole Harbor, on the island's eastern shore, by a series of lakes, streams, and portages.

### Little Norway

Peter Buschmann's success in Petersburg inspired many of his countrymen to follow him to Alaska in search of fjords, fishing, and opportunity. Nicknamed Little Norway, the town reflects its Norwegian heritage in the decorative details on buildings and the souvenirs on offer. On the weekend nearest Norwegian Independence Day on May 17, the town celebrates the Little Norway Festival *(see p46)* with a Norwegian feast and *bunad*

(traditional dress) fashion show. The *Valhalla* leads a parade of revelers clad in Norwegian flags and Viking attire. Even if it rains – and it usually does – a good time is had by all.

# ⑩ Sitka

One of Alaska's most beautiful towns, Sitka sits beside an island-studded sea on the west coast of Baranof Island. The lure of hunting sea otters for their pelts led the Russians to set up Redoubt St. Michael in the year 1799. After local Tlingit destroyed the fort in 1804, the Russians established the fortified town of Novo Archangelsk. By 1808, this was the capital of Russian America and was flourishing economically and culturally. When the US bought Alaska in 1867, the town's name was changed to Sitka, a contraction of Shee Atiká, the Tlingit name for the settlement. Today, Sitka's economy is based on tourism and a large fishing and cold-storage industry.

Tlingit totem poles on display at the Sheldon Jackson Museum

Detail of ceremonial Native canoe, Sitka History Museum

### 🏛 Sitka History Museum
330 Harbor Dr. **Tel** 747-6455, 747-5516 (performance information). **Open** mid-May–late Sep: 9am–5pm Mon–Fri, 10am–4pm Sat–Sun; late Sep–mid-May: 10am–4pm Tue–Sat. 🏛 donations accepted. 👟 📷 �W sitkahistory.com

Housed in the Harrigan Centennial Hall, this museum outlines Sitka's history from the Russian era to the present, including exhibits on mining, forestry, and World War II. In addition to a model of Sitka at the time of its transfer to the United States, the museum's highlights include Tlingit art, tools, and spruce baskets. There are also trade beads, Russian weapons, historic photographs, and a unique "tea brick." These bricks of compacted Cantonese tea were acquired by the Russians from the Chinese in exchange for the sea otter pelts that formed the basis of Russian Alaska's economy.

Outside, a large Haida ceremonial canoe is on display beneath a canopy. In the summer, the New Archangel Dancers perform in traditional Russian costume for tourists.

### ✝ St. Michael's Russian Orthodox Cathedral
240 Lincoln St. **Tel** 747-8120. **Open** May–Sep: 9am–4pm Mon–Fri, or when cruise ships are in port; winter: by appt. 🏛 👟 limited. ✝ 6pm Sat, 9:30am Sun. �W oca.org/parishes/oca-ak-sitsmk

This onion-domed cathedral is the quintessential Sitka landmark. The cornerstone was laid by Bishop Veniaminov (see p78) in 1844, and construction was completed in 1848. The present church is a replica of the original, which burned down in a fire in 1966. Although locals managed to rescue the paintings, icons, chandelier, and the partially melted bronze bells, the large library of works in Russian, Tlingit, and Aleut languages was lost. One surviving artifact, the Madonna of Sitka, has been credited with miraculous healing. The reconstruction, in fire-resistant materials, took from 1967 to 1972, and the new cathedral was consecrated in 1976. Visitors can attend services.

Dome and spire of St. Michael's Russian Orthodox Cathedral

### 🏛 Sheldon Jackson Museum
104 College Dr. **Tel** 747-8981. **Open** summer: 9am–5pm Tue–Sat; winter: 10am–noon, 1–4pm Tue–Sat. 📷 free for under 18s. 👟 📷 �W museums.alaska.gov

From 1888 to 1898, the Presbyterian Reverend Sheldon Jackson traveled

around Alaska representing the US educational system. In the course of his travels, he collected the indigenous artifacts that are displayed here, including hunting tools, masks, kayaks, and reindeer sleighs. Each summer, Native artisans come to the museum to demonstrate their crafts. The museum shop offers a variety of Native hand-crafted goods and artwork.

### ⚡ Alaska Raptor Center

1000 Raptor Way. **Tel** 747-8662.
🚌 Community Ride. **Open** May–Sep:
8am–4pm daily; Oct–Apr: 10am–
3pm Mon–Fri. 🅿️ 🛍️ 🚻 ♿
🅦 **alaskaraptor.org**

One of the state's best raptor
hospital and rehabilitation
centers, the non-profit Alaska
Raptor Center treats injured
ravens and raptors such as
eagles, falcons, owls, and
hawks, and tries to re-adapt
them to life in the wild. Seriously
wounded birds become Raptors-
in-Residence and are used in
educational programs for visitors.

### 🏛️ Russian Bishop's House

Lincoln & Monastery Sts. **Tel** 747-
0110/07. 🚌 Community Ride. **Open**
May–Sep: 8:30am–5pm daily; winter:
by appt. 🅿️ 🛍️ ♿ 🅦 **nps.gov/sitk**

The oldest building in Sitka, this
1843 structure is one of the few
surviving examples of secular
Russian architecture. The original
building was made from spruce
by Finnish woodworkers,
who introduced Baltic-

Bald eagle in the compound of the Alaska
Raptor Center

style opulence to Russian
America. Despite the building's
flamboyance, its first occupant,
Bishop Veniaminov, lived a
simple monastic life.

Over the years, the building
has served as an orphanage,
seminary, and school. The last
Russian bishop moved out
in 1969 and the building was
purchased in 1972 by the US
National Park Service for restoration. On the main floor is a model
of Novo Archangelsk as it looked
in 1845 and a collection of icons
and relics. To see the library,
chapel, and Bishop's quarters, it
is necessary to join a guided tour.

Russian cemetery, where
hundreds of graves recall 18th-
and 19th-century Russian Sitka.

### 🏛️ Sitka National Historical Park

103 Monastery St. 🛈 747-0110. **Open**
May–Sep: 6am–10pm daily; Oct–Apr:
7am–8pm daily. **Closed** public hols.
🛍️ ♿ 🏛️ 🅦 **nps.gov/sitk**

Alaska's oldest federal park was
established in 1910 to commemorate the 1804 Battle of Sitka. In
1802, Tlingit warriors of the Kiks.
ádi tribe attacked the Russian
redoubt, killing most of the
Russian and Aleut personnel.
The Russians returned with four
ships and beseiged the Tlingit
fort. After much bloodshed,
Russians entered the fort to find
that it had been abandoned by
the Tlingit. Today, the site is part
of the park. From the visitors'
center and museum, trails lead
through rainforest past nearly a
dozen Northwest Coast totem
poles. To the east is the site of
the Tlingit fort and the actual
battleground, while to the
north, across the creek, trails
lead to the Russian Memorial.

Map scale:
0 metres — 300
0 yards — 300

## Sights at a Glance

① Sitka History Museum
② St. Michael's Russian Orthodox
  Cathedral
③ Sheldon Jackson Museum
④ Alaska Raptor Center
⑤ Russian Bishop's House
⑥ Blockhouse and Russian
  Cemetery
⑦ Sitka National Historical Park

### 🏛️ Blockhouse and Russian Cemetery

Kogwantan & Marine Sts. Blockhouse:
**Open** late May–early Sep: noon–4pm
Sun. Cemetery: **Open** 24 hrs.

North of St. Michael's sits a
reconstruction of an octagonal
two-story blockhouse used by the
Russians to shield their redoubt
from the Tlingit. Just behind the
Blockhouse lies the overgrown

Prince of Wales Island totem pole, Sitka
National Historical Park

# ⑬ Juneau

Often described as a little San Francisco due to its hilly setting, Alaska's capital is located between Mount Juneau and Mount Roberts along Gastineau Channel. Joe Juneau and Dick Harris' 1880 discovery of gold in Gold Creek and Juneau's strategic location on the route to the Klondike goldfields established its importance and led to it taking over the role of Alaska's capital from Sitka in 1900. In the mid-1970s, Alaskans voted to move the state capital to Willow, but due to projected costs, they reversed the decision in 1982.

Gold Rush-era mining display at the Alaska State Museum

Pleasure craft and fishing boats anchored in Juneau

## 🏛 Alaska State Capitol Building

4th & Main. 🚌 3 & 4. **Open** mid-May–mid-Sep: 8:30am– 5pm Mon–Fri, 9:30am–4pm Sat & Sun; winter: 8am–4:30pm Mon–Fri. 📷 🖥 alaska.org/detail/alaska-state-capitol-building

Designed to serve as the seat of Territorial Government, this marble Art Deco building was completed in 1931. It now houses the Alaska State Legislature and the offices of the Governor and Lieutenant Governor. A state map made from a slice of the Alaska Pipeline is on display near the staircase, and decorative details throughout showcase aspects of Alaska's culture and economy. Free tours are available daily in summer. The Legislature is in session January to March.

Facade of the Alaska State Capitol Building

## 🏛 Alaska State Museum

395 Whittier St. **Tel** 465-2901. 🚌 3 & 4. **Open** for new opening hours following closure for renovations, telephone or see website. 📷 ♿ 📷 🖥 **museums.alaska.gov**

The Alaska State Museum has an impressive collection reflecting many facets of Alaskan history, ranging from prehistoric times to modern days. On the ramp to the second floor is a mock rainforest, complete with recorded birdsong and a replica bald eagle nest. Displayed along the walls of the ramp are a range of Native artifacts, including dolls, masks, baskets, and models of traditional canoes. There is also a collection of Native ivory "billikens" upstairs. These chubby elf-like figurines have now become mainstays of the Alaskan tourist trade. Russian America is represented by a collection of icons and samovars, while numerous mining tools bring the Gold Rush to life. Other high-lights include a mineral collection, the pen used by President Dwight Eisenhower to sign the bill that gave Alaska its statehood, and a children's area with hands-on activities.

| 0 meters | | 200 |
| 0 yards | | 200 |

## Sights at a Glance

① Alaska State Capitol Building
② Alaska State Museum
③ Wickersham State Historical Site
④ Red Dog Saloon
⑤ Mount Roberts Tramway

*For hotels and restaurants in this area see pp243–4 and pp253–4*

## 🏛 Wickersham State Historical Site

213 7th St. **Tel** 586-9001. **Open** mid-May–late Sep: 10am–5pm Sun–Thu; winter: by appt. 🏛 donations accepted. 🌐 **dnr.alaska.gov/parks/units/wickrshm.htm**

The historic Wickersham house, built in 1898, was once the home of Judge James Wickersham, who served as the voice of the law in over half of Territorial Alaska. As a delegate to the US Congress, the judge introduced an Alaska Statehood Bill in 1916, planting the seeds of an idea that would come to fruition in 1959. After his death in 1939, his niece Ruth Allman opened the house to the public. In 1984, the house and its relics were purchased by the state and turned into a museum.

## 🍺 Red Dog Saloon

278 S Franklin St. **Tel** 463-3658. 🚌 3 & 4. **Open** 11am–11pm daily. 🚻 ♿ 💳 📷 🌐 **reddogsaloon.com**

During Juneau's mining heyday in the late 19th century, the Saloon offered alcohol, entertainment, and dancing to travelers and local miners. The Harris family bought the place in 1973 and turned it into a bar. Popular with cruise passengers and other visitors, it offers meals and drinks in a retro setting that includes a collection of interesting memorabilia, plus live music.

## 🚡 Mount Roberts Tramway

490 S Franklin St. **Tel** 463-3412. 🚌 3 & 4. **Open** May–Sep: 8am–9pm daily. 🚗 ♿ 🚻 💳 📷 🌐 **mountroberts tramway.com**

The tramway up the slopes of Mount Roberts offers panoramic views along Gastineau Channel and across to Douglas Island. At the summit, the Mountain House has a gift shop, restaurant, and the Chilkat Theater, which screens a film on Tlingit culture. The short Alpine Loop trail winds through meadow and forest, past several Tlingit carvings, with a short side trip to Father Brown's Cross. The energetic can forgo the tramway and hike up the mountain from the end of Sixth Street.

Mount Roberts Tramway cable car moving past forested slopes

## 🏛 Last Chance Mining Museum

1001 Basin Rd. **Tel** 586-5338. **Open** mid-May–late Sep: 9:30am–12:30pm, 3:30–5:30pm daily. 🏛

The only remnants of the Juneau goldfields are the historic buildings and relics of the Last Chance Mining Museum. It is located in the mine's old service center, which once housed dormitories, assay offices, and machine repair shops. The museum displays what was once the world's largest air compressor, mining tools, and a three-dimensional representation of the mine tunnels that wind through the adjacent mountain.

*Map labels:*
Last Chance
ing Museum
1 mile (2 km)
SIN ROAD
KENNEDY ST
EAST STREET
HARRIS STREET
EAST STREET
STREET
St. Nicholas
N 4TH STREET
GOLD STREET
N FRANKLIN ST
STREET
2ND STREET
1ST STREET
Cinema
FRONT STREET
SOUTH FRANKLIN STREET
SHATTUCK ST
SEWARD ST
GASTINEAU AVENUE
FERRY WAY
Marine Park
Visitor Dock
4 Red Dog Saloon
Library
Gastineau Channel
Cruise Ship Dock
Mount Roberts 5 Tramway
THANE

View of downtown Juneau from the upper Mount Roberts Tramway station

# Exploring Beyond Juneau

Downtown Juneau lies between the Coast Range and Gastineau Channel, so most of the city's residential areas are found on the coast of precipitous Douglas Island, as well as in the scenic side valleys and along the coastal, forest-studded Glacier Highway to the northwest. The city bus system extends only as far as the Mendenhall Valley loop, but with a rental car, it is possible to explore the spectacular hinterlands. More adventurous visitors can join helicopter tours of the Juneau Icefield.

## Sights at a Glance

① Macaulay Salmon Hatchery
② Alaskan Brewing Company
③ Glacier Gardens
④ Juneau Icefield
⑤ Mendenhall Glacier
⑥ Shrine of St. Therese de Lisieux

### Key

▢ Juneau
▬ Highway
┄ Minor road

## 🏛 Macaulay Salmon Hatchery

2697 Channel Dr, 3 miles (5 km) N of downtown Juneau. **Tel** 463-4810. 🚌 3 & 4. **Open** May–Sep: 10am–6pm Mon–Fri, 10am–5pm Sat & Sun; fish ladder: year-round. 🅿 🔊 🛗 📷
ⓦ adfg.alaska.gov/index. cfm?adfg=southeastviewing. juneaumacaulaysalmonhatchery

A working hatchery that provides fry to stock streams in many areas of Southeast Alaska, the interesting Macaulay Salmon Hatchery has over 100 species of local sealife on view in a number of large saltwater aquariums. Outside the building, walkways lead past several tanks where fry of various ages are fed and reared until they are ready for release into the surrounding waterways. Small salmon are also released into nearby Twin Lakes for recreational anglers. Between June and October, a 450-ft (135-m) fish ladder provides easy access for pink and chum salmon returning to the hatchery to spawn and produce their fry. Visitors can purchase a range of salmon products in the hatchery shop.

## 🏛 Alaskan Brewing Company

5429 Shaune Dr. **Tel** 780-5866. 🚌 3 & 4. **Open** May–Sep: 11am–7pm daily; Oct–Apr: 11am–5:30pm Mon–Sat. 🔊 🛗 📷 ⓦ alaskanbeer.com

Home-brewers Geoff and Marcy Larsen started the Alaskan Brewing Company in 1986 when they uncovered an ingredient list for a popular beer brewed during the 19th-century Gold Rush. This recipe became the base for their winning formula for Alaskan Amber. The popularity of their beers grew, and today their company is the state's largest fully-fledged brewery. In 1987, they produced 1,600 barrels of Amber and currently, the company annually distributes about 125,000 barrels of award-winning amber, pale ale, stout, and smoked porter throughout the western states.

A free hour-long tour explains the brewing process and includes displays of brewing equipment. Beer samples are available, and it is also possible to buy discounted cases of beer.

## 🏵 Glacier Gardens

7600 Glacier Hwy. **Tel** 790-3377. 🚌 3 & 4. **Open** May–Sep: 9am–6pm daily. 🅿 🔊 🛗 📷
ⓦ glaciergardens.com

Nearly surrounded by the Tongass National Forest, the 52-acre (21-ha) Glacier Gardens is a pleasant blend of groomed gardens and natural rainforest, including a series of artificial streams and ponds flanked by lovely plantings. A collection of upended tree stumps, salvaged from a devastating 1984 mudslide, form planters for colorful hanging gardens of petunias, begonias, and fuschias.

From the greenhouse, a succession of rainforest trails leads to boardwalks and a platform offering dramatic views of Gastineau Channel. For those who do not want to climb the steep hillside, the admission price includes transport by an electric golf cart through the woods, as well as a running commentary on the rainforest environment.

Unusual tree-stump planters, Glacier Gardens

Mendenhall Glacier on the shores of Mendenhall Lake near Juneau

### Juneau Icefield

accessible by flightseeing or helicopter tour only.

The Juneau Icefield sprawls across 1,500 sq miles (3,885 sq km) of the Coast Range, with its highest peak, the 8,584-ft (2,616-m) Devil's Paw, straddling the US-Canada border.

The icefield feeds about 40 large and 100 small glaciers. Of all Juneau Icefield's glaciers, only Taku Glacier continues to advance and calve into Taku Inlet.

The most readily accessible portion of the icefield is the retreating Mendenhall Glacier. A hike to the rest of the vast white wilderness of the icefield can be quite challenging, and most visitors opt for helicopter or flightseeing tours, some of which additionally offer adventurous summer dog sled rides across the ice. Also available are ice climbing classes, with instruction and gear provided.

### Mendenhall Glacier

8150 Mendenhall Loop Rd. 3 & 4.
789-0097. **Open** May–Sep: 8am–7:30pm daily; Oct–Apr: 10am–4pm Fri–Sun. **Closed** Apr summer only; free in winter.
fs.usda.gov/main/tongass/home

Spilling into the Mendenhall Valley from the Juneau Icefield, the large Mendenhall Glacier was first called Auke Glacier after the nearby Tlingit village, Aak'w Kwaan. In 1892, it was renamed in honor of physicist Thomas Mendenhall, who surveyed the international border between Canada and Southeast Alaska.

Several trails access the glacier. The East Glacier Loop follows the glacial trimline, while the West Glacier Trail goes up to the glacier's west face. The Moraine Ecology Trail has information panels explaining the regeneration of vegetation on deglaciated areas. The Photo Point Trail is lined with benches and interpretive panels, and provides the best vantage points to capture panoramic shots of the glacier.

At **Mendenhall Lake**, which is often choked with icebergs calved from the glacier, the huge curving glass wall of the visitor center offers fabulous views of the glacier across the lake. An exhibit hall has information on glaciers, and a theater shows films on icefield geology. A salmon-viewing platform and a fish-cam provide views of spawning salmon moving up Steep Creek.

### Shrine of St. Therese of Lisieux

21425 (Mile 22) Glacier Hwy.
**Tel** 780-6112. **Open** Apr–Sep: 8:30am–10pm; Oct–Mar: 8:30am–8pm. limited. late May–early Sep: 1:30pm Sun.
shrineofsainttherese.org

This peaceful Catholic pilgrimage site lies on Shrine Island at the end of a 400-ft (120-m) pedestrian causeway from the mainland. The serene chapel, built of beach stone, occupies a lovely forested spot with views across the sea to the distant peaks of the Chilkat Range. It is dedicated to the 19th-century French saint Therese de Lisieux, who was chosen by the first Bishop of Alaska, Joseph Raphael Crimont, as the patron saint of the state. The shrine also contains the 14 Stations of the Cross, a prayer labyrinth, and the Marian Gardens.

The Shrine of St. Therese on a forested islet west of Juneau

*For hotels and restaurants in this area see pp243–4 and pp253–4*

# ⑭ Glacier Bay National Park

The 5,000-sq mile (13,000-sq km) area surrounding Glacier Bay was designated a National Park in 1980 and declared a UNESCO World Heritage Site in 1992. Historically, the park has served as an open-air laboratory for studies on the recolonization of formerly glaciated lands by plants and wildlife. For visitors, Glacier Bay is best known for its tidewater glaciers and deep fjords, and is also a popular destination for wildlife enthusiasts. Its forests and alpine areas are home to bears and mountain goats, while in the summer, its waters are alive with migrating humpback whales. Although most visitors take an organized cruise, kayaking is also an enjoyable option.

**Locator Map**

▨ Glacier Bay National Park

★ **Margerie Glacier**
Of the seven tidewater glaciers that calve icebergs into the bay, Margerie Glacier is the most visited. It was once a tributary of the Grand Pacific Glacier, which has retreated 70 miles (112 km) in the past 200 years.

★ **Fairweather Range**
The forbidding Fairweather Range, which culminates at the 15,300-ft- (4,590-m-) high Mount Fairweather, was the source of the ice that created the park's deeply indented fjords. The range continues to feed the glaciers on the western peninsula of the park.

*For hotels and restaurants in this area see pp243–4 and pp253–4*

**Whale-watching at Glacier Bay**
Black and white killer whales (orcas) and humpback whales can frequently be spotted, along with sea otters, sea lions, and harbor porpoises. Boats are not allowed within 500 yards (450 m) of the whales, so bring binoculars.

**★ Bartlett Cove**
Several easy hikes are available around Bartlett Cove, the only developed area within the park. It has a visitor center, park headquarters, a lodge, a campground, and the lovely Tlingit tribal house, Xunaa Shuká Hít.

## Exploring the Park

*While short, easy hikes loop through the forests around Bartlett Cove, the best views of Glacier Bay are from the water, and most visitors see the park either on cruises or organized boat tours that typically go up to the face of Margerie and Grand Pacific Glaciers. Smaller boats provide drop-off services for people wishing to explore on their own.*

**Gustavus**
The village of Gustavus, outside the southeast corner of the park, prospered in the 1920s as an agricultural homestead area. It offers lodging and visitor services, and operators run tours and rent kayaks for private trips.

**For keys to symbols** *see back flap*

Former officers' quarters at Fort Seward, Haines

### ⑮ Haines

75 miles (120 km) NW of Juneau.
**Transport map** E4. 🚂 2,500. ✈ to
Juneau & Skagway. 🚌 ℹ 122 2nd
Ave, 766-2234. 🎭 Great Alaska Craft
Beer & Home Brew Festival (4th week
of May), Southeast Alaska State Fair
(last weekend of Jul), Alaska Bald
Eagle Festival (2nd week of Nov).
🌐 **visithaines.com**

Founded in 1881 by Presbyterian
missionaries, Haines sits on a site
known to indigenous peoples
as Dei-Shu, or "end of the trail."
Early residents were quick to
take advantage of the plentiful
fish in adjacent Lynn Canal, the
country's deepest and longest
fjord. By 1900, commercial fishing
and canning had grown into
major enterprises. The building
of Fort Seward brought further
economic benefits. In 1939, a
sawmill was developed to support a nascent timber industry.

Haines boasts a mild climate and
spectacular setting and over the
years has attracted many artists
and entrepreneurs. In addition
to having several galleries and a
renowned microbrewery, it hosts
an annual competition between
breweries from around the state.
There are excellent
hiking trails around
town, including the
Mount Ripinsky and
Mount Riley Trails and
the easy 2-mile (4-km)
Battery Point Trail.

#### 🏛 Fort Seward
**Open** 24 hrs. 🚷 🚻
Named for William
H Seward, President
Andrew Johnson's
Secretary of State who insti-
gated the purchase of Alaska,
Fort Seward was built in 1903.
Complete with barracks, officers'
quarters, carpentry shops, and

Indigenous copper
shield

smithies, the fort was the state's
first permanent army post and
the mainstay of Haines' economy.
Locally refered to as Chilkoot
Barracks to avoid confusion with
the town of Seward (see pp102–3),
the fort was used as a training
base during the two World Wars.
Decommissioned in 1947, it was
bought by five World War II
veterans who set up a series
of small businesses. Today, it
houses art galleries, restaurants,
a replica Tlingit clan house, and
a center for Native arts.

#### 🏛 Sheldon Museum
11 Main St. **Tel** 766-2366. **Open** mid-
May–mid-Sep: 10am–5pm Mon–Fri,
1–4pm Sat & Sun; mid-Sep–mid-May:
1–4pm Mon–Sat. 🚷 📷
🌐 **sheldonmuseum.org**

Established in 1924, this museum
grew around a private collection
of artifacts from the
early days of European
settlement in the
upper Chilkat Inlet area.
The original collection
has been augmented by
relics from the Gold Rush
era and the fishing and
timber industries, as well
as by Chilkat blankets,
basketry, and a single-
log dugout canoe. The
area's Russian history is
reflected in colorfully painted
Russian trunks. There are also
shipping artifacts, including
an old lens from Lynn Canal's
Eldred Rock Lighthouse.

Eldred Rock Lighthouse sitting in the middle of spectacular Lynn Canal

Model woodcarver at the Hammer Museum

## ⊞ Hammer Museum

108 Main St. **Tel** 766-2374.
**Open** May–Sep: 10am–5pm Mon–Fri,
10am–2pm Sat; all other times: by
appt. **Closed** public holidays. 🎦 📷
🅦 hammermuseum.org

The Hammer Museum is
Alaska's contribution to the
world's most unique museums.
Over 1,500 hammers of varying
sizes are on display, all painstak-
ingly collected by owner Dave
Pahl. They served a variety of
purposes, from blacksmithing
and mining to cracking nuts
and stunning cattle. Highlights
include Colonial-era and
Industrial Revolution hammers,
and an 800-year-old Tlingit
slave-killing hammer found on a
Southeast Alaska beach, all put
into historical context. There are
also some model woodcarvers
salvaged from the Smithsonian
Institution in Washington, DC.
Visitors are invited to identify
hammers whose purpose is
not yet known.

## ❁ Mount Ripinsky

Rising above Haines, the
3,610-ft (1,083-m) Mount
Ripinsky affords the best view
over the town and its stunning
hinterlands, extending as far as
Skagway and almost to Juneau.
North of the town center, from
the trailhead at Young Road, a
trail winds up the peak. Climbing gently for about 3 miles
(5 km), it then ascends steeply
through alpine meadows to
the summit. Hikers should carry
bear spray and plenty of water,
and allow at least seven hours
for the strenuous round trip.
Overnight camping is also
possible beyond the North
Summit. The less energetic can
opt for an easier hike up 1,760-ft
(528-m) Mount Riley, which is
accessed by a trail from Mud
Bay Road near Fort Seward,
or along a spur trail from the
Battery Point Trail that starts at
the end of Beach Road, south
of the town center.

## ⌨ Chilkat Bald Eagle Preserve

Mile 9.4 to Mile 25, Haines Cut-Off.
🅚 limited. American Bald Eagle
Foundation Center: 113 Haines Hwy.
**Tel** 766-3094. **Open** May–Sep: 9am–
5pm Mon–Fri, noon–4pm Sat; Oct–
Apr: 9am–3pm Mon–Fri. 🎦 🅚 📷
🅦 baldeagles.org

In the summer, Haines hosts a
modest number of bald eagles
that can be seen at the waterfront or along streams. In
October and November, however, cottonwood trees along
the Chilkat and Klehini River
valleys in the 75-sq-mile (195-sq-
km) Chilkat Bald Eagle Preserve
fill with up to 3,500 eagles, who
arrive to feed on Alaska's last
salmon run after most other
waterways have frozen solid.
Within the preserve, several pull-
offs along the Haines Cut-Off
afford excellent viewing of this
phenomenon, known as the
Gathering of the Eagles, which
has inspired Haines' annual
Alaska Bald Eagle Festival.

Summer visitors who will miss
this November event can stop
by the **American Bald Eagle
Foundation Center** in town,
only 20 miles (32 km) away,
dedicated to the protection
and preservation of bald eagles.
Using a diorama of the Chilkat
Preserve, this non-profit center
gives visitors a better understanding of how the eagles live
in a delicate balance with their
environment. The center also
has a screening room where
visitors can watch videos of
the Gathering of the Eagles.

## Bald Eagles

The national bird of the US, the bald eagle *(Haliaeetus leucocephalus)* is the only eagle unique
to North America. In this case, the word "bald" means not hairless, but white, a reference to its
distinctive head color. In 1963, the bald eagle
population in the Lower 48 states included
just 417 breeding pairs, but by 2004 stringent
conservation measures had raised that number
to about 10,000 pairs. Currently, North America is
home to 100,000 bald eagles – about half of which
live in Alaska – leading the US Fish and Wildlife
Service to suggest that they can be removed from
the official threatened species list. While the Bald
Eagle Protection Act makes it illegal to transport,
trade, or possess any part of an eagle without
a permit, indigenous peoples are allowed to
use eagle feathers in their traditional dresses
and ceremonies.

Bald eagle taking flight from a tree

# ⑯ Skagway

After pioneers George Washington Carmack, Skookum Jim Mason, and Dawson Charlie discovered gold in the Klondike in the late 1890s, steamboat captain William Moore founded Skagway as a gateway to the goldfields. Over 30,000 hopeful prospectors passed through in the first year, seeking supplies and entertainment and helping the town to boom. The 1900 completion of the White Pass and Yukon Route Railroad (WP&YR) made the trip easier, but the Gold Rush was already subsiding. Skagway was revived in the 1940s as an Alaska Highway construction staging camp, and today, the town's economy is driven mainly by tourism.

**Locator Map**

— Area illustrated

★ **Arctic Brotherhood Hall**
The front of this building, housing the Skagway Visitor Information Center, is decorated with thousands of pieces of driftwood.

★ **Red Onion Saloon**
The 1898 Red Onion still retains the bar from the days when it served as a saloon and brothel. It offers the Brothel Tour, conducted by appropriately clad young ladies.

**White Pass and Yukon Route Railroad Depot**
In the summer, trains set off from here daily, offering journeys through stunning scenery (see pp152–3).

**Key**

 Suggested route

**Klondike Gold Rush NHP Visitors' Center**
Now the Klondike Gold Rush National Historical Park Visitors' Center, the original WP&YR depot, built using packing crates and salvaged lumber, was hurriedly constructed in 1898 to handle the flood of prospectors.

*For hotels and restaurants in this area see pp243–4 and pp253–4*

**Corrington Museum**
Built in 1975, the Corrington Building houses an ivory gift shop and displays Native basketry, a mammoth tusk, and a collection of walrus ivory scrimshaw.

**Eagle's Hall**, built in 1898, hosts the Days of '98 show, re-creating the Frank Reid-Soapy Smith shootout.

**Nome Saloon**, a Gold Rush drinking hall, now houses a jewelry shop.

Library

STATE STREET

7TH AVENUE

8TH AVENUE

U.S.
Post Office

5TH AVENUE

6TH AVENUE

BROADWAY

Mollie Walsh
Park

Moore
House

**★ Skagway Museum**
The 1899 faux-Gothic McCabe College first functioned as a private school, then the Federal Courthouse, jail, and Town Hall. It now houses the town museum, with displays on the Gold Rush, local Tlingit culture, and the infamous Soapy Smith.

| 0 meters | 100 |
|---|---|
| 0 yards | 100 |

**Moore Cabin**
Built in 1888 by Captain Moore, the town's founder, this is Skagway's oldest building. Its walls are papered with newspapers from the late 1800s.

## Soapy Smith

Born Jefferson Randolph Smith in Georgia in 1860, Soapy earned his nickname after a swindle involving soap. In 1896, he arrived in Skagway, opened a saloon, and set himself up as an underworld boss and local philanthropist. His most notorious scams included a phony freight company and a fake telegraph office that would "wire" money across non-existent wires. In 1898, this uncrowned "king" of Skagway was killed after a shootout with city surveyor Frank Reid.

Historic image of Soapy Smith at the bar of his saloon

# ⑰ Gold Rush Routes

Along the old Gold Rush trail from Skagway, three separate routes link the port with the interior. The most famous is the Chilkoot Trail, starting at the site of Dyea and crossing Chilkoot Pass to Bennett Lake in Canada's British Columbia. Hikers can return by the narrow-gauge 1898 White Pass and Yukon Route Railroad, which runs from Skagway past vertical cliffs, over old bridges, and through tunnels from sea level to the 2,865-ft (860-m) high White Pass in just 20 miles (32 km). The third route, the picturesque Klondike Highway, is a good driving route that passes spectacular scenery on the opposite side of the Skagway River from the railway and continues to the Yukon Territory.

Rafting on the Chilkoot River at Dyea near Skagway

**③ Chilkoot Pass**

After struggling up the 3,525-ft (1,058-m) Chilkoot Pass on the US-Canada border, hikers can look forward to a down-hill run all the way to Bennett Lake. During the Gold Rush, stampeders crossing the border had to stop here to pay customs duties to the Royal Canadian Mounted Police.

**② Canyon City**

In 1898, Canyon City had 1,500 residents and 24 businesses, but the town had disappeared within two years. All that is left today is the remains of a boiler once owned by a transportation company.

**④ Lindeman**

Now a campsite, Lindeman was a bustling lakeside tent town of 4,000 during the Gold Rush. While stampeders and their gear were carried by a steamer and barges across the lake in the summer, they had to walk across the frozen lake in the winter.

Mount Hoffman
6,080 ft

Irene Glacier

Mount Yeatman
5,670 ft

Taiya

Mount Carmack
6,229 ft

Goat Lake

U
(AL

Skagway

0 km        2
0 miles      2

**① Dyea**

Although it rivaled Skagway as Alaska's largest town during the Gold Rush *(see pp56–7)*, nothing remains of Dyea but a few harbor pilings, a cemetery, and the wooden frontage of a land office. Thousands of prospectors, also called stampeders, set off from Dyea for the Klondike. Today, it is the trailhead for the Chilkoot Trail.

**⑤ Bennett Lake, British Columbia**
In the winter of 1897, a town of over 20,000 people sprang up at Bennett Lake, as stampeders waited for the ice to break up. In May 1898, in the week after the thaw, about 7,000 boats set off for the goldfields. For modern hikers, the lake is the end of the Chilkoot Trail.

## Tips for Walkers

**Starting point:** Dyea. Hikers returning on the WP&YR Railroad must pre-book at 983-2217.
**Length:** the Chilkoot Trail is 35 miles (56 km) and takes three to five days to hike.
**Getting there:** 9 miles (14 km) N of Skagway on Dyea Rd. There are private taxis to Dyea.
**Permits:** needed for back-country travel; available at the Chilkoot Trail Center, Broadway & 1st Ave, Skagway.
**Immigration:** hikers must carry passports and clear Customs at the Chilkoot Trail Center, Skagway, tel 983-9234.
W nps.gov/klgo

**Key**

≡ Klondike Highway

- - Chilkoot Trail

— White Pass and Yukon Route Railroad

■ ■ International border

△ Peak

**CANADA
(BRITISH COLUMBIA)**

Bennett Lake

Lindeman Lake

Homan Lake

Long Lake

Lindeman

ater ake

Bernard Lake

Summit Lake

**⑥ Fraser, near Bernard Lake**
Beside beautiful Bernard Lake in an alpine valley, Fraser is a stop on the modern White Pass and Yukon Route Railroad. It also serves as Canada's Customs and Immigration post for travelers on both the railway and the Klondike Highway.

**⑧ Denver**
At Denver, the railway line crosses the east fork of the Skagway River. Here, the US Forest Service rents out a public use cabin sited in a historic railway caboose.

**⑦ White Pass**
About 7 miles (11 km) from Fraser, the railway crosses White Pass where, during the Gold Rush, Canadian police checked the grubstakes (see p56) of stampeders on the White Pass Route. The modern trains, made up of 1890s rolling stock, are pulled by either steam or diesel locomotives.

**For keys to symbols** *see back flap*

# ⑱ Haines Cut-Off Tour

The scenic 146-mile (234-km) Haines Cut-Off, or Haines Highway, links Haines with the Alaska Highway. From Haines, the route follows the Chilkat and Klehini Rivers northward. Near the Canadian border, the road climbs steeply, gaining 3,000 ft (900 m) over 18 miles (29 km). For the next 50 miles (80 km), the road passes through the high alpine country of northern British Columbia before dropping into Yukon's lake-studded forests to join the Alaska Highway at Haines Junction.

## Tips for Drivers

**Starting point:** Haines.
**Length:** 146 miles (234 km).
**Stopping-off points:** there is excellent whitewater rafting at Tatshenshini-Alsek Park at Dalton Post off the Haines Cut-Off. An overlook at Mile 78 offers photo opportunities. Dezadeash Lake at Mile 114 has primitive campsites.

### Key

- ▦ Alaska Highway
- ▦ Tour
- ▦ Major road
- ▪▪ International border
- – – Provincial border
- △ Peak

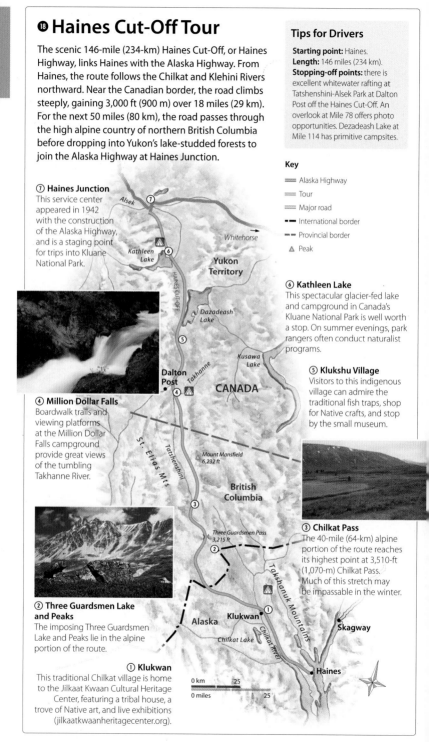

### ⑦ Haines Junction
This service center appeared in 1942 with the construction of the Alaska Highway, and is a staging point for trips into Kluane National Park.

### ⑥ Kathleen Lake
This spectacular glacier-fed lake and campground in Canada's Kluane National Park is well worth a stop. On summer evenings, park rangers often conduct naturalist programs.

### ⑤ Klukshu Village
Visitors to this indigenous village can admire the traditional fish traps, shop for Native crafts, and stop by the small museum.

### ④ Million Dollar Falls
Boardwalk trails and viewing platforms at the Million Dollar Falls campground provide great views of the tumbling Takhanne River.

### ③ Chilkat Pass
The 40-mile (64-km) alpine portion of the route reaches its highest point at 3,510-ft (1,070-m) Chilkat Pass. Much of this stretch may be impassable in the winter.

### ② Three Guardsmen Lake and Peaks
The imposing Three Guardsmen Lake and Peaks lie in the alpine portion of the route.

### ① Klukwan
This traditional Chilkat village is home to the Jilkaat Kwaan Cultural Heritage Center, featuring a tribal house, a trove of Native art, and live exhibitions (jilkaatkwaanheritagecenter.org).

**For keys to symbols** *see back flap*

# ⑲ Tatshenshini-Alsek Rivers

**Transport map** E4. 🚌 🚲 🚗 🏕️
Permits: mandatory, contact the Visitor
Reception Center, Haines Junction, YT.
**W** env.gov.bc.ca/bcparks/explore/
parkpgs/tatshens

The Tatshenshini River and its
tributary, the Alsek, which are
considered two of the world's
best whitewater rafting and
kayaking rivers, rise in the
St. Elias Range of British Columbia
and the Yukon Territory, respectively. From there, they flow
160 miles (256 km) through
canyons and rapids and past
numerous glaciers to the coast
at the northern end of Glacier
Bay National Park *(see pp146–7)*.
Once a vital Tlingit trade route,
the Tatshenshini supports
productive salmon runs, and
visitors to Klukshu can see how
the First Nations once caught
salmon with fish traps and dried
them for use in the winter.

The usual put-in site for the
glacial Alsek is near Haines
Junction, while Tatshenshini
rafters put in at Dalton Post,
near the Yukon Territory-British
Columbia border. Most rafters
run the rivers with commercial
operators and experienced
guides. For private trips on the
Alsek, rafters need a wilderness
permit from Canada's Kluane
National Park. Rafters on both
rivers must also obtain a permit
for Glacier Bay National Park,
citing a pre-specified take-
out time from Dry Bay at the

Floating houses in Yakutat's harbor with Mount Augusta in the distance

mouth of the Alsek, which will
require a bush flight to Haines
or Yakutat.

Rafters on the Alsek should be
aware that the 10-mile (16-km)
stretch through Turnback
Canyon in British Columbia
presents serious whitewater, and
must be bypassed using a pre-
organized helicopter portage.
A highlight is the paddle past
the icebergs of Alsek Glacier.
There are no services along the
way, so river runners need to be
fully self-sufficient.

# ⑳ Yakutat

225 miles (362 km) NW of Juneau.
**Transport map** E4. 🛩️ 660. 🚤 ⛴️
🛈 Yakutat Chamber of Commerce
784-3933. 🎣 Fairweather Days (early
Aug). **W** yakutatalaska.com

Located on the Gulf of Alaska at
the southern edge of Wrangell-
St. Elias National Park *(see
pp192–3)*, Yakutat is just 70 miles

(110 km) from the 18,008-ft
(5,490-m) Mount St. Elias, the
second highest peak in the US.

The Russians were among the
first outsiders in Yakutat, whose
name means "where the canoes
rest" in the Tlingit language.
In 1805, the Russian-American
Company built a fur trading post
here, but it was destroyed by the
Tlingit, who had been denied
access to their traditional
hunting and fishing lands. In
1886, minor gold deposits were
discovered in the beach sands,
but the area's economy took off
only in 1903, when a cannery,
sawmill, and railroad were
established. Yakutat also served
as a garrison and airstrip during
World War II.

Due to its remote location,
modern Yakutat sees few casual
visitors. However, it has been
discovered by fly-fishermen, who
come for steelhead, and surfers
who head to **Cannon Beach**, a
popular place to surf the waves.
The town also enjoys
good views of a host of
peaks and glaciers,
including the galloping
**Hubbard Glacier** *(see
p31)* and the vast
**Malaspina Glacier**,
which is one of the
largest in North America.
Yakutat is a good base
for exploring the
southeast corner
of Wrangell-St. Elias
National Park, while the
Russell Fjord Wilderness,
which includes
Harlequin Lake and
Yakutat Glacier, is a
26-mile (42-km)
drive away.

Rafters passing through a calm section of the Tatshenshini River

*For hotels and restaurants in this area see pp243–4 and pp253–4*

# WESTERN INTERIOR ALASKA

The landscape of the sparsely populated Western Interior is covered with boreal forest, muskeg, taiga, and lakes. Dominated by a continental climate that creates the state's greatest climatic extremes, the region enjoys long summer days with almost round-the-clock sunlight and dramatic storms, and long, cold winter nights illuminated by the undulating colors of the aurora borealis.

This territory was first settled by Native Athabaskan peoples who, despite its exceedingly harsh environment, found it a region rich in wildlife and capable of providing meat for food, and skins for clothing and shelter during the bitterly cold winters. While much of the land is deemed unproductive by modern definitions, the first Europeans in the area, like the Athabaskans before them, managed to eke out a living in these bleak and difficult conditions. These pioneers, including early 20th-century prospectors near Fairbanks, built up a semblance of civilization in what was then considered the country's last frontier.

By the 1920s, engineers were using dredges to exploit deep seams of gold after placer gold *(see p57)* started to play out. World War II boosted the region's fluctuating fortunes and population, when huge military bases were set up to counter the Japanese threat *(see p59)*. There was another growth spurt in the 1970s when Fairbanks was chosen as the logistical headquarters of the Trans-Alaska Pipeline.

Across the heart of the region stretches the massive Alaska Range, crowned by Denali. Located within the popular Denali National Park, the peak is now the area's main draw. Denali and various state parks provide excellent hiking and wildlife viewing. Winter activities range from Nordic skiing to soaking in hot springs and viewing the aurora. Attractive towns, including Fairbanks, Alaska's second-largest city, historic gold dredges, and whitewater rafting all combine to draw steadily increasing numbers of visitors.

Brilliant aurora borealis undulating across the sky

◀ A Riverboat Discovery cruise on the Chena River near Fairbanks

# Exploring Western Interior Alaska

Dominating the landscape of the Western Interior is Denali, North America's highest mountain. Popular Denali National Park, home of the massive peak, is on the itinerary of nearly every visitor to the state. Beyond Denali, summer visitors also enjoy Denali State Park, the rustic little town of Talkeetna, and the excellent museums of Fairbanks. The region also contains such little-known gems as Nancy Lake State Recreation Area to the south and Chena Hot Springs to the north. The uncrowded and mostly untarred Elliott, Steese, and Denali highways, which lead into the heart of the northern wilderness, make not-to-be-missed drives.

Rafting the Nenana on the border of Denali National Park

## Key

▬▬ Highway

▭▭ Minor road

— Alaska Railroad

△ Peak

## Sights at a Glance

### Towns and Cities

**1** Big Lake

**2** Houston

**4** Willow

**5** Talkeetna

**7** Cantwell

**10** Denali Village

**12** Healy

**13** Nenana

**14** Ester

**15** Fairbanks

### National and State Parks

**3** Nancy Lake State Recreation Area

**6** Denali State Park

**9** Denali National Park pp166–9

### Area of Natural Beauty

**11** Nenana River

### Tours

**8** Denali Highway Tour p165

**16** Steese Highway Tour p179

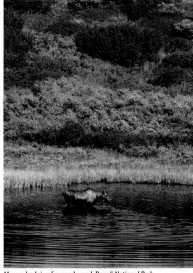

Moose dredging for pond weed, Denali National Park

## Getting Around

The Western Interior has evolved around one thin lifeline, the Parks Highway, which connects the northern part of the Mat-Su to Fairbanks. Daily summer bus and train services link Anchorage, Denali National Park, and Fairbanks. Daily flights operate between Anchorage and Fairbanks; the Interior's largest city is also the most convenient airport for scheduled and chartered flights to bush communities in Arctic and Western Alaska. Radiating out from Fairbanks, the Chena Hot Springs Road, the Steese Highway, and the Elliott Highway link the city with outlying areas that are best accessed with an organized tour or by car.

0 kilometers    50

0 miles          50

A floatplane flying across Denali and the Alaska Range

*For hotels and restaurants in this area see p244 and pp254–5*

Cottages lining the shoreline along Big Lake

# ❶ Big Lake

60 miles (96 km) N of Anchorage.
**Transport map** E3. 3,300.
3261 Big Lake Rd, 892-6109.
Big Lake Ice Fishing Derby (Mar).
**W** biglakechamber.org

Dubbed Alaska's "Year Round Playground", Big Lake lives up to the moniker. In the summer, the lake echoes with the roars of motorboats, floatplanes, jet skis, and fireworks, while in the winter, it buzzes as snow-machiners take to the trails.

While the community itself is small, most of the surrounding lakes are lined with the vacation cabins of city dwellers trying to get away to the outdoors. However, in contrast to Big Lake's constant hum of activity, many of these lakes, including the Papoose Twins, Big Beaver Lake, and Horseshoe Lake, are quieter. Most have public boat launches that offer access to quiet sailing, kayaking, and canoeing, as well as the chance to view otters, muskrats, and nesting waterfowl. Devastating forest fires in 1996 burned much of the area, but it now provides a first-hand look at the regeneration of the boreal forest.

# ❷ Houston

60 miles (96 km) N of Anchorage.
**Transport map** E3. 1,900.
Anchorage–Fairbanks.

Stretched out along the Parks Highway, this small service center is the only place in the Matanuska-Susitna Valley where fireworks can be purchased

legally. They are banned in some parts of the state, including Anchorage and much of the Mat-Su, due to the possibility of setting wildfires. Fireworks stands are permitted in only one area near the southern end of the town, and it is worth visiting for their advertising alone. The most imaginative is Gorilla Fireworks, featuring enor-mous inflatable gorillas and a range of psychedelic vehicles.

# ❸ Nancy Lake State Recreation Area

Nancy Lake Parkway, Mile 67.3 Parks Hwy. **Transport map** E3. Ranger Station, Mile 1.3 Nancy Lake Parkway, 495-6273. **dnr. alaska.gov/parks/units/nancylk/ nancylk.htm**

The Susitna Valley landscape is dominated by the winding ridges and small hills – eskers and drumlins – left behind by retreating glaciers. Here, low-lying bogs, forested slopes, and lakes of Nancy Lake State Recreation Area provide a serene environment for canoeing, fishing, and wildlife watching. The highlight is the two-day **Lynx Lake Loop** canoe trail, which winds through 14 lakes and ponds. Canoes can be rented at South Rolly Lake in the summer. Many lakes in this area have beaver lodges and dams, and every lake has at least one pair of loons, whose haunting calls punctuate summer evenings. During the winter, the park's trails and canoe route become excellent Nordic ski trails and snowmachine routes.

# ❹ Willow

70 miles (113 km) N of Anchorage.
**Transport map** E3. 2,100.
Anchorage–Fairbanks. 495-9000. **W** willowchamber.org

Founded in 1897 after the discovery of gold in the Talkeetna Mountains, Willow flourished until the 1940s, when mining stopped and the town lapsed into obscurity. It gained national visibility in 1976, when voters selected it as their new state capital. Investment poured in, land prices skyrocketed, and myriad plans surfaced for the new "capital in the wilderness." The hype evaporated after a 1982 referendum in which Alaskans declined to fund the predicted costs of the move from Juneau. The town now serves as a Parks Highway snack stop, and, more importantly, as the restart location for the Iditarod (see p49).

Small roadside museum on the Parks Highway at Willow

# The Boreal Forest

Most of Interior Alaska is cloaked in the vast circumpolar boreal forest that also covers much of subarctic Canada, northwestern Russia, Scandinavia, and Siberia. In hilly or well-drained regions, the term "boreal forest" includes dry lands, such as the rolling country around Fairbanks, which are typically covered in white or black spruce and birch. This region also includes taiga, "little sticks" in Russian, which refers to the stick-like black spruce forest that dominates the typically boggy and low-lying muskeg that prevails in much of Alaska's Interior. These rich, lake-dotted lands produce a wealth of berries and are home to most of Alaska's lynx, bears, and forest-dwelling rodents such as beavers, porcupines, martens, and ermines.

**Shrubs, mosses, and lichens** form the ground cover beneath the trees.

**White spruce, birch, and aspen** dominate Alaska's dryer areas and highlands.

## Boreal Fauna

*At different stages in its regrowth after a wildfire, the boreal forest supports a changing succession of wildlife. Northern hawk owls are among the first to inhabit the forest, followed by red foxes, martens, and spruce hens as the forest matures.*

**Black-capped chickadees**, tiny song birds, do not migrate in the winter and are evident all year round.

**Red squirrels** spend summer cutting and storing green spruce cones. They nest in trees, using ground burrows mostly as caches.

**Spruce hens**, marked by mottled feathers, usually nest in exposed bluffs or under spruce trees.

**Northern hawk owls** are atypical of most owls because they hunt during the day, preying on voles, mice, and occasionally small birds.

**Martens**, who feed mainly on voles, have non-retractable claws, used for climbing as well as holding prey.

**Red foxes** are recognized by their white-tipped tails and black "stockings." These omnivores are found across the Alaskan Interior in hilly, forested country.

# ❺ Talkeetna

114 miles (183 km) N of Anchorage.
**Transport map** E3. 🚂 900.
✈️ 🚂 Anchorage–Fairbanks.
🚌 Anchorage–Fairbanks. ℹ️ Parks
Hwy & Talkeetna Spur Rd, 733-2688 or
(800) 660-2688. 🎭 Bachelor Auction
and Wilderness Woman (1st weekend
in Dec). 🌐 talkeetnadenali.com

Climbers planning a trip at the Walter Harper Talkeetna Ranger Station

Possibly the only town to have
had a tabby cat – Stubbs –
as town mayor for 16 years
until his retirement in 2015,
Talkeetna, meaning "meeting
of the rivers" in Athabaskan,
began in 1896 as a trading
post and grew into a riverboat
port supplying the 1910
Susitna Valley Gold Rush.
There was a second wave
of development when
the Alaska Engineering
Commission set up
its headquarters
here during the
construction
of the Alaska
Railroad. Modern
growth has been fueled
by its favorable location
near Denali.
　Any illusions of
Talkeetna being the
prototype of a small, quiet,
pioneer town will be quickly
dispelled by the summer
crowds. Although the town was
bypassed by the Parks Highway

**AIRCRAFT CROSSING**

Road sign,
Talkeetna

when it was built in the early
1970s, it still attracts a lot of
traveler traffic: busloads of
tourists admire its old-fashioned
air, young backpackers wonder
how to settle in permanently,
and prospective climbers hope
to scale Denali. Popular
activities include flightseeing trips over the
mountain and
touring the
junction of the
Susitna, Talkeetna,
and Chulitna rivers
with **Mahay's Riverboat
Service**. Mahay's also
runs Denali wilderness
tours and fishing tours
on the Talkeetna river.

**Mahay's Riverboat Service**
Main St, Talkeetna. **Tel** 733-2223.
🌐 mahaysriverboat.com

## Walter Harper Talkeetna Ranger Station

22241 B St. **Tel** 733-2231. **Open** mid-
Apr–early Sep: 8am–5:30pm daily;
winter: 8am–4:30pm Mon–Fri. ♿
🌐 nps.gov/dena/planyourvisit/
walter-haper-trs.htm

Maintained by the National
Park Service, this ranger station,
named for the first known climber
to summit Denali, provides year-
round information for prospective climbers of Denali and other
peaks of the Alaska Range. The
staff also mails out free information on mountaineering regulations and fees. Inside, there is
a reference library of books
and maps on mountaineering
and Denali. Rangers conduct
free orientation programs for
climbing expeditions, as well
as general interest programs at
the Talkeetna Historical Society
Museum and the Talkeetna
Alaskan Lodge.

## 🏛️ Talkeetna Historical Society Museum

Off 1st St. **Tel** 733-2487. **Open** early
May–late Sep: 10am–6pm daily;
winter: 11am–4pm Sat & Sun. 📷
🌐 talkeetnahistoricalsociety.org

Located next to the old
airstrip, the Talkeetna Historical
Society Museum consists of
a complex of seven buildings.
The main displays are housed
in the red 1937 **Schoolhouse**,
which had rooms for teachers
on the floor above. Used as a
school until 1971, it became the
museum headquarters three
years later. Today, it is packed
with pioneer artifacts, photographs, and articles on old
Talkeetna, including relics
of bush pilot Don Sheldon
and mountaineer Ray Genet.

Climbers and bush plane on Kahiltna Glacier

## Mountaineers and Glacier Pilots

Denali, looming on the horizon, is Talkeetna's main draw. In 1947,
Bradford and Barbara Washburn pioneered the West Buttress
Route, which is the standard route in use today. Starting with
a flight to the 7,200-ft (2,160-m) level of Kahiltna Glacier, it
eliminates a long walk on Muldrow Glacier from Denali's northern
slope. Talkeetna legend Ray Genet became the first Denali guide,
and his friend Don Sheldon ferried climbers to and from Kahiltna
Glacier. Today, dozens of Talkeetna pilots fly climbers, skiers, and
sightseers to Denali's slopes.

The museum also includes the 1933 **Railroad Depot**, complete with a historic ticket office, which replaced the original 1920s structure that burned to the ground. It was moved from the railway yard to its present location in 1990. The 1923 **Railroad Section House** was originally the home of the railway foreman and his family and crew. It now houses a mountaineering exhibit, including a 12-sq-ft (3.5-sq-m) scale model of Denali that is based on aerial photographs taken by renowned photographer, Bradford Washburn.

The town's oldest building, the 1916 **Ole Dahl Cabin**, home of miner and barber Ole Dahl, was also salvaged by the museum, as were the 1924 **Harry Robb Cabin** and the 1920s **stables** operated by Belle McDonald.

### 🏛 **Fairview Inn**
101 Main St (corner of D St)
**Tel** 733-2423.

Built by Ben Nauman in 1923 as the overnight stop on the Alaska Railroad between Seward and Fairbanks, the Fairview Inn holds the laudable distinction of having possessed Talkeetna's first bathtub. Decorated with antlers, pelts, and local memorabilia, it was a community hall and drinking den for both locals and visitors. In 2003, it was decreed that no building in downtown

Fairview Inn sign, downtown Talkeetna

Denali Climbers Memorial in Talkeetna's wooded cemetery

Talkeetna could be higher than the inn. After closing briefly, the Fairview reopened in 2006 and is now a buzzing place for an evening out, with occasional live bands. It's also a great spot for meeting locals and climbers.

### 🏛 **Nagley's Store**
13650 E Main Street. **Tel** 733-3663.
**Open** 7:30am–10pm Sun–Thu, 7:30am–11pm Fri & Sat. 📷
🌐 nagleysstore.com

Across the street from the Fairview Inn, the charming Nagley's Store boasts that it was 'established before most of you were born'. Horace Nagley ran a shop at Susitna Station on the Big Su (the Susitna River), but dismantled it and reconstructed it on the Talkeetna riverfront between 1917 and 1921. In 1945, it was moved again on log rollers to its current site. Amazingly, it stayed open during the move. The store houses the town's

only grocery and general store. Farther down Main Street is the 1930s **Ole Dahl Cabin No. 2**, the home of miner Ole Dahl, the 1930s Norwegian-style **Helmer Ronning House**, and the 1917 **Frank Lee Cabin and Barn**, now housing the popular Talkeetna Roadhouse.

### 🏛 **Talkeetna Cemetery**
2nd & F Sts.
Talkeetna's quiet cemetery would be of little interest to visitors if it were not for the memorial commemorating climbers who have died on Denali over the years. It is a sobering reminder to those setting out that the mountain and its weather can be harsh opponents. Among the headstones is that of Talkeetna glacier pilot Don Sheldon, whose exploits are immortalized in the book, *Wager with the Wind*. He died in 1975 at the age of 56. Talkeetna's other hero, Ray Genet, is missing here as he was lost on Mount Everest in 1979 at the age of 48 and his body never found.

Historic Nagley's Store in downtown Talkeetna

The enormous concrete Igloo at Mile 188.5 of the Parks Highway

## ❻ Denali State Park

135 miles (215 km) N of Anchorage.
**Transport map** E3. 🚌 Anchorage–
Fairbanks. 🛈 Alaska State Parks Office
(Wasilla), 745-3975. ♿ limited. ⛺
**W** dnr.alaska.gov/parks/units/
denali1.htm

The majority of travelers drive
past Denali State Park en route
to the better-known Denali
National Park (*see pp166–9*),
effectively creating this park's
quieter charm. Established in
1970, Denali State Park sprawls
over 507 sq miles (1,313 sq km),
which is about half the size of
Rhode Island.

The park offers uncrowded
campgrounds, fabulous hiking
trails, and views that equal
those of its more renowned
neighbor. **Denali Viewpoint
South**, at Mile 134.7 of the
Parks Highway, which bisects
the park, offers the best
panorama of Denali along the
road system. The park's **Kesugi
Ridge Trail**, a challenging 13-
to 35-mile-(21- to 56-km-) long
hike, follows an alpine ridge
east of the Parks Highway, with
superb mountain and glacier
views from beginning to end.
It is accessed from Little Coal
Creek Trailhead at Mile 163.9
of the Parks Highway, with
exits back to the highway via
the Troublesome Creek, Ermine
Hill, or Cascade Trails. At the
Cascade trailhead by Byers Lake,
there is a campground, a visitors'
center (summer only), and a
tasteful Veterans' Memorial.

The flora of the park is dominated
by white spruce and paper birch,
as well as moss campion and
mountain avens. The park's varied
landscape, with valley glaciers
and great alpine ridges, as well
as meandering lowland streams
and Arctic tundra, make it the
favored habitat of a wide range
of wildlife, including caribou,
moose, bears, wolves, and lynx.
Beavers and muskrats inhabit the
park's wet areas, while both marmots and pikas (small rabbit-like
mammals) can be seen on treeless hillsides and rocky outcrops.

Other notable sights just
north of the park include the
spectacular **Hurricane Gulch** at
Mile 174 and the **Igloo** at Mile
188.5. Built in the 1970s, this
enormous, now abandoned
structure roughly marks
the midway point between
Anchorage and Fairbanks.

## ❼ Cantwell

210 miles (340 km) N of
Anchorage. **Transport map** E3.
🚐 220. 🚌 Anchorage–Fairbanks.

This small village takes its
name from the Cantwell
River, the former name of
the Nenana River. This scenic
area was originally inhabited
by itinerant Athabaskan
hunters, but the first person
to settle there was trapper
Oley Nicklie in the early
20th century. As more
people settled there, Cantwell
was designated a federally
recognized tribal commu-
nity. Today, a quarter of its
residents are of Native descent.
Cantwell, with a food shop
and a lodge, is a convenient
refueling stop. It is also the
western terminus of the
Denali Highway.

### No-See-Ums

The biting midges known as no-see-ums are the smallest of
the biting flies. Their peskiness quotient often surpasses that of
mosquitoes, as they appear in thick swarms that are impossible
to ignore. Alaska has 50 midge species, of which only a few
actually bite. The variety found in the boreal forests of Interior
Alaska, *Culicoides sanguisuga*
(the Latin name appropriately
means bloodsucker), raises
large itchy welts, and can make
life intolerable from late June
through July. A DEET-based
repellant will be effective,
although some people swear
by the widely available Avon
Skin-So-Soft moisturizer, which
acts as a repellant.

Tiny midges appear in swarms in
the summer

# ❽ Denali Highway Tour

A trip across the fabulously scenic Denali Highway is an unforgettable experience. Built in 1957, it was the only link between Anchorage and Denali National Park until the completion of the Parks Highway in 1972. The Alaska Range runs along its length, offering spectacular views, and tundra and taiga forests on the route are home to moose, caribou, and grizzlies. Except for the first 21 miles (34 km) westward from Paxson and the last couple of miles, the route is gravel that ranges from smooth to rough and rutted.

## Tips for Drivers

**Starting point:** Paxson.
**Length:** 134 miles (214 km).
**Accommodation:** Tangle River Inn, Mile 20 (Tangle Lakes). **W** tangleriverinn.com Gracious House, Mile 82 (Susitna River). **W** gracioushouse lodge.com
Maclaren River Lodge, Mile 42. **W** maclarenlodge.com
**Stopping-off points:** waysides and parking areas along the route offer great photo opportunities.
**Note:** the highway is closed to traffic from October to mid-May.

### Key

— Tour route
═ Main road

### ⑥ Brushkana River

The highway crosses the Brushkana River at Mile 104.3. The campsite near the bridge is ideal for fishing.

### ⑤ Susitna River

The 260-mile (416-km) Susitna River, popularly called the Big Su, has its headwaters in the Susitna Glacier in the Alaska Range. The river has Class III to Class V rapids between here and Talkeetna.

### ④ Clearwater Creek Controlled Use Area

Gold was mined in the Clearwater Creek area in the early 20th century. Today, there is good hunting and fishing available here.

### ③ MacLaren Summit

At 4,086 ft (1,226 m), this is Alaska's second highest highway pass. The view north takes in several glaciers, including Susitna Glacier.

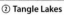

### ② Tangle Lakes

Tangle Lakes, the headwaters of the Delta River, are popular for kayaking and fishing. The surrounding 350-sq-mile (900-sq-km) area includes several ancient Native hunting sites.

### ① Summit Lake

Around Mile 4, several highway turnouts afford great views north to Summit Lake and Gakona Glacier.

# 🌀 Denali National Park

Alaska's top attraction, the expansive Denali National Park, sprawls across 9,420 sq miles (24,395 sq km) and is larger than the entire state of New Hampshire. Its highlight is, of course, the 20,320-ft (6,194-m) Denali, which dominates the surrounding landscape and is North America's highest peak. The park is world-renowned for its wildlife viewing, and visitors can expect to see a wide variety of animals. In the summer, Denali's tundra regions explode with wildflowers, while in September, they blaze with autumnal yellows, reds, and oranges. Just one road penetrates the backcountry; after Mile 15 this single route is accessible only in summer by the park's shuttle buses, crossing open tundra, boggy lowlands, and mountain passes to wind up at beautiful Wonder Lake.

**Alaska Railroad**
The train is a convenient way to reach the park from Anchorage or Fairbanks.

**★ Wonder Lake**
Wonder Lake, near the end of the park's shuttle route, affords one of the finest views of Denali. Visitors will find excellent late-summer blueberry picking around the lake campground.

## Exploring the Park

*With a full day, it is possible to take an early morning shuttle bus to Wonder Lake and still have an hour or two to explore on foot before catching the last bus back. As long as no wildlife is visible in the area, day hikers can get off the bus wherever they like and flag down a later bus back on a space-available basis. Some of the finest day hiking is found around the Eielson Visitor Center. Backcountry hiking and camping can be strenuous and requires a permit from the Backcountry Information Center.*

Kantishr

McKinley

Denali
20,320 ft

Mount Foraker
17,400 ft

Mount
14,5...

Alaska Range

Yentna Glacier

Lacuna Glacier

Kahiltna Glacier

Kahiltna Glacier

Bell Glacier

**Denali**
This massive snow-clad peak looms over its surroundings and is visible from many points on the Denali National Park Road. Originally named Mount McKinley for Ohio Congressional candidate (and later president) William McKinley, its name was officially changed back to the Athabaskan Denali in 2015 (see p64).

**Polychrome Pass**
The Park Road crosses four high passes between Riley Creek and Wonder Lake. The overlook on Polychrome Pass offers a fabulous view across a wildly multicolored landscape.

**Whitewater Rafting**
The Nenana River *(see p172)*, on the park's eastern boundary, offers exciting whitewater rafting.

`0 km` `20`
`0 miles` `20`

## Wildlife Viewing at Denali

Wildlife viewing is one of Alaska's major attractions, and Denali National Park offers excellent opportunities to see Alaska's "Big Four" – grizzlies, moose, caribou, and Dall sheep *(see p33)*. A variety of other animals and birds are routinely sighted, including the well-known wolf packs of Denali.

**Grizzly bear roaming the park**

**Moose dredging for pond weed**

**Caribou browsing on the tundra**

## Key
═══ Highway
─── Minor road
─── Alaska Railroad
- - Park boundary
△ Peak

**For keys to symbols** *see back flap*

# Exploring Denali National Park

Most summer visitors to Alaska have Denali National Park on their itineraries, so a smooth visit requires pre-booking and advance planning. In the June to August peak season, it is not uncommon to have to wait several days for shuttle tickets or campsite bookings. For hikers, the park is divided into 43 backcountry units, each of which accommodates one group per night. Backcountry permits cannot be reserved, so access to high-demand units can require long waits. To get to the most appealing parts of the park, those without bookings should stop off at the Wilderness Access Center to organize their visit. Note that no private vehicles are allowed on the Denali National Park Road beyond Savage River.

Horseshoe Lake, a popular and easy hike from Park Headquarters

## Denali National Park Headquarters Area

PO Box 9, Denali National Park.
**Tel** 683-2294. ♿ 🚲 📷 ⛺

The Park Headquarters area, near the main entrance at the eastern end of the park, is a necessary stop for all visitors. Around the Denali Visitor Center, which has an information desk, there is a general store, a restaurant, a bookshop, a gas station, showers, and lockers. A mile (1.6 km) away, the Wilderness Access Center handles shuttle bus tickets and campsite reservations, while next door, the Backcountry Information Center issues free backcountry permits. Also worth a visit are the **Sled Dog Kennels**, accessible by free shuttle bus from the Denali Visitor Center. Since the 1920s, rangers have used dog sleds to patrol the park. The dogs are so popular that rangers now offer mushing demonstrations in the summer. The entrance area also has some

smooth, well-managed trails. The Rock Creek and Mount Healy Overlook Trails both take half a day, while the Horseshoe Lake and Taiga Trails take an hour or two. As the park proper has no managed trails, hikers must be prepared for rough terrain and unbridged river crossings. They need to carry their camping gear and food, and must be adept at route-finding with a map and a compass or GPS.

Park shuttles go to all six of the park's campgrounds. All the sites have toilets; four have potable tap water. Reserve a place as far in advance as possible.

## 🚌 Denali National Park Road

**Tel** (866) 761-6629 (bus reservations). 🚌 late May–mid-Sep: 6am–3pm at half-hour intervals from Wilderness Access Center; reserve in advance. ♿ 🚲 on some buses. 🌐 **reservedenali.com**

The Denali National Park Road leads 85 miles (136 km) into the

heart of the park through a picturesque and wildlife-rich forest and tundra landscape. The area between the Park Headquarters and **Savage River**, 15 miles (24 km) west of the entrance, is moose habitat. In the spring, visitors should look out for cow moose with calves. Beyond the river, the road grows increasingly scenic as it climbs onto alpine tundra, with herds of Dall sheep often visible on Primrose Ridge to the north.

Winding past braided rivers and colorful peaks, the road continues above the treeline to **Sable Pass**. **Polychrome Pass** at Mile 45 is another highlight. The stunning, vividly colored rocks of Polychrome Mountain were formed by volcanic action about 50 million years ago. Wolves sometimes hunt migrating caribou in this area, and visitors

Park shuttle buses at the Stony Hill Overlook on the Denali National Park Road

*For hotels and restaurants in this area see p244 and pp254–5*

might spot a lone wolf on the road in the summer. Shortly after the road's highest point at the 3,980-ft (1,213-m) **Highway Pass**, visitors get their first good view of Denali at the **Stony Hill Overlook**. The road continues west to the **Eielson Visitor Center**. West of here, the road passes the foot of **Muldrow Glacier** and follows the wildly braided McKinley River to Wonder Lake. The one-way trip from Park Headquarters to the lake takes about six hours.

In an effort to control traffic pollution, only park shuttle buses are allowed on the Park Road beyond Savage River. The only exceptions are RV drivers who have a minimum three-night stay booked at the Teklanika campground.

### 🏕 Wonder Lake

Mile 85, Denali National Park Road. 🚐 from Wilderness Access Center. 🏔

The aptly named Wonder Lake, at an altitude of just 2,090 ft (627 m), enjoys an unobstructed view of Denali, which rises a dramatic 18,230 ft (5,569 m) above the level of the lake. By comparison, the 29,035-ft- (8,710-m-) high Mount Everest rises only about 10,000 ft (3,000 m) from its base. On rare clear days, visitors are treated to the remarkable sight of the mountain reflected in the still waters of Wonder Lake. The

The original log-built 1919 Kantishna Roadhouse

region around the lake, characterized by expanses of tundra and blueberry bushes, is favored grizzly habitat, and campers at the Wonder Lake Campground frequently see bears and caribou. In nearby ponds, beavers can often be seen cutting willows, and moose can be spotted dredging for pond weed. For most visitors, the lake is the end of the usual route through the park, although the road and shuttle bus services continue on to Kantishna.

### Kantishna

93 miles (150 km) W of Denali Village. 🏔 *130.* ✈ air taxi from Denali Village. 🚐 from Wilderness Access Center.

Located 7 miles (11 km) beyond Wonder Lake, tiny Kantishna is

one of many Alaskan settlements that started as mining camps. In 1905, the initial rush brought in at least 2,000 stampeders, who arrived to profit from the area's deposits of gold, silver, lead, zinc, and antimony. After ANILCA was passed in 1980 *(see p61)*, Denali National Park was expanded and Kantishna found itself surrounded by the park. In 1985, all mining, including that on private claims, was banned.

Today, Kantishna is little more than an airstrip and a collection of lodges. The 1906 recorder's and assayer's office and the original 1919 **Kantishna Roadhouse** can still be seen near the current roadhouse. Anglers who hold a state fishing license can also fish around Kantishna.

## The Wolves of Denali

While most people come to Denali to see the "Big Four" – grizzly bears, moose, caribou, and Dall sheep – a very lucky few also have the chance to see timber wolves in the wild, or hear their haunting choruses. These canines number only 7,000 to 10,000 in Alaska, and only 100 or so individuals, in about a dozen packs, inhabit Denali National Park. Each pack, which includes an alpha male, a female, and their pups, requires between 200 and 800 sq miles (518 to 2,072 sq km). Adults usually weigh around 100 lb (45 kg), and have a brain twice as large as that of a domestic

Timber wolf wandering through the scrub, Denali National Park

dog. Currently, Alaska's wolf population is healthy, but some sport and subsistence hunters maintain that wolves kill too many moose and caribou, and the state government has instituted highly controversial predator control programs. Denali's wolves are safe from officially sanctioned hunts, but once a pack roams beyond the boundaries of the park, there are no guarantees. Wolf researchers in Denali employ aircraft, radio collaring, and genetic studies to track and study the packs.

Idyllic view of the majestic Denali peak ▶

Denali Village, the main service center for Denali National Park

## ❿ Denali Village

124 miles (200 km) S of Fairbanks.
**Transport map** E3. 🚌 170.
🚐 Anchorage–Fairbanks.
🚌 Anchorage–Fairbanks, park
shuttle buses.

This cluster of huge hotels, RV
parks, lodges, restaurants, and
outdoor activity operators is
the main service center for the
Denali National Park area *(see
pp166–9)*. Normally referred
to as either Denali Village or
Denali Park, this place was
formerly just a roadside stretch
of development, but a growing
number of hotels, shops, and
tourist-driven businesses have
earned it the moniker "Glitter
Gulch." By any name, however,
it would still be one of Alaska's
villages in the summer. Since
the demolition of the Denali
National Park Hotel, which
provided well-heeled
accommodations inside
the park, visitors who want to
appreciate Denali in comfort
usually take hotel rooms here.

Visitors can also opt for less
expensive options in Healy
to the north, or Carlo Creek,
13 miles (21 km) south on
the Parks Highway.

## ⓫ Nenana River

S of Nenana Bridge in Denali Village.
**Transport map** E3.

Rising on Nenana Mountain in
the Alaska Range, the 150-mile
(240-km) long Nenana River
tumbles down to join the Parks
Highway at Mile 215. From
this point on, the river and
highway flow side by side.
Spruce occasionally topple
off the eroding banks, forming
"sweepers," logs that float in the
water and are a real navigation
hazard for rafts and canoes.
   Beyond Healy, the Nenana
enters the flats north of the
Alaska Range and flows more
lethargically until it merges with
the Tanana River at the village
of Nenana. From the south side
of the Nenana Bridge in Denali

Park, thrilling whitewater rafting
through the steep-sided Nenana
Canyon is provided by three
main outfitters: **Nenana Raft
Adventures**, the **Denali Outdoor
Center**, and **Denali Raft
Adventures**. Difficulty levels
range from easy Class I rapids
to more challenging Class IV
white-water. In the price of
a half-day trip are included
raingear, boots, personal
flotation devices, and transfers
to and from hotels in the area.

**Denali Outdoor Center**
Mile 238.5, Parks Hwy.
**Tel** 683-1925, (888) 303-1925.
🌐 denalioutdoorcenter.com

**Denali Raft Adventures**
Mile 238, Parks Hwy. **Tel** 683-2234,
(888) 683-2234. 🌐 denaliraft.com

**Nenana Raft Adventures**
Mile 238, Parks Hwy. **Tel** (800) 789-
7238. 🌐 raftdenali.com

## ⓬ Healy

113 miles (182 km) S of Fairbanks.
**Transport map** E3. 🚌 1,000.
🚌 Anchorage–Fairbanks.
ℹ 5 Healy Spur Rd; 683-4636.
🌐 denalichamber.com

North of Denali, the village of
Healy has long been the service
center for the Usibelli coal
fields 3 miles (5 km) to the east.
Discovered by Emil Usibelli in
1943, these fields contain the
state's largest deposits of sub-
bituminous coal. The mine now
provides energy for Alaska's
military bases, fuels Fairbanks'
power plant, and exports
coal. Healy is best known as an
inexpensive place to stay and

Thrilling whitewater rafting on the Nenana River

*For hotels and restaurants in this area see p244 and pp254–5*

plan a visit to Denali National Park. It is also well-known for the rough winter route from here to Kantishna (see p169). Known as the **Stampede Trail**, the route is accessible by snowmachine in winter, but river crossings make it practically impassable in the summer. About 4 miles (6 km) north of Healy, the trail passes an old Fairbanks city bus. It was here that 24-year-old Chris McCandless died of injury and starvation in 1992. He intended to live off the land, away from civilization, and to experience the raw Alaskan wilderness. His story is documented in Jon Krakauer's book Into the Wild and film of the same name.

## ⓭ Nenana

58 miles (93 km) S of Fairbanks. **Transport map** E3. 🚐 400. 🚌 Anchorage–Fairbanks. 🛈 A St & Parks Hwy, 832-5446. 🎿 Nenana Ice Classic (Feb–Apr). 🔗 **nenana.org**

The little service center of Nenana lies at the confluence of the Nenana and Tanana Rivers. At the turn of the 20th century, it was known as Tortella or Tortilli, apparently derivations of a long forgotten

Old river tug, the *Taku Chief*, outside the Nenana Visitor Center

Athabaskan word. The town began as a trading post for river travelers, and eventually came to be called Nenana, which means "a good campsite between the rivers." In the 1920s, it served as a railroad construction camp, and gained fame on July 15, 1923, when President Warren G Harding drove in the golden spike that completed the Alaska Railroad between Seward and Fairbanks.

The old railroad depot at the end of Main Street houses the **Alaska Railroad Museum**. A block away, the log-built **St. Mark's Mission Church** is worth a visit, as is the *Taku Chief*, a river tug that once pushed barges down the Tanana. Today, it stands outside the Nenana Visitor Center. The **Alfred Starr Cultural Center** has displays on Native culture, plus a small gift shop.

Nenana is the site of the **Nenana Ice Classic** competition.

Each year, people from all across the state place bets on when the ice will go out on the Tanana. Any surge in the river ice shifts a four-legged "tripod" on shore, which pulls a cord, which in turn trips the clock on the adjacent tower. All correct entries split half the take and the organizers get the other half.

Four-legged "tripod" for determining ice breakup

## ⓮ Ester

6 miles (10 km) W of Fairbanks. **Transport map** E3. 🚐 2,400. 🚌 Anchorage–Fairbanks. 🔗 **fairbanks-alaska.com/ester-alaska.htm**

Northeast of Nenana on the Parks Highway is the old mining and Gold Rush town of Ester. In 1906, in its heyday, Ester had a population of 5,000. The Fairbanks Exploration Company built the Ester Gold Camp in the mid-1930s to service the area's dredging operations. The camp closed in the 1950s, but enjoyed a stint as a mining-themed tourist camp from 1958 to 2008. Today, Ester retains a small mining village ambience, but is entering a new phase as a growing suburb of Fairbanks. Most residents are employed in Fairbanks or at the University of Alaska Fairbanks (see p175), although there are some small local businesses: a saloon, a library, fire station, post office, arts and crafts studios, three active gold mines and a summer farmers' market.

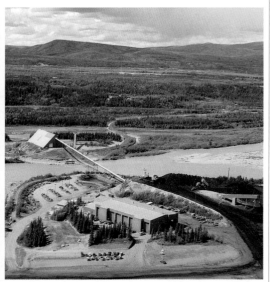
Now open only for testing, the Healy Clean Coal Plant once generated energy using Usibelli coal

# ⓯ Fairbanks

Known as Alaska's Golden Heart, Fairbanks sprawls across the broad Tanana Valley. Italian immigrant Felix Pedro, who discovered gold near Chatanika, met miner E T Barnette, who was forced ashore here when his boat ran aground, and together, they founded Fairbanks in 1901. The two men convinced Dawson prospectors to come to Fairbanks, swelling its population to 18,000. Most boomers left when the seam played out in the 1920s, but the town's economy was bolstered by World War II and the construction of the Trans-Alaska Pipeline in the mid-1970s. Today, Alaska's second largest city enjoys a sense of stability that has outlasted both its rapid urbanization and its economic fluctuations.

Sandhill crane at Creamer's Field Migratory Waterfowl Refuge

The broad Chena River curving through the city of Fairbanks

### 🏛 Morris Thompson Cultural & Visitor Center

101 Dunkel St. **Tel** 459-3700. 🚌 Blue and Red Lines. **Open** mid-May–mid-Sep: 8am–9pm daily; mid-Sep–mid-May: 8am–5pm daily. ♿
🌐 morristhompsoncenter.org

On the Chena River in the heart of Fairbanks, this lovely modern building has state-of-the-art exhibits portraying traditional cultures and the natural world. Watch artisans at work, or enjoy a film on Alaskan life. A block away, Golden Heart Plaza's fountain features Malcolm Alexander's sculpture, *The Unknown First Family*, depicting an Inuit family and dedicated to the spirit of all Alaskans.

### 🏛 Fairbanks Ice Museum

500 2nd Ave. **Tel** 451-8222. 🚌
**Open** May–Sep: 9am–8pm daily. 📷
📷 🌐 icemuseum.com

Housed in the historic Lacey Street Theater, the Fairbanks Ice Museum displays beautifully carved ice sculptures at a chilly -7° C (20° F). The World Ice Art Championships in early March draws top ice sculptors from around the world, who turn massive 7,800-lb (3,500-kg) blocks of ice into works of art. Children can enjoy the ice slides and mazes.

### 🦅 Creamer's Field Migratory Waterfowl Refuge

1300 College Rd. **Tel** 452-5162. 🚌 Red Line. **Open** 24 hrs. Visitors' center: **Open** Jun–mid-Sep: 10am–5pm daily; winter: noon–4pm Sat. 📷 Jun–Aug: 10am Mon–Thu, 7pm Wed. ♿ 📷 Bird banding: May: 6:30am–noon daily; Jun–mid-Jul & mid-Aug–Sep: 6am–noon daily.
🌐 creamersfield.org

The refuge was originally a dairy farm but was sold to the state in 1975, and as it had always attracted migratory birds, the Alaska Conservation Society expanded the acreage to turn it into Creamer's Field Migratory Waterfowl Refuge. Today, the site

offers good opportunities to view harriers, falcons, and swans. Sandhill cranes can be seen performing their unique dance, consisting of a series of bowing and hopping movements, through much of the summer. Visitors can watch birds being banded at the Alaska Bird Observatory near the edge of the refuge.

## Pioneer Park

2300 Airport Way. **Tel** 459-1087. Blue & Red Lines. **Open** year-round. for some attractions. Museums: **Open** Mar & Apr: 1–5pm Fri–Sun; early May: 1–5pm daily; mid-May–mid-Sep: 11am–8pm daily; late Sep: 1–5pm daily. **w** fairbanks-alaska.com/alaskaland.htm

This historical theme park features gold panning, a reconstructed Gold Rush town, the railway car that President Warren G Harding used while visiting Nenana in 1923, and the SS *Nenana*, a sternwheeler which operated on the Chena River from 1933 to 1956. The Alaska Native Museum highlights Athabaskan culture, while the Alaska Pioneer Museum outlines the lives of early settlers. Don't miss the **Pioneer Park Air**

Vintage mining equipment in Pioneer Park

**Museum**, with its collection of vintage aircraft and exhibits on Alaska's aviation history.

## University of Alaska Museum of the North

907 Yukon Dr, University of Alaska Fairbanks. **Tel** 474-7505. Blue, Yellow, & Red Lines. **Open** Jun–Aug: 9am–7pm daily; Sep–May: 9am–5pm Mon–Sat. **w** uaf.edu/museum Georgeson Botanical Garden: 117 W Tanana Dr, UAF. **Open** Jun–Aug: 8am–8pm daily. **w** georgesonbotanicalgarden.org LARS: 2220 Yankovich Rd, UAF. **Tel** 474-5724. **Open** mid-Jun–early Sep: 9:30am–7pm Wed, 9:30am–4:30pm Thu–Sun. 10am, noon, & 2pm daily. **w** uaf.edu/lars

Packed with natural history, cultural, and geographical displays, the old wing of the University of Alaska Museum of the North is well worth a visit. Exhibits include the famous Blue Babe, a mummified Ice Age bison, a large collection of Inuit carvings, and Native costumes. The architecturally inspiring new wing is designed to represent mountain ridges, ice, the aurora, and the tail flukes of a sounding whale. Inside, the two-story glass view of the Alaska Range complements the Rose Berry Gallery of Alaska

## VISITORS' CHECKLIST

**Practical Information**
357 miles (574 km) N of Anchorage. **Transport map** E3. 35,000. 101 Dunkel St, 456-5774 or (800) 327-5774. summer: Wed & Sat. World Ice Art Championships (early Mar), Midnight Sun Festival (Jun 21), Fairbanks Golden Days (3rd week of Jul), World Eskimo-Indian Olympics (mid-Jul). **w** explorefairbanks.com **w** fairbankschamber.org/goldendays

**Transport**
Anchorage–Whitehorse.

Art, which exhibits works by renowned Alaskan artists. The university's **Large Animal Research Station (LARS)**, which studies musk oxen and caribou, and the **Georgeson Botanical Garden** are also open to visitors.

## Riverboat Discovery

1975 Discovery Dr. **Tel** 479-6673. Yellow Line. **Open** mid-May–mid-Sep: 9am & 2pm daily. **w** riverboatdiscovery.com

Perhaps the town's most popular attraction, Riverboat Discovery offers three-hour-long stern-wheeler riverboat cruises down the Chena River on the *Discovery I*, *Discovery II*, or *Discovery III*. En route, a bush pilot displays field take-offs and landings from a grass runway on the bank. There are visits to the kennels of the late Iditarod champion Susan Butcher and to a reconstructed Athabaskan village, where guides explain Native traditions. The cruise also sails past the confluence of the clear black waters of the Chena River and the silty, glacial Tanana River.

## Sights at a Glance

The striking building of the University of Alaska Museum of the North

**For keys to symbols** *see back flap*

# The Aurora Borealis

The Fairbanks area is one of the best places in the world to see the aurora borealis, or northern lights. The effect is visible as faint green, light yellow, or rose curtains, pillars, pinwheels, wisps, and haloes of undulating, vibrating light. During the greatest auroral storms, it appears as bright yellow, crimson, or violet streaks of light across the sky. While summer visitors will miss out due to the 24-hour daylight, there is a good chance of catching the celestial show on clear nights between late September and early April. Indigenous peoples had various explanations for these dancing lights. One legend said that they were the spirits of their ancestors, while another held that they were past and future events playing out across the sky.

**Auroral undulations** are due to the eddies, fluctuations, and directional changes in the earth's magnetic field. During a single storm, the aurora can produce up to a trillion watts of electricity with a million-amp current. Some people claim that they can hear the aurora crackling and whirring, or feel its charged particles, although scientists doubt this.

## The Northern Lights Phenomenon

*The aurora is caused by the interaction of the Earth's magnetic field with charged particles from the sun. As the sun fuses hydrogen into helium, it emits particles of radiation – protons and electrons – that are shot into space. When this plasma stream of particles, known as the solar wind, blows past the earth, the earth's lines of magnetism draw them toward the points where these lines converge, at the north and south magnetic poles. As the particles arrive in the ionosphere, they collide with gas atoms, causing them to emit light. The type of gas determines the color of the aurora.*

Rare crimson aurora borealis over spruce and birch trees, Fairbanks

Vivid green aurora borealis shining above Bear Lake on Eielson Air Force Base

# Exploring Beyond Fairbanks

Moving away from Fairbanks into the Fairbanks North Star Borough, the population thins and the vistas open up. This landscape of seemingly endless forested hills, broad river flats, and distant views of snow-capped peaks is the essence of Interior Alaska. Typically blue summer skies oversee it all, and in the winter, the aurora borealis is clearer and brighter than in Fairbanks, where it is obscured by the city lights.

## Sights at a Glance

① North Pole
② Chena River State Recreation Area
③ Chena Hot Springs
④ Gold Dredge No. 8
⑤ Elliott Highway

**Key**

▬▬ Main road
══ Minor road
– – Trail
— Alaska Railroad

## North Pole

15 miles (24 km) SE of Fairbanks.
🚗 2,100. 🚌 Fairbanks' Green Line.
ℹ️ 125 Snowman Lane, 488-2281.
🌐 **northpolealaska.com** Santa Claus House: 101 St. Nicholas Dr. **Tel** 488-2200. **Open** late May–early Sep: 10am–6pm Mon–Sat, noon–6pm Sun; winter: hours vary. 🌐 **santaclaushouse.com**

This town is nowhere near the North Pole, or even within the Arctic Circle, but here, the name is everything. Homesteaded in 1944, it was eventually sold to a developer who hoped to attract toy manufacturers by naming the new town North Pole. While manufacturers never materialized, the name inspired a Christmas spirit, as evidenced by such street names as Mistletoe Lane and Reindeer Alley. The charming **Santa Claus House**, next to the Richardson Highway, attracts youngsters with its enormous Christmas store, live reindeer, and the chance to speak with Santa. The Christmas season is ushered in with a tree-lighting ceremony.

## 🏞️ Chena River State Recreation Area

Mile 26, Chena Hot Spring Rd. **Tel** 269-8400. 🏕️ 🌐 **dnr.alaska.gov/parks/units/chena**

A wonderful park in Fairbanks' backyard, the Chena River State Recreation Area follows the clear Chena River as it winds between low, forested hills topped by rocky tors sprouting from alpine tundra. The river is ideal for Arctic grayling fishing as well as for easy kayaking.

The surrounding hills have hiking trails, from short walks to multi-day routes. One popular walk goes uphill through birch and spruce to Angel Rocks, large outcrops with superb views. The excellent two-day **Granite Tors Trail** leads up into the hills to a free shelter overlooking the Plain of Monuments, a wide expanse dotted with towering volcanic rocks. It loops back down through forest and over boardwalks across a berry-studded muskeg bog. The three-day 29-mile (46-km) **Chena Dome Trail** climbs above the timberline onto alpine tundra, with views across the wilderness. In the winter, there is plenty of scope for Nordic skiing and aurora viewing.

## 🏞️ Chena Hot Springs

Chena Hot Springs Rd, 57 miles (91 km) E of Fairbanks. **Tel** 451-8104. 🌄 Chena Hot Springs. **Open** 7am–midnight daily. 🍴 📷 🏊 🎿 💻 🛏️ 🌐 **chenahotsprings.com**
Aurora Ice Museum: **Open** tours daily at 11am, 1pm, 3pm, 5pm, & 7pm.

The most developed thermal spa in the state, Chena Hot Springs has functioned since 1905. It offers a complete resort experience with hot springs, pools (adults only), an indoor pool, spa therapies, and many other activities such as canoeing and fishing.

Nordic skiing, sleigh rides, snowmachining, dog sledding, and, of course, aurora viewing make the spa more popular in the winter. An addition is the unique **Aurora Ice Museum**. It boasts an ice bar, elaborate ice carvings, and average room temperatures of -2° C (28° F).

Visitors enjoying a soak in a rock pool at Chena Hot Springs

**For keys to map symbols** see back flap

### 🏠 Gold Dredge No. 8

1803 Old Steese Hwy N. **Tel** 479-6673, (866) 479-6673. **Open** mid-May–mid-Sep: tours daily at 10:30am and 1:45pm (advance booking required).
🚗 ♿ 🖥 W **golddredge8.com**

A brief taste of the Fairbanks Gold Rush of 1902 can be experienced at Gold Dredge No. 8, which gives visitors a two-hour long tour that faithfully explains gold-mining methods used in the early days. The tour begins with a ride on a replica of the Tanana Valley Railroad, with commentary and, if longtime conductor Earl is on board, old-time country songs along the way. First stop is by a section of the Trans-Alaska Pipeline, which carries approximately 15 per cent of the nation's oil production. (Top tip: stand under the pipe, raise your arms and have your photo taken "holding up" the structure.)

The train then moves on to Dredge No. 8 – a huge, mechanical gold pan which between 1928 and 1959 extracted over 7.5 million ounces (210,000 kg) of gold. Miners demonstrate the use of a sluice box and also give a brief history of mining in Alaska. Prospectors then demonstrate panning and washing gravel to extract the gold, and the guides encourage visitors to try it themselves using "pay dirt." Any gold found is weighed to determine its current value, and can then be kept by the lucky finder. Exit is, inevitably, through the gift shop, where your gold

Historic Manley Roadhouse in the village of Manley Hot Springs

pannings can be encased in a locket if you wish, while everyone enjoys complimentary coffee and cookies.

This attraction is run by the Binkleys, a fifth-generation Alaskan steamboating family who also operate the Riverboat Discovery trip on a picturesque sternwheeler *(see p175)*; the two tours can be combined in a day.

### 🛶 Elliott Highway

Starts 11 miles (18 km) NW of Fairbanks, off the Steese Highway. **Tolovana Hot Springs** 100 miles (160 km) W of Fairbanks. **Tel** 455-6706.
🚗 W **tolovanahotsprings.com**
**Manley Hot Springs** 152 miles (245 km) W of Fox. **Tel** 672-3171. 🚗

Connecting Fairbanks with **Manley Hot Springs**, the winding, undulating Elliott Highway is a 152-mile (245-km) wilderness route through some of Interior Alaska's finest scenery. The landscape it passes through is especially lovely in early September, with the fall colors of the birch and aspen forests.

At the tiny village of Livengood, the Dalton Highway *(see pp222–3)* turns north toward Prudhoe Bay while the Elliott Highway continues westward. At Mile 87, the road begins to climb to the trailhead for **Tolovana Hot Springs**, 11 miles (18 km) off the highway to the southeast. Pre-booking is essential for the springs and lodge. At Mile 98, the view opens up to take in the lake-studded Minto Flats, and a few miles later, a long side road turns south to the Athabaskan village of Minto.

The Elliott Highway ends at the pretty village of Manley Hot Springs, which boasts the Gold Rush-era Manley Roadhouse. The village's growth dates from 1902, when the site became a supply center for the nearby Tofty and Eureka Mining Districts. Today, the hot springs consist of three tubs in a spring-fed greenhouse filled with tropical plants.

Gold Dredge No. 8 moored along the Old Steese Highway

### Dredging for Gold

After early prospectors had taken most of Alaska's easily available gold, large mining companies employed mechanical dredges, which resembled massive houseboats beset with machinery. To get at the gold-bearing quartz, water cannons blasted away soil and gravel permafrost layers. Upon reaching the bedrock, a dredge was brought in, usually to a streambed, to gouge out the rock using steel buckets on a conveyor belt. The rock was then sifted by screens of diminishing size until it reached a riffle board, where mercury was introduced to bind with the gold. Dredges crawled slowly upstream, creating dredge ponds in front of them and leaving artificial moraines behind.

Steel bucket used in gold dredging

# ⑯ Steese Highway Tour

From its start in Fox, the Steese Highway winds through the Alaskan Interior to Circle on the Yukon River *(see pp198–9)*. Built in 1927, the highway follows an early mail route. After passing rolling hills and low-lying muskeg, it travels through several river valleys, which are choked with mining residue, and then crosses a scenic alpine stretch. After Twelvemile Summit, it starts descending into the flatlands around the Yukon River. While the first 44 miles (71 km) are tarred, the rest of the route is gravel of variable quality.

## Tips for Drivers

**Starting point:** Fox, 11 miles (18 km) N of Fairbanks.
**Length:** 161 miles (259 km).
**Accommodation:** Chatanika Gold Camp Lodge at Mile 28.5 Steese Highway has rooms and a good restaurant. At Mile 39, the Upper Chatanika River State Recreation Site has wooded riverside campsites, as does Cripple Creek Campground at Mile 60.

### Key

▬ Tour route
═ Minor road
– – Trail
△ Peak

```
0 km            20
0 miles         20
```

### ⑥ Circle

The highway ends at Circle, the largest town in the region until the rise of Dawson in the late 1890s. Early settlers chose its name believing that it lay astride the Arctic Circle – it is, in fact, about 55 miles (88 km) south of it.

### ⑤ Central

Unique exhibits at the town museum detail the history of Central, which was the heart of the Circle Mining District during the Gold Rush.

### ④ Birch Creek Access

River runners can launch at a facility at Mile 94, and put-in for a float to Mile 147.

### ③ Pinnell Mountain Trail

This 27-mile (43-km) trail follows an alpine ridge from Eagle Summit to Twelvemile Summit. Two free public shelters provide a roof for hikers along the route.

### ② Chatanika and Gold Dredge No. 3

Chatanika was built in 1925 to supply local dredging operations. Dredge No. 3, which closed in 1962, stands a short hike away from Chatanika Lodge.

### ① Fox

This former gold-mining camp is the site of such attractions as the Howling Dog Saloon. Also worth visiting is the nearby Gold Dredge No. 8.

# EASTERN INTERIOR ALASKA

The heart of the Klondike Gold Rush of 1898, the wild Eastern Interior reflects the popular image of Alaska for most outsiders. This "great, big, broad land 'way up yonder," so evocatively extolled in the poetry of Robert Service, is typified by hills laced with the gold-bearing streams that were the destinations of hopeful prospectors, and the icy peaks and glacial valleys that barred their way.

During the Gold Rush, towns sprang up in remote areas along the Yukon River and its tributaries. Dawson City, lying at the confluence of the Yukon and Klondike Rivers in Canada's Yukon Territory, became the commercial heart of the region. After most of the claims had been staked and the readily accessible gold had been extracted, many penniless prospectors opted to stay to homestead and pursue frontier lifestyles.

Shortly after the Gold Rush ended, copper was discovered at the turn of the century near Kennicott in the Wrangell Mountains, and the Copper River and Northwestern Railway was built from Cordova to export ore to the outside world. World War II necessitated the construction of the Alaska Highway in 1942, and the road not only opened up an access route through the Interior, but also boosted the economy of the region. In the 1970s, the area experienced a new boom – a black gold rush – as the Richardson Highway became the corridor for the Trans-Alaska Pipeline that connected the Prudhoe Bay oilfields with the Valdez terminal.

With the creation of Wrangell-St. Elias National Park in 1980, a thriving tourist industry took shape in the region. The park, a UNESCO World Heritage Site, is now on the itinerary of an increasing number of visitors. Visitors are also drawn by the numerous wildlife refuges and the mighty Yukon River, which flows across the northern part of the region, as well as by adventure activities, scenic drives, and historic towns.

An oil pipeline going through the forest at Copper Center

◄ Abandoned buildings at Kennicott within Wrangell-St. Elias National Park

# Exploring Eastern Interior Alaska

Eastern Interior Alaska takes in not only vast swaths of landscape crossed by gold-bearing streams, but also the peaks of the Wrangell-St. Elias Mountains and the eastern Alaska Range. Cutting through Wrangell-St. Elias National Park is one of North America's most scenic drives, the Edgerton Highway/McCarthy Road, which leads to Kennicott, an abandoned mining town that is one of the state's most unusual attractions. Paxson is famous for hosting the Arctic Man, a demanding snowmachining challenge, while farther north lie the appealing communities of Eagle and Chicken. The mighty Yukon River and its tributaries offer adventurous canoeing, kayaking, and whitewater rafting.

Guided hiking across the Matanuska Glacier

## Sights at a Glance

### Towns and Cities
- **3** Glennallen
- **4** Copper Center
- **5** Paxson
- **6** Delta Junction
- **8** Kennicott pp188–9
- **11** Tok
- **13** Northway
- **15** Chicken
- **18** Eagle
- **20** Dawson City

### National and State Parks
- **2** Lake Louise State Recreation Area
- **9** Wrangell-St. Elias National Park pp192–3
- **12** Tok River State Recreation Site
- **14** Tetlin National Wildlife Refuge
- **16** The Fortymile Country
- **17** Yukon-Charley Rivers National Preserve

### Areas of Natural Beauty
- **1** Matanuska Glacier
- **7** Edgerton Highway/McCarthy Road
- **10** Tok Cut-Off
- **19** The Yukon River pp198–9

*For hotels and restaurants in this area see p245 and p255*

**Key**

▬▬▬ Alaska Highway

▬▬▬ Highway

:::::: Minor road

▬▬▬ International border

△ Peak

0 km    50
0 miles    50

Fall colors in the forests around Dawson City, Canada

Swift-flowing creek in Wrangell-St. Elias National Park

## Getting Around

In this region of great distances, a car or SUV will open up the spectacular country along the Alaska, Glenn, and Richardson Highways. There are relatively few public transport links. One bus line connects Whitehorse, in Canada, with Anchorage and Fairbanks via the Glenn and Alaska Highways, respectively. In the summer, there is a daily van service between Anchorage, Tok, Glennallen, and McCarthy. Popular guided tours serve as *de facto* bus links between Fairbanks, Tok, Chicken, Dawson City, and Eagle. In the summer, a riverboat operates daily along the Yukon River between Eagle and Dawson City. Bush planes provide transport to remote destinations, such as the wilder part of Wrangell-St. Elias National Park.

**For keys to symbols** *see back flap*

The wide face of the Matanuska Glacier visible from the Glenn Highway

## ❶ Matanuska Glacier

30820 (Mile 101) W Glenn Highway.
**Transport map** E3. **Tel** 745-2534,
(888) 253-4480. **Open** May–mid-Oct.
🎿 📷 🖥 🏠 W **matanuskaglacier
adventures.us**

Drivers on the Glenn Highway
cannot fail to notice the
Matanuska Glacier, a broad,
blue river of ice, descending
12,000 ft (3,600 m) to its 2-mile
(3-km) wide face. It is thought
that about 18,000 years ago,
the glacier filled the entire
Matanuska Valley and probably
even flowed into Knik Arm near
Palmer. Presently, it is advancing
a foot (30 cm) a day.

Access to the glacier is via the
privately owned Glacier Park,
where hiking to the glacier face
is permitted. Mica Guides leads
ice treks and climbing classes
on the ice. Drivers can stop at
the free Matanuska Glacier State
Recreation Site, which provides
a lofty vantage point and
interpretive panels. The Edge
Nature Trail loops from here to
another point with fine views.

## ❷ Lake Louise State Recreation Area

Mile 160 on the Glenn Highway.
**Transport map** E3. ℹ 441-7575.
**Open** May–Sep.

Not often visited by outsiders,
the 26-sq-mile (67-sq-km) Lake
Louise lies 19 miles (30 km)
north of the Glenn Highway.
It was named in 1889 by Major

Edwin F Glenn of the US
Geological Survey who reported
its existence. Much of the lakeshore lies within the Lake Louise
State Recreation Area, which
offers camping, swimming, berry
picking, boating, and fishing
for trout and grayling in the
summer, and snowmachining
and ice fishing in the winter.

## ❸ Glennallen

Mile 187 on the Glenn Highway.
**Transport map** E3. 🚌 480.
🚌 Anchorage–Whitehorse.
ℹ 'The Hub', 189 Glenn Hwy, 822-
5555. W **coppervalleychamber.com**

Deriving its name from two
early explorers in the Copper
River Valley, Major Edwin F
Glenn and Lieutenant Henry
T Allen, Glennallen is mainly a
food and fuel service center at
the junction of the Glenn and
Richardson Highways, with a
supermarket, restaurants, and
a hotel. Despite an unusually
high mosquito population,
Glennallen has a beautiful
location, and its approaches

are dominated by vistas of the
mountains Sanford, Drum, and
Wrangell. Rising from the flats,
they appear unimaginably
lofty, and become even more
dreamlike in the haze from
humidity or wildfires.

## ❹ Copper Center

100 miles (161 km) N of Valdez.
**Transport map** E3. 🚐 330.
🚌 Glennallen–McCarthy.
W **oldtowncoppercenter.com**

Dotted with historic buildings,
this small town makes a worthwhile side trip off the Richardson
Highway. In operation since 1896,
the Old Town Copper Center
Inn and Restaurant offers rooms
and meals. In an old bunkhouse
next to it, the **George I Ashby
Memorial Museum** is filled with
artifacts such as birch baskets,
an enormous mouse trap,
and a kerosene tin cradle. It also
has information on the Copper
River and Northwestern Railway
(see p187). The annex next
door displays old tools and an
antique snowmachine. A block

Abandoned cabins around the small town of Copper Center

away, in the Copper Rail Depot Pub, a 1:24 scale replica of the CR&NW railway winds around the beer garden, and a collection of historic railway photos decorates the walls. The town also boasts the region's first church, the 1942 log Chapel on the Hill; occasionally, the church screens historic videos.

Outside town, the beautiful **Wrangell-St. Elias National Park Visitors' Center** *(see pp192–3)* features a shop, information office, interpretive displays, and a nature trail.

### George I Ashby Memorial Museum

Copper Center Loop Road.
**Open** Jun–mid-Sep: 11am–5pm daily. donations accepted.

Rivers winding by the Denali Highway near Paxson

### Paxson

176 miles (283 km) SE of Fairbanks.
**Transport map** E3. 40. from Fairbanks to Valdez. Arctic Man Classic (early–mid-Apr).
arcticman.com

The eastern anchor of the Denali Highway, the tiny village of Paxson consists of little more than a road junction – the nearest gas station is at Tangle Lakes. However, for five days in early April, attendance at the Arctic Man Classic contest *(see box, above)* makes it the fourth largest city in the state.

The area is dotted with vacation cabins along the shores of Paxson and Summit Lakes, and Paxson Lake has one of the best-maintained campgrounds in Alaska. The lake itself serves as

## The Arctic Man

The Arctic Man Classic held annually at Paxson is unsurpassed for sheer craziness. The contest attracts as many as 15,000 spectators to this tiny hamlet. Each team consists of a snowmachine driver and a skier. After schussing down 1,700 ft (518 m) in less than 2 miles (3 km), the skier grabs a tow rope attached to the snowmachine. Pulled uphill at 80 miles (128 km) an hour, the skier lets go of the rope, slides over another mountain, and descends 1,200 ft (360 m) to the finish line.

Team participating in the Arctic Man Classic, Paxson

a launching point for four-day rafting and kayaking trips on the Gulkana River, with Class II to Class III rapids *(see p266)*.

North of Paxson, the area around Summit Lake provides long views across open tundra and beyond to glaciers on the southern slopes of the mighty Alaska Range.

### Delta Junction

98 miles (158 km) SE of Fairbanks.
**Transport map** E3. 1,000. from Fairbanks to Valdez. Richardson Hwy, 895-5068. Deltana Fair (last weekend in Jul). deltachamber.org

In 1910, Delta Junction was little more than a roadhouse on the wagon road from Valdez to Fairbanks, but in the early 1920s, it grew as a construction camp for the Richardson Highway. After the Alaska Highway connected with the Richardson Highway here in the early 1940s, the town developed into a major service center. Several private and governmental

projects were set up here, including an Alaska Pipeline pump station and reindeer, yak, and elk farms. There were also bison farms, following the relocation of a herd from the Lower 48 states in the 1920s.

Delta Junction remains a small, rural outpost. The 1905 **Sullivan Roadhouse Museum** reveals pioneer life in Interior Alaska. Once located in the wilderness 14 miles (22 km) west of the modern town, it was moved here in 1996. Just outside town, the **Big Delta State Historical Park** includes the historic Rika's Roadhouse, with sweeping views along the Tanana River.

### Sullivan Roadhouse Museum

266 Richardson Hwy. **Tel** 895-5068.
**Open** May–Sep: 10am–5pm daily. donations accepted.

### Big Delta State Historical Park

Mile 275, Richardson Hwy. **Tel** 451-2695. **Open** mid-May–early Sep: 8am–8pm daily. dnr.alaska.gov/parks/units/deltajct/bigdelta.htm

Log facade of Rika's Roadhouse in Big Delta State Historical Park

# The Trans-Alaska Pipeline

When oil was discovered at Prudhoe Bay in 1968, no one knew how to transport it to market. It was eventually decided to lay an 800-mile (1,280-km) pipeline from the North Slope oilfields to the ice-free port of Valdez, where a pipeline terminal and shipping facility were to be built to handle the crude. Through the early 1970s, the Alyeska Pipeline Service Company worked on the pipeline design. Construction began on April 29, 1974, and was completed three years later at a cost of $8 billion. The first tanker, the *ARCO Juneau*, left Valdez filled with crude on August 1, 1977. Now run by a consortium, the pipeline transports 450,000 barrels of oil per day.

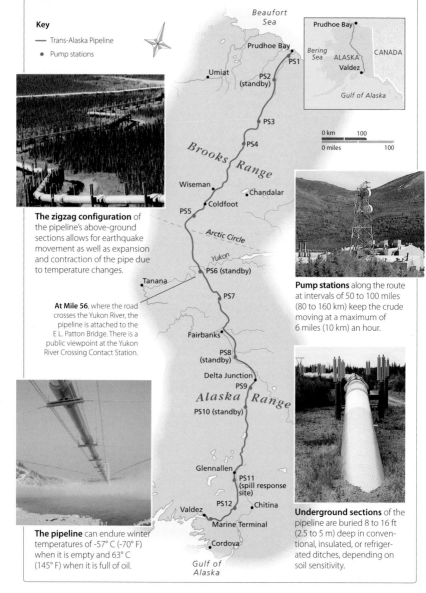

**Key**

— Trans-Alaska Pipeline

● Pump stations

Beaufort Sea

Prudhoe Bay
PS1

Umiat

PS2 (standby)

PS3

PS4

*Brooks Range*

Wiseman
Chandalar

Coldfoot

PS5

*Arctic Circle*

*Yukon*

PS6 (standby)

Tanana

PS7

Fairbanks

PS8 (standby)

Delta Junction

PS9

*Alaska Range*

PS10 (standby)

Glennallen

PS11 (spill response site)

PS12
Chitina

Valdez

Marine Terminal

Cordova

*Gulf of Alaska*

Prudhoe Bay

Bering Sea
ALASKA
CANADA

Valdez

Gulf of Alaska

0 km 100
0 miles 100

**The zigzag configuration** of the pipeline's above-ground sections allows for earthquake movement as well as expansion and contraction of the pipe due to temperature changes.

**At Mile 56**, where the road crosses the Yukon River, the pipeline is attached to the E. L. Patton Bridge. There is a public viewpoint at the Yukon River Crossing Contact Station.

**Pump stations** along the route at intervals of 50 to 100 miles (80 to 160 km) keep the crude moving at a maximum of 6 miles (10 km) an hour.

**Underground sections** of the pipeline are buried 8 to 16 ft (2.5 to 5 m) deep in conventional, insulated, or refrigerated ditches, depending on soil sensitivity.

**The pipeline** can endure winter temperatures of -57° C (-70° F) when it is empty and 63° C (145° F) when it is full of oil.

The pristine falls at the Liberty Falls State Recreation Site

# ⦿ Edgerton Highway/McCarthy Road

Off the Richardson Hwy at Mile 82.6. **Transport map** E3. 🚌 Backcountry Connection shuttle bus.

The Edgerton Highway/McCarthy Road is among the most picturesque drives in North America. It begins calmly, gradually descending from the Richardson Highway into the Copper River Valley, with long views of the river's characteristic eroded bluffs. Entering Wrangell-St. Elias National Park *(see pp192–3)* at Chitina, the often rutted and dusty road follows the Copper River and Northwestern Railway (CR&NW) as it twists along above the Chitina River. Dramatically crossing the Kuskulana River, the road parallels the glaciated Wrangell Mountains to McCarthy, deep inside the park.

## Chitina

66 miles (106 km) SE of Glennallen. 🏙 130. ✈ scheduled flights. 🚌 Glennallen–McCarthy. 🛈 Chitina Ranger Station, 823-2205.

Huddling in a narrow valley, Chitina was founded in 1908 as a halt on the CR&NW railway and a supply center for the copper mines at Kennicott. Of the few remaining original buildings, the former tinsmith's shop is the best restored and now houses an art gallery.

About 10 miles (16 miles) short of Chitina, the road passes camping and picnic spots at the **Liberty Falls State Recreation Site**. Entering a narrow canyon, it passes three lovely blackwater lakes before it reaches Chitina. Heading east from town, the road crosses the 1,378-ft- (413-m-) long Copper River Bridge, where subsistence fish wheels are visible. The river current turns the wheels, trapping salmon in the rotating baskets.

## 🚌 Kuskulana Bridge and Gilahina Trestle

🚌 Glennallen–McCarthy.

Perhaps the most dramatic reminders of the days when ore trains clattered along the CR&NW route are the two large railway trestles between Chitina and McCarthy. The incredible Kuskulana Bridge at Mile 17, built in 1910, is a three-span former trestle above the roiling Kuskulana River. At Mile 29, the road crosses the Gilahina River just downstream from the towering wooden Gilahina Trestle.

## McCarthy

60 miles (96 km) W of Chitina. 🏙 30. 🚌 Glennallen–Kennicott River bridge, then on foot or by shuttle bus.

Homesteaded in 1906, McCarthy was a lively rest and supply town for workers at the Kennicott Mine in the early 20th century. During World War I, the rise in copper prices boosted McCarthy's economy. The town declined in 1938 when the mines and railway closed down, but its fortunes revived in the 1980s with the creation of Wrangell-St. Elias National Park.

Scenic little McCarthy retains much of its original flavor due to the well-preserved and restored buildings, some of which are still in use. The free **McCarthy-Kennicott Museum**, housed in the old Railway Depot, features historic photographs and artifacts from the two towns. Kennicott can be accessed by a shuttle bus or on foot along the Old Wagon Road out of McCarthy.

🏛 **McCarthy-Kennicott Museum** Kennicott Road. **Tel** 259-4550. **Open** late May–early Sep: 1–7pm daily, also 10am–noon Mon–Sat. 🆆 mccarthy kennicotthistoricalmuseum.com

The one-lane Kuskulana Bridge 283 ft (85 m) above the Kuskulana River

## Copper River and Northwestern Railway

With the discovery of copper in the Wrangell Mountains in 1900, railway builder Michael J Heney began surveying the route and laying the track for the Copper River and Northwestern Railway from Cordova to the copper veins in the mountains. Given the difficult terrain, pessimists dubbed it the "Can't Run and Never Will." The Kennecott Corporation started a rival operation, but when a storm destroyed their railhead, they bought Heney's project and with an investment of $23 million, completed the railway in 1911.

# ❸ Kennicott

Overlooking the spectacular Kennicott Glacier, Kennicott is a fascinating historical attraction. In 1900, while exploring the mountain east of the glacier, prospectors Clarence Warner and "Tarantula Jack" Smith discovered some of the richest deposits of copper ever found. Mining engineer Stephen Birch convinced wealthy East Coast families to finance the completion of the Copper River and Northwestern Railway to transport ore to Cordova. Over the years, nearly $200 million in copper was mined, but declining copper deposits and the high cost of railway maintenance led to the closure of the mine in 1938.

Kennicott Glacier Lodge, housed in a replica of a historic mine building

Mine buildings against the Wrangell Mountains

## KEY

① **Workers' cottages**, dotted around the site and perched on the hillsides are now used as private homes.

② **Electrical shop**

③ **Storage shed**

④ **The machine shop**, one of the most prominent buildings at Kennicott, held the metal-working and maintenance operations of the mine.

⑤ **The General Manager's Office**, Kennicott's oldest standing structure, had a large drafting room and was the heart of the mine's operations.

★ **Power House**
Power at Kennicott was generated by the large power plant which overlooks Kennicott Glacier. In this now partially restored building, four coal-fired steam boilers and two diesel generators provided enough steam and electricity for the entire mining operation.

**★ Concentration/Crusher Mill**
In Kennicott's heyday, low-grade ore was processed in the mill, which is the most striking building in the town. Remnants of the tramways that brought ore from the Bonanza and Jumbo Mines to the mill are still visible.

### VISITORS' CHECKLIST

**Practical Information**
5 miles (8 km) NE of McCarthy.
**Transport map** F3. 🚐 50.
ℹ️ Visitors' Center at the old General Store, 822-5234. 🎫 ♿
✏️ 🚮 ⛺ informal camping along the Root Glacier Trail.
🆆 nps.gov/wrst

**Transport**
✈️ scheduled or charter flight to McCarthy, then 5 miles (8 km) on foot or by shuttle bus.
🚌 Glennallen to McCarthy.

**★ Ammonia Leaching Plant**
Here, copper carbonates were extracted from treated ore that had passed through the crusher mill.

**Plan of the site**

Bonanza Tramway

Jumbo Tramway

The General Manager's Office

Trail to Bonanza & Jumbo Mines

Nation of Creek

**Key**
— Minor road
— Illustrated area

East Bunk House

Hospital

Workers' Cottages

Concentration/ Crusher Mill

National Creek Bunk House

Kennicott Glacier Lodge

Silk Stocking Row

Root Glacier Trail

Power House

Ammonia Leaching Plant

Old Wagon Road

West Bunk House

McCarthy 5 miles (8km)

0 meters 100
0 yards 100

Morning view of the scenic mountains at Tok Cut-Off ▶

# ❾ Wrangell-St. Elias National Park

Wrangell-St. Elias National Park, the largest national park in the US – six times the size of Yellowstone – is a 20,000 sq mile (52,500 sq km) wilderness sprawling across the southeast corner of the Alaskan mainland. Dominated by the volcanic Wrangell Mountains and the glaciated St. Elias Range, the park has nine of the 16 highest mountains in the US. Designated a UNESCO World Heritage Site in 1992, the park contains remnants of historic mining sites and harbors a wealth of wildlife. Major activities include hiking, whitewater rafting, and taking flightseeing tours over the park's vast expanses.

**Locator Map**

▨ Wrangell-St. Elias National Park

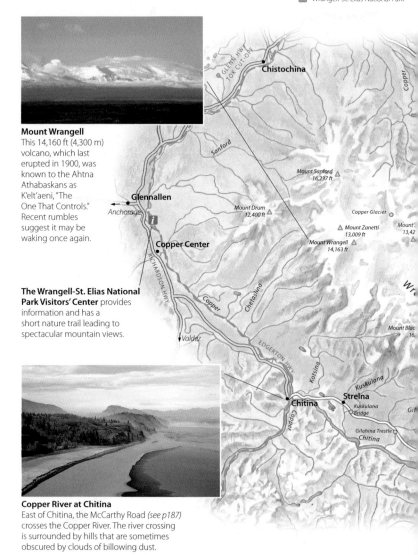

**Mount Wrangell**
This 14,160 ft (4,300 m) volcano, which last erupted in 1900, was known to the Ahtna Athabaskans as K'elt'aeni, "The One That Controls." Recent rumbles suggest it may be waking once again.

**The Wrangell-St. Elias National Park Visitors' Center** provides information and has a short nature trail leading to spectacular mountain views.

**Copper River at Chitina**
East of Chitina, the McCarthy Road *(see p187)* crosses the Copper River. The river crossing is surrounded by hills that are sometimes obscured by clouds of billowing dust.

★ **Nabesna Road**
Built in 1933 to access Nabesna Mine, this 42-mile (67-km) gravel road leads through muskeg and hills to the eponymous village. At Mile 36, a tough 5-mile (8-km) loop hike explores the area around the inactive Skookum Volcano.

**Key**

— Highway

— Minor road

-- Trail

-- Park boundary

△ Peak

*Skookum Volcano 5,800 ft* ■ **Nabesna**

*Nabesna*

*Nutzotin Mountains*

△ *Mount Gordon 9,040 ft*

**Chisana** •

*Chisana Glacier* ○

*Nabesna Glacier* ○

△ *Regal Mountain 13,845 ft*

*Root Glacier* ○ *Bonanza Mine* ○

*Kennicott Glacier* ○

⛺ ✈ • **McCarthy**

*Nizina*

*Chokina* *Chitina*

★ **Kennicott**
In the early 20th century, Kennicott *(see pp188–9)* was the site of rich copper mines. In the summer, rangers conduct tours of the abandoned buildings.

## Exploring the Park

*Given the distances, flights are needed to get to the heart of the park. Only the Nabesna and McCarthy Roads (see p187) penetrate the park, which offers hikes of varying lengths and difficulty levels. Two short trails at Kennicott, the easy 3-mile (5-km) return hike to Root Glacier and the straightforward but strenuous 9-mile (14-km) return hike to Bonanza Mine, offer magnificent views. Longer routes are accessible off the McCarthy Road, including the challenging Dixie Pass Trail and the easier Nugget Creek Trail, both two- to four-day hikes.*

★ **McCarthy**
The old mining town of McCarthy *(see p187)* was a supply and support center for the workers at Kennicott. It is now accessed via a short walk or shuttle ride from the Kennicott River footbridge.

**For keys to symbols** *see back flap*

Swans paddling in a lake, just off Tok Cut-Off

centuries, the modern town came up as a housing site for workers during the construction of the Alaska and Glenn Highways in the 1940s. Tok's economy was later enhanced by a fuel line from Haines to Fairbanks in 1954 and the opening of a Loran station, built in 1976 as an aid to long-range navigation.

Tok is now a service center with a range of accommodation, RV parks, eateries, and gas stations. It also has three information centers: the Tok Main Street Visitors Center, the Alaska Public Lands Information Center next door, and a Tetlin National Wildlife Refuge ranger station about 5 miles (8 km) southwest of town. The Fortymile Country (see p196), a gold mining region with historic and active claims, stretches north over undulating landscape along the Taylor Highway to the Yukon River.

## ❿ Tok Cut-Off

Gakona Junct. to Tok. **Transport map** E3. 🚌 Anchorage–Whitehorse. ⚠

For drivers heading from Anchorage to the Alaska Highway, the scenic 125-mile (200-km) Tok Cut-Off links Glennallen with the village of Tok. The southern half of the route looks eastward on to broad vistas of Mount Drum, Mount Sanford, Mount Jarvis, and Mount Blackburn in the Wrangell Mountains. At Mile 60 is the junction with the Nabesna Road, which leads east, past the town of Slana and several hiking trailheads into the northern reaches of Wrangell-St. Elias National Park (see pp192–3).

The Native village of Mentasta Lake, the northernmost outpost of the Ahtna Athabaskans, lies in the heart of the Mentasta Mountains, which form the easternmost extent of the Alaska Range. About 16 miles (26 km) short of Tok, the Eagle Trail State Recreation Site includes a large campground and a steep 2-mile (3-km) trail to spectacular views over the surrounding hills and valleys.

## ⓫ Tok

206 miles (331 km) SE of Fairbanks. **Transport map** F3. 🚶 1,300. 🚌 from Fairbanks and Anchorage to Whitehorse. 🛈 Tok Main St Visitors Center, Mile 1314, Alaska Hwy; 883-5775. 🆆 **tokalaskainfo.com**

Situated in the upper Tanana River Valley, at the junction of the Tok Cut-Off and the Alaska Highway, Tok is the first major Alaskan town west of the Canadian border. While there have been Athabaskan settlements in the region for

Arctic poppies produce a burst of color in the village of Tok

## ⓬ Tok River State Recreation Site

5 miles (8 km) E of Tok at Mile 1309, Alaska Hwy. **Transport map** F3. 🚌 Anchorage–Whitehorse. **Open** mid-May–mid-Sep: daily. 🎣 ⚠ 🆆 **alaskastateparks.org**

Located beside a sandy beach on the eastern bank of the Tok River, the Tok River State Recreation Site is a popular venue with both locals and highway travelers. Families spend sunny afternoons fishing and picnicking at this lovely site, which also offers good boating opportunities. Although the area was burned in the Tok wildfire in 1990 and in the devastating fires of 2004, the campground itself was spared and remains a pleasantly green place to stop and take a break.

In addition to 43 campsites, 10 of which have room for RVs up to 60 ft (18 m) long, there is a picnic shelter with drinking water and facilities, a boat launch, a short nature loop, and interpretive sign boards that describe the human and natural history of this part of Interior Alaska. A campfire area is provided on the beach.

## ® Northway

59 miles (95 km) E of Tok. **Transport map** F3. 🛩 70. ✈ charter plane only. 🚌 Anchorage–Fairbanks.

This small village was named in 1942 to honor the local Athabaskan chief, Walter Northway, who passed away in 1993 at the age of 117. During the 1940s, the village served as an airstrip on the Northwest Staging Route, a chain of air bases and radio ranging stations that were built every 100 miles (160 km) from Edmonton, Alberta in Canada to Fairbanks, Alaska, to provide defense during World War II.

Visitors' Center at the Tetlin National Wildlife Refuge

Today, Northway remains the main US port of entry for private aviators arriving from the Lower 48 states. It is also the first US village for travelers arriving via the Alaska Highway. The modern settlement consists of three separate sectors. Northway Junction lies right on the Alaska Highway, with a café, lodge, and gas station. The airstrip is on the Northway Road, 6 miles (10 km) south of the Alaska Highway, and another 2 miles (3 km) to the south is the Athabaskan Native village of Northway, where visitors can purchase basketry, Native moosehide and fur clothing, hats, gloves, and shoes decorated with fine beadwork.

Sandhill crane, a migratory visitor

## ® Tetlin National Wildlife Refuge

E of Tok on the Alaska Highway. **Transport map** F3. 🚌 Anchorage–Whitehorse. ℹ Mile 1229, Alaska Highway, 883-5312. **Open** mid-May–mid-Sep: 8am–4:30pm daily. 🚻 ♿ visitors' center only. 📷 ⚠ 🅦 **tetlin.fws.gov**

Snow-capped peaks, glacial rivers, open tundra, lakes, and muskeg flats mark the 1,140-sq mile (2,955-sq km) Tetlin National Wildlife Refuge. Along with the Kenai National Wildlife Refuge (see p109), it is one of the few Alaskan refuges that are accessible by road. Situated under a bird migration corridor, the refuge attracts over 185 species of waterfowl, songbirds, and raptors. At least 115 of these, including the once threatened trumpeter swan, breed and nest here, and the annual migrations of sandhill cranes through the Tetlin corridor are spectacular events. In addition, some 25 hardy bird species remain in the refuge through the frigid winters of the Alaskan Interior.

The northern boundary of the refuge runs along the Alaska Highway, with seven interpretive turnouts and two free campsites. At Mile 1229 of the Alaska Highway, just west of the Canadian border, the visitors' center presents a wealth of natural history, wildlife, and cultural exhibits, as well as a spectacular view from its elevated deck.

Wildfire raging through forests in Interior Alaska

### Wildfires in Alaska

In 2004, a record-breaking 10,156 sq miles (26,304 sq km) of Alaskan forest was destroyed by wildfires. Fires burning every 80 to 200 years are a necessary part of forest development, as they consume dead vegetation and recycle vital nutrients without destroying the soil's organic matter, so fires that do not threaten populated areas are allowed to burn. After the fire, vegetation returns in a well-defined succession. As the forest matures, leaf litter collects on the forest floor, until a lightning strike restarts the cycle.

The wild and beautiful Charley River, flowing through the mountains in the Yukon-Charley Rivers National Preserve

## ⓯ Chicken

71 miles (114 km) N of Tok. **Transport map** F3. ⓐ 7. 🚌 tour bus from Tok to Eagle. 🎣

Chicken reputedly got its unusual name when early gold miners were unable to spell the chosen name, Ptarmigan, which is a bird that somewhat resembles a chicken. Today, the chicken theme is rather pronounced, with chicken T-shirts, stuffed chickens, a cutout of a chicken-pulled dog sled, and even a set of Chicken Poop outhouses.

Modern Chicken, south of the Taylor Highway, is divided into three main communities, Chicken Center, Beautiful Downtown Chicken, and Chicken Gold Camp. The Pedro Creek Dredge, which operated on Chicken Creek in the 1960s, lies on the grounds of Chicken Gold Camp and can be viewed on a guided tour. The historic town lies north of the highway. The Goldpanner in Chicken Center arranges guided tours, including panning opportunities and taking in the schoolhouse made famous in Anne Purdy's 1976 book, *Tisha*.

## ⓰ The Fortymile Country

Mile 75 to Mile 112, Taylor Highway. **Transport map** XX. 🛈 BLM Field Office, 474-2200 or (800) 437-7021. 🌐 **blm.gov/ak/st/en/prog/nlcs/ fortymile_nwsr.html**

Passing through some of Alaska's richest gold-bearing country,

the Fortymile National Wild & Scenic River descends from the highlands around the southern end of the Taylor Highway, down through forested canyons, and past the Canadian border to the mighty Yukon River. It was given this name by Gold Rush prospectors because it joins the Yukon River about 40 miles (64 km) below Fort Reliance, an old Canadian trading post.

Gold mining in the region began as early as 1881 when gold was discovered on the North Fork of the Fortymile River. It proved to be one of the richest veins in Alaska, with its ore assaying $20,000 per ton (900 kg). Relics from the past lie all along the graveled highway, as do a large number of active gold claims that are off limits to visitors. Bureau of Land Management (BLM) recreation sites and waysides are also closed to recreational panning.

Outdoor adventurers can choose from several canoe, raft, or kayak trips on the Fortymile. At the South Fork Bridge Wayside at Mile 75 of the Taylor Highway, a popular two-day whitewater trip, with rapids up to Class III, winds past historic Gold Rush sites from the 1880s to the Fortymile Wayside take-out at Mile 112. Alternatively, it is possible to take a week or more and continue all the way to the Yukon River (canoers will have several portages) and then downstream to Eagle. A passport is necessary for the border crossing.

## ⓱ Yukon-Charley Rivers National Preserve

12 miles (20 km) N of Eagle. **Transport map** F2. 🚢 Dawson–Eagle cruise. 🛈 1st Ave West End, Eagle; 547-2233. 🏠 🌐 **nps.gov/yuch**

Administered by the US National Park Service, the Yukon-Charley Rivers National Preserve spreads over 3,906 sq miles (10,117 sq km), protecting 115 miles (185 km) of the Yukon River and the entire Charley River basin. This New Jersey-sized preserve, with only 30 year-round residents, is one of the wildest places in the US.

During the Klondike Gold Rush, the rivers in the area served as the main highways for prospectors trying to reach their claims along smaller gold-bearing streams. Today, most visitors are canoers, kayakers, and rafters who use free public use cabins scattered along the wilderness floodplain of the Yukon River. Most trips begin in Dawson City, in Canada's Yukon Territory, or in Eagle, and float down the Yukon to Eagle or Circle respectively. To raft the more challenging Charley River requires good whitewater skills and a chartered bush flight to the Finger-Charley or Golvins airstrips within the park, with a take-out at Circle. The preserve's visitor center in Eagle provides maps, and canoes can be hired in either Dawson City or Eagle.

# ⑱ Eagle

166 miles (267 km) NE of Tok.
**Transport map** F2. 🚌 90. 🚤
Dawson–Eagle cruise. ℹ️ 1st Ave
West End, 547-2325.

The historical town of Eagle
sits beside the Yukon River
*(see pp198–9)* at the end of
the Taylor Highway. Started as
the Belle Isle Trading Post, just
12 miles (19 km) west of the
Canadian border, the town
was founded in 1897 by
unsuccessful Klondike
Gold Rush prospectors. They
named it Eagle after the birds
nesting on the bluff.

As the Gold
Rush boomed, the
founders staked 400
town lots and sold
them to settlers for
a $5 recording fee. By
1898, the settlement
had grown into the
military, judicial, and
commercial heart of
the region. New settlers set
up gambling halls, saloons,
restaurants, and businesses.
Fort Egbert was established
in 1899, and a year later, the
legendary Judge Wickersham
*(see p143)* chose Eagle as the
site of the Interior's first federal
courthouse. In 1905, Norwegian
explorer Roald Amundsen
mushed a dog team from
the Beaufort Sea to Eagle to
announce that his ship, the
*Gjoa*, had successfully negoti-
ated the Northwest Passage.
In 2009, a devastating flood
destroyed the entire riverfront,

Cannon turned monument at the historic site of Fort Egbert

Welcome sign at
Eagle Village

but the town has rebuilt
and offers much to explore.
A popular town tour takes
in the historical sights,
the stroll to the
BLM campground
is pleasant, and the
summit of Eagle
Bluff offers great
views. The 8–10
day "float" down the
Yukon from Dawson
is a popular paddling
trip for canoe enthusiasts.

### 🏛️ Fort Egbert

4th St Extension. **Open** late May–
early Sep: 9am–5pm daily. 🎫 Eagle
Historical Society, 547-2325.

Fort Egbert was established
by the US Army in 1899 and
five of its 46 original buildings
at the fort were restored by
the BLM between 1974 and
1979. Open to the public as
a National Historic Landmark,
the buildings include the **Mule
Barn**, built in 1900 to house
the army's horses and mules.
It now holds tools used in early

mining, woodcutting, trapping,
agriculture, and transportation.
The distinctive **Waterwagon
Shed** was used in the winter to
prevent the fort's water supply
from freezing. Sliding doors
admitted the horse-drawn
wagons and sleds that
delivered water. The building
now houses transportation
exhibits and vintage vehicles.
The Scandinavian-style
**Non-Commissioned Officers
Quarters**, built in 1901, is now
set up as a military residence,
complete with period furnishings.
There is also an 1899 **Quarter-
master Storehouse** and a
1903 **Storehouse**, which now
features an interpretive display
on the restoration.

### 🏛️ Eagle Historical Society Museum Tour

Wickersham Courthouse. **Tel** 547-
2325. **Open** late May–early Sep. 
🕘 9am daily (duration 3 hrs). 

Many of Eagle's finest historic
buildings are still in place, and
in the summer, the Historical
Society conducts a walking tour
of the prominent sights. Built by
Judge James Wickersham, the
1901 **Wickersham Courthouse**
still contains his original
courtroom, and also houses
a museum of town history.
The old **Customs House**, part
of Fort Egbert, contains a period
residence. The tour also covers
the 1904 **Improved Order of
Redmen Lodge** (now the home
of the Historical Society), and the
town icon, the 1903 **Wellhouse**.
The 2009 flood damaged
much of the commercial center,
however, fortunately, most
of Eagle's historic structures
escaped the flooding.

Log cabin gift shop decorated with moose and caribou antlers, Eagle

# ⑲ The Yukon River

Rising in the high peaks of northwestern British Columbia in Canada and flowing 2,300 miles (3,680 km) across the Yukon Territory and Alaska to the Bering Sea, the Yukon River provides a vital transport route for the people who live along it. Only four bridges cross the river – at Tagish, Whitehorse, and Carmacks in Canada, and at Mile 56 of Alaska's Dalton Highway. In the winter, the frozen river is a venue for a part of the Yukon Quest International Sled Dog Race, while in the summer, it offers adventure activities ranging from afternoon paddles and catamaran cruises to longer expeditions from the river's headwaters to the Bering Sea.

**Locator Map**
◼ Area illustrated

★ **Alaska Pipeline Crossing**
The E L Patton Bridge spans the river at Mile 56 of the Dalton Highway (see pp222–3), providing a crossing for both the highway and the Trans-Alaska Pipeline (see p186).

★ **Yukon-Charley Rivers National Preserve**
This vast swath of wilderness floodplain (see p196) offers a range of activities, including hiking, skiing, and rafting on the Yukon and the more challenging Charley River.

**Key**

━━ Alaska Highway
━━ Highway
━━ Minor road
▬ ▬ International border
▬ ▬ Park boundary
••• Trans-Alaska Pipeline

**KEY**

① **Circle**, a village on the Yukon River (see p179), offers beautiful wilderness views across braided river channels.

For keys to symbols *see back flap*

**Eagle**
Founded by unsuccessful Gold Rush prospectors, Eagle *(see p197)* is one of Alaska's most interesting towns with numerous old artifact-filled buildings, most of which survived the damaging floods that hit the town in 2009.

**Dawson City, Canada**
One of the main centers of the Klondike Gold Rush, Dawson City *(see pp200–201)* has preserved its architectural legacy and makes a lovely stop on a Yukon tour.

**Whitehorse, Canada**
As the start of the readily navigable portion of the Yukon, Whitehorse developed as a launching point for Gold Rush prospectors who had come over Chilkoot Pass *(see p152)*. Today, the city is the capital of the Yukon Territory and a major stop on the Alaska Highway.

★ **Canoe Trips**
The Yukon offers exciting adventures for canoeists, kayakers, and rafters. The most popular routes are the 8–10 day float from Whitehorse to Dawson, the four-day float between Dawson and Eagle and the five-day trip from Eagle to Circle. Fly-in options and vehicle shuttles are available at Dawson, Eagle, and Circle.

*For hotels and restaurants in this area see p245 and p255*

# ⑳ Dawson City

Over the international border in the Yukon Territory of Canada, Dawson City is a worthwhile side trip for visitors to Interior Alaska. Once an Athabaskan fishing camp at the confluence of the Yukon and Klondike Rivers, the area boomed in 1896 when gold was discovered in Rabbit Creek. In 1898, when the Yukon became a Canadian Territory, Dawson was designated its first capital. Along with government agencies, the thriving town was packed with saloons, brothels, and dance and gambling halls. Designated a Parks Canada National Historic Site in the 1960s, Dawson City is now a living museum. Although gold mining continues, the town's most reliable source of income is tourism.

The Yukon River curving past the Gold Rush town of Dawson City

### 🏛 Tr'ondëk Hwëch'in Dänojà Zho Cultural Center

1131 Front St. **Tel** (867) 993-7100.
**Open** Jun–mid-Sep: 10am–5pm
Mon–Sat. 🖼 🎦 2pm & 3pm daily.
🚻 🏠 ⓦ trondekheritage.com/danoja-zho

This center provides an insight into the cultural history and traditions of the Tr'ondëk Hwëch'in, the original inhabitants of the region. During the Klondike Gold Rush, many members of this Native group moved away to Moosehide, about 4 miles (6 km) down the Yukon River. Some returned in the 1950s, eventually setting up the center in an effort to preserve their traditions.

The center's award-winning modern architecture reflects the traditional housing and fish drying racks that were so prominent in the indigenous way of life. Inside are displays of archeological artifacts, reproductions of traditional tools, historical photographs, and costumes. The center also hosts cultural events such as traditional dance performances.

### 🎭 Palace Grand Theatre

King St between 2nd & 3rd. **Tel** (867) 993-7210. **Open** late May–early Sep: 9am–5pm daily. 🎦 for tours. 🎥 🚻 limited.

Built from the remnants of two wrecked sternwheelers in 1899 by the Wild West showman and notorious gunslinger "Arizona Charlie" Meadows, the Palace Grand Theatre was at Dawson's cultural heart during the Gold Rush. Everything from Wild West shows to opera was staged in its opulent auditorium. After gold was discovered in Nome *(see*

Historic Palace Grand Theatre, built in 1899 and reconstructed in the 1960s

*pp233–5)*, Dawson began to decline, and in 1901, the theater was sold. Saved from destruction by the Klondike Visitors Association and reconstructed in the 1960s by the Canadian government, it is now open for tours.

### 🎰 Diamond Tooth Gertie's

4th Ave & Queen St. **Tel** (867) 993-5525. **Open** mid-May–mid-Sep: 7pm–2am daily; mid-Jun–early Sep: 2pm–2am Sat & Sun; late Sep–mid-Oct & late Jan–early Apr: some Fri & Sat nights; shows 8.30pm, 10pm, & midnight. 🖼 🚻 ✏ 🅿 🏠 ⓦ dawsoncity.ca/diamond-tooth-gerties

Constructed in 1910, the building was used for the town's important social gatherings. In the 1970s, it was transformed into a casino and named after a popular dance hall queen. Diamond Tooth Gertie's is currently the only legalized gambling hall in the Yukon Territory. It is run by the non-profit Klondike Visitors' Association, who use the proceeds to promote tourism in Dawson City. Slot machines and all the major games are on offer for gaming enthusiasts. Nightly shows of garter-wearing, high-kicking dance hall girls attempt to re-create the bawdy atmosphere of the Gold Rush days.

### 🏠 Robert Service Cabin

8th Ave & Hanson St. **Tel** (867) 993-7210. **Open** May–Sep: 9am–5pm daily. 🖼 🎦 1pm & 7pm daily.

One of Dawson City's most popular attractions is the humble two-room cabin once owned by "the Bard of the Yukon," Robert Service (1874–1958). Nestled amid willows and alders at the edge of town, the cabin is typical of the era. Built of logs and chinked with moss, it was originally heated with a wood stove and illuminated with coal oil lamps.

Although Service spent only three years in Dawson, between 1909 and 1912, he absorbed the essence of this wild region. His seminal works, "The Cremation of Sam McGee," "The Shooting of Dan McGrew," "The Call of the Wild," and "The Spell of the Yukon" have long defined the Gold Rush era and the magic of the North. Today, Service's poetry is brought

Exterior of the original log cabin of Gold Rush poet Robert Service

## VISITORS' CHECKLIST

### Practical Information
328 miles (525 km) N of Whitehorse. **Transport map** F3. 2,000. Front & King St, (867) 993-5566. **dawsoncity.ca**

### Transport
from Whitehorse, Canada, & Fairbanks. from Fairbanks (Alaska/Yukon Trails) & Whitehorse (Husky Buslines). **alaskashuttle.com** **huskybus.ca**

to life through the interpretations of engaging Park Service actors, who tell his story and recite his most popular works.

### Jack London Cabin
8th Ave & Firth St. **Tel** (867) 993-5575. **Open** mid-May–mid-Sep: 11am–3pm daily. noon & 2:30pm.

The renowned author Jack London (1876–1916) first came to the Yukon in search of gold, but instead found a wealth of material for the tales of adventure he spun about frontier life. The cabin he lived in was located on the North Fork of Henderson Creek, 72 miles (120 km) south of Dawson City. Local trappers rediscovered his cabin in 1936, and it was dismantled and shipped to Dawson in 1965 by Yukon author and Jack London researcher Dick North. Two replicas were made from the original logs, one of which is on view in Oakland, London's California hometown. The other remains in Dawson and houses relics, photographs, documents, and articles from the Gold Rush days. Every summer, Dick North interprets the site for visitors.

Situated across the road from Jack London Cabin, the 1920s **Frank Berton Cabin** is worth a visit. The building now houses the Berton House Writer's Retreat Program.

### The Goldfields
10 miles (16 km) SE of Dawson City on Bonanza Creek Rd. only for tours. can be arranged with Husky Buslines; **Tel** (867) 993-3821. **klondikeexperience.com**

Although numerous Gold Rush prospectors worked gravel for alluvial gold, the real environmental impact of mining came after 1910 with the introduction of dredges. For a close look at the effects of large-scale gold extraction, it is worth making a trip to Dredge No. 4. This enormous wooden-hulled dredge functioned from 1912 to 1966, when it was turned into a Parks Canada Historic Site. Down the road at Discovery Claim, a monument marks the spot where George Carmack found ore in 1896, launching the Gold Rush that changed the area forever. Nearby, Claim No. 6 is open to visitors for panning free of charge.

## Sights at a Glance

① Tr'ondëk Hwëch'in Dänojà Zho Cultural Center
② Palace Grand Theater
③ Diamond Tooth Gertie's
④ Robert Service Cabin
⑤ Jack London Cabin
⑥ Frank Berton Cabin

Top of the World Hwy

Tr'ondëk Hwëch'in Dänojà Zho Cultural Center ①

Palace Grand Theater ②

Diamond Tooth Gertie's ③

Commissioner's Residence

Victory Gardens

Minto Park

⑥ Berton Cabin
④ Robert Service Cabin
⑤ Jack London Cabin

The Goldfields
10 miles (16 km)

Yukon River

0 meters 200
0 yards 200

**For keys to symbols** see back flap

# SOUTHWEST ALASKA

The arc of volcanoes that form the Alaska Peninsula and Aleutian Islands stretches through Southwest Alaska like a fiery necklace. Lying across the fault line where the North American and Pacific tectonic plates collide, flanked by the North Pacific and the Bering Sea, and almost continuously battered by the forces of the wind and sea, this is a land of great extremes.

The original inhabitants of the region were the Aleut islanders and the Alutiiq of the Alaska Peninsula. Over the millennia, they wrested a living from the stormy seas and managed to thrive despite the forbidding climate and volcanic activity.

The first outsiders to arrive were the Russians in the mid-1700s. As the first point of contact for the Russians in Alaska, the Southwest experienced tempestuous cultural clashes. The newcomers' quest for the valuable pelts of seals and sea otters led them to first employ the locals for their hunting expertise and to later forcibly exploit them for their labor.

Today, visitors to the region come for both the culture and the incredible wealth of natural beauty. The opulent churches that dominate nearly every town and village are a lasting legacy of the Russian era. Kodiak, the second-largest island in the US, was once the capital of Russian America and is the heart of the Alutiiq culture today.

While the national parks of the Alaska Peninsula are among the most remote in the US National Park System, they attract growing numbers of visitors with opportunities to view brown bears and hike through stark volcanic landscapes. Enthusiastic naturalists head to the remote Pribilof Islands, where cliffs are packed with thousands of nesting birds and basking seals. The ride down the stormy Aleutian chain on the ferry *Tustumena* makes an adventure-filled excursion.

The lovely Church of the Holy Ascension overlooking Illiuliuk Bay, Dutch Harbor/Unalaska

◄ Brown bears fishing for salmon at Brooks Falls, Katmai National Park

# Exploring Southwest Alaska

Lying on the Pacific Ring of Fire and beset by stormy weather, this region is among the most difficult to access, but visitors who manage to get this far off the beaten track marvel at the region's history, abundant wildlife, and ethereal beauty. Aniakchak National Monument features the striking Surprise Lake, while Wood-Tikchik State Park's river systems are popular with boaters. Wildlife enthusiasts will enjoy Katmai National Park, which has the world's largest population of brown bears, and the Pribilofs, world-renowned for their bird and fur seal populations. Kodiak, part of a beautiful, rainy archipelago, has the area's largest town. It is also a busy fishing port, as are Dutch Harbor/Unalaska and Dillingham.

Horned puffins on St. Paul Island

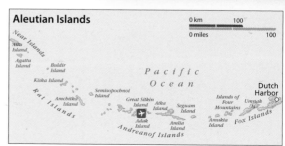

Hoop

Has

Mekoryuk

*Nunit Islan*
△
*Rober Mounte 1,668*

PRIBILOF
ISLANDS 13
St. Paul

St. George

*B e r i n g
S e a*

0 kilometers   100

0 miles   100

*Pogromni Volcano 6,547 ft* △   Fals

*Makushin Volcano 6,658 ft*   Akutan   *Unimak Pass*   U

DUTCH HARBOR/ 12
UNALASKA

*Fox Islands*

## Sights at a Glance

### Towns and Cities

1 Kodiak
2 King Salmon
3 Dillingham
9 Sand Point
10 King Cove
11 Cold Bay and Izembek
National Wildlife Refuge
12 Dutch Harbor/Unalaska

### National and State Parks

4 Walrus Islands State Game
Sanctuary
5 Wood-Tikchik State Park
6 Lake Clark National Park
7 *Katmai National Park*
*pp210–11*
8 Aniakchak National
Monument

### Area of Natural Beauty

13 *Pribilof Islands pp216–17*

### Key

===== Minor road
– – Ferry route
△ Peak

## Aleutian Islands

0 km   100

0 miles   100

*Near Islands*
*Attu Island*
*Agattu Island*
*Buldir Island*
*Kiska Island*
*Semisopochnoi Island*
*Rat Islands*
*Amchitka Island*
*Great Sitkin Island*
*Atka Island*
*Adak Island*
*Amlia Island*
*Seguam Island*
*Andreanof Islands*
*Islands of Four Mountains*
*Amukta Island*
*Umnak Is.*
*Fox Islands*

*P a c i f i c
O c e a n*

Dutch
Harbor

## Getting Around

No place in Southwest Alaska is accessible by road, so travel within the region is by ferry or by air. Scheduled flights access Kodiak, Iliamna, King Salmon, Dillingham, Cold Bay, Dutch Harbor/Unalaska, and St. Paul. In the summer, the Alaska Marine Highway ferry *Tustumena* does a twice-monthly run between Homer and Dutch Harbor/Unalaska, stopping at otherwise hard-to-reach Alaska Peninsula ports of call. Other towns and national parks – Aniakchak, Lake Clark, and Katmai – are accessible by chartered floatplane.

Russian Orthodox church overlooking Karluk Lagoon, Kodiak Island

**For keys to symbols** *see back flap*

Looking down on Kodiak town from Pillar Mountain

# ❶ Kodiak

150 miles (241 km) SW of Homer.
**Transport map** D4. 🚗 6,100.
✈ from Anchorage. 🚢 from Homer.
ℹ 100 Marine Way (Marine Hwy
Terminal building), 486-4070. 🎿 Pillar
Mountain Golf Classic (late Mar), Crab
Festival (Memorial Day weekend), State
Fair & Rodeo (1st weekend in Sep).
Ⓦ kodiak.org

Known as Alaska's Emerald Isle,
Kodiak Island and its surroundings are best known for rain,
bears, and fishing. Kodiak was
settled by Alutiiq hunters and
fishermen as many as 7,000 years
ago. Its name, in fact, comes from
the Alutiiq word Qiq'rtaq, which
simply means "island" and was
corrupted by the Russians to
Kodiak. The first Russian explorer
landed here in 1763, and the
village came up in 1784. About a
decade later, Alexander Baranov
set up a trading post, designating
it the capital of Russian America.
    Kodiak suffered two major
natural disasters in the last
century: the 1912 explosion
of Novarupta (see p211) and
the 1964 earthquake (see p29).
The island was once largely
treeless, but spruce seeds and
pollen blowing across from
the mainland have taken
hold of the northern end of the
archipelago and the forests are
slowly spreading southward.

## ❶ Holy Resurrection Russian Orthodox Cathedral

410 Mission Road. **Tel** 486-3854.
🕙 late May–early Sep: 1–2pm daily.
🚻 🕇 6pm Sat, 9am Sun.

Following Russian colonists to
Alaska in the 18th and 19th
centuries, Orthodox priests

converted large numbers of
Natives, whose descendants
still follow the faith. The
present Holy Resurrection
Russian Orthodox Cathedral
is, in fact, the third on
this site. A scale replica of
the original 1794 church
is kept at St. Herman's
Theological Seminary
next door. The second
church, built in 1874,
was destroyed by fire
in 1943. The current
building, with blue
onion domes and gold-
flecked windows, contains an
original 1790s Russian icon,
ornate candlestands, and the
reliquary of the 18th-century
Russian monk, St. Herman,
canonized here in 1970. The
neighboring chapel houses
a collection of 17th-century
manuscripts and a hand-carved
chandelier. Each August, some
300 boats join a pilgrimage to
nearby Spruce Island, the saint's
retreat in his later years.

Samovar at the
Baranov Museum

## 🏛 Baranov Museum

101 Marine Way. **Tel** 486-5920.
**Open** summer: 10am–4pm Mon–Sat;
winter: 10am–3pm Tue–Sat. 🅿 📷
Ⓦ baranovmusèum.org

The Kodiak Historical Society's
Baranov Museum occupies the
white weatherboard Erskine
House, built by Alexander
Baranov in 1808 as a warehouse
for otter pelts, and named after
one of its later owners. Although
minor changes have been made,
this is the oldest existing building
on the US West Coast. The
museum features such oddities
as an unusual three-seat *baidarka*
(skin boat) and a Russian sealskin banknote. It also holds
Alutiiq and Aleut artifacts
such as woven grass bas-
kets, seal gut bags, and
bone carvings. The Russian
era is reflected in a beautiful collection of brass
samovars and icons,
and the 1912 Novarupta
eruption is chronicled
in a photographic
display. The archives
and extensive library
are open to the public.

## 🏛 Alutiiq Museum

215 Mission Road. **Tel** 486-7004.
**Open** mid-May–mid-Sep:10am–
4pm Mon–Fri, noon–4pm Sat.
**Closed** Mon in winter. 🅿 ♿ 📷
Ⓦ alutiiqmuseum.org

With the arrival of the Russians
in Alaska in the late 18th century, many aspects of Alutiiq
culture on Kodiak and on the
Alaska and Kenai Peninsulas
were lost, but more than
1,000 archeological sites
around the region reveal
the original ways of the
Alutiiq. This museum has
put together an archive
and collection of his-
torical artifacts, including Alutiiq ornaments,
a replica of an 1883
ground squirrel parka,
and a fabulous *awirnaq*
(spruce root hat), shared
between this museum
and the Anchorage
Museum (see pp72–3)
in alternating years.
The renowned Alutiiq
Dancers occasionally
perform here.

Holy Resurrection Russian Orthodox Cathedral

Clouds hanging over the peaks of Afognak Island, north of Kodiak

### 🏛 Fort Abercrombie State Historical Park

Miller Point Road, 5 miles (8 km) E of Kodiak. **Tel** 486-6339. **Open** park: 24 hrs; visitors' center: 8:30am–noon, 1–5pm Mon–Fri. 🏕 🌐 **dnr.alaska. gov/parks/units/kodiak/ftaber.htm**

The lovely Fort Abercrombie State Historical Park lies on Miller Point along Rezanof Road. In June 1941, fearing a Japanese attack on Alaska, President Franklin D Roosevelt authorized the establishment of a 780-acre (312-ha) military post at Miller Point. After the attack on Pearl Harbor, coastal defense gun emplacements were installed on the site. Although the garrisons were removed some time ago, remnants of the searchlight bunkers, pillbox bunkers, ammunition dumps, and gun emplacements can still be seen around the lovely wooded site.

The **Kodiak Military History Museum**, with a wealth of military artifacts, is housed in the Ready Ammunition Bunker on the Miller Point Headland.

The park, crisscrossed by numerous short hiking trails, is accessed on a forest road that leads past the picnic site at Lake Gertrude, where anglers can fish for stocked rainbow trout and grayling. Beyond is a campsite in lush, mossy spruce forest.

### 🏛 Kodiak Military History Museum

1417 Mill Bay Rd. **Tel** 486-7015. **Open** Jun–Aug: 1–4pm Fri–Mon; May & Sep: 1–4pm Sat & Sun. 🌐 **kadiak.org**

### ⚔ Kodiak National Wildlife Refuge

SW of Kodiak. ✈ chartered floatplane from Kodiak. 🚤 from Kodiak. ℹ 402 Center St, 487-2626. 🏕 🏔 🌐 **fws. gov/refuge/kodiak**

Established in 1941 to protect the Kodiak bear and sea mammals, the Kodiak National Wildlife Refuge covers most of the southwestern end of Kodiak Island, as well as Uganik and Ban Islands and much of the Red Peaks area on Afognak Island. This wild area sprawls over 3,405 sq miles (8,820 sq km) of rugged mountains, lakes, bogs, and meadows, and includes hundreds of miles of convoluted shoreline. It is

Alaskan wildflower

currently home to about 3,500 Kodiak brown bears, as well as 50 million wild salmon, representing all five Alaskan species. There are also 250 bird species and 1.5 million seabirds. The refuge has no roads or trails, so access is limited to floatplane, bush flights, or watercraft from Kodiak town. The most popular activity is taking a half- or one-day flightseeing trip to prime bear-viewing areas such as Frazer Lake and Karluk Lake. The refuge also offers backcountry camping, rafting, hunting, and fishing opportunities at the popular Karluk and Ayakulik Rivers.

## Kodiak Bears

The Kodiak archipelago is home to around 3,500 Kodiak brown bears (*Ursos arctos middendorffi*), the world's largest land carnivores. While sows weigh 400 to 600 lbs (180 to 270 kg), the boars weigh from 800 to 1,500 lbs (360 to 675 kg) and can stand up to 12 ft (4 m) tall on their hind legs. The omnivorous

Solitary Kodiak bear on Kodiak Island

bears stay at sea level during spring, feeding on grasses, but as summer progresses, they move uphill to eat alpine shoots. In mid-July, they begin congregating around streams to partake in a feast of spawning salmon. Pregnant sows enter their winter dens, usually natural rock outcrops, in fall. They bear two to three cubs by late January, who emerge from the den when they are about four months old. Cubs typically stay with their mother for two to three years.

Boats docked at the bustling harbor in Dillingham

# ❷ King Salmon

285 miles (459 km) SW of Anchorage.
**Transport map** D4. 🛬 370. 🛫
ℹ️ Airport terminal, 246-2450.

The rugged little village of King Salmon occupies a lovely setting amid wide open spaces. The town overlooks the banks of the Naknek River, 15 miles (24 km) upstream from the fishing port of Naknek on Bristol Bay. Much of the current population of King Salmon is descended from people who were forced to relocate after the 1912 eruption of the Novarupta volcano, in what is now Katmai National Park *(see pp210–11)*.

As the gateway to Katmai National Park, King Salmon features an airstrip and lodging for those without reservations at Brooks Camp inside the national park. The Katmai National Park tourist office at the airport has natural history displays and videos on the park, as well as a gift shop selling maps and books.

# ❸ Dillingham

481 miles (774 km) SW of Anchorage.
**Transport map** C4. 🛬 2,300. 🛫
ℹ️ 348 D St, 842-5115. 🆆 dillingham chamberofcommerce.org

Founded by Russian fur traders in 1822 as a fort called Alexandrovski Redoubt, Dillingham is the largest community in the Bristol Bay region, as a result of its renowned commercial fishing industry. In 1884, after the US took possession of Alaska, enormous runs of salmon in the Wood and Nushagak Rivers made Dillingham a logical fish processing and canning site. Today, up to 10,000 tons (9 million kg) of fish is processed every year from the Bristol Bay salmon fishery.

The chief attraction here is the **Sam Fox Museum**, named for Yup'ik carver Sam Fox, featuring a large collection of his works as well as skin and fur pieces and basketry.. The town is a staging point for visits to Togiak National Wildlife Refuge, Walrus Islands State Game Sanctuary, and Wood-Tikchik State Park.

🏛️ **Sam Fox Museum**
306 D St W. **Tel** 842-4831.
**Open** 8am–5:30pm Mon–Fri, 10am–2pm Sat. ♿ 📷

# ❹ Walrus Islands State Game Sanctuary

100 miles (160 km) W of Dillingham.
**Transport map** C4. 🛫 Dillingham, then by charter boat. ℹ️ 267-2189.
**Open** May–mid-Aug. 🎫 Permits: 10 available for each 5-day period from Alaska Department of Fish and Game.
🆆 adfg.alaska.gov

Located in the northwestern reaches of Bristol Bay, the Walrus Islands State Game Sanctuary is an archipelago of seven rocky islands. The most popular destination in the sanctuary is **Round Island**, where lounging walruses cover the beaches.

After the northern pack ice recedes in the spring, male walruses – as many as 14,000 a day – haul out onto the rocky, exposed beaches between feeding excursions at sea. In the summer, the surrounding seas abound with harbor seals, as well as gray, orca, and humpback whales. The beaches of Round Island and the neighboring islands also attract several hundred breeding Steller sea lions, and the cliffs above bustle with nearly 400,000 nesting sea birds. Red foxes roam the beaches to feed on seabird eggs and fallen chicks.

Access to Round Island is by permit only. Visitors need to be self-sufficient with gear that will accommodate a range of climatic conditions.

### The Tusky Pinniped

Closely packed walruses lying on Round Island

The Pacific walrus *(Odobenus rosmarus divergens)*, a resident of the western Gulf of Alaska, Bristol Bay, the Bering Sea, and the Chukchi Sea, is a large, brown pinniped covered with coarse hair. Its most distinctive features are its shaggy "old man" moustache and its two ivory tusks, which are actually enlarged canine teeth. While breeding, males use the tusks to vanquish competitors for females. They also use the tusks to anchor themselves to the sea bottom while digging for mollusks. Male walruses can grow up to 12 ft (4 m) in length and weigh in at 3,700 lbs (1,480 kg). Only Alaska Natives are permitted to hunt walruses for food and for ivory, which they turn into their renowned scrimshaw carvings.

Red fox in Wood-Tikchik State Park

## ❺ Wood-Tikchik State Park

25 miles (40 km) N of Dillingham.
**Transport map** C4. ✈ Dillingham,
then by floatplane or bus. ℹ Ranger
Station, Dillingham, 842-2641. ⌖
ⓦ dnr.alaska.gov/parks/units/
woodtik.htm

America's largest state park,
the 2,345-sq mile (6,070-sq km)
Wood-Tikchik State Park is
a vast landscape of two
interconnected lake systems,
that of the Wood River in the
south and the Tikchik River in
the north. The park is situated
in a biological transition zone
between coniferous forest and
tundra, with willow and alder
thickets as well as spruce and
birch forests. Its eastern side
consists of low, boggy wetlands
studded with lakes and streams,
while to the west rise the wild
and untracked Wood
River Mountains.
The remoteness of
the park makes it
especially good wild-
life habitat. Brown
bears, caribou, and
moose are abundant,
as are porcupines,
wolverines, marmots,
beavers, land otters,
and foxes. Through-
out the park, well-
appointed fly-in
lodges serve as
staging points
for canoeing and
fishing trips. Anglers will find
all five Alaskan salmon species,
especially sockeyes (reds),
plus trout, Arctic char, Arctic
grayling, and northern pike.

The most usual access for
independent groups is to fly in
to one of the lakes on the Wood
River system, and then canoe
downstream to Aleknagik on
Lake Aleknagik, accessible from
Dillingham via a gravel road. On
the Tikchik system, most people
fly into one of the lakes and then
float downstream along the
Nuyakuk and Nushagak Rivers,
to be picked up at the airstrips
at Ekwok or New Stuyahok.

Visitors who are considering
an expedition but not planning
to stay in one of the fly-in
lodges should keep in mind
that well-honed survival skills
are essential for trips into the
park's wilderness.

## ❻ Lake Clark National Park

200 miles (320 km) SW of Anchorage.
**Transport map** D4. **Tel** 781-2217.
✈ Iliamna, then charter plane to Port
Alsworth. ⌖ only in Port Alsworth.
ⓦ nps.gov/lacl

When ANILCA was passed in
1980 (see p61), the 6,250-sq mile
(16,187-sq km) Lake Clark
National Park came into being
to protect the 50-mile- (80-km-)
long Lake Clark and its surrounding ecosystems. These include
the shores of Cook Inlet, which
is prime bear territory, and the
glaciated heights of the Chigmit
Mountains and the Aleutian
Range. The twin volcanoes,
Mount Iliamna and Mount
Redoubt, are also included. The
park boasts an array of wildlife,
most prominently brown bears
and migrating herds of caribou.
Activities include canoeing,
kayaking, fishing, and hiking,
but the only marked hiking
trail leads from Port Alsworth
to Tanalian Falls. A worthwhile
destination is Dick Proenneke's
cabin on Twin Lakes, which
features in the film Alone in
the Wilderness.

Port Alsworth, the park's
headquarters, has several small
lodges, but the park has no other
services, so non-lodge visitors
will need to carry camping and
cooking gear. Access to remote
parts of the park is by chartered
bush flight only.

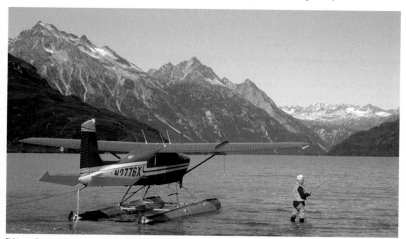

Fishing in Crescent Lake, surrounded by the Chigmit Mountains in Lake Clark National Park

# ❼ Katmai National Park

Katmai was proclaimed a National Monument in 1918 to preserve the unique geological features that were formed after the eruption of Novarupta in 1912. Designated a National Park when ANILCA was passed in 1980 *(see p61)*, it now encompasses 6,400 sq miles (17,000 sq km) of cold lakes, scenic valleys, volcanic landscapes, and wild seacoasts. Lakes and marshes serve as nesting sites for waterfowl, including swans, ducks, grebes, loons, and Arctic terns. The Brooks River, which flows past Brooks Camp, and the McNeil River to the northeast draws large numbers of visitors to view bears feeding at the red salmon runs into Bristol Bay.

**Fishing at Naknek Lake**
Anglers flock to the park's rivers and lakes to fish for salmon, trout, and Arctic char.

**★ Brooks Camp**
This prime bear-viewing spot lies on the shores of Naknek Lake. It consists of a campground, ranger station, lodge, and elevated viewing platforms overlooking the Riffles and iconic Brooks River Falls.

## Exploring the Park

*From Brooks Camp, a rough 23-mile (37-km) road accesses the Valley of 10,000 Smokes. A steep trail descends into the valley, from where trails lead to Ukak Falls and the confluence of River Lethe and Windy River. A chartered bush plane is necessary to access remote areas of the park, while hiking to Mount Katmai or Novarupta is challenging and requires good backcountry skills. Camping is allowed throughout the park, but a backcountry permit is needed.*

Map labels:
Kukak
Alagnak
Nonvianuk Lake
Lake Coville
KING SALMON–NAKNEK RD
Naknek Lake
**King Salmon**
**Brooks Camp**
Lake Brooks
Mount Kelez 3,250 ft
Iliuk Arm
Mou La G 3,18.
**Three Forks**
Mount Mart 6,05C

**★ Valley of 10,000 Smokes**
After the 1912 Novarupta eruption, thousands of fumaroles steamed from this bleak landscape of ash deposits, which is now slashed by deep river canyons.

0 km    10
0 miles    10

*For hotels and restaurants in this area see p245 and p255*

Brown bear with yearlings at McNeil River State Game Sanctuary

## McNeil River State Game Sanctuary

The McNeil River State Game Sanctuary, at the northeast boundary of Katmai, provides reliable summer bear viewing. Often, a big group of brown bears congregates at the falls to feast on salmon, offering good opportunities for photographs. Access is by lottery permit only.

### VISITORS' CHECKLIST

**Practical Information**
290 miles SW of Anchorage.
**Transport map** D4. 🛈 King Salmon Airport, 246-3305/365-2267. 🚌 🎫 daily guided bus tour from Brooks Lodge to Valley of 10,000 Smokes. 🏕 Permits required for Brooks Camp Campground: 🔲 **recreation. gov**; 🔲 **nps.gov/katm** McNeil River State Game Sanctuary: N of Katmai National Park. **Tel** 267-2182.

**Transport**
✈ charter floatplane to Brooks Camp & Kulik Lodge. ✈ from Homer. 🔲 **adfg.alaska.gov**

**Mount Douglas**
At the summit of this 7,000-ft (2,100-m) volcano is an active fumarole field and a warm, highly acidic crater lake. The park contains at least 14 active volcanoes.

★ **Mount Katmai and Novarupta**
In June 1912, severe earthquakes around Mount Katmai led to a cataclysmic eruption that covered the surrounding tundra with volcanic debris. It was initially thought that Mount Katmai had erupted, but Novarupta proved to be the source. As Novarupta's explosion emptied Mount Katmai's magma chamber, Katmai's summit collapsed, leaving a caldera with a crater lake.

**For keys to symbols** see back flap

### Key

══ Minor road

■ ■ Park boundary

△ Peak

Colorful iron springs at Surprise Lake in the Aniakchak Caldera

## ❽ Aniakchak National Monument

200 miles (320 km) SW of Kodiak.
**Transport map** D5. ✈ King Salmon,
then chartered floatplane to Surprise
Lake. ℹ King Salmon airport terminal, 246-3305. 🌐 **nps.gov/ania**

With the unofficial distinction
of being the least visited unit
in the US National Park System,
Aniakchak National Monument
is tucked away in a remote
corner of the Alaska Peninsula.
The park's most striking feature
is the 2,000-ft (600-m) deep,
6-mile (10-km) wide **Aniakchak
Caldera**, an ash-filled bowl
formed 3,500 years ago when
Aniakchak Volcano collapsed
into its own empty magma
chamber. Over the millennia,
minor eruptions, including one

in 1931, have added several
small cinder cones and lava
flows to the crater.

Located within the caldera,
Surprise Lake is the remnant
of a larger lake that once
existed here. After a weakness
developed in the caldera's
southeastern wall, the lake
drained. The resulting whitewater Aniakchak River created
the canyon known as The
Gates and flowed 27 miles
(43 km) to the Gulf of Alaska.
Fed by brilliant red iron
springs, Surprise Lake provides
floatplane access to the park
and is the put-in point for
whitewater rafting trips. The
park has excellent hiking
opportunities, but hikers
and rafters need to be self-
sufficient and prepared for
long weather-related delays.

## ❾ Sand Point

440 miles (710 km) SW of Kodiak.
**Transport map** C5. 🗺 975. ✈ ⛴
🌐 **sandpointak.com**

Situated on the northwest
coast of Popof Island, the town
of Sand Point was settled in
the late 19th century by the
Russians. Like nearby King Cove,
it has Aleut and Scandinavian
heritage, and these two groups
still constitute the majority of its
population. As with the rest of
the region, the area's economy
has always been based on the
fishing industry. In 1898, a
trading post and cod fishing
station were set up by a San
Francisco seafood company,
and by the 1930s, fish processing
had become the dominant
activity. Today, Sand Point is home
to one of the largest fishing
fleets in the Aleutian region.

Visitors can view the large
flocks of bald eagles that
gather near the shore, ride the
popular 14-mile (23-km) bike
trail, and visit the 1933 Russian
Orthodox Church, which is
listed on the National Register
of Historic Places.

To visit Sand Point, travelers
will most likely take the Marine
Highway ferry *(see pp282–3)*
from Kodiak. The first stop
on the journey is the tiny,
beautifully situated village of
**Chignik**, which is flanked by
snow-capped peaks. Farther
south is Perryville, founded by
villagers from Katmai who
migrated after their homes were
destroyed in the 1912 eruption

Magnificent lagoon at the mouth of the Aniakchak River in Aniakchak National Monument

*For hotels and restaurants in this area see p245 and p255*

The active Shishaldin Volcano, best viewed from the Izembek National Wildlife Refuge

of Novarupta *(see pp210–11)*. The ferry arrives at Sand Point nine hours after leaving Chignik.

## ❿ King Cove

551 miles (887 km) SW of Kodiak.
**Transport map** C5. 🏔 750. ✈ 🚢
ℹ️ 497-2340. 🆆 cityofkingcove.com

Founded in 1911, King Cove developed around a salmon cannery belonging to the Pacific American Fisheries. The first settlers in the village were Scandinavian, Aleut, and Anglo fishermen who either hauled in the fish or worked in the processing plant. The plant operated until 1976, when it was damaged by fire and replaced by the Peter Pan Seafood Cannery.

Today, half the residents are of Native descent, while the rest are descended primarily from the early Scandinavian settlers. They continue to fish commercially or work for the cannery, which has grown into one of Alaska's most successful commercial operations. Locals also engage in subsistence fishing and hunting for geese, caribou, and ptarmigan.

Most visitors arrive on the Alaska Marine Highway's twice-monthly ferry between Homer and Dutch Harbor/Unalaska, which stops long enough for a visit to the Russian Orthodox Church. The church's bells and interior icons were brought here in the 1980s by residents who

moved from the abandoned town of Belkofski, 12 miles (19 km) to the southeast.

Visitors should be wary of the unusually large numbers of bears that invade town, chasing dogs, tipping over trash cans, and trying to break into buildings.

## ⓫ Cold Bay and Izembek National Wildlife Refuge

579 miles (930 km) SW of Kodiak.
**Transport map** C5. 🏔 100. ✈
🚢 Izembek National Wildlife
Refuge: ℹ️ Izembek St, 532-2445.
🆆 coldbayak.org 🆆 fws.gov/
refuge/izembek

The small town of Cold Bay, within view of the dramatic 9,370-ft (2,850-m) Shishaldin Volcano, officially came into existence in August 1941 as a covert US military base to ward off Japanese attacks. Its construction was classified and its military contractor, General William Buckner, assumed a civilian name and claimed to have built a salmon cannery.

Even after Fort Randall was constructed here in 1942, the Japanese failed to realize its military significance. In 1945, the US and Russia forged an alliance and made Fort Randall a training site for over 12,000 Russian troops. During the Vietnam War in the 1960s, Cold Bay sprang back to life as a

freight hauling base and the headquarters of the famed Flying Tigers squadron. Today, its massive airport provides an emergency landing site for trans-Pacific travel.

The main attraction is the beautiful 650-sq mile (1,700-sq km) **Izembek National Wildlife Refuge**, partly accessible via gravel roads from Cold Bay. The refuge protects the habitat of bears, caribou, seals, sea lions, and whales. At the 150-sq mile (390-sq km) brackish Izembek Lagoon, 10 miles (16 km) from Cold Bay, vast beds of eelgrass provide food for migrating birds. These include 98 percent of the world's population of Pacific black brant, a small dark goose. Visitors can watch the wildlife from the Grant Point viewing hide at the lagoon.

Caribou grazing in Izembek National Wildlife Refuge

# ⑫ Dutch Harbor/Unalaska

For thousands of years, Dutch Harbor and its sister town Unalaska have provided shelter from stormy seas. The Aleuts, or the Unangan, have lived here for centuries, fishing and hunting sea mammals from *iqax* (skin boats). The first outsiders to arrive were the Russians. Settling on Iliuliuk Bay, the site of Unalaska, in 1759, they conscripted the Aleuts to hunt fur seals and sea otters. After buying Alaska, the US also used the islands as a seal hunting base and, during World War II, as a military outpost. The king crab boom of the 1970s and the growth of the fishing industry have made this ice-free port the largest in the US in terms of the weight and value of the catch.

Fishermen repairing crab pots at Dutch Harbor

## Sights at a Glance

① Church of the Holy Ascension
② Museum of the Aleutians
③ Aleutian World War II National Historical Park
④ Mount Ballyhoo

| 0 meters | 500 |
| 0 yards | 500 |

## 🏛 Church of the Holy Ascension

Broadway Rd. **Tel** 581-6404.
🕐 groups by appt. ✉ 🏛 6:30pm Sat & 9:30am Sun.

The focal point of Unalaska, the cruciform Church of the Holy Ascension stands on a small spit at the western end of the village. In 1808, it was the site of Alaska's first Russian Orthodox church, a basic structure that Bishop Veniaminov *(see p78)* reconstructed in a more opulent style in 1827. A third structure was built in 1858 by Aleut priest Innokenti Shaishnikov. The present building, dating from 1896, had suffered so much damage from Aleutian storms that by 1990 it needed repairs. The renovated church was rededicated in 1996, in time for its centenary.

Its interior is filled with a rich collection of icons from abandoned villages around Unalaska Islands, as well as an ornate candelabra, bronze bells, and paintings. The adjacent 1882 Bishop's House reflects a style characteristic of 1880s San Francisco.

Church of the Holy Ascension in Unalaska

## 🏛 Museum of the Aleutians

314 Salmon Way. **Tel** 581-5150.
**Open** noon–6pm Tue–Sat. 🅿 ♿ 📷
🌐 aleutians.org

Opened in 1999 on the site of an old World War II warehouse, the museum is one of the finest attractions in the area. The modern building, with lovely terrazzo tiles in the entryway, has an extensive collection that includes historic photographs, drawings, and relics from the Russian era, as well as objects salvaged from the World War II defense of the islands and a 1920s herring fishery.

Also on display are Aleut artifacts uncovered in several archeological digs around Unalaska, Amaknak, and other Aleutian Islands, including many of the 100,000 items recovered from the adjacent Margaret Bay village site. Once a flourishing fish camp, this village is thought to have thrived about 2,000 years ago. Volunteers and students are

---

*Map labels:*
Mount Ballyhoo ④ 1,634 ft
Ferry Dock
AMAKNAK ISLAND
BALLYHOO ROAD
TUNDRA ROAD
Dutch Harbor
Aleutian World War II ③ National Historical Park
Unalaska Bay
DUTCH HARBOR
BIORKA DR
E POINT ROAD
Summer Bay 1 mile (2 km)
AIRPORT BEACH ROAD
Ounalaska Native Corporation
② Museum of the Aleutians
Iliuliuk Harbor
Iliuliuk Bay
SUMMER BAY ROAD
Church of the ① Holy Ascension
Bunker Hill △ 421 ft
Small Boat Harbor
UNALASKA
BAY VIEW ROAD
Library ℹ
HENRY SWANSON DRIVE
CAPTAIN'S BAY RD
Iliuliuk Clinic
BROADWAY RD
Captain's Bay
South Channel
CAPTAIN'S BAY ROAD
Unalaska Lake

Summer Bay Road winding across the tundra toward Ugadaga Pass

welcome to apply to participate in the ongoing museum-
sponsored digs around the
Aleutian Islands.

### 🏛 Aleutian World War II National Historical Park

Dutch Harbor Airport. **Tel** 581-9944.
**Open** year-round; visitor center:
1–6pm Wed–Sat or by appt. 🅿 ♿
🖥 nps.gov/aleu

Known as Unangax Tenganis,
which means "Our Islands" in
Aleut, the Aleutian World War II
National Historical Park was
designated by the US Congress
in 1996. It aims to showcase the
little-known war history of the
state, focusing on the culture
and role of the Aleuts and their
islands in the defense of the US.

The visitor center, at the
airport in Dutch Harbor, occupies the renovated Naval Air
Transport Service's Aerology
Building. Its displays include
a 1940s-era radio room and
exhibits on the mass evacuation
of the Aleuts. The area's
remaining World War II structures and ruins convey the
grand scale of the war effort
mounted in the islands.

### 🏔 Mount Ballyhoo

During World War II, Mount
Ballyhoo was the site of Fort
Schwatka, one of Dutch
Harbor's four coastal defense
posts. It was named for
Lt. Frederick Schwatka, who
was responsible for surveying
the Aleutians in the 1880s.

At this strategic location,
897 ft (269 m) above the
harbor, engineers built over 100
buildings designed to withstand
nature's fury. Today, the fort is a
part of the Aleutian World War II

National Historical Park. A stroll
across the site reveals concrete
bunkers, observation posts, and
gun emplacements from the
1940s. The site also offers views
across the sea and toward the
Makushin Volcano. While it is
possible to negotiate the steep,
twisting road with a hardy
vehicle, a pleasant day hike is
also an option.

### 🏕 Summer Bay

Heading east from Unalaska, a
gravel road along the scenic
coastline of Iliuliuk Bay turns
north to reach the beautiful
inlet known as Summer Bay.
Behind coastal sand dunes that
attract picnickers, the pristine
freshwater Summer Bay Lake
reflects the surrounding green

hills and magical Aleutian
light. At the head of the lake,
the road winds uphill across
the tundra to Ugadaga Pass.
From here, a relatively easy
hiking trail leads down to
Ugadaga Bay on the east
coast of Unalaska Island. In
fine weather, this makes an
excellent day hike.

Just northeast of Ugadaga
Bay at Ugadaga Head, it is
possible to see remnants of
another of the island's coastal
defense posts. The last mile
(2 km) or so is rough, so park
your vehicle and walk. Local
companies provide guided
birding and historical tours.

MV *Tustumena* sailing in Kachemak Bay

### The Trusty Tusty

Built in 1964, the 296-ft- (89-m-) long ferry MV *Tustumena*, which is
affectionately known as the "Trusty Tusty," plies some of the roughest
waters on earth. Once a month from April to September, this sturdy
vessel – the oldest ship in the fleet of the Alaska Marine Highway
(see pp282–3) – does the difficult, stormy four-day run from Homer
to Dutch Harbor/Unalaska. This spectacular trip attracts adventurous
visitors hoping to see one of the most remote corners of the world.
Be forewarned though that the amenities are basic. Deck-class
passengers have access to a solarium where they can stake out
a warm spot to roll out their sleeping bags.

# ⓭ Pribilof Islands

In 1786, Gerassim Pribilof claimed the Pribilof Islands for Russia, and set up Russian trade interests based on the large fur seal colonies he found there. These five islands in the middle of the Bering Sea have been dubbed the "Northern Galapagos" due to their dense concentrations of breeding pinnipeds and nesting birds. While the larger islands of St. Paul and St. George have small Aleut communities, Otter Island, Walrus Island, and Sea Lion Rock are inhabited only by wildlife. Bird-watching groups dominate island tourism, but an increasing number of visitors also come to appreciate the local Aleut culture, the profusion of summer wildflowers across the volcanic landscapes, and the stark beauty of the islands.

*St. Paul Island*

**St. Paul**

*Bering Sea*

**St. George**

*St. George Island*

**Key**

=== Minor road

Village houses and the Russian Orthodox church, St. Paul Island

### St. Paul Island

🏔 480. ✈ 🚤 ℹ Tanadgusix Corporation, PO Box 88, St. Paul; 546-3100. 🎫🎫🎫🎫 St. Peter and Paul Feast Day (Jul 12). 🏕 **Permits** needed to camp on the island; see 🌐 tanadgusix.com St. Paul Island Tours: **Tel** 278-2312, (877) 424-5637. 🌐 stpaultour.com

St. Paul Island, with an area of only just over 40 sq miles (104 sq km), lies in the Bering Sea, 375 miles (600 km) west of the mainland. The island's only village, also called St. Paul, has the state's largest Aleut community, with 86 percent of the population consisting of indigenous people.

Life in the community revolves around the St. Peter and Paul Russian Orthodox Church, which is the only church on the island. For visitors, highlights include forays to the island's spectacular bird cliffs and northern fur seal rookeries, as well as the opportunity to hike through the wild interior to see reindeer

herds, volcanic formations, numerous small lakes, and a changing tableau of wildflowers. While it is possible to visit the island independently, tours are available only through St. Paul Island Tours, operated by the Native Tanadgusix Corporation.

### St. George Island

🏔 100. ✈ 🚤 ℹ St. George Tanaq Corporation, St. George, 859-2255 or 4141 B St #301, Anchorage, 272-9886. 🎫 🏕 🏕 **Permits** needed to camp on the island; issued by the St. George Tanaq Corporation. 🌐 stgeorgetanaq.com

Lying 47 miles (75 km) south of St. Paul, St. George Island is less visited, but is considered to be even more spectacular than its more easily accessed neighbor. Much wilder than St. Paul Island, it has six fur seal rookeries, harboring up to 250,000 animals, and the highest and most prolific bird cliffs in the Pribilofs.

About 90 percent of the islanders are Aleut or belong to other indigenous groups.

As with St. Paul Island, the beautiful Russian Orthodox church of St. George the Martyr dominates the local social scene and is one of the island's main attractions. Hiking around St. George or camping are other interesting options, but it is worth noting that there are few roads or trails, and in places, the going can be quite rough. Visits are organized by the St. George Tanaq Corporation, which is headquartered in Anchorage.

Towering cliffs with St. George village in the distance

# Wildlife of the Pribilof Islands

The biodiversity of the Pribilof Islands is largely due to the Bering Sea, which is rich in fish, shellfish, seaweed, and plankton, as well as to the island's range of habitats, which include sand dunes, tundra, beaches, lagoons, and towering cliffs. Half of the world's population of northern fur seals breeds on St. Paul and St. George, while Steller sea lions breed on Walrus Island and harbor seals on Otter Island. In the summer, the spectacular cliffs that gird the islands hum with millions of nesting birds. Sea ice that once reached this far south from the Arctic brought a substantial population of Arctic foxes to the Pribilofs, while a reindeer herd that was introduced to St. Paul in the early 20th century still inhabits the interior of the island.

**Bird cliffs** are alive with thousands of nesting birds such as murres, a type of auk.

**Horned puffins** are awkward fliers, but can dive up to 20 ft (6 m) and swim underwater while retrieving the small fish that form their main diet.

**The crested auklet** sports a distinctive plume of dark feathers during the breeding season.

## Birds

*The towering cliffs of these tundra-covered, treeless islands annually attract over two million birds of at least 200 species, including Asian migrants that are blown off course by strong westerly winds.*

**Red-legged kittiwakes** are similar in size and shape to black-legged kittiwakes (*see p119*), but have red legs and darker wing undersides.

## Animals

*The abundance of wildlife attracts visitors to the Pribilofs, who come to view the world's largest colony of northern fur seals. Arctic foxes, reindeer, and harbor seals are easily spotted, while Steller sea lions are seen occasionally.*

**Arctic foxes** den in grassy bluffs, foraging for sea bird eggs and chicks. They have both blue and white phases, when their coats change color, but the blue phase is most common in the Pribilofs.

**Northern fur seals** are "eared" seals, with a waxy coating in their ears and nostrils that prevents water from entering during dives. Their large bare flippers regulate body temperature by shedding heat while on land. Hunting them is now restricted to Alaska Natives, who take around 2,000 animals a year.

**The reindeer herd** on St. Paul Island, introduced in 1911, was originally of Russian stock. These domesticated caribou are shorter and stockier than their wild counterparts.

# ARCTIC AND WESTERN ALASKA

Covering nearly two-thirds of Alaska, the vast coastal plains and wild peaks stretching from the Canadian border to Norton Sound is a quintessentially Arctic region. While this pristine wilderness is home to only a few thousand people, Arctic wildlife is abundant: great herds of caribou live on the tundra, musk oxen inhabit the North Slope, and millions of migrating birds flock to the region's lakes in summer.

Although the winters along the lonely coastline are not as harsh as those of the Alaskan Interior, the early Athabaskans chose to continue onward to the forested lands to the south, leaving the coast to the Inupiat and Yup'ik peoples that arrived later. Remarkably, these hardy groups thrived in this barren region. They subsisted mainly on fish and sea mammals such as seals, sea lions, walrus, and whales, using their skins to make clothing and their fat to provide heat and light. While long-standing Native traditions are still followed to some extent, Native people now lead an increasingly modern way of life. Alaskans were the last Native people to be contacted by Europeans, mainly because they inhabited a wasteland with few natural resources. However, in the early 20th century, the Nome area experienced a boom, as the beach sands were found to bear gold. Today, while the attractions of the region are undeniably spectacular, they are also universally difficult and expensive to access. This relative inaccessibility has resulted in swathes of untouched wilderness in parks such as the Arctic National Wildlife Refuge and Gates of the Arctic National Park. Several designated "Wild Rivers" offer rafting and fishing, and excellent bird-watching is available around Nome and Gambell. The Dalton Highway is more accessible and follows the Trans-Alaska Pipeline through spectacular wilderness.

Caribou crossing the Alatna River, Gates of the Arctic National Park

◄ Spectacular aurora borealis display reflected in icy water in the Brooks Range

# Exploring Arctic and Western Alaska

Most visitors venture north of the Arctic Circle to experience the region's fierce, desolate beauty. Of the three major towns, historical Nome has roads leading into spectacular country, Barrow is the largest Inupiat community in Alaska, and commercial Kotzebue is a gateway to four remote national parks. The rewarding Arctic National Wildlife Refuge is one of America's last true wildernesses and Prudhoe Bay displays the harsh conditions involved in Arctic oil extraction. Gambell and Nome are world-renowned bird-watching venues, and the Kobuk, Noatak, John, Kongukut, and Hulahula Rivers provide excellent kayaking, rafting, fishing, and access to wildlife habitat.

Kayaking on Walker Lake in the Brooks Range

## Sights at a Glance

### Towns and Cities

② Prudhoe Bay
⑤ Barrow
⑥ Kotzebue
⑩ Nome
⑫ Gambell

### Tour

① *Dalton Highway Tour pp222–3*

### National and State Parks

③ Arctic National Wildlife Refuge
④ Gates of the Arctic National Park
⑦ Kobuk Valley National Park
⑧ Noatak National Preserve
⑨ Cape Krusenstern National Monument
⑪ Bering Land Bridge National Preserve

Atigun River flowing along the Dalton Highway

## Key

- ----- Minor road
- ▬▬ International border
- △ Peak
- )( Pass

Native whalers launching an *umiak* (skin boat) into the Arctic Ocean near Barrow

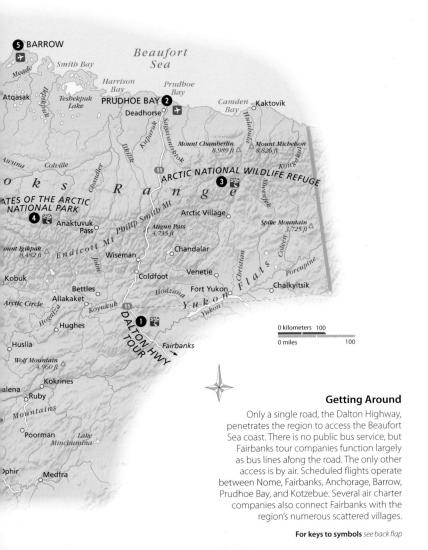

## Getting Around

Only a single road, the Dalton Highway, penetrates the region to access the Beaufort Sea coast. There is no public bus service, but Fairbanks tour companies function largely as bus lines along the road. The only other access is by air. Scheduled flights operate between Nome, Fairbanks, Anchorage, Barrow, Prudhoe Bay, and Kotzebue. Several air charter companies also connect Fairbanks with the region's numerous scattered villages.

**For keys to symbols** *see back flap*

# Dalton Highway Tour

Originally built in the 1970s to supply equipment to the Prudhoe Bay oilfields and provide a service corridor for the Trans-Alaska Pipeline, the Dalton Highway is the only road in Alaska that crosses the Arctic Circle. Also known as the Haul Road, it was initially accessible only to supply trucks, but in the 1990s, the full route was opened to private drivers. While astoundingly scenic, much of the highway is a bone-jarring gravel route that should not be taken lightly. Services are available in a handful of places but supplies are not, and drivers should travel with essentials such as food, water, a first aid kit, spare tires, and fuel.

**⑥ Sukakpak Mountain**
This dramatic 4,460 ft (1,360 m) peak was once a limestone deposit before heat and pressure metamorphosed it into marble.

**⑤ Wiseman**
The village of Wiseman was founded in 1907 as a camp to service the gold strike at nearby Nolan. Today, the site is home to a historic church an open-air museum.

**④ Arctic Interagency Visitors' Center, Coldfoot**
An essential stop in Coldfoot, the center has exhibits and interpretive programs on the Arctic. Also worth a look is Coldfoot's temperature sign, which describes the day in 1989 when the temperature dropped to -63° C (-82° F), the coldest ever recorded in North America.

**③ Arctic Circle Wayside**
The highway crosses the Arctic Circle at Mile 115, where there is a wayside with a picnic area, a basic campsite, and interpretive signs.

**① E. L. Patton Yukon Bridge**
This 2,295-ft- (688-m-) long bridge carries both the Dalton Highway and the Alaska Pipeline. Built in 1975, this is the only US bridge across the Yukon (*see pp198–9*).

**② Finger Mountain**
Distant views from the Finger Mountain wayside take in the Caribou Mountain and a lovely tor-studded landscape.

### Tips for Drivers

**Starting point:** Livengood on the Elliot Highway, 73 miles (117 km) N of Fairbanks.
**Length:** 414 miles (662 km).
**Accommodation:** Coldfoot at Mile 175 has a hotel and café. There are campgrounds at Marion Creek. Wiseman at Mile 188.6 has lodging and a general store. The Prudhoe Bay Hotel in Deadhorse serves meals.
**Note:** there are only four gas stations on the Dalton Highway – at Yukon Crossing, Five-Mile Camp, Coldfoot, and Deadhorse.

⑦ **Atigun Pass**
The highway crosses the Brooks Range at the 4,800-ft- (1,440-m-) high Atigun Pass, the highest point on Alaska's road system. Its steep grades demand extreme caution.

**Key**

⎯ Tour route
⎯ Highway
••• Trans-Alaska Pipeline
△ Peak

⑧ **Trans-Alaska Pipeline**
Near the northern end of the highway, the gleaming pipeline winds across a vast tundra landscape along the western edge of the Arctic National Wildlife Refuge.

⑨ **Franklin Bluffs**
The iron-rich soil on the east bank of the Sagavanirktok River on the plains of the North Slope gives Franklin Bluffs their striking yellow, tan, and orange hues.

Pipelines crisscrossing the oilfields at Prudhoe Bay on the North Slope

## ❷ Prudhoe Bay

487 miles (784 km) N of Fairbanks.
**Transport map** E1. 🚠 2,100.
🛫 from Anchorage. 🚌 tour bus
from Fairbanks. 🛈 Prudhoe Bay
Hotel, 100 Airport Way; 659-2449.
🌐 **prudhoebayhotel.com**

The North Slope oilfields, often
collectively called Prudhoe
Bay, make up the largest
oil-producing field in North
America. While geologic surveys
took place in the 1950s, the first
major discovery was made only
in 1968. The Alyeska Pipeline
Service Company was formed a
year later to construct a pipeline
*(see p186)* across the state to the
ice-free port of Valdez. Today,
the vast oilfields use the latest
technology to minimize their
impact on the delicate tundra.

Deadhorse, the oilfields'
service center, has a shop, a gas
station, a hotel, and restaurants.
Prudhoe Bay and the Arctic
Ocean coast, which lie beyond
a checkpoint, can only be
accessed on tours run by the
Prudhoe Bay Hotel.

## ❸ Arctic National Wildlife Refuge

200 miles (320 km) N of Fairbanks.
**Transport map** E1. 🛫 air taxi to Fort
Yukon, Arctic Village, Deadhorse, or
Kaktovik, then bush plane. 🚌 tour
bus to Galbraith Lake, then hike.
🛈 101 12th Ave, Fairbanks; 456-0250,
(800) 362-4546. **Open** year-round.
🌐 **arctic.fws.gov**

The 30,000-sq mile (78,000-sq
km) Arctic National Wildlife
Refuge (ANWR, pronounced
AN-wahr) was established in
1960 to protect the region's

abundant wildlife, flocks of
migratory birds and its range
of ecosystems. However,
studies of the ANWR coastal
plain east of Prudhoe Bay have
determined that the northwestern corner of the refuge
holds vast amounts of natural
gas and oil. Political forces have
long tussled over ANWR, with
pro-development organizations
lobbying to allow oil drilling
on the coastal plain, while
environmental groups oppose
opening the wildlife refuge
to oil exploitation.

Scenically stunning, ANWR
is bisected by the Brooks
Range and crossed by the
Sheenjek, Kongukut, Hulahula,
and other "Wild Rivers" that
are popular for rafting trips.
Wildlife enthusiasts may
have the chance to spot
all of Alaska's bear species,
as well as musk oxen, wolves,
caribou, and over 140 species
of birds. ANWR has no trails or
facilities, and visitors need to
be self-sufficient.

## ❹ Gates of the Arctic National Park

200 miles (320 km) NW of Fairbanks.
**Transport map** D1. 🛫 to Anaktuvuk
Pass, Bettles, Coldfoot, or Kotzebue,
then bush plane. 🚌 tour bus to
Coldfoot, then bush plane. 🛈 Bettles
Visitors' Center, 692-5494. Also
Anaktuvuk Pass Ranger Station &
Arctic Interagency Visitors' Center
(Coldfoot). Note: no roads or facilities
in national park. 🌐 **nps.gov/gaar**

The second-largest national
park in the US after Wrangell-
St. Elias *(see pp192–3)*, Gates
of the Arctic National Park
encompasses 12,500 sq miles
(32,000 sq km). The park got
its name in the 1930s when
wilderness advocate Bob
Marshall described Frigid Crags
and the Boreal Mountains as
the "gates" to the Arctic Slope.
The heart of the park is the
Brooks Range, the northernmost
extent of the Rocky Mountains.
The abundant wildlife includes
black and grizzly bears, caribou,
moose, and migratory birds,
and the vegetation away from
the bare, glaciated peaks ranges
from boreal forest of spruce,
birch, and aspen to alder
thickets, taiga, and muskeg.
Most visitors fly in for hiking
or rafting *(see p266)* on National
Wild and Scenic Rivers such as
the Kobuk, John, and Noatak.
Commercial trips are available,
but lone travelers usually take
an air taxi to Bettles, and then a
bush plane to a drop-off point.
Lodges at Bettles provide
accommodation and meals.

The mighty Brooks Range, Gates of the Arctic National Park

# The Arctic Tundra

Lying north of the Brooks Range, Alaska's North Slope encompasses 88,000 sq miles (227,920 sq km) of largely flat, open Arctic tundra. Derived from the Finnish *tunturia*, meaning "treeless land," this circumpolar environment is characterized by low temperatures and thin topsoil that supports only ground-hugging vegetation such as reindeer mosses, sedges, lichens, liverworts, berries, dwarf birch, and miniature wildflowers. This thin surface is underlain by permanently frozen ground known as permafrost. Tundra areas typically have little precipitation, a growing season of less than 60 days, and average temperatures of 12° C (54° F) during the summer and around -34° C (-30° F) in the harsh winter. The average temperature in Anaktuvuk Pass in January, the coldest month, is -23° C (-9° F).

**Vibrant miniature wildflowers** carpet the tundra during the short flowering season in summer. Alaska has about 400 species of wildflowers.

### Landscape
*Underlying the thin tundra surface is permafrost. This permanently frozen ground cannot absorb surface water, resulting in millions of small shallow ponds and bogs.*

**Crater lakes** are sometimes found in *pingos*, domed ice-cored mounds of earth. The expanding ice may cause the summit of the pingo to crack. This exposes the ice core and allows part of it to melt, forming the crater lake.

### Wildlife
*The tundra teems with wildlife, including Arctic hares, caribou, Arctic foxes, polar bears, and wolves, species that are well-adapted to the severe climatic conditions.*

**The Arctic ground squirrel** digs burrows in the ground and hibernates through the long, cold winter.

**Musk oxen** live year-round on the open tundra, protected from the extreme cold by a soft insulating layer of hair known as *qiviut*. Musk oxen eat a wide variety of plants, including grasses, sedges, and woody plants.

**Caribou** have broad hooves that provide support in soft tundra and snow, function as paddles when the animal swims, and, in winter, help to scrape away snow to expose the limited grazing below. Unlike moose, both bulls and cows grow antlers.

# ❺ Barrow

The northernmost town in the US and seat of the vast North Slope Borough, Barrow sits on the tundra beside the Beaufort Sea. Its Inupiat name, Utqiagvik, means "the place to hunt snowy owls." Offshore ice huddles close to the shore almost all year round, retreating for just a few weeks in July and August. This isolated community experiences the midnight sun for 84 days in the summer; conversely, the sun does not rise at all for the same period in the winter. At 300 miles (480 km) north of the Arctic Circle, many people of this Inupiat outpost continue to live on subsistence fishing and hunting, as they have always done.

Whalers towing a whale out of the sea, Barrow

### 🏛 Ukkuqsi Archeological Site
Stevenson St.

Along the coast at the western end of town, a series of sod ruins and remnants of archeological digs sit on the bluffs overlooking a lonely stretch of beach. While contact between Europeans and indigenous peoples began around 1825, trade was not common until the 1870s. For that reason, the types of items unearthed – ivory points, weapons, tools, and artwork – are still familiar to the older residents of the town, who usually participate in the excavations. This grassy bluff makes a pleasant place to stroll and enjoy the views out over the Arctic Ocean.

### 🏛 Will Rogers and Wiley Post Monument
Akhovak & Momegana Sts. ♿

This memorial honors the renowned pilot Wiley Post and his friend, Cherokee humorist Will Rogers. Post, famous for setting 1920s distance records in his Lockheed Vega, decided to survey an air route from California to Russia in 1935. Funded by interested airlines, he built a low-wing monoplane. In July 1935,

Post and Rogers left Seattle for Alaska. Near Barrow they encountered bad weather and made an emergency landing. However, soon after they took off again, the engine failed and the plane plunged into a lagoon, killing both men. Visitors can hire ATVs or hike to the crash site 15 miles (24 km) to the south.

### 🏛 Inupiat Heritage Center
5421 North Star St. **Tel** 852-0422.
**Open** 8:30am–5pm Mon–Fri.
**Closed** public holidays. 🎟 📷 ♿
📷 🅦 nps.gov/inup

Affiliated with the US National Park Service, the Inupiat Heritage Center was set up in recognition of Inuit contribution to whaling. For hundreds of years, the Inuit hunted whales from their *umiaks*, and in the 19th and 20th centuries, crewed on whaling ships and provided shelter for shipwrecked sailors.

In addition to the whaling connection, the center celebrates Inupiat culture, displaying diverse facets of local life, such as a whale baleen kayak, spirit masks, and ivory implements. A large performance area hosts singing, drumming, and dance performances.

### 🏛 Whalebone Arch
Stevenson St.

This lonely spot at Browerville on the Arctic Ocean coast is the historic site from where generations of Inuit whalers have set out across the icy seas in hopes of killing a whale to feed the community through the winter. An arch made from the massive jawbone of a

Prominent whalebone arch at Browerville on the Arctic Ocean coast

## Polar Bears

Polar bears (*Ursus maritimus*) are marine mammals that wander across the Arctic ice in search of walruses and seals. Rivaling Kodiak bears as the world's largest four-footed carnivores, these bears keep warm due to their

Polar bear on Alaska's coastal plains

hollow tube-like hairs which seem white in the sunlight. Currently, about 3,000 to 5,000 polar bears live in Alaska, and one of the best places to see them is around Barrow's rubbish dump or on the nearby sea ice and gravel beaches. Sadly, recent climatic factors, resulting in decreasing ice, may make it increasingly difficult for them to hunt.

### VISITORS' CHECKLIST

**Practical Information**
580 miles (928 km) N of Fairbanks.
**Transport map** D1. ⚐ 4,200.
ℹ Momegana & Ahkovak St, 852-5211. ✈ Kivqiq Midwinter Festival (early Feb), Piuraagiaqta Spring Festival (Apr), Nalukataq (late Jun). Ⓦ **north-slope.org**

**Transport**
✈

bowhead whale commemorates this indigenous tradition. Next to the arch is the former trading post (closed to the public) of the first European settler, Charles Dewitt Brower, who arrived in Barrow in 1884. Married twice to Inupiat women, he acted as postmaster, census taker, military recruiter, and unofficial surgeon. Brower's grave, marked by whalebones, is located beside the nearby lagoon.

### 🐾 Point Barrow

12 miles (19 km) N of Barrow. 🖼
North of Barrow, a coastal gravel road leads to the lonely cape, Point Barrow, which is the northernmost point of land in the US and divides the Chukchi Sea in the west from the Beaufort Sea in the east. At about 71 degrees N, it is roughly at the same latitude as North Cape in Norway, but without the warming waters of the Gulf Stream, it experiences considerably harsher climatic conditions. In the winter and spring, polar bears den in the area. Any sort of food will attract their attention so visitors should ensure they leave no waste on the beach.

Along the route to Point Barrow is the local Ilisagvik College, which works with the Barrow Arctic Science Consortium to research the Arctic environment.

Stress test being conducted on Arctic sea pack ice, Point Barrow

## Sights at a Glance

① Ukkuqsi Archeological Site
② Will Rogers and Wiley Post Monument
③ Inupiat Heritage Center
④ Whalebone Arch

Point Barrow
12 miles (19 km)

BROWERVILLE

Whalebone Arch ④

Arctic Ocean

Tasigrook Lagoon

③ Inupiat Heritage Center

Isatqoaq Lagoon

Ukkuqsi Archeological Site ①

Bus Station

② Will Rogers and Wiley Post Monument

OKPIK STREET

OGROOK STREET

PISOKAK STREET

Airport Buildings

Freshwater Lake | Will Rogers and Wiley Post Crash Site
1 mile (2 km) | 15 miles (24 km)

0 meters        200
0 yards         200

# 6 Kotzebue

550 miles (880 km) NW of Anchorage.
**Transport map** C2. ⛰ 3,200. ✈
ℹ 258A 3rd Ave, 442- 3401.
ⓦ cityofkotzebue.com

Located on the shores of the Chukchi Sea, Kotzebue, with a 75 percent Native population, is the commercial, economic, and political center of the Northwest Arctic Borough. A gateway to the Kobuk Valley National Park, the site, which has been occupied since at least the 15th century, lies 26 miles (43 km) north of the Arctic Circle on a 3-mile- (5-km-) long sandspit at the end of the Baldwin Peninsula. Kikiktagruk, its Inupiat name, simply means "the peninsula," and its modern name honors Otto von Kotzebue, a German who arrived in 1816.

The economy of modern Kotzebue depends largely on the Red Dog Mine, a lead and zinc mine 100 miles (160 km) north of town, which employs hundreds of workers and provides a good income for the Northwest Arctic Native Association (NANA). Kotzebue also has Alaska's only power grid that is supplemented by electricity generated by windmills.

Kotzebue is not a major tourist destination, however visitors to the area will get an idea of what life is like in this harsh place where the winters

An Inuit woman drying salmon near Kotzebue

are long and summers are brief and intense. Take a walk along the shore south of town to view local fish camps where fish, seal, and walrus meat are smoked and dried. In the heart of town, the cemetery is well worth a visit for its beautifully decorated graves, or head out on the dirt road east from Kotzebue to explore the rolling tundra stretching to the horizon. Be sure to pack head nets and mosquito repellent, as well as a good supply of water.

The National Park Service's **Northwest Arctic Heritage Center** has a wealth of exhibits on Kobuk Valley National Park, Cape Krusenstern National Monument, Noatak National Preserve, and Bering Land Bridge. These offer visitors a taste of some of the least-visited units

in the US National Park Service. (The parks themselves are very remote and require bush flights and total self-sufficiency for the duration of the trip.) The heritage center also provides an interesting introduction to Inupiat culture and houses a bookstore and gift shop. Educational programs are offered, along with occasional Native dance performances and blanket tosses.

**Northwest Arctic Heritage Center**

171 3rd St. **Tel** 442-3890, (800) 478-7252. **Open** Jun–Aug: 9am–6:30pm Mon–Fri, 10am–6:30pm Sat; Sep–May: 9am–noon & 1–6:30pm Mon–Fri. ♿
ⓦ nps.gov/kova

# 7 Kobuk Valley National Park

125 miles (200 km) E of Kotzebue.
**Transport map** D2. ✈ charter plane from Kotzebue. ⛴ charter boat from Ambler. ℹ 171 3rd Ave, Kotzebue; 442-3890, (800) 478-7252.
ⓦ nps.gov/kova

Situated between the Baird and Waring Mountains, Kobuk Valley National Park is a sanctuary for the area's range of Arctic wildlife, including caribou, grizzlies, and wolves.

The park's most visited attraction is the Great Kobuk Sand Dunes which lie along Kavel Creek, a tributary of the Kobuk. Covering over 25 sq miles (65 sq km), the dunes,

Fall migration of caribou through Kobuk Valley National Park

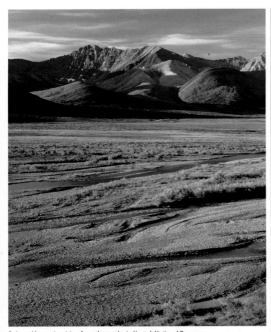

DeLong Mountains rising from the tundra in Noatak National Preserve

headwaters in the Brooks Range inside Gates of the Arctic National Park *(see p224)*, is the preserve's main highway. River runners regard the wild 350-mile (550-km) descent of the Noatak as one of Alaska's best river trips. The trips, which can take up to three weeks, involve a bush flight into the Noatak headwaters from either Kotzebue or Bettles, with a pickup in Noatak village.

## ❾ Cape Krusenstern National Monument

50 miles (80 km) NW of Kotzebue. **Transport map** C2. ✈ charter bush plane from Kotzebue. 🛈 171 3rd Ave, Kotzebue; 442-3890, (800) 478-7252. 🆆 **nps.gov/cakr**

The broad coastal plain of the haunting Cape Krusenstern National Monument is made up of 114 parallel limestone bluffs and ridges that create the Chukchi Sea coastline. In the autumn, this changing landscape of alternating lagoons and beaches attracts migrating waterfowl with its swarms of protein-rich insects. There is also rewarding bird-watching, hiking, and wildlife viewing.

The monument's only facility is a lonely summer ranger station at Anigaaq, near the beach ridges. There are no roads, trails, cabins, or campsites, and visits must be carefully planned.

which rise as high as 250 ft (75 m), were created when glacier-ground rock was deposited and built up in an area where vegetation could not take hold.

The park is popular with river runners, who fly to Walker Lake and raft, canoe, or kayak 260 miles (416 km) down the Kobuk River over three weeks to the village of Kiana. Those who prefer a tamer adventure fly to Ambler, just east of the park entrance, and float the relatively mild 85-mile (136-km), six-day section to Kiana.

## ❽ Noatak National Preserve

200 miles (320 km) NE of Kotzebue. **Transport map** C2. ✈ charter bush plane from Kotzebue. 🛈 171 3rd Ave, Kotzebue; 442-3890, (800) 478-7252. 🆆 **nps.gov/noat**

The wonderfully wild Noatak National Preserve, between the DeLong and Baird Mountain Ranges, encompasses some of the loneliest landscapes in the country and protects an array of plants and wildlife. The Noatak River, with its

### The Blanket Toss

The blanket toss, in its most traditional form, is performed using a large walrus hide blanket held by a dozen or more people. The jumper stands in the middle of the blanket and while those holding the sides count to three, he or she makes increasingly higher jumps, as on a trampoline. Once a bit of altitude and momentum are gained, those holding the fringes provide a serious boost, and the jumper is propelled high into the air. Historically, the toss was used to allow lookouts to gain a bit of elevation over the largely flat coastline and determine whether whales, seals, walrus, or polar bears were visible on the ice or out at sea. Today, it is used mostly in celebration of a successful whaling season, hence the Inupiat name of Barrow's main festival, Nalukataq, which means "blanket toss." Blanket tosses are also staged for visitors in Barrow and at the Alaska Native Heritage Center in Anchorage. Although they will not have a chance to be tossed in the air, they can participate as blanket holders.

Propelling a jumper skyward at a blanket toss, Kotzebue

# Alaskan Wildflowers and Berries

Beginning in the spring and through the short northern summer, a series of wildflowers splash color across the Alaskan landscape. Plants of the same species may bloom as much as six weeks apart, depending on their location. Perhaps the finest show is in the Pribilof Islands, where the summer-long sequence of wildflower displays is renowned. Throughout Alaska, from mid- to late summer, edible berries emerge, many developing from the flowers of the early summer. In the late summer, after the salmon runs, this rich harvest provides sugar for the bears, to fatten them before they take to their winter dens.

**Salmonberries** can be either red or yellow in color.

**Wild blueberries** are popularly used in pies and desserts.

**Lowbush cranberries** are tart fruits that grow in both muskeg and tundra.

## Berries

*Wild strawberries grow in southern and central Alaska in late June, followed by the cloudberries and blueberries that carpet many parts of the state. Rose hips and lowbush cranberries ripen in late summer.*

**Labrador tea** grows mainly in muskeg.

**The aromatic leaves** can be used as tea.

**The chocolate lily**, also called skunk lily due to its smell, is found in damp woodlands and open meadows.

**Lupines**, found in a range of elevations, bloom in June.

## Wildflowers

*During Alaska's short flowering season in the summer, the forests, bogs, and meadows are alive with the brilliant colors of blooming wildflowers. Tiny northern anemones and delicate pasqueflowers appear first, often just after the snow melts. At the height of summer, bright fireweed, lemon yellow Arctic poppies, skunk cabbage, and other flowers carpet the landscape.*

**The alpine forget-me-not**, Alaska's state flower, blossoms between May and August.

**Fireweed in full bloom**

### Fireweed

Every summer, large swathes of the landscape turn purple as fireweed blooms. The young stems and leaves are rich in vitamins A and C, and Athabaskans have long eaten them either boiled or raw, and used raw cut stems to draw infection from boils. When the blooms go to seed and turn to cotton fluff, leaving only the topmost flower, Alaskans say that the winter is only six weeks away.

**Villous cinquefoil**, one of the first wildflowers to bloom, grows in cracks in boulders and cliff faces.

# ⑩ Nome

650 miles (1,050 km) W of Fairbanks.
**Transport map** C2. ⚙ 3,600. ℹ 301
Front St, 443-6555. 🏁 Iron Dog
Snowmobile Race (mid-Feb), Iditarod
Finish, Bering Sea Ice Classic Golf
Tournament (both after the Iditarod,
mid-Mar), Midnight Sun Festival (Jun
21). ⓦ visitnomealaska.com

Nome's curious name probably
dates from the 1850s, when a
British officer scrawled "?Name"
across a naval chart. It is said
that a draughtsman later misread
this as "Nome." Attractively
situated on the shores of Norton
Sound, this mixed Inupiat and
Anglo community is the
commercial and transport hub
for northwest Alaska.

A former Gold Rush town,
Nome is today less busy than
it was in its heyday in the late
1890s, when "The Three Lucky
Swedes", Jafet Lindberg, Erik
Lindblom, and John Brynteson,
discovered gold in nearby
Anvil Creek. In 1899, gold was
also found in the beach sands
(see pp56–7). Over 30,000
people staked claims, sparking
a boom that lasted until 1906,
when Nome quickly slipped
into obscurity.

However, gold fever has
not entirely faded in modern
Nome. The public beach, from
the end of the seawall to the
roadhouse, is open for

Semipalmated sandpiper in the meadows
around Nome

recreational mining and in the
summer, a motley colony of
hopeful prospectors camp
here. Clad in wet suits, they
brave the freezing, ice-choked
waters of Norton Sound, using
diesel-powered dredges to
process the sands and collect
what remains of the gold.

Nome is also famous for its
superb bird-watching and as the
finish line of the Iditarod. Visitors
in January can see the whimsical
Nome National Forest, created
each year when residents plant
their old Christmas trees in the
sea ice just outside town.

### 🎫 The Burled Arch

Front St. ⓦ iditarod.com
Each March, the official finish
line, called the Red "Fox"
Olson Trail Monument and
better known as the Burled

Arch, becomes the ultimate
destination of all Iditarod
mushers (see pp42–3). The
original arch, with the inscrip-
tion "End of the Iditarod Dog
Race," was erected for the first
Iditarod in 1975. It succumbed
to dry rot after 26 years and was
replaced with a large burled
spruce log, which rests outside
the Town Hall in the summer.
During the race, a kerosene
lantern hangs from the arch
until the last competitor crosses
the finish line and retrieves it,
winning the Red Lantern Award.
This tradition recalls the early
days of transport in Alaska,
when mushers carrying goods
or mail would look for the
lanterns hanging outside
roadhouses along the route.

### 🏛 Carrie M. McLain Museum

223 Front St. **Tel** 443-6630.
**Open** noon–6pm Tue–Sat.
🖼 ♿ ⓦ nomealaska.org/
museum

Named after its founder, this
renovated city-run museum
reveals Nome's colorful history
with original displays on its Gold
Rush days. Other exhibits focus
on modern Nome, as well as on
historic aviation, the arts and
culture of the Bering Strait Inuit,
the world-famous Iditarod, and
the original Nome Kennel Club
and its All Alaska Sweepstakes
sled dog race.

### ✝ Old St. Joseph's Catholic Church

279 King Place, Anvil City Square.
**Tel** 443-7856.
Nome's oldest building, the
1901 St. Joseph's Catholic
Church, was built on the
waterfront as a counterpoint
to the rollicking Gold Rush
atmosphere of the time. On
its steeple, a cross lit by electric
lights served as a beacon to
guide mushers and miners into
town. Eventually, the building
fell into decay and a new one
was built. In 1996, the old church
was moved to its present site,
restored, and given a new
steeple. The church is now a
community hall. In front of it are
statues of Lindberg, Lindblom,
and Brynteson. The building is
only open for special events.

Dog team finishing the Iditarod in Nome

# Exploring Beyond Nome

Located on the Seward Peninsula, Nome may be remote, but it is the hub of an extensive wilderness road system. Most visitors rent a vehicle or join a tour to explore the area's wild hinterlands. The drive east along the coast to Council includes fine bird-watching and the remains of a failed railroad, while the Kougarok Road accesses remote hot springs. The Teller Road leads through spectacular scenery to the end-of-the-world village of Teller on the windswept coast of the Bering Sea.

## Sights at a Glance

① Council Road
② Kougarok Road
③ Teller Road

## Key

═══ Minor road
── Trail

### 🏕 Council Road

72 miles (115 km) to Council.

The causeway-like Council Road follows the coastline east of Nome past campsites of wildcat prospectors, who mine the beach sands with gas-powered dredges. Passing superb bird-watching sites at the marshes of **Safety Sound**, it arrives at the photogenic **Last Train to Nowhere**, three locomotives and several decrepit railcars of the 1881 Council City and Solomon River Railroad that stand rusting on the tundra at Mile 33. The railway was envisioned as part of a link between Nome and the Lower 48, but the plans were abandoned in 1907 due to a lack of funds. At this point, the road turns inland, through the tiny village of **Solomon**, now virtually abandoned. After crossing scenic Skookum Pass, the road reaches its end at the Niukluk River. There is a ford into the Gold Rush village of **Council**, but the village is best accessed with the help of local boat owners.

### 🏕 Kougarok Road

89 miles (143 km) to Kougarok Bridge.
**Pilgrim Hot Springs** Turn-off at Mile 62. **Tel** 443-5252.

Also known as the Taylor Road, the wonderfully scenic Kougarok Road passes through the Kigluaik Mountains, paralleling the Wild Goose Pipeline, which was built in 1909 to transport water to Nome but never used. North of the mountains, a graveled spur road leads to an oasis of cottonwood trees at **Pilgrim Hot Springs**. The site has a simple wooden hot tank, which visitors can use after getting a permit from the Nome Visitor Center. Beyond the springs, the road passes through wetlands and tundra to its end at **Kougarok Bridge**. From here, a rough track leads to Taylor.

### 🏕 Teller Road

66 miles (110 km) to Teller.

Leaving Nome, this beautiful, lonely road follows clearwater streams, grasslands, and steep climbs on its way to **Teller**. Passing through the Kigluaik Mountains, it reaches rolling tundra, where there is a good chance of seeing wild musk oxen and domestic reindeer. Teller, at the westernmost tip of this westernmost road in North America, lies on a gray gravel spit at Port Clarence on the Bering Sea. It is known as the site where Norwegian explorer Roald Amundsen landed after his legendary 70-hour airship flight over the North Pole in 1926.

Rusting engines and railcars of the Last Train to Nowhere, on the tundra east of Nome

**For keys to symbols** *see back flap*

Granite tors at the Bering Land Bridge National Preserve

## ⓫ Bering Land Bridge National Preserve

100 miles (160 km) N of Nome.
**Transport map** C2. 🛩 charter bush plane from Nome or to Deering, then hike. 🛈 Sitnasuak Building, 214 Front St, Nome; 471-2352. **Open** year-round. 🅰 🆆 nps.gov/bela

Designated a National Monument in 1978, Bering Land Bridge received National Preserve status when ANILCA was passed in 1980 *(see p61)*. Encompassing 4,200 sq miles (10,900 sq km), the preserve commemorates the 55-mile- (88-km-) long and 1,000-mile- (1,600-km-) wide land bridge that once connected North America and Asia *(see p53)*. It is believed that during the last major Ice Age, this bridge allowed the passage of both prehistoric wildlife and early human settlers from Asia into North America. Around 15,000 years ago, the melting of the ice caused a gradual rise in sea level, and the land bridge disappeared beneath the waves of the newly formed Bering Strait.

The broad Arctic landscape of the preserve includes wide expanses of tundra, as well as scenic granite tors that bear testament to the area's distant volcanic past. The six public use cabins scattered around the preserve, and the 20-bed bunkhouse and hot tub at the preserve's main attraction, **Serpentine Hot Springs**, may be used free of charge and require no reservations, although users may have to share the space with other parties. The preserve's visitor center in Nome has exhibits, maps, and videos showcasing its cultural and natural history.

Access into the preserve is almost exclusively by bush plane in the summer and snowmachine in the winter, although a few people do hike the 40 miles (64 km) to Serpentine Hot Springs from Kougarok Bridge.

## ⓬ Gambell

230 miles (370 km) E of Nome.
**Transport map** B3. 🚹 680. 🛩 from Nome. Permits: needed to access lagoons and other areas.

The small Siberian Yup'ik village of Gambell sits on beach gravel at the northwestern corner of St. Lawrence Island, which measures 70 miles (112 km) in length and includes the even more isolated village of **Savoonga**. Lying near the Siberian coast, the island is one of Alaska's most remote outposts.

When ANCSA was passed in 1971 *(see p60)*, Gambell and Savoonga decided not to participate, and thus gained title to about 1,780 sq miles (4,600 sq km) of land. The villagers are therefore able to charge an "outsider tax" from non-residents wishing to access the lagoons and areas around the village and farther afield.

Getting around the island requires an ATV, and visitors can usually get rides from the villagers for a small fee. Most visitors to the island come to view birds not seen elsewhere in North America, including several incidental Eurasian species such as Lapland longspurs. Summer visitors can also spot flocks of eider ducks, murres, kittiwakes, puffins, and auklets either nesting or heading north.

In addition to the birdlife, the island's main attractions include the unique boneyards south of the village and at the base of Sivaquaq Mountain, where waste from Native hunts – mainly whalebones – is tossed. Walrus ivory from the yards is now carved and sold to visitors.

The remote Yup'ik village of Gambell on St. Lawrence Island

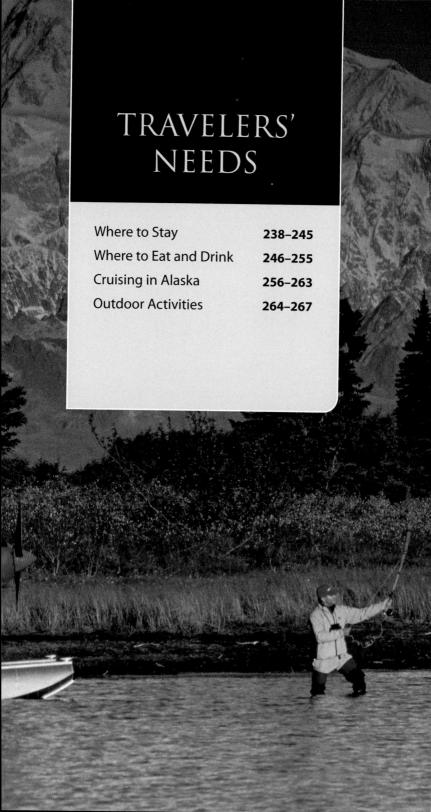

# TRAVELERS' NEEDS

Where to Stay                  238–245

Where to Eat and Drink         246–255

Cruising in Alaska             256–263

Outdoor Activities             264–267

# WHERE TO STAY

The extensive range of accommodation offered in Alaska ranges from rustic campsites along remote hiking trails to business-class hotel rooms in Anchorage, Fairbanks, and Juneau. Those who prefer to experience local flavour have a choice of bed-and-breakfast accommodation ranging from simple lodges to well-appointed houses with home-grown vegetables and gourmet cuisine. Budget travelers will find a selection of low-priced hostels accessible by public transport. In the bush, a number of hunting, fishing, and wildlife-viewing lodges offer wilderness luxury far from the well-trodden routes. For more information, refer to the detailed listings on pages 242–245.

Hotel Captain Cook in downtown Anchorage *(see p242)*

### Seasonal Pricing

While the summer months of June, July, and August offer the year's finest weather, summer prices in Alaska are often two to three times the off-season rates. Between October and April, many of the hostels, hotels, and bed-and-breakfasts located away from urban areas are closed, as are most federal and state campsites. In larger cities, winter hotel rates for luxury rooms may be a true bargain. Exceptions are the Alyeska Ski Resort and those hotels in the Interior that cater to visitors wishing to see the aurora borealis. Here high season can last all year. During the Fur Rondy and the Iditarod Trail Sled Dog Race *(see p49)* in February and March, prices in Anchorage and some other places along the race route may be higher than the usual winter discount rates.

Generally, Alaska has two shoulder seasons, in May and September. Hoteliers may offer discounts of up to 25 percent during these months.

### Choosing a Hotel and Getting There

In nearly every town, hotels compete for visiting business travelers by offering convention facilities and wireless Internet connections. Fairbanks, Juneau, Ketchikan, and Anchorage have the most expensive business hotels. Most towns also have comfortable motels providing decent, relatively inexpensive accommodation, as well as historic and independent hotels filled with period furnishings and run with meticulous attention to detail. Virtually all historic Alaska hotels are non-smoking. In addition, a selection of mid-range and budget choices offer travelers a simple bed, a hot shower, and basic amenities.

Some of the better hotels have free telephone links in the baggage claim areas at Anchorage, Fairbanks, and Juneau airports, as well as at many Alaska Marine Highway terminals. Travelers can use these to arrange rooms or free shuttle transport from the airport or ferry terminal to the hotel. Most cruise ship passengers will have pre-booked rooms in finer establishments near tourist sites.

Most bed-and-breakfasts within a few minutes' drive of a ferry terminal or airport are happy to provide transport for booked guests. Hikers and backpackers hoping to stay in hostels or campsites will have to rely on rental cars or taxis.

### Hostels

Alaska has a network of more than 25 official **Alaska Hostel Association** hostels scattered around the state. Largely offering no-frills amenities, these inexpensive options provide a basic place to sleep, most often in a shared dormitory setting with toilets and showers down the hall, as well as communal cooking facilities. Dorms are usually single sex, although, if requested, a private room may

Dating from 1916, the Historic Anchorage Hotel *(see p242)* with its old-time ambiance

◄ Fishing adventure by floatplane, with Denali in the background

Kenai Princess Wilderness Lodge *(see p242)* in Cooper Landing on the Kenai Peninsula

occasionally be arranged for couples traveling together. While hostels usually provide basic bedding and linen, travelers often bring their own sheets or sleeping bags.

Most hostels offer lockers where luggage or valuables can be stored, as well as a games or television room and laundry facilities. In several places guests are locked out between 9am and 5pm. For this inconvenience, hostelers can expect to pay less than 50 percent of the price of a bed in an inexpensive hotel.

## RV Parks

Driving through Alaska in a recreational vehicle or RV *(see pp288–9)* is an extremely popular way of seeing the state. While most RVs can be accommodated at "pull-through" sites in public campgrounds, only private RV parks offer such amenities as hook-ups and dump stations. The better RV parks also provide hot showers, bathrooms, and laundromats. Some even have cable TV and Wi-Fi access. Full hook-up facilities can cost up to $80 per night. Normally, even those not staying at the site can use the showers for a small fee. RV parks are found in most cities and towns along the highway system, as well as in most Marine Highway ports in Southeast and Southcentral Alaska.

## Hotel Chains

Anchorage and other large cities have many hotel chains, including **Sheraton Hotels**, **Hilton**, **Hawthorn Suites**, **Embassy Suites**, **Extended Stay**, **Hampton Inn**, **Super 8 Hotels**, **Best Western**, **Marriott Inns**, and **Holiday Inn**. There is little to differentiate one from the other, apart from desired price and location. Many of the newer hotels have large rooms, Wi-Fi access, buffet breakfasts, small fridges and microwaves, and king-size beds. Shuttle services to and from the airport are often available. For cruise ship passengers and visitors looking for a lavish wilderness experience, **Princess Lodges** offer interesting architecture and comfortable accommodation in and around major tourist sites.

## Bed-and-Breakfasts

While the bed-and-breakfast idea is relatively new to Alaska, it has rapidly become popular. B&Bs come in many shapes and sizes, but unlike their European counterparts, they are not a budget option. Guests should be prepared to pay at least what they would for an average mid-range hotel room.

The advantage offered by B&Bs is the chance to meet friendly locals and fellow guests while staying in cozy, comfortable homes rather than in impersonal hotels. Many of these places are lovingly tended by people who take pride in their gardening and culinary skills, and who treat their guests not only to excellent breakfasts but often to memorable experiences. Some of the best B&Bs are in quiet neighborhoods or idyllic rural areas, while the more convenient ones in town centers tend to be functional places.

For those who have not pre-booked, a good way to find a B&B is via the brochures stacked in every airport, ferry terminal, and tourist office. Many, but not all B&Bs, are members of the **Bed and Breakfast Association of Alaska**, which can help in finding and booking a room. Some of the best choices are included in the listings on pp242–5.

The facade of the Historic Anchorage Hotel *(see p242)*

Talon Loge, on a private island, offers superb views of the Sitka shoreline

## Campgrounds

Alaska has two main types of campgrounds – public and private. Generally, public campgrounds occupy scenic sites in national and state parks, wildlife refuges, forests, recreation areas, and game sanctuaries. The **Alaska Public Lands Information Centers (APLIC)** provide details on public campgrounds, most of which are not reservable. **Lifetime Adventures** makes reservations for some **Alaska State Park** campgrounds. **Reserve Denali** takes bookings for that popular park. It is worth arriving early on summer weekends to find a good camping spot.

While public campgrounds offer few amenities, they do provide spacious individual campsites and easy access to scenic outdoor attractions. Sites located in government campgrounds along the road system will offer parking spaces, picnic tables, and a basic barbecue pit. Communal facilities usually include outhouses and public water pumps.

A few of the campgrounds administered by the **Chugach National Forest** or **Tongass National Forest** may be used free of charge. However, most of the state and nationally administered sites charge nightly fees for pitching a tent or parking an RV. Some campgrounds include pre-cut firewood in the price of the site. Most of these places are open from mid- or late May to early September. Those that stay open through the winter generally shut down the water supply in early September.

## Public Use Cabins

In the Chugach and Tongass National Forests, as well as in several state parks and recreation areas, more than 200 cabins are available for overnight use. Most of these public use cabins are in remote areas or along hiking trails. Access to these isolated cabins is almost always on foot, by boat, or by floatplane.

Many cabins have wood stoves and ranger-provided firewood. They usually contain bunks for eight or more people. Mattresses are not provided and travelers need to bring their own ground pads and sleeping bags. Alaskan public use cabins require pre-booking, and with few exceptions, are available to only one party at a time. Because they get booked up quickly between June and August, reserve in advance, especially in popular locations such as Chugach State Park, Nancy Lake State Recreation Area, and in the Chugach National Forest. National forest cabins may be booked up to six months in advance at **www.recreation.gov**, while state park cabins can be booked with **Alaska State Parks Public Use Cabins**.

Private cabin, Kachemak Bay State Park

## Wilderness Lodges

Dotted around the wildest parts of Alaska, wilderness lodges offer accommodation in remote areas off the road system. Usually accessed by boat or bush plane, most have their own dock, airstrip, or floatplane landing facility. While many are hunting or angling lodges, several cater to visitors interested in photography, wildlife viewing, and hiking. Their prices reflect not only the undeniable beauty of the sites, but also the exclusivity of the lodge, the quality of the experience, and the difficulties of accessing and supplying such remote locations. In the most expensive places, prices include accommodation, meals, activities, guides, and local boat or plane transport. Many fishing lodges also provide fishing equipment and freezer space. In the mid-priced lodges, guests can expect to pay a set rate for accommodation, as well as a substantial charge for a bush flight or boat transport and additional charges for meals and activities. While those

The comfortable House of the Rock B&B in Valdez

willing to share rooms or cabins with other guests may be able to get a discount, the tariff will still be two or three times what a traveler would usually pay at a hotel in town. Details of some of the best lodges are included in the listings (see pp242–5).

### Recommended Hotels

The hotels on the pages that follow have been carefully selected to cover a variety of accommodation options, from historic city hotels, extended

stay and bed-and-breakfast places, to the most modern high-rises and luxury wilderness lodges. The list also includes youth hostels, campgrounds for backpackers and RV guests and lodging for travelers on a budget. Entries labelled as DK Choice highlight places that stand out in some way; this might be for their exceptional surroundings, historic architecture, excellent service, friendly hosts, or fine on-site restaurants. For map references to Anchorage see pp68–9.

## DIRECTORY

### Hostels

**Alaska Hostel Association**
W alaskahostel association.org

### Hotel Chains

**Best Western**
Tel (888) 780-7234.
W bestwesternalaska.com

**Embassy Suites**
Tel (800) 362-2779.
W embassysuites.com

**Extended Stay**
Tel (800) 804-3724.
W extendedstay america.com

**Hampton Inn**
Tel (800) 426-7866.
W hamptoninn.com

**Hawthorn Suites**
Tel (800) 337-0202.
W hawthorn.com

**Hilton**
Tel (800) 445-8667.
W hilton.com

**Holiday Inn**
Tel (888) 465-4329.
W holidayinn.com

**Marriott Inns**
Tel (888) 236-2427.
W marriott.com

**Princess Lodges**
Tel (800) 426-0500.
W princesslodges.com

**Sheraton Hotels**
Tel (800) 325-3535.
W starwoodhotels.com

**Super 8 Hotels**
Tel (800) 8454-2313.
W super8.com

### Bed-and-Breakfasts

**Bed and Breakfast Association of Alaska**
W alaskabba.com

### Campgrounds

**Alaska Public Lands Information Center**
Anchorage
605 W 4th Ave, Suite 105.

Tel 644-3661.
W alaskacenters.gov/ anchorage.cfm

**Fairbanks**
101 Dunkel St. Tel 459-3730. W alaskacenters.gov/fairbanks.cfm

**Ketchikan**
50 Main St. Tel 228-6220.
W alaskacenters.gov/ketchikan.cfm

**Tok**
Mile 1314 Alaska Hwy.
Tel 883-5667.
W alaskacenters.gov/tok.cfm

**Alaska State Parks**
Tel 269-8400.
W dnr.alaska.gov/parks

**Chugach National Forest**
161 East 1st Ave, Door #8, Anchorage. Tel 743-9500.
W fs.usda.gov/chugach

**Lifetime Adventures**
Tel (800) 952-8624.
W lifetimeadventures.net

**Reserve Denali**
Mile 237 George Parks Highway No. 3.
Tel (866) 761-6629.
W reservedenali.com

**Tongass National Forest**
648 Mission St, Ketchikan.
Tel 225-3101. W fs.usda.gov/tongass

### Public Use Cabins

**Alaska State Parks Public Use Cabins**
550 W 7th Ave, Suite 1260, Anchorage. Tel 269-8400.
W dnr.alaska.gov/parks/cabins

**Recreation.gov**
Tel (877) 444-6777.
W recreation.gov

# Where to Stay

## Anchorage

### Downtown

**Anchorage Downtown Hotel** $$
Boutique     **Map** C5
*826 K St, 99501*
**Tel** *866-258-7669*
W theanchoragedowntown
hotel.com
Convenient for the ocean, shops
and galleries, and the green space
of Delaney Park. Rooms have com-
fy beds, free Wi-Fi, coffee maker,
microwave, and fridge. There's
an airport shuttle in summer.

**Anchorage Grand Hotel** $$
Modern     **Map** C4
*505 W 2nd Ave, 99501*
**Tel** *907-929-8888*
W anchoragegrand.com
Comfortable downtown suites
with full kitchens, plus a business
center. Near the 5th Ave Mall and
five blocks from the Coastal Trail.

**Copper Whale Inn B&B** $$
B&B     **Map** B5
*440 L St, 99501*
**Tel** *866-258-7999*
W copperwhale.com
In a historic building with pretty
gardens just a block from the
Coastal Trail. The 15 rooms, some
en suite, are small but clean and
charming, with views across Cook
Inlet. There's one two-room suite.

**Historic Anchorage Hotel** $$
Boutique     **Map** D4
*330 E St, 99501*
**Tel** *907-272-4553*
W historicanchoragehotel.com
Opened in 1916 and fully
restored in 1989; convenient for
shopping, the 5th Avenue Mall
and Coastal Trail. Free Wi-Fi,
breakfast, fitness center, business
center. Helpful staff include a 24-hr
concierge. Rooms are spacious
and clean, if a bit dated in décor.

### DK Choice

**Hotel Captain Cook** $$$
Luxury     **Map** B5
*939 W 5th Ave, 99501*
**Tel** *907-276-6000*
W captaincook.com
One of Downtown's premier
business hotels, this high-rise
comes with a gym, pool, spa,
business center, hair stylists, and
four restaurants. Several rooms
boast spectacular views of Cook
Inlet. The top floor suites and
some tower rooms offer a lounge
with free breakfast and snacks.

**Sheraton Anchorage**
**Hotel & Spa** $$$
Luxury     **Map** F5
*401 E 6th Ave, 99501*
**Tel** *907-276-8700*
W sheratonanchorage.com
Rooms are large, with big flat-
screen TVs and fridges. The
business and fitness centers are
open 24 hours; the Ice Spa is a
highlight, with treatment rooms
overlooking Cook Inlet.

### Greater Anchorage

**Spenard Hostel International** $
Hostel     **Map** E1
*2845 W 42nd Ave, 99517*
**Tel** *907-248-5036*
W alaskahostel.org
Clean, basic bunks with linens
provided; three kitchens and
common areas, book exchange
and travel library, yard with
barbecue and off-street parking.

**11th Avenue Bed & Breakfast** $$
B&B     **Map** E1
*334 W 11th Ave, 99501*
**Tel** *855-446-1410*
W 11thavenue.net
In a quiet historic area; rooms
are simply furnished, with private
bath and premium bedding.
Full breakfast and 24-hour
snack service.

**Oscar Gill House** $$
B&B     **Map** E1
*1344 W 10th Ave, 99501*
**Tel** *907-279-1344*
W oscargill.com
Three clean, unassuming rooms
in a charming restored 1913
home, situated in a quiet
neighborhood bordering Cook
Inlet, but close to downtown and
the Coastal Trail. Two rooms have
a shared bathroom.

The Historic Anchorage Hotel offers comfort
and traditional décor

**Dimond Center Hotel** $$$
Luxury     **Map** E2
*700 E Dimond Blvd, 99515*
**Tel** *907-770-5000/866-770-5002*
W dimondcenterhotel.com
Sleek architecture, and art from
the Kachemak Bay region. The
large, modern rooms have
oversized tubs. Airport shuttle,
fitness center, free breakfast
buffet, and business center.

**Embassy Suites Anchorage** $$$
Modern     **Map** F1
*600 E Benson Blvd, 99503*
**Tel** *907-332-7000*
W embassysuitesanchorage.com
Well-equipped suites midtown,
with lots of amenities and extras,
from a pool and spacious hot tub
to complimentary full breakfast
cooked to order. Good service.

## The Kenai Peninsula

**COOPER LANDING: Kenai**
**Princess Wilderness Lodge** $$
Wilderness Lodge     **Map** B3
*17245 Frontier Circle, 99572*
**Tel** *907-595-1425* **Closed** *Oct–Mar*
W princesslodges.com
Frequently booked by Princess
Tour Groups, this rustic lodge
in a beautiful location features
vaulted ceilings, wood-burning
stoves, a river-view deck, and
a massive central fireplace.

**HOMER: Land's End Resort** $$$
Luxury     **Map** A4
*4786 Homer Spit Rd*
**Tel** *800-478-0400*
W lands-end-resort.com
Beautifully situated near the ferry
terminal at the end of Homer Spit,
this nautical-themed resort offers a
spa, sauna, hot tub, a fitness center,
and fine seafood dining. Ocean
charters can be organized.

**KENAI: Diamond M Ranch** $
Wilderness Lodge     **Map** A3
*48500 Diamond M Ranch Rd, 99611*
**Tel** *907-283-9424*
W diamondmranchresort.com
Bunkhouse rooms, cabins, or suites
in the main lodge; good amenities,
a fish-cleaning station, and free
Wi-Fi. Organized potluck and
campfire socials are a highlight.

## DK Choice

**KENAI: Hi-Lo Charters and Riverside Lodge** $$$
Wilderness Lodge **Map** A3
*1105 Angler Dr, 99611*
**Tel** *907-398-4162*
W hilofishing.com
Here at Beaver Hole on the lower Kenai River, a top fishing location, lodging consists of suites, each with two bedrooms, one bath, a full kitchen, and an outdoor deck or patio. Social activities include picnicking, horseshoes, and evening cocktails.

**NIKISKI: Grouchy Old Woman B&B** $
B&B **Map** A3
*48570 N Earl Dr, 99611*
**Tel** *907-776-8775*
W grouchyoldwoman.homestead. com
Located on Daniels Lake in Nikiski, north of Kenai, with flower gardens and a rural setting. Refrigerator space and laundry service available, and one room has a private bath. Full cooked breakfast.

**SEWARD: Van Gilder Hotel** $$
Boutique **Map** A3
*308 Adams St*
**Tel** *907-224-3079*
W vangilderhotel.com
This historic hotel, built in 1916, is listed in the National Register of Historic Places. The period furnishings, including brass beds and a library of Alaskana, provide a unique experience of staying amid modern Alaskan history.

**SOLDOTNA: Best Western King Salmon Motel** $$
Modern **Map** A3
*35545 Kenai Spur Hwy, 99669*
**Tel** *907-262-5857*
W bestwestern.com
Laundry facilities, restaurant on site. Rooms are basic and clean, with coffee maker, fridge and microwave. Fitness center, ample parking, free Wi-Fi and breakfast.

## Prince William Sound

**VALDEZ: Best Western Valdez Harbor Inn** $$
Modern **Map** E4
*100 N Harbor Dr, 99686*
**Tel** *907-835-3434*
W valdezharborinn.com
Standard décor, but large, comfortable beds and a harbor-side location. Rooms and suites have lots of amenities and free Wi-Fi. Restaurant and bar on site; breakfast is complimentary.

**VALDEZ: House on the Rock B&B** $$
B&B **Map** E4
*613 S Moraine Dr, 99686*
**Tel** *907-831-9027*
W houseontherockbandb.com
In town close to the docks, shops and trail. Rooms are "rustic Alaska" but with private baths, free Wi-Fi and flat-screen TVs. Common areas include kitchen and diner, laundry, and a popular massage chair.

**WHITTIER: The Inn at Whittier** $$
Modern **Map** E4
*5A Harbor Loop Rd*
**Tel** *907-472-3200*
W innatwhittier.com
Perched above the rocky shore of Passage Canal on Prince William Sound, this coastal-themed place overlooks Whittier's small boat harbor. The acclaimed dining room features local seafood.

## Southeast Alaska

**JUNEAU: Alaskan Hotel & Bar** $
Boutique **Map** F4
*167 S Franklin St, 99801*
**Tel** *907-586-1000/800-327-9347*
W thealaskanhotel.com
The oldest hotel in downtown Juneau, built in 1913, is on the National Register of Historic Places. Choose a room with shared or private bath or a suite. Décor is dated but clean.

**JUNEAU: Historic Silverbow Inn** $$
Boutique **Map** F4
*120 2nd St, 99801*
**Tel** *907-586-4146*
W silverbowinn.com
In a convenient downtown location, with free Wi-Fi, full breakfast, and on-site restaurant and wine bar. Rooftop deck with hot tub. Rooms are spacious and simply furnished, with private baths. One has a whirlpool tub.

**JUNEAU: Westmark Baranof** $$
Luxury **Map** F4
*127 N Franklin St, 99801*
**Tel** *907-586-2660*
W westmarkhotels.com
Located near the harbor, museums, shopping, and restaurants, this Art Deco hotel is a favorite of business travelers. Clean, simple rooms have standard modern furnishings and free Wi-Fi. Fitness center, lounge, two restaurants.

The Historic Silverbow Inn with its rooftop hot tub

## DK Choice

**JUNEAU: Alaska's Capital Inn** $$$
B&B **Map** F4
*113 W 5th Street, 99801*
**Tel** *907-586-6507*
W alaskacapitalinn.com
This 1906 Arts & Crafts mansion sits in a quiet residential neighborhood overlooking the waterfront, and is an easy walk to downtown. The large rooms feature period furnishings; some have whirlpool tubs and fireplaces. Lush garden with a covered hot tub, and a lavish cooked breakfast.

**KETCHIKAN: Cape Fox Lodge** $$
Wilderness Lodge **Map** F5
*800 Venetia Way, 99901*
**Tel** *866-225-8001*
W capefoxlodge.com
Ski lodge-style hotel surrounded by big trees, with Native art, restaurant, comfortable lounge and views of the Tongass National Forest. Rooms are spacious.

**KETCHIKAN: Inn at Creek Street and New York Hotel** $$
Boutique **Map** F5
*207 Stedman St, 99901*
**Tel** *907-225-0246*
W thenewyorkhotel.com
Historic building overlooking the Thomas Basin and Inside Passage. Accommodations range from modern loft units, rooms with period furnishings in a former brothel on the waterfront, and apartment-size suites with full kitchens. Flat-screen TVs, free Wi-Fi, on-site restaurant.

**For more information on types of hotels** see pp238–41

## DK Choice

### KETCHIKAN: Silverking Lodge $$$
Wilderness Lodge     **Map** F5
*Grant Island, 20 miles NW of Ketchikan, 99901*
**Tel** *800-813-4363*
W silverkingalaska.com
A family-run lodge situated on a private island with a boardwalk built over the water. After fishing excursions that are included in the price, visitors are welcomed with a comfortable room, a hot shower, a home-cooked meal, and a lounge with an open fire.

### SITKA:
Sitka International Hostel    $
Hostel     **Map** E5
*109 Jeff Davis St, 99835*
**Tel** *907-747-8661*
W alaskahostelassociation.org
Housed in the historic Tillie Paul Manor, this quiet and clean hostel is near the sea and just blocks away from downtown. Guests enjoy an entertainment room, a library, laundry services and a kitchen.

### SITKA: Alaska Ocean View Bed & Breakfast $$
B&B     **Map** E5
*1101 Edgecumbe Dr, 99835*
**Tel** *907-747-8310*
W sitka-alaska-lodging.com
Three rooms with lovely down comforters on the beds. Free organic breakfast, outdoor barbecue, hot tub, and croquet.

## DK Choice

### SITKA: Talon Lodge & Spa $$$
Wilderness Lodge     **Map** E5
*Private island, Sitka, 99835*
**Tel** *1-800-536-1864*
W talonlodge.com
A short boat trip from Sitka, with unspoiled views of the Inside Passage and the ocean. Private and multi-room lodging is offered. Gourmet meals are prepared each night. Package prices also include local transport, guides, boats, and equipment.

### SITKA: Wild Strawberry Lodge $$$
Wilderness Lodge     **Map** E5
*724 Siginaka Way, 99835*
**Tel** *907-747-3232*
W wildstrawberrylodge.com
Everything is about fish here, and packages include salmon and halibut charters, fishing gear, and fish-cleaning with chefs who prepare the catch. Accommodations include suites, cabins, and a three-bedroom house.

Cabin-style accommodation at Mount Aurora Lodge

### SKAGWAY: Chilkoot Trail Outpost $$
B&B     **Map** E4
*In Dyea beside National Park campgrounds*
**Tel** *907-983-3799*
W chilkoottrailoutpost.com
Get away from it all in individual, well-equipped log cabins, one off site. There's a campfire pit, a nearby waterfall, and a retreat center. Breakfast included.

## Western Interior

### DENALI HIGHWAY: MacLaren Lodge $$
Wilderness Lodge     **Map** E3
*Mile 42 Denali Hwy*
**Tel** *907-269-4370*
W maclarenlodge.com
This secluded lodge at the McLaren River offers rooms, cabins, bunks, a remote glacier camp, and a very Alaskan roadhouse café. Wilderness canoe trips are available.

### DENALI VILLAGE: Crow's Nest $$
Wilderness Lodge     **Map** E3
*Mile 238.5 Parks Hwy*
**Tel** *907-683-2723*
W denalicrowsnest.com
The cabins of this rustic lodge climb the hillside above Denali Village. There is an atmospheric bar and dining room, all with panoramic views. Free shuttle to Denali National Park headquarters.

### FAIRBANKS: Ah, Rose Marie Downtown Bed & Breakfast $
B&B     **Map** E2
*302 Cowles St, 99701*
**Tel** *907-456-2040*
W ahrosemarie.com
Two quaint 1930s historic homes an easy walk to downtown. Accommodating hosts offer rooms furnished with antiques with private baths and full breakfasts.

### FAIRBANKS: Billie's Backpackers Hostel $
Campground/Hostels     **Map** E2
*2895 Mack Blvd, 99709*
**Tel** *907-479-2034*
W alaskahostel.com
Good for aurora viewing: stay in a dorm, private room, gazebo, or tent. Free linens, storage, bike use, Wi-Fi, phone, coffee/tea, showers.

### FAIRBANKS: Aurora Borealis Chalet & Lodge $$
Modern     **Map** E2
*1906 Ridge Run Rd, 99707*
**Tel** *907-389-2812*
W auroracabin.com
Twenty miles north of Fairbanks, in an ideal spot for aurora viewing (the two-bedroom chalet has a viewing platform). Spacious rooms.

### FAIRBANKS: Aurora Express Bed & Breakfast $$
B&B     **Map** E2
*1550 Chena Ridge Rd, 99708*
**Tel** *907-474-0949*
W fairbanksalaskabedand breakfast.com
Fabulously quirky accommodations in authentic railroad cars refitted Victorian-style, on tracks overlooking the Tanana Valley. Breakfast is served in the dining car.

### FAIRBANKS: Mount Aurora Lodge $$
Modern     **Map** E2
*2320 Fairbank Creek Rd, 99712*
**Tel** *907-389-2000*
W mountauroralodge.com
A former gold miner bunkhouse and mess hall remade as cabin-style rooms. Spacious lounge, full breakfast. Near skiing and town.

## DK Choice

### FAIRBANKS: Chena Hot Springs Resort $$
Wilderness Lodge     **Map** E2
*Mile 56.5 Chena Hot Springs Rd*
**Tel** *451-8104*
W chenahotsprings.com
This charming, environmentally sound resort is the best place for comfortable rooms, along with the best hot springs soaks and aurora-viewing in Alaska. Camping and budget yurts are also available.

### TALKEETNA: Denali Fireside Cabins & Suites $$
Modern     **Map** E3
*22647 Talkeetna Spur Rd, 99676*
**Tel** *907-733-2600*
W denalifireside.com
Suites and cabins in rustic Alaskan style, have gas fireplaces, private baths and kitchenettes, and private decks with scenic views.

**TALKEETNA: Denali Overlook Inn** $$$
Modern **Map** E3
29198 Talkeetna Spur Rd, 99676
**Tel** 907-733-3555
**w** denalioverlookinn.com
Spectacularly situated, with views of Denali. The spacious rooms, suites and one cabin have free Wi-Fi. Full cooked breakfasts.

## Eastern Interior

**COPPER CENTER: Copper River Princess Wilderness Lodge** $$
Wilderness Lodge **Map** E3
1 Brenwick Craig Rd, 99573
**Tel** 907-822-4000
**w** princesslodges.com
Ski lodge-style, with forest or mountain views. Basic rooms, free Wi-Fi, restaurant, bar, and coffee shop. Wilderness excursions arranged. Daily shuttle service to the nearby Wrangell-St. Elias National Park visitor center.

### DK Choice

**KENNICOTT: Kennicott Glacier Lodge** $$$
Wilderness Lodge **Map** F3
15 Kennicott Millsite, 99588
**Tel** 907-258-2350
**w** kennicottlodge.com
An exceptional location amid glorious scenery. Rooms in the main lodge share bathrooms and are small but clean; the newer south wing rooms have private baths but no phones, TVs, or other amenities. The restaurant serves breakfast, lunch, and family-style dinner.

**TOK: Burnt Paw Cabins** $$
B&B **Map** F3
Mile 1314.3 Alaska Hwy, 99780
**Tel** 907-883-4121
**w** burntpawcabins.com
Rustic log cabin rentals with breakfast, private bath, satellite TV, microwave, fridge, and Wi-Fi. Dog team equipment on show, as are puppies when available.

## Southwest Alaska

**DILLINGHAM: Beaver Creek B&B** $$
B&B **Map** C4
1800 Birch Cir, 99576
**Tel** 907-842-7335
**w** dillinghamalaska.com
Rooms in the main house and large cottages and cabins. Full kitchens, phones, TV, limited Internet, laundry facilities.

**DUTCH HARBOR: Grand Aleutian Hotel** $$
Modern **Map** B5
498 Salmon Way
**Tel** 907-581-3844
**w** grandaleutian.com
This enormous chalet-style hotel rises above the waters of Margaret Bay affording superb views of the surrounding sea and mountains. Rooms are simple but clean. There are a variety of dining options.

**KING SALMON: Brooks Lodge** $$$
Wilderness Lodge **Map** D4
Brooks Camp, Katmai National Park
**Tel** 907-243-5448
**w** katmailand.com/brooks-lodge
A short hike from the famous Brooks Falls, this basic lodge and restaurant provides comfortable access to bear-viewing and the Valley of 10,000 Smokes. Packages include transport from Anchorage.

### DK Choice

**KING SALMON: Alagnak Lodge** $$$
Wilderness Lodge **Map** D4
Alagnak River north of King Salmon
**Tel** 800-877-9903
**w** alagnaklodge.com
A dream destination for serious anglers, poised on a bluff overlooking the Alagnak River and Bristol Bay watershed. Guides, boats, and all meals provided; the cooking is of a high order, the rooms clean and comfy, and the ambiance conducive to swapping of tall fishing tales.

**KODIAK: Best Western Kodiak Inn and Convention Center** $$
Modern **Map** D4
236 W Rezanof Drive, 99615
**Tel** 907-486-5712
**w** bestwestern.com
Standardized décor, as one might expect, but great on amenities, with a fitness center and hot tub, restaurant, bar, free cooked breakfast, self-service laundry, airport shuttle, and business facilities. Rooms are spacious, with TV, coffee maker, fridge and microwave.

**KODIAK: Afognak Wilderness Lodge** $$$
Wilderness Lodge **Map** D4
Afognak Island, 99697
**Tel** 360-799-3250
**w** afognaklodge.com
This remote lodge in Afognak Island State Park prides itself on its eco-tourism options. Rates include a room or cabin, fishing gear and transport, kayaking, use of the sauna, and family-style meals.

## Arctic & Western Alaska

### DK Choice

**BARROW: Top of the World Hotel** $$$
Modern **Map** D1
3060 Eben Hopson St, 99723
**Tel** 907-852-3900
**w** tundratoursinc.com
Exceptional rooms, with clean modern furnishings, coffee maker, free Wi-Fi, and Arctic Ocean views. 24-hour front desk, ATM, fitness room, coin laundry, kitchen facilities, and an on-site restaurant where you can sample traditional Native foods.

**NOME: Dredge No. 7 Inn** $$
Modern **Map** C2
1700 Teller Hwy, 99762
**Tel** 907-304-1270
**w** dredge7inn.com
In a private location near to town. Free Wi-Fi and clean rooms with historic ambiance. Private baths, TV, fridge, microwave.

**NOME: Nome Nugget Inn** $$
Modern **Map** C2
315 Front St, 99762
**Tel** 877-443-2323
**w** nuggetinnhotel.com
Expect the usual mod cons here: private bath, free Wi-Fi, fridge, microwave, on-site bar. Ocean-view rooms tend to be quieter.

**PRUDHOE BAY: Prudhoe Bay Hotel** $$
Modern **Map** E1
100 Main St, 99734
**Tel** 907-659-2449
**w** prudhoebayhotel.com
Near the airport and geared to local workers and visitors. Excellent wildlife viewing. Popular buffet restaurant, gift shop, Internet access. Shared or private baths.

The beautiful Grand Aleutian Hotel reflected in Margaret Bay

# WHERE TO EAT AND DRINK

Most of the larger cities in Alaska have a variety of eateries serving better-than-average fare that spans a range of cuisines reflecting the many immigrant communities that are part of the Alaskan population. Anchorage provides the widest selection, including Indian, Japanese, Vietnamese, and Greek restaurants. Fairbanks, Juneau, Homer, and some of the smaller towns also present a number of fine choices. Nearly all mid-sized communities have Chinese, Mexican, and fast food restaurants, and even the smallest bush community will usually have a basic eatery, a coffee shop, supermarket, food stalls, or a cannery canteen. Mobile or static lunch wagons provide welcome pitstops in many remote areas. Alaskan cuisine includes hearty, filling dishes, featuring well-prepared steak and a range of seafood. Portions are generous and may come with large starters, and as many baskets of bread or tortilla chips as are requested by the diners.

## Types of Restaurants

The most expensive options are the true gourmet restaurants, which are found only around Anchorage or in larger towns, but many mid-range restaurants in other areas offer dishes that approximate gourmet standards.

The majority of Alaskan restaurants are individual and family-run and range from satisfying to superb. In small highway towns and along the road system, roadhouses provide excellent breakfasts, lunches with homemade soups, and a variety of filling dinners. The larger hotels usually have their own restaurants, which in wilderness areas may be the only places to eat in the vicinity. The larger towns have chain restaurants that offer decent food at good prices and in very generous portions that few people can finish. The assumption is that most diners will pack up the leftovers in a doggy bag to eat later. Many supermarkets have bakeries, delis, noodle bars, sushi bars, and cafés for quick and filling fare.

Towns of all sizes have at least one fast food joint serving up the usual range of burgers, fried chicken, sub sandwiches, pizzas, or tacos.

## Reservations and Dress Codes

While dining in Alaska is most often casual and informal, advance dinner reservations are recommended for upscale places, and in the case of popular restaurants that don't accept bookings, it pays to arrive as early as possible. When it comes to dress, Alaska is possibly the most relaxed state in the country, and only a few of the finest restaurants request jackets and ties.

## When to Eat

In Alaska, breakfast is often served as early as 6am to allow guests to eat and get a good start on the day's activities. The

The Exit Glacier Salmon Bake in Seward knows how to reel in a crowd

first meal of the day can be anything from fruit, toast, and coffee to a hearty spread that includes juice, eggs cooked to order, ham, steak, bacon, or sausage. Fried potatoes, biscuits and gravy, pancakes, and several Mexican possibilities involving eggs, beans, vegetables, salsa, tortillas, and cheese may also be on the menu.

Lunch, therefore, can often be a lighter meal than breakfast, especially when there are so many daytime activities to choose from. Staples include appetizing soups – often fish chowder – and salads, burgers, or sandwiches.

Dinner is the main meal of the day, and is usually eaten between 5 and 9pm. In the long daylight hours of summer, Alaskans tend to eat late, after recreational activities are finished for the day, and outdoor evening barbecues are very popular. Dinner usually includes fish or meat – beef, pork, chicken, and occasionally moose or even reindeer – as well as a vegetable dish, a salad, and potatoes.

A converted railway tram car houses Smoke Shack in Seward

Pleasant outdoor seating at a restaurant on Homer Spit

## What to Eat

Alaskan cuisine (see pp248–9) is hearty, as befits its heritage as an adventurous, outdoorsy state, and has some of the world's finest fish and game. In urban restaurants, meals range from the usual Alaskan meat-and-potatoes fare to international options such as Italian, Greek, Mexican, Thai, Chinese, Korean, and Japanese food.

Above all, Alaska has access to superlative seafood, from plump, cold-water Kachemak Bay oysters and Alaska king crab to halibut and, of course, wild Alaska salmon, one of the most popular products of the state. In the summer, restaurants and tourist-oriented businesses in many towns organize salmon bakes – often served in an all-you-can-eat style – with freshly caught wild salmon.

## Prices and Tipping

Despite the fact that shipping distances dictate higher prices than those found in the Lower 48, visitors will find that restaurant meals in Alaska generally represent good value. In fact, in hotels, locally run places, and sit-down chain restaurants, generous portions of tasty, filling food will cost only a bit more than if you prepared them yourself. What the food might lack in sophistication, it amply makes up for in quantity and taste. Even fine-dining restaurants are reasonably priced and provide value for money.

As with any restaurant in the country, tipping is essential. Restaurant employees are typically paid low wages under the assumption that customers will liberally tip the servers and bus staff. Tips are usually determined by the quality of the service received, with the average being around 15–20 percent. A tip of 10 percent will make it clear that the service was lacking, while 20 percent will indicate an appreciation of outstanding service.

## Vegetarian Choices

Despite the local fondness for fish and game, vegetarians will be happy to find that most Alaskan restaurants cater to a wide variety of preferences, and that Anchorage, Juneau, and Fairbanks have some excellent places specializing in vegetarian cuisine. In small towns, Asian places are usually the best bet for vegetarian meals, and wilderness lodges offer buffets with both vegetarian and meat-oriented selections. Visitors on cruises or organized tours will also find that their culinary preferences are almost universally accommodated.

## Children

Most Alaskan restaurants cater to children with simple meals that include hot dogs, French fries, burgers, and other items that appeal to the younger set. These will typically cost around half the price of an adult meal. In addition, many places provide high chairs, play areas, coloring books, and crayons to keep kids busy while they wait for their meals.

## Accessibility

The US is perhaps one of the world's most progressive countries in terms of providing easy access to public buildings for guests with mobility challenges, and new buildings are designed with accessibility in mind. Still, many restaurants in Alaska's small towns are in older buildings that date from the Gold Rush era and have not been modernized. In remoter areas where dining options are limited, it might be wise to check online or call ahead.

## Recommended Restaurants

The best way to find a decent meal is to ask locals, including hotel staff and taxi drivers, who are usually pleased to promote their favorite spots. Tourist offices can provide listings but may not make recommendations.

The restaurants on pp250–55 offer options for every region to suit every budget and taste. The DK Choice heading highlights establishments that offer terrific food, exceptional service, or perhaps occupy an unrivalled location; they may simply be the locals' favorite for brunch or a great steak and beer, or elevate food from the mediocre to the sublime with innovative use of ingredients, often sourced locally from nearby fisheries and gardens. Whatever the reason, they will offer a memorable dining experience.

For map references to Anchorage see pp68–9.

Ketchikan's popular Bar Harbor Restaurant (see p253)

# The Flavors of Alaska

From Alaska's cold waters, commercial deep-sea fishermen harvest some of the world's best wild salmon, halibut, and cod, as well as three species of crab and other shellfish. Seafood is served grilled, baked, or broiled, or preserved by smoking, drying, or canning. Hunters bring in game meat such as Dall sheep, moose, caribou, and black-tailed deer, which are prepared in a variety of creative ways. A range of local produce, including potatoes, carrots, and other "winter" vegetables, is grown commercially in Delta Junction and the Mat-Su Valley; some of these grow to gargantuan proportions in the long daylight hours of the Alaskan summer *(see p88).*

Alaskan crowberries and lowbush cranberries

Commercial crab fisherman off Juneau in Southeast Alaska

### Alaskan Food

Alaska's cuisine reflects the variety of people who have come to the state from all over the US and other parts of the world. However, most ethnic foods have been adapted to local tastes. Local specialties include pizzas made with reindeer sausage, bolognaise sauces made with moose meat, and taco fillings that include carrots and halibut. Fresh vegetables play less of a role than they do in the Lower 48. Instead, most Alaskans favor hearty fare that is heavy on meat and fish. In the summer, barbecued meat or grilled fish is accompanied by sourdough bread, salads, light soups, and local vegetables, while in the winter, a typical meal would include a bowl of warming chili or beef, game, or chicken stew, along with potato dishes and vegetable casseroles topped with cheese and breadcrumbs.

The most reliable places to find authentic Alaskan "home cooking" are wilderness lodges and roadhouses along the highway system, which serve up hearty, filling fare that usually features meat, potatoes, and cold-weather vegetables.

Salmon filet

Salmon steak

Halibut filet

Trout

Shrimp

Scallops

A selection of fresh seafood available in Alaska

### Alaskan Dishes and Specialties

Alaskan sourdough

Most fine Alaskan restaurants serve local seafood using various creative recipes for wild salmon and halibut, as well as king, Dungeness, and snow crab. Available in season, these are most often served as a pile of legs and claws, accompanied by a selection of dipping sauces. Game meat is also a staple and a few restaurants offer options such as reindeer sausage. Potatoes figure prominently in most meals, and the most popular vegetables used are hardy varieties that can be grown in cold climates. Meals may also feature Alaskan sourdough bread, which was popularized during the Gold Rush. It is made with a starter, which contains a yeast that causes the dough to rise. The periodic addition of sugar keeps the yeast growing and some starters in use today date from the early 1900s. Desserts include pies, tarts, or cobblers made from local wild berries.

**Salmon**, an iconic Alaskan dish, is served grilled, baked, or alder-smoked with lemon, dill, and melted butter. Alaska has five species of Pacific salmon.

Sampling beer at the Alaskan Brewing Company *(see p144)* in Juneau

## Vegetables and Fruits

Alaska's main agricultural area, the Matanuska Valley, produces a wide range of cold-climate vegetables such as carrots, squash, zucchini (courgettes), potatoes, kohlrabi, rutabagas (swedes), cauliflower, broccoli, and turnips. These are usually used in stews, baked into casseroles, or eaten as stand-alone dishes after being baked, boiled, or mashed. The climate of Anchorage, the Kenai Peninsula, and the Mat-Su is also suitable for growing orchard fruits such as apples and cherries, although not in commercial quantities. Rhubarb and a wide variety of berries grow well through much of the southern half of the state. Most are cultivated in gardens and canned, made into jams and jellies, or baked into delicious pies.

## Beer and Wine

The state has seen a growth of microbreweries in the larger towns, where many pubs and brewhouses will offer a selection of craft ales. Alaska's largest fully fledged brewery is the Alaskan Brewing Company in Juneau. Its range of award-winning beers include stout, amber, pale ale, and both summer and winter ales, which are available all over Alaska, as well as in the western states.

Alaska's climate is too cold for growing wine grapes, but that does not stop a few enterprising winemakers producing refreshing wines, either from imported grape must or from local flowers, fruits, and other produce – birch sap, honey, and even potatoes, onions, and carrots. In Homer, Bear Creek Winery produces rhubarb, blueberry, and raspberry wines. Anchorage's Denali Winery imports grapes to produce palatable vintages.

### Native Foods

**Akutaq** "Eskimo ice cream" is made by the Inuit from seal oil, whipped berries, and snow.

**Caribou, moose, black-tailed deer** Hunted by Alaska Natives in Southeast, Interior, and Arctic Alaska, wild game meat is dried, frozen, or eaten in any meat-based recipe.

**Dried fish** Fish are preserved by drying them on large racks.

**Smoked fish** Fish are smoked in a wood-fired smoker, usually using alder wood, which adds a fine flavor.

**Whale** This beef-like meat is a favored part of the local diet. Inupiat villages are allowed to harvest a quota of whales.

**Muktuk** Whale blubber, the fatty layer beneath the outer skin, is chewed raw or softened by boiling or pickling.

**Berries** Historically, berries such as salmonberries, elderberries, and blueberries were the main source of sugar in the Native diet.

**Crab legs and claws** are steamed or boiled and served with a variety of sauces. Diners need a crab-cracker to extract the meat from the shell.

**Reindeer sausage pizza** is a thick crust pizza spread with marinara sauce and cheese, topped with reindeer sausage, roasted peppers, and onions.

**Wild blueberry pies** are made by baking berries with sugar, cornstarch, and lemon juice in a pie shell. They are served with whipped cream.

# Where to Eat and Drink

## Anchorage
### Downtown

**Alaska's Gourmet Sub** $
Café       Map D5
601 W 7th Ave, 99501
**Tel** 907-297-7827     **Closed** Sun
A favorite with local workers for
a quick lunch featuring soups
and subs. A good choice of
breads, dressings, and fillings,
including several veggie options.
Also serves gyros, wraps, pizzas,
and a daily special. Lunch only.

**Brown Bag Sandwich Co.** $
Pub       Map D4
535 W 3rd Ave, 99501
**Tel** 907-277-0202
Hearty sandwiches are good
value at $10. A favorite is grilled
spicy roast beef made with
London broil, cheddar, Dijon
mustard, and horseradish on
marble rye. Local beers. Open
only for lunch.

**Midnight Sun Café** $
Café       Map E4
245 W 5th Ave, 99501
**Tel** 907-743-0572
Breakfast bagels, croissants,
muffins, and scones. For lunch,
deli and grilled sandwiches,
paninis, salads, smoothies.
Lots of teas and fresh-roasted
specialty coffee.

**Humpy's Great Alaskan
Alehouse** $$
Pub       Map D5
610 W 6th Ave, 99501
**Tel** 907-276-2337
Steamer clams, chowder, wings,
salads, burgers, sandwiches, and
fresh seafood. The selection of
craft beers is outstanding. There's
live music through the week, and
an outdoor patio.

**The Red Chair Café** $$
Café       Map E1
337 E 4th Ave, 99501
**Tel** 907-270-7780
Slick urban atmosphere. Lots of
vegetarian and vegan options,
as well as burgers, steaks, and
sandwiches, omelets and other
breakfast dishes. Beer and wine.

**Snow City Café** $$
Café       Map E1
1034 W 4th Ave, 99501
**Tel** 907-272-2489
Popular for all-day breakfast and
brunch, with omelets, breakfast
sandwiches, biscuits and gravy,
and eggs Benedict. Vegan and
gluten-free options.

**White Spot Café** $$
Café       Map E4
109 W 4th Ave, 99501
**Tel** 907-279-3954
No-frills diner serving breakfast
and lunch with super-fast service
– a good spot for quick family
meals. Breakfast is the favorite,
especially biscuits and gravy.

**Club Paris** $$$
Steakhouse       Map D5
417 W 5th Ave, 99501
**Tel** 907-277-6332
Cozy and unpretentious, often
voted Anchorage's best steak
house. Sandwich meats are
smoked or roasted in-house.
Steaks include filet mignon,
New York, rib eye, and prime
rib; there's also fresh Alaskan
seafood, combos of meat and
fish, a few simple salads and
sides, and desserts such as tart
key lime pie and chocolate sweet
potato pie. Limited wine list, big
beer list.

**Crush Wine Bistro & Cellar** $$$
Café       Map D5
343 W 6th Ave, 99501
**Tel** 907-865-9198     **Closed** Sun
More than 40 wines by the
glass and a wide choice of
beers. Salads, soups, desserts,
and light dishes change daily
and are offered with wine
pairings. Hip, cozy atmosphere.
Wine shop upstairs.

**Ginger** $$$
Asian       Map D5
425 W 5th Ave, 99501
**Tel** 907-929-3680
Pacific Rim-style food such
as tamarind-cashew shrimp,
spring rolls, spicy ahi tuna
and Korean BBQ ribs. Lots of
salads and vegetarian options;
separate bar menu. Sleek,
stylish interior.

### DK Choice

**Glacier Brewhouse** $$$
Pub       Map D5
737 W 5th Ave Ste 110, 99501
**Tel** 907-274-2739
This is a popular local gathering
spot and is busy most evenings.
It has a big, rowdy, rustic wood
dining room, serving up fresh
seafood, wood-grilled steaks,
ribs and chicken, pastas, pizzas,
sandwiches, and salads. Kids'
and gluten-free options for
lunch, dinner, and dessert.
Huge selection of craft beers
on tap.

### Price Guide

The price ranges cover a main dish with
sides, taxes, and service charges, but
exclude alcoholic beverages.

$          up to $25
$$        $25 to $50
$$$      over $50

### DK Choice

**The Marx Bros Café** $$$
Seafood       Map D4
627 W 3rd Ave, 99501
**Tel** 907-278-2133   **Closed** Sun &
Mon
Fine dining in a simple, quiet
dining room. The limited
seating makes reservations a
necessity. Appetizers include
seared foie gras, fresh Alaska
oysters, and Neapolitan seafood
mousse. Favorite entrées are
wild-caught salmon, braised
rabbit, tea-smoked duck, and
grilled scallops. Desserts are
elegant and there's a huge
wine selection. Dinner only.

**Sacks Café and Restaurant** $$$
Seafood       Map D4
328 G St, 99501
**Tel** 907-276-3546
Contemporary diner-style décor at
this friendly place serving lunch and
dinner, with brunch too on Saturday
and Sunday. Menu selections
include seafood, pastas, risottos,
pork, and duck, imaginatively
prepared. Daily home-made soup
and salads. Good wine list.

**Sullivan's Steakhouse** $$$
Steakhouse       Map D5
320 W 5th Ave, 99501
**Tel** 907-258-2882
This upscale chain features hefty
steaks, from an 8-oz filet to a
26-oz rib eye. Live music in the
evening, specialty cocktails, and
a large wine list.

The popular Glacier Brewhouse with its big
rustic dining room

## Greater Anchorage

### Great Harvest Bread Co. $
Café **Map** F1
*570 E Benson Blvd, 99503*
**Tel** *907-274-3331* **Closed** *Sun*
Different fresh-baked breads
including wonderful pesto
bread, cookies, scones and
pound cakes daily. Treats
include chocolate chip oatmeal
cookies, blueberry scones, and
tasty ham and cheese rolls.

### Taco King $
Mexican **Map** F1
*113 W Northern Lights, 99503*
**Tel** *907-276-7387*
This is a simple restaurant
serving food as authentic as
the one served in the street
cafés of Mexico. Open for lunch
and dinner.

### Gwennie's Old Alaska
### Restaurant $$
Roadhouse **Map** E2
*4333 Spenard Rd, 99517*
**Tel** *907-243-2090*
This traditional roadhouse-style
place is renowned for its hearty
breakfasts, big enough to keep
you going all day. It serves equally
generous lunches and dinners
and is packed with Alaskans.

### Moose's Tooth Pub & Pizzeria $$
Pizzeria **Map** F1
*3300 Old Seward Hwy, 99503*
**Tel** *907-258-2537*
Legendary pizza place with a
huge and inventive selection of
toppings, plus succulent chicken
wings, wide choice of in-house
beers, and brewed root beer.
Come early or prepare for a wait.

### Samurai Sushi Garden $$
Japanese **Map** F1
*1265 Muldoon Rd, 99504*
**Tel** *907-332-1020*
Classic, very fresh Japanese sushi
rolls, California rolls, bento boxes,
tempura, and soups. Children's
menu. A good selection of sake
and beer; fast service.

### Spenard Roadhouse $$
Café **Map** E1
*1049 W Northern Lights Blvd, 99503*
**Tel** *907-770-7623*
A clean, modern dining spot with
a varied menu, including Thai
curry, jambalaya, flatiron steak,
fish and chips, soups, salads, and
sandwiches. Local beers and
small-batch bourbon.

### Thai Kitchen $$
Thai **Map** E4
*3405 E Tudor Rd, 99507*
**Tel** *907-561-0082*
A modest yet always packed, long
time local-favourite is known for

Distinctive graffiti at Gwennie's Old Alaska Restaurant in Great Anchorage

bringing the best of Bangkok to
Anchorage. The home-cooked
Thai cuisine is delicious and the
atmosphere friendly.

### DK Choice

**Double Musky Inn $$$**
Cajun/Creole **Map** E4
*3 Crow Creek Rd, 99587*
**Tel** *907-783-2822* **Closed** *Mon*
An extremely popular and
often cited as Alaska's finest
dining, the Double Musky Inn
has a lively atmosphere.
It specializes in gourmet New
Orleans-style Cajun cuisine
and serves scrumptious dishes
such as shrimp etouffee,
salmon au poivre and sausage
jambalaya. Reservations are
not accepted.

### Jen's Restaurant $$$
Seafood **Map** F1
*701 W 36th Ave, 99503*
**Tel** *907-561-5367* **Closed** *Sun*
Jen's boasts an ever-changing
Alaskan/Danish menu, which
features fresh-caught oysters,
salmon, rockfish, and scallops, as
well as farm-raised duck, pork,
lamb, and beef specialties.
House-made pastas and salads
complement the big wine list.
Paintings by local artists adorn
the elegant dining room.

### Kincaid Grill & Wine Bar $$$
Seafood **Map** E2
*6700 Jewel Lake Rd, 99502*
**Tel** *907-243-0507* **Closed** *Sun &*
*Mon*
Fine dining on Alaskan game
and seafood, and steaks. Try the
roasted beet salad with goat
cheese frittata, salmon with
chimichurri, tomato bacon jam
and grilled asparagus, then
chocolate bourbon soufflé. Large
wine list, boutique coffees, and
attentive service. Dinner only.

### Kinley's Restaurant & Bar $$$
Seafood **Map** F1
*3230 Seward Hwy, 99503*
**Tel** *907-644-8953* **Closed** *Sun*
Varied menu featuring fresh
seafood, pastas, salads, home-
made soups, burgers, and steaks.
Good vegetarian and gluten-free
options, wide wine list.

### DK Choice

**Villa Nova Restaurant $$$**
Mediterranean **Map** E2
*5121 Arctic Blvd, 99503*
**Tel** *907-561-1660* **Closed** *Sun–*
*Mon*
Sicilian Chef Georgio makes
everything from scratch,
and the menu features fresh
seafood choices that change
daily with the catch. Count
on classics such as veal
parmigiano, chicken piccata,
home-made pastas and sauces,
and tiramisu. Good wine list;
quaint Italian décor.

## The Kenai Peninsula

### DK Choice

**COOPER LANDING: Gwin's**
**Roadhouse $**
Roadhouse **Map** B3
*14865 Sterling Hwy, 99572*
**Tel** *907-595-1266*
A rustically atmospheric
pub, Gwin's Roadhouse
first opened in 1952. This
quintessentially Alaskan spot
is a favorite with anglers, who
stop by for refills and to swap
fish stories. Try the superb
home-made chili, smoked
salmon chowder and Mexican
specialties. Try the famous
fruit pies. Pre-packaged
lunches are also available.

**For more information on types of restaurants** *see pp246–7*

**COOPER LANDING: Sackett's Kenai Grill** $$
Café      Map B3
*16201, Mile 50.4 Sterling Hwy, 99572*
**Tel** *907-595-1827*
Combination pizzeria, barbecue joint, and bakery. Smoked prime rib sandwich for lunch is popular. Draft beer. Casual dining on picnic tables in good weather.

**HALIBUT COVE: Saltry Restaurant** $$$
Seafood      Map A4
*1 W Ismilof, 99603*
**Tel** *907-226-2424*
Enjoy fresh seafood in a dining room that offers wide ocean views. Words local, homemade, fresh, and organic feature heavily on the menu. The friendly waitstaff are adept at helping pair meals with the extensive selection of wines and beers.

**HOMER: Captain Pattie's Fish House** $$
Seafood      Map A4
*4241 Homer Spit Rd, 99603*
**Tel** *907-235-5135*    **Closed** *Mon*
Fresh local salmon and halibut, as well as king crab, oysters, and scallops are the best choices. The menu also offers steak, pastas and chicken, burgers, salads, and soups. Come early or make a reservation.

**HOMER: Chart Room Restaurant** $$$
Seafood      Map A4
*4786 Homer Spit Rd, 99603*
**Tel** *907-235-0400*
A sweeping view of the bay, with an outdoor deck for good weather dining. Baked halibut topped with crab is the signature dish. Fish specials according to the catch. Experienced waitstaff, full bar, and good wine list.

**KENAI: Burger Bus** $
Café      Map A3
*912 Highland Ave, 99611*
**Tel** *907-283-9611*    **Closed** *Sun*
Known for the biggest and best burgers in town, with the Kenai King a favorite – a succulent beef patty with bacon, jalapeno, cheese, onion, tomato, and home-made fries. Service is from a converted school bus, to eat or takeout; there are picnic tables for good weather.

**KENAI: Playa Azul** $
Mexican      Map A3
*104 Haller St, 99611*
**Tel** *907-283-2010*
Ignore the exterior and come for the Mexican favorites, including fresh fish tacos, carne asada, chimichangas and salsa bar.

**KENAI: Veronica's Old Town Coffee House** $
Café      Map A3
*604 Peterson Way, 99611*
**Tel** *907-283-2725*
Home-made soups, salads, sandwiches, quiches, and desserts. Specialty teas and coffees. Try the cinnamon apple pie with ice cream. Live entertainment Fri–Sat.

**KENAI: Louie's Steak & Seafood** $$
Seafood      Map A3
*47 Spur View Dr, 99611*
**Tel** *907-283-3660*
Stuffed wildlife and old Alaska artifacts in a lodge-style dining room. Portions of stroganoff, steamers, salmon, chowder, and halibut are huge, and the service is efficient and friendly.

**KENAI: Paradiso's Restaurant** $$
International      Map A3
*811 Frontage Rd, 99611*
**Tel** *907-283-2222*
Longtime favorite serving a mix of cuisines: Italian chicken Parmesan, Mexican enchiladas, Greek pizzas and gyros, American steaks, and seafood. Will deliver.

**NIKOLAEVSK: Samovar Café** $$
Russian      Map A4
*Nikolaevsk Village*
**Tel** *907-235-6867*
Enjoy traditional Russian fare at this tiny café located in Alaska's Old Believer community. Run by the engaging Nina Fefelov, this cafe is sought after for the experience it offers.

**SEWARD: Nature's Nectars** $
Café      Map B4
*1313 4th Ave, 99664*
**Tel** *907-422-0688*
Small, friendly takeout stand with specialty coffees, plus fruit and veggie smoothies made to order from fresh local ingredients.

Saltry Restaurant, perched above the water in Halibut Cove

**SEWARD: Le Barn Appetit** $$
Café      Map B4
*11786 Old Exit Glacier Rd, 99664*
**Tel** *907-224-8706*
Specializing in crepes and Belgian waffles; a favorite is the reindeer sausage with spinach and egg. Portions are huge, but seating limited (just 21 covers), so there are often long lines.

**SEWARD: Smoke Shack** $$
Café      Map B4
*411 Port Ave, 99664*
**Tel** *907-224-7427*
A fun venue with limited seating in a converted railway train car. Expect long lines for breakfast and take-out barbecue. Snow crab eggs Benedict, spicy breakfast burritos, French toast, biscuits and gravy, and hash are the specialties.

**SOLDOTNA: Firehouse BBQ** $
Steakhouse      Map A3
*43837 Kalifornsky Beach Rd, 99669*
**Tel** *907-252-7747*
All types of barbecue, such as pulled pork sandwiches, brisket and ribs, with beans and slaw. Stuffed potatoes are favorites. Dine in, drive-up to order for takeout, or eat at picnic tables in good weather.

**SOLDOTNA: The Moose is Loose** $
Bakery      Map A3
*44278 Sterling Hwy, 99669*
**Tel** *907-260-3036* **Closed** *Sun & Mon*
Doughnuts and other baked goods are the draw here, from cinnamon rolls to cookies and breads. The champagne cake doughnuts are a favorite. Lots of moose-themed trinkets and gifts in the adjoining gift shop.

**SOLDOTNA: Odie's Deli** $
Café      Map A3
*44315 Sterling Hwy, 99669*
**Tel** *907-260-3255*
A local institution, with a second location at Kenai Airport. Home-made soups change daily. Sandwiches are prepared with breads baked on the premises. Fresh salads, local beer on tap. Live music on Fridays.

**SOLDOTNA: St. Elias Brewing Company** $$
Pub      Map A3
*434 Sharkathmi Ave, 99669*
**Tel** *907-260-7837*    **Closed** *Mon*
Fresh pizzas, salads, sandwiches, and desserts served in a simple, bar-style setting, with outdoor seating for summer. As many as 11 ales are available on tap from the on-site brewhouse, as well as a large wine list with some Alaskan labels.

# Prince William Sound

**CORDOVA: Baja Taco** $
Mexican **Map** E4
*137 Harbor Loop Rd, 99574*
**Tel** *907-424-5599*
This quirky place with the kitchen
in a parked bus, a ramshackle
dining hall, and outdoor seating,
is popular for its huge servings of
Alaskanized Mexican staples.

**VALDEZ: Old Town Burgers** $
Café **Map** E4
*139 E Pioneer St, 99686*
**Tel** *907-831-0999*
Huge omelets and chicken-fried
steak are breakfast favorites.
Double cheeseburger serves two
and fish and chips are top rated.
Simple diner with picnic tables.

**VALDEZ: A Rogue's Garden** $
Café **Map** E4
*354 Fairbanks Dr, 99686*
**Tel** *907-835-5880* **Closed** *Sun*
A natural foods store and café
with organic espresso and
smoothie bar, fresh baked
pastries, and home-made soups,
salads, and sandwiches.

**VALDEZ: Alaska Halibut
House** $$
Seafood **Map** E4
*208 Meals Ave, 99686*
**Tel** *907-835-2788*
Fried halibut and shrimp platters
with home-made waffle fries
are to die for. Fresh and plentiful
portions in a modest setting.

**VALDEZ: Totem Inn Restaurant** $$
Café **Map** E4
*144 Egan Ave, 99686*
**Tel** *907-835-4443*
All types of fish and burgers, huge
breakfasts with the chili cheese
omelet a favorite. Busy, diner-type
ambiance. Fast, efficient service.

**WHITTIER: Varly's Swiftwater
Seafood Café** $$
Café **Map** E4
*Waterfront Triangle, 99693*
**Tel** *907-472-2550* **Closed** *winter*
Overlooking the harbour, this little
café uses fresh seafood. Try the
fish and chips made with halibut
and the desserts prepared from
local berries and rhubarb.

# Southeast Alaska

**JUNEAU: Alaskan Crepe Escape** $
Café **Map** F4
*350 S Franklin St, 99802*
**Tel** *907-586-1846* **Closed** *winter*
Big variety of sweet and savory
crepes. Try the Gastineau with

Shops and restaurants lining Front St, Ketchikan

salmon, cream cheese, spinach,
lemon, and herbs. Good
sandwiches and smoothies too.

**JUNEAU: Hangar on
the Wharf** $$
Seafood **Map** F4
*2 Marine Way, 99801*
**Tel** *907-586-5018*
Situated beside Gastineau
Channel, this aviation-themed
restaurant is housed in an old
floatplane dock. It specializes in
a wide range of Alaskan seafood
dishes, creative burgers and
salads. Bar features local
and imported beers.

**JUNEAU: Island Pub** $$
Pizzeria **Map** F4
*1102 2nd St, 99824*
**Tel** *907-364-1595*
In a newly refurnished historic
building on Douglas Island,
offering soups and salads,
chicken skewers, wraps and
wood-fired pizzas; the pizza
dough and focaccias are made
on site daily.

**JUNEAU: The Rookery Café** $$
Café **Map** F4
*111 Seward St, 99801*
**Tel** *907-463-3013* **Closed** *Sun*
Fresh baked goods, burgers,
sandwiches, and salads during
the day; a more refined menu
for dinner, prepared by an award-
winning chef.

**JUNEAU: Sandpiper Café** $$
Café **Map** F4
*429 W Willoughby Ave, 99801*
**Tel** *907-586-3150*
A favorite breakfast and brunch
spot; opt for French toast with
mounds of fresh fruit, eggs
Benedict, burritos, or a smoked
salmon omelet. Prepare to wait
for seating; contemporary décor.

## DK Choice

**JUNEAU: Tracy's King Crab
Shack** $$
Seafood **Map** F4
*406 S Franklin St, 99802*
**Tel** *907-723-1811*
On the pier at the cruise ship
dock. Feast on succulent
Bristol Bay king crab legs
fresh from the sea, king crab
bisque, and spicy crab cakes
or rolls; plus snow crab, scallops,
shrimp, and Dungeness crab
in the summer. The only sides
are garlic rolls, rice, and slaw.

**KETCHIKAN: Burger Queen** $
Café **Map** F5
*518 Water St, 99901*
**Tel** *907-225-6060* **Closed** *Sun*
Excellent, juicy, creatively
prepared burgers, chicken,
fish and chips, and thick
milkshakes in a plain little diner
with just four tables. Will also
deliver to all local areas.

**KETCHIKAN: Sweet Mermaids** $
Café **Map** F5
*340 Front St, 99901*
**Tel** *907-225-3287*
Specialty coffees and a good
variety of pastries, including
cakes, cookies, croissants, and
pies. Fresh chowder, sandwiches,
and salads too, plus free Wi-Fi,
make this a local favorite.

**KETCHIKAN: Bar Harbor
Restaurant** $$
Steakhouse **Map** F5
*55 Schoenbar Ct, 99901*
**Tel** *907-225-2813*
Attentive service and a varied
menu that includes juicy pot
roast, fresh seafood, steaks,
salads, pastas, and home-made
breads and desserts.

**SITKA: Highliner Coffee** $
Café                         Map E5
*327 Seward St, 99835*
**Tel** *907-747-4924*   **Closed** *Sat & Sun*
Drive-through and café with
house-roasted gourmet coffees,
teas, and fresh-baked pastries.
Wi-Fi and a selection of gifts in
the comfortable café; a popular
local hangout.

**SITKA: Homeport Eatery** $
Café                         Map E5
*209 Lincoln St, 99835*
**Tel** *907-966-2336*   **Closed** *Sun*
Rustic old cable house with
ocean views. Hot and cold
sandwiches, coffees and pastries,
chowder, big brunch selection.
Live music on weekends.

### DK Choice

**SITKA: Ludvig's Bistro** $$
Mediterranean               Map E5
*256 Katlian St, 99835*
**Tel** *907-966-3663*   **Closed** *Sun and Oct–Jan*
Famous for its service and its
cuisine: rustic Mediterranean
specialties featuring local
seafood and local produce.
Try the Alaskan rockfish, grilled
lamb chops with lentils, bistro
steak or fresh halibut. There's
also a wine bar and gallery
with an outdoor deck. Booking
is essential; limited offerings
in winter.

**SITKA: Channel Club** $$$
Steakhouse                  Map E5
*2906 Halibut Point Rd, 99835*
**Tel** *907-747-7440*
Elegant dining with a view of
Mt Edgecumbe. Attentive service.
Salmon and halibut specials,
prime rib and steaks cooked over
wood fires. Full wine list.

**SKAGWAY: Bites on Broadway** $
Café                         Map E4
*648 Broadway, 99840*
**Tel** *907-983-2166*
Friendly owners and service.
Breakfast sausage or bacon
and cheese biscuits are huge and
fresh; try chili or chowder for lunch.
Desserts include German
chocolate cake or red velvet cake.

**SKAGWAY: Red Onion Saloon** $
Pub                          Map E4
*205 Broadway, 99840*
**Tel** *907-983-2414*
Lodged in a gold-rush era bordello
dating from 1897, this lively saloon
shares the historic building with
a red-light-themed museum.
Popular for its pub meals and
diverse pizzas named after historic
madams, and a range of brews.

# Western Interior

**FAIRBANKS: Alaska Coffee
Roasting Co.** $
Café                         Map E2
*4001 Geist Rd, Ste 12, 99709*
**Tel** *907-457-5282*
Fresh-roasted coffee and fresh-
baked goods such as cinnamon
and pecan rolls. Savory flatbreads,
sandwiches, pizzas and soups.
Biscuits and gravy on weekends.

**FAIRBANKS: The Crepery** $
Café                         Map E2
*535 2nd Ave, 99701*
**Tel** *907-450-9192*
Filling and inventive crepes such
as savory smoked salmon or brie
and cranberry. For dessert, try the
crème brûlée and cheesecake
with fresh berries. Limited seating.

**FAIRBANKS: Fudge Pot** $
Café                         Map E2
*515 1st Ave, 99701*
**Tel** *907-456-3834*
Specializing in desserts, including
home-made fudge in 30 different
flavors; blueberry and cranberry
are made from Alaskan berries.

**FAIRBANKS: Pita Place** $
Middle Eastern              Map E2
*3300 College Rd, 99709*
**Tel** *907-687-2456*   **Closed** *Sun, Mon, and winter*
Perfectly spiced falafel and huge
pitas with sauces and veggies to
eat at picnic tables or take away.
Authentic Turkish coffee.

**FAIRBANKS: Bad 2 da Bone
BBQ** $$
Grill                        Map E2
*80 5th St, 99701*
**Tel** *907-699-2663*
Authentic pit barbecue ribs,
pulled pork, juicy brisket, chicken,

Try an Alaskan favorite, juicy steak, at one
of the region's steak houses

tri-tip beef, and home-made
sauces from a little place attached
to a gas station, and in summer
from a roving mobile food truck.

**FAIRBANKS: The Cookie Jar** $$
Café                         Map E2
*1006 Cadillac Ct, 99701*
**Tel** *907-479-8319*
Breakfast all day, with fresh baked
goods and large portions of eggs,
meats, and potatoes. Pastas, soups,
salads, and burgers for lunch;
steaks and seafood at dinner.

**FAIRBANKS: The Pump
House** $$
Seafood                      Map E2
*796 Chena Pump Rd, 99701*
**Tel** *907-479-8452*   **Closed** *Mon*
Enjoy Alaskan seafood, especially
fresh salmon dishes in the
historic Chena Pump House
overlooking the Chena River.

**FAIRBANKS: Thai House
Restaurant** $$
Thai                         Map E2
*412 5th Ave, 99701*
**Tel** *907-452-6123*   **Closed** *Sun*
Favorites from the large menu
include classic pad Thai, drunken
noodles, shrimp fried rice, and
red curry vegetables.

**FAIRBANKS: Wasabi Bay** $$
Japanese                     Map E2
*1448 S Cushman St, 99701*
**Tel** *907-452-0521*
Traditional and American-style
sushi with fresh-caught fish. Try
the salmon and white tuna, the
Caterpillar, or Cherry Blossom.

### DK Choice

**FAIRBANKS:
Lavelle's Bistro** $$$
Steakhouse                  Map E2
*575 1st Ave, 99701*
**Tel** *907-450-0555*
Friendly staff and excellent wine
list, with seating in the bar or
romantic main room. Menu
options include prime rib, filet,
halibut, lobster cakes, red prawn
curry, fresh local vegetables, and
Caesar salad. Crème brûlée
and double chocolate mousse
cake are popular desserts.
Reservations recommended.

**TALKEETNA: Flying Squirrel
Bakery Café** $
Café                         Map E3
*26205 Mile 11, Talkeetna Spur Rd, 99676*
**Tel** *907-733-6887*
Home-made soups served with
artisan bread, breakfast pastries,
desserts, deli salads and wraps.
Wood-fired pizzas on weekends.

**TALKEETNA: Spinach Bread** $
Café **Map** E3
*Main St, 99676*
**Tel** *907-354-8080* **Closed** *winter*
Addictive toasted bread topped with spinach, garlic, and cheese, and lovely Ethiopian coffee, served from a silver Airstream trailer.

**TALKEETNA: Mountain High
Pizza Pie** $$
Pizzeria **Map** E3
*22165 C St, 99676*
**Tel** *907-733-1234*
Crispy pizzas with more than 30 toppings, as well as salads and salmon mac and cheese. Jaunty décor, local beers on tap, and live music most summer evenings.

## DK Choice

**TALKEETNA: Talkeetna
Roadhouse** $$
Café **Map** E3
*13550 E Main St, 99676*
**Tel** *907-733-1351*
Huge meals served family-style in a frontier roadhouse more than 100 years old. Breads and pastries are made from scratch. The sourdough hotcakes, cream cheese brownies, Granny's chocolate potato cake, and gingersnaps are favorites. Try the Roadhouse Standard breakfast: eggs, home fries, and peppered bacon.

## Eastern Interior

**DELTA JUNCTION: The Cave
Wine Bar and Grille** $$
Grill **Map** E3
*266 Richardson Hwy, 99737*
**Tel** *907-895-1074* **Closed** *Sun*
Generous portions of steak, pasta, burgers, salads, and appetizers are served at this cosy restaurant and bar with a small-town atmosphere.

**COPPER CENTER: Tonsina River
Lodge Restaurant** $$$
Russian **Map** E3
*Mile 79 Richardson Hwy, 99573*
**Tel** *907-822-3000*
Try classics such as borscht, meat or veggie *blinchiki* (crepes), grilled steak or fish, or home-made soups. Family-style dining room and bar.

**KENNICOTT: Tailor Made
Pizza** $$
Pizzeria **Map** F3
*Lot 9, Mile 59 Edgerton Hwy,
Wrangell-St Elias National Park, 99588*
**Tel** *907-554-2324* **Closed** *winter*
Friendly diner in a converted bus near the mine, with terrific views. Fresh salads and local veggies, pizzas, noodle bowls, and wraps.

Enjoy Russian classics at Tonsina River Lodge

**TOK: Fast Eddy's Restaurant** $$
Café **Map** F3
*Mile 1313 Alaska Hwy, 99780*
**Tel** *907-883-4411*
Solid American fare – burgers, curly fries, milkshakes, hefty breakfasts with eggs, biscuits, and gravy, very fresh salad bar. Crowded and at times pretty boisterous, this is a local favorite.

## Southwest Alaska

**DILLINGHAM: Bayside Diner** $$
Café **Map** C4
*Bristol Inn, 104 Main St, 99576*
**Tel** *907-842-1013*
Fresh salads, sandwiches, and crab and shrimp dinners. Breakfasts are hearty and meat-centric, with bacon, ham, or reindeer sausage and fresh eggs.

**KING SALMON:
Eddie's Fireplace Inn** $
Pub **Map** D4
*1 Main St, 99613*
**Tel** *907-246-3435*
A fair option in this remote spot for burgers, pizzas, chicken strips, fish and chips, and sandwiches. Pizza served in the bar after the restaurant is closed. Breakfasts are huge, with specialty coffees.

**KODIAK: Java Flats** $
Café **Map** D4
*11206 Rezanof Dr, 99619*
**Tel** *907-487-2622* **Closed** *Mon*
The heavenly fresh-baked cookies are the stars, but breakfasts, light meals and vegetarian options, prepared with local produce are also great.

**KODIAK: Old Powerhouse
Restaurant** $$
Seafood **Map** D4
*516 E Marine Way, 99615*
**Tel** *907-481-1088* **Closed** *Sun lunch*
Enjoy some of the West Coast's freshest sushi at this restaurant housed in a historic power station right on the shore.

## Arctic and Western Alaska

**BARROW: Sam & Lee's** $$
Asian/American **Map** D1
*1052 Kiogak St, 99713*
**Tel** *907-852-5556*
The menu includes kimchi, pizza, egg drop soup, chicken-fried rice, and more Japanese, Chinese, and Korean dishes, plus American favorites such as breakfast pancakes.

**KOTZEBUE:
Bayside Restaurant** $
Café **Map** C2
*303 Shore Ave, 99752*
**Tel** *907-442-3600*
Famous for its extensive and eclectic menu, from sushi to cheeseburgers. Try the home-made strawberry lemonade. The Wi-Fi is free and fast.

**NOME: Airport Pizza** $$
Pizzeria **Map** C2
*406 Bering St, 99762*
**Tel** *907-443-7992*
Try the giant breakfast burrito, spicy pepper pizza, or Philly-style cheese steak. Dozens of combinations for pizzas and meals throughout the day. Some veggie options; free Wi-Fi.

## DK Choice

**NOME: Pingo Bakery-Seafood
House** $$
Café **Map** C2
*308 Bering St, 99762*
**Tel** *907-387-0654* **Closed** *Mon &
Tue*
In a turn-of-the-century Gold Rush house, offering fresh baked breads and pastries, seafood fresh from Norton Sound, and home-made desserts, all to eat in or take out. Seafood omelets are favorites, as are the chocolate chip cookies to go.

# CRUISING IN ALASKA

Wildlife sightings on land and sea, tide-water glaciers and snowcapped peaks, and the cultural heritage of Alaska's indigenous peoples provide the big draw for cruising the Inside Passage *(see pp38–9)* and the Gulf of Alaska *(see pp40–41)*. For many travelers, an Alaskan cruise is a once-in-a-lifetime experience, providing a luxurious way to see some of the wildest places on earth. Rates vary greatly depending upon the cruise line, the season, and national economic conditions. Cruise lines like to appeal to as wide a market as possible, offering numerous itineraries on various classes of ship, resort-style amenities, and a range of shore excursions. All travelers need to be prepared for Alaska's unpredictable weather. While the parkas may end up packed away the entire time, so may the swimsuit and sandals.

### Best Times to Go

While weekly cruises to tropical islands operate all year round, the Alaska cruise season lasts less than five months, typically from mid-May to mid-September. Sun worshippers can aim for cruises that depart at the end of June and through July. With a decrease in the likelihood of storms, this is considered peak season, and cruise lines charge accordingly. Also, as the summer solstice nears, the northern latitudes make for exceptionally long days. This translates into late evenings and technicolor sunsets almost at midnight.

If price matters more than the weather, it is best to hunt for deals in the September and May shoulder seasons *(see p270)*. Generally, the later in the season that travelers depart, the greater the likelihood of damp weather. However, passengers need to be prepared at all times for Alaska's erratic weather.

### Choosing a Cruise Line and Ship

Budget may be the most important factor in influencing the choice of a cruise. Also, it is essential to decide which is more important – the ship or the itinerary. For some, cruising is all about low fares, fresh air, and the destination itself. For others, imaginative itineraries and creature comforts matter more.

Cruise lines rate themselves according to a star system that is, however, fast losing definition. Six-star lines offer smaller, more intimate ships, the best cuisine, superior accommodation, and services to match. Naturally, such luxury comes at a price, but travelers may be able to find fares that include round-trip air travel, onboard expenses, and excursions. Mass market ships advertise the lowest rates. No line with less than four or five stars will mention their rating, while others may exaggerate their status. Be sure to research the ship's age and when it began to sail under its current name. Lastly, do not judge a ship by the cruise line. Even mass-market cruise lines offer new ships with design features and amenities that approach luxury.

### Choosing an Itinerary

Consult cruise route maps *(see pp38–41)* to get your bearings. The Inside Passage has the largest concentration of accessible towns, glaciers, fjords, and forests. Popular stops include Glacier Bay, Haines, Hoonah, Juneau, Skagway, Sitka, Ketchikan, and Misty Fiords. The Gulf of Alaska has fewer ports of call, but benefits include the glaciers, deep fjords, and marine life of Hubbard Glacier and Prince William Sound.

Week-long round-trip cruises between Juneau and Seattle, San Francisco, and Vancouver in Canada take in the Inside Passage and are especially

Multi-level cruise ship moored in Juneau's Gastineau Channel

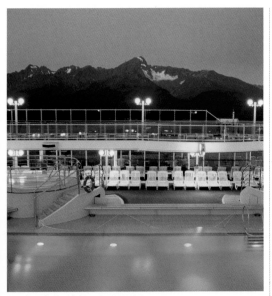

Cruise ship with a large decktop swimming pool

popular. As the route heads north from Canada or the US to Juneau, Seward, or Whittier, signs of modern civilization recede gradually with each passing day. Another popular itinerary goes across the Gulf of Alaska between Seward or Whittier and Juneau, and includes points of interest both in the Gulf and in the Inside Passage as far south as Misty Fiords National Monument.

## Planning and Research

To ensure a great vacation, it would be wise to devote some time to planning and research. The Internet offers extensive information on cruise lines and is a fast and efficient way to compare the best deals. **Alaska Cruises**, **Cruise Critic**, **Cruise Reviews**, and **Cruise Mates** all maintain websites with comprehensive, insightful reviews and information on how to book a cruise. For proprietary cruise information, browse through the websites of cruise companies.

Travel bookstores are also an invaluable resource, as are travel-related websites such as **Expedia Travel**. For the latest deals, consult the travel sections of leading newspapers in early spring.

## Major Cruise Lines

Most major cruise lines have in their fleet at least two or more ships that are large enough to carry hundreds or even thousands of passengers. Common facilities on board include restaurants and buffets, health spas and salons, theaters, themed lounges, bars, dance clubs, swimming pools and hot tubs, and children's clubs.

Large and midsized cruise ships are offered by **Regent Seven Seas Cruises**, **Celebrity Cruises**, **Holland America Line**, **Princess Cruise Line**, **Royal Caribbean Line**, **Norwegian Cruise Line**, **Disney Cruise Line**, **Silversea Cruises**, and **Carnival Cruise Lines**. Silversea vessels are among the best in Alaskan waters, while Holland America and Princess Cruises have tied up with Alaska Railroad to offer rail tours (see pp284–7).

## Small Ships

The only way to sail into secluded villages and hidden coves that large ships cannot approach is to cruise with small-ship operators or off-the-beaten-track adventure specialists. There's often a high standard of comfort and good food on these trips, but the glitzier cruise entertainments are traded for on-board experts in subjects such as marine biology and photography, and shore excursions may range from informal encounters with local culture to two-day forest hikes. **Alaskan Dream Cruises**, **Discovery Voyages**, **Un-Cruise Adventures**, and **Lindblad Expeditions** are excellent choices for this type of cruise.

## What's Included

Fares on all mass market cruise ships include meals, snacks, shows, and complimentary drinks at a "Captain's Meet and Greet" cocktail party. Passengers have some control over the amount of gratuities, but more and more lines include a nominal fee for wait staff and room stewards on the final bill. Luxury ships may offer complimentary alcoholic beverages or wine during meals, while other upscale lines stock cabins with bottles of liquor. Economy ships charge for everything at every turn. All purchases made on board are added to the final bill.

## Special Deals

Promotional fares are easily available in the weeks just before the peak season. The first and last weeks of the season have the cheapest fares. All major lines also offer air add-ons and hotel stays, and in Alaska, that can mean extended rail tours to Denali and other points of interest in the Interior.

Look out for special deals offered on the websites of cruise lines and travel agencies. Travel clubs, academic societies, and other membership associations organize charters to take advantage of group rates. Large cruise lines sponsor themed cruises and these might occasionally offer a good bargain.

## Traveling Solo

Fares are always based on double occupancy unless stated otherwise. However, a single traveler can find deals that waive or reduce what is called the single supplement – an additional fee added on to single fares that can sometimes equal another full fare. When such deals are not available travel agents can help book cabins to be shared by single travelers of the same gender. Most large cruise lines also arrange onboard events and parties meant for singles.

## Cabin Types

Experienced cruisers have two opposing views on how to choose cabins. One opinion holds that as most passengers merely sleep, bathe, and dress in their cabins, it makes little sense to reserve a deluxe stateroom with all possible amenities. However, under certain conditions, comfortable cabins can make all the difference. Travelers should consider booking either an inexpensive inside cabin or an outside one with portholes (or windows that increase in size with every category upgrade). Cabins with balconies are ideal for romantic and restful settings and usually sell first, despite being considerably more expensive. However, many cruisers argue that the same views are available for free from the public decks.

Deluxe cabins may include mini-suites with sitting areas or apartment-style penthouses with separate rooms that can sleep four. Some modern ships have taken this category to new heights, creating opulent spaces for six people, complete with conference facilities, butlers, private hot tubs, and large secluded patios on the ship's top deck.

## Cabin Facilities

While all standard cabins include a bathroom, beds for two, sufficient storage, a room safe, television, cabin phone,

Atrium bar offering a chic sitting area on a cruise ship

toiletries, and most importantly, lifejackets, all facilities improve with higher fares. Amenities can include a refrigerator, wider and thicker mattresses, softer pillows, and plush comforters. Bathrooms in high-priced cabins offer superior quality toiletries.

## Location Within the Ship

The websites of all cruise lines provide the deck plans of each ship and a layout showing cabin locations. Cabins can be situated aft, forward, or amidships. Depending on the quality of the ship, lower aft cabins can be subject to muted engine noise, vibrations, and heat. In rough seas, lower forward cabins experience the maximum vibrations from wave impact. Even so, if wind and wave height create heavy sway, those subject to seasickness would do well to book a lower cabin amidships, as motion intensifies the higher one goes. However, for some, watching waves splash against their portholes can cause anxiety – such travelers may prefer an upper cabin. It is wise to select a cabin near an elevator

if the ship has over a dozen decks. With an upper outside cabin, check that a lifeboat does not obstruct the view.

Restaurants and bars can be located anywhere on the ship, while buffets are generally higher up near the pools.

## Public Areas

Framed art and sculpture line the stairways and hallways of virtually every ship. While the art can range from sedate to postmodern and whimsical, travelers will almost always find some vestiges of the classic Art Deco era – the

Ship library providing a quiet retreat

glory era of cruise ships – whether in the details of the handrail design or in themed restaurants. Towering atriums are *de rigueur*, and passengers with vertigo should steer clear of the overlooks. Most include comfortable bars and lounges on the periphery, or generic sitting areas with splendid views out to sea.

Large ships stage Vegas- and Broadway-themed shows in plush theaters, full of glitz and glamor. More sophisticated ship theaters come complete with multiple stage lifts, large orchestras, and a huge revue staff of singers and dancers. Other cruise lines, while well funded, choose to economize by investing little or nothing in stage musicians, using pre-recorded soundtracks instead.

Quiet libraries and card rooms are common, especially in cruise lines popular with the retired set. Most lines have Internet facilities, and some offer Wi-Fi to those with their own laptop computers.

## Spa, Fitness, and Beauty Salons

Every large or midsized ship boasts a spa and salon with trained staff who pamper

The luxurious lobby of an onboard spa and salon

passengers with spa treatments and massages. Onboard spas reduce their rates when the ship is in port and as the cruise proceeds, but only for more expensive packages.

To maintain your at-home fitness regimen, exercise rooms of large ships have a range of equipment, including climbers and treadmills. They almost always offer hot tubs, some provide saunas, and a few offer steam baths. Fitness centers often remain open round the clock, while salons keep long hours. Fitness programs can include yoga, Pilates, and personal training.

To prepare for formal or gala nights, salons will generally offer passengers total makeovers, as well as hair styling and facials.

## Medical Facilities

All cruise ships will have a licensed medical professional on board to deal with illness, emergencies, and patient evacuations. If travelers have special needs or require specific medical equipment, it is best to check before making your reservations. While no cruise ship pretends to be a floating hospital, some do advertise such equipment as dialysis machines. Costs can vary from ship to ship, but in general the fee for visits and medication is significantly higher than on land.

## DIRECTORY

### Planning and Research

**Alaska Cruises**
W alaskacruises.com

**Cruise Critic**
W cruisecritic.com

**Cruise Mates**
W cruisemates.com

**Cruise Reviews**
W cruisereviews.com

**Expedia Travel**
W expedia.com/cruises

### Major Cruise Lines

**Carnival Cruise Lines**
Tel (800) 764-7419.
W carnival.com

**Celebrity Cruises**
Tel (800) 647-2251.
W celebrity.com

**Disney Cruise Line**
Tel (800) 951-3532.
W disneycruise.com

**Holland America Line**
Tel (877) 724-5425, (877) 932-4259.
W hollandamerica.com

**Norwegian Cruise Line**
Tel (800) 327-7030.
W ncl.com

**Princess Cruise Line**
Tel (800) 774-6237.
W princess.com

**Regent Seven Seas Cruises**
Tel (800) 784-0022.
W regentcruises.com

**Royal Caribbean Line**
Tel (866) 562-7625.
W royalcaribbean.com

**Silversea Cruises**
Tel (877) 215-9986.
W silversea.com

### Small Ships

**Alaskan Dream Cruises**
Tel (855) 747-8100.
W alaskandreamcruises.com

**Discovery Voyages**
Tel (907) 653-1957, (800) 324-7602.
W discoveryvoyages.com

**Lindblad Expeditions**
Tel (800) 397-3348.
W expeditions.com

**Un-Cruise Adventures**
Tel (888) 862-8881.
W un-cruise.com

# Life on Board

The day-to-day goings on of a cruise to Alaska mirror life on board any other cruise, but with a few major exceptions – there is unlikely to be a white sand beach for tanning, and there may be more hiking boots than sandals on deck. Likewise, ship staff never try to re-create tropical themes, leaving the grandeur of Alaska to speak for itself with every passing seascape, fjord, and glacier-topped peak. However, it is still a cruise, and passengers can expect levity, dancing, late-night parties, theater productions, and casino action, as they would on a cruise anywhere in the world.

Enjoying sunshine and a wide-ranging view from the deck

## Entertainment and Activities

Ship theaters on the larger lines boast professionally lit stages with state-of-the-art audio, and draw full-house crowds for events on each night of the cruise. Talent and musicianship vary among cruise lines, and the Vegas- and Broadway-style productions alternate with stand-up comics. Some of the latter have content older than the ocean, while others present risqué humor. Bigger ships often maintain a separate venue for game shows hosted by cruise directors who urge audiences to participate.

A good ship will also have country singers, jazz crooners, string trios and quartets, and classical pianists to entertain lounge patrons, atrium visitors, and strollers on the ship's interior promenades.

Art shows represent an outlet for buyers interested in originals or numbered prints signed by the artist. Onboard art auctions usually manage to bring in a large crowd of cruisers.

Given the variable climate, Alaskan lines make none of the promises that tropical operators do. Ships shy away from planning too many outdoor activities that could suffer cancellations due to bad weather. However, deck parties do take place, along with midnight fiestas, usually with a Mexican theme.

Glitzy stage show providing live onboard entertainment

## Casinos

After shopping and sunning on deck, spending time and money in the casino is one of the popular cruise pastimes, despite poor odds of winning.

Gambling options depend on the cruise line and the class of the ship and can range from craps, roulette, and simple slot machines to blackjack, poker, and baccarat. Most ship casinos also offer video poker machines. Ship casinos have a vested interest in educating their clients, so the house often offers classes on how to play some of the more esoteric games.

A shipboard casino is more or less like a land-based one, but with a few differences. It is open only while the ship is actually sailing in international waters. Only passengers over 21 years of age are allowed to play, although anyone may pass through when it is closed to take pictures. It would be considered unusual, and possibly an infringement of casino rules, to photograph ongoing games or people gambling. While every ship has a bar that exclusively serves the casino, patrons are usually not offered free drinks, except at occasional promotional events, such as when the casino first opens.

## Shopping

Those interested in buying luxury items such as tobacco, spirits, designer clothing and cosmetics, digital cameras, and jewelry will find them at excellent prices, all tax- and duty-free. Usually designed to resemble upscale shopping malls, onboard arcades can sprawl over two decks, or simply consist of a string of interconnected shops. All through the cruise, selected merchandise is also sold at slashed prices in hallways or outside on the upper deck, and liquor tastings are also common. Passengers should note that they cannot take possession of their alcohol purchases until their last night on board the ship.

Crew members preparing a buffet barbecue

## Meals

For many travelers, cruising is all about the cuisine. In addition to three heavy meals a day, served in the main dining rooms, hot and cold buffets, snack bars, cafés, and deckside grills cater to the huge demand.

Large ships manage the rush by establishing at least two main seatings for dinner and assigning tables for the duration of the cruise. Dinner typically begins at 6pm and 8:30pm. Passengers who are dissatisfied with their seating or table may consult the ship's *maître d'* after the first night to ask for a change, but there is no guarantee of one. Tables for two may not be easy to find, even if passengers make the request prior to booking. Many ships now have more flexible dining programs and a range of onboard restaurants that require no bookings.

The tradition of dining with the captain is mostly historical, and not a common practice. A good alternative is attending the captain's cocktail party to meet him and his senior officers.

## Expenses

Costs mount rapidly during a cruise. Onboard purchases, beverages, and casino expenses can reach unimaginable heights. The need for ready cash almost disappears on a ship, as passengers have the convenience of paying with a swipe of a key card. Many generous passengers do dole out bills as tips to room stewards and other crew members. Note that all cruise lines assert that tipping is optional while stating clearly their policy of adding a basic rate of gratuity for services rendered during the cruise. Passengers are free to accept, raise, or lower that amount at the Purser's Desk.

## Dress Code

Check the ticket packet for details of the ship's dress code for the main dining room. Most disallow jeans, sleeveless T-shirts, shorts, or tennis shoes for dinner, but relax the rules for other meals and buffet restaurants. Dress rules and styles change all the time, but even aboard luxury ships the trend towards casual lifestyles has prevailed. Still, the classic cruise tradition of formal nights persists for at least one night of the week. Black tie dinners are solely in the province of six-star ships.

For formal nights, men can wear suits; tuxedos are in the minority on most ships. Women wear cocktail dresses or gowns. Semi-formal nights require sports coats and tie and slacks for men, and cocktail dresses for women. Resort casuals such as cotton dresses for women and khaki pants and button-up shirts for men apply on other nights. Except on the most sophisticated ships, restaurant staff rarely turn away inappropriately dressed passengers.

## Traveling with Children

Virtually all ships have relaxed their restrictions in recent years and allow children of all ages. Most cruise ships come equipped with facilities exclusively for children. Activities range from crafts and treasure hunts for young kids, to teen discos, talent shows, and karaoke events for older children. Baby-sitting fees are incurred for child care when the formal programs end, usually after 10pm. Many programs do not accept children under two or three years of age unless accompanied by a parent. Famous for its family cruises, Disney Cruise Line now visits Alaska's Inside Passage.

### What to Pack

On average, cruise lines provide four baggage tags per person. To carry anything beyond that, passengers must check with the cruise line. Essentials for an Alaskan cruise include:

- Cell phone and charger
- Rain shell, hat, and warm sweater
- Comfortable walking or hiking boots
- Toiletries and cosmetics
- Medication and first aid, including sunscreen
- Passport, travel insurance, cruise documents
- Camera, memory card, and batteries
- Formal, semi-formal, and resort casual wear
- Shorts, swimwear, sunglasses and sandals
- Laptop computer
- Portable music player
- Books and magazines
- Spare luggage for purchased items

Hiking boots for excursions

# Shore Excursions

While not all the tourists who flock to Alaska each year travel via cruise ships, the ones who do often consider shore excursions to be the main event. Tours emphasize Alaska's geological wonders such as tidewater glaciers and vast temperate rainforests, while nature sightseeing focuses on wildlife. Historical tours, on the other hand, offer engaging presentations of human history from the earliest Native American settlements to the first Europeans. No cruise passenger has the time or opportunity to try each tour, but with careful planning, visitors can return home with a deeper understanding of what makes Alaska magical.

tours fill up. Most ships also have drop boxes for filled-out registration forms, to eliminate waiting in line. However, most travelers still prefer to sign up in person, which ensures a face to face meeting with shore tour staffers.

Sometimes a shore operator may cancel the tour if too few people register, or the weather is unfavorable. Always check for postings that identify cancellations, and conversely, if any new tours have been added to the inventory.

Small pleasure craft moored next to a giant cruise ship in Whittier

## What's Included

Ticket packets, cruise line websites, and flyers placed at the shore excursion desk on board the ship give brief descriptions of each excursion along with the duration and degree of physical stamina required. Usually, all that passengers need are sun or rain protection, water if none is provided, and a willingness to share the experience with fellow passengers. It always helps to ask a few questions before signing up about the chances of cancellation, how large the group will be, and whether food or water will be provided during the excursion.

## Booking

More and more cruise lines allow online bookings for the dozens of shore excursions offered during week-long cruises. Online booking saves passengers the trouble of filling out forms soon after boarding, which is the recommended time to make choices before

## Excursion Prices

The fee per person per tour varies widely from one cruise line to another. A walking tour around historic neighborhoods may cost less than $40, and kayaking less than $100. Tours that involve dog sledding, glacier travel, flightseeing by floatplane to remote areas, or heli-skiing can cost hundreds of dollars per person. Depending on the location, luxury cruise lines offer upscale tour programs that can cost over $10,000.

Cancellation policies vary, but in general, there is a 24-hour window before the tour in which visitors can change their minds. After the excursion, refunds are rare, although shore tour staff can reduce or waive the entire fee if a passenger can justify being completely dissatisfied.

Grizzly bear with cubs at Denali National Park

Creek Street, part of a Ketchikan walking tour, a popular shore excursion

## Going Ashore

Information printed on tour tickets tells passengers where and when to meet, either on the ship or the pier. Private shore tour operators usually hold up boards clearly marked with the tour's name making it easy for passengers to spot where they need to be. Passengers taking tours enjoy priority status once the gangway opens. Some ports cannot handle large ships at the pier, so small launches bring dozens of cruisers ashore, starting with the passengers taking tours.

## Independent Travel

Cruise lines have made it easier for passengers to book tours with the introduction of online billing systems, among other innovations, and tend to mark up tour costs because tourists usually pay willingly for the convenience.

However, some travelers prefer to arrange hotel stays, rail journeys, and tours entirely on their own. Before taking such matters into your own hands, it is wise to consider all the factors. Research the company and find out about the level of experience of the staff and how long the operator has been in business,

and if it makes customer testimonials available. Remember also that you will be without a tour representative, and will have to get to the tour start point alone. No matter how you book, additional expenses will arise, gratuities, food, and drink among them.

Getting back to the ship after a tour poses other challenges. While ships usually depart promptly at a well-publicized time, they will wait a few minutes for stray passengers after courteous public announcements. The only exception to this rule, and one that will certainly delay a departure, is if a shore excursion group booked via the shore desk is delayed.

Being completely alone may appeal to the adventurous, but travelers need to plan very carefully and stay well-informed.

## Safety on Shore

Alaskan life in small seaside towns is slow and steady, with few residents and not much bustle. Even in the larger cities along the coast, personal safety poses no real concern. However, while most locals will be glad to help you navigate to where you want to go, as with any travel away from home, keep your valuables protected.

## Best Shore Excursions

Providing shore excursions for their passengers has become a gigantic industry for cruise lines. Holland America Line and Princess Cruise Line, for example, offer hundreds of tours in Alaska and are specialists in the field. Among the interesting shore excursions visitors can expect to find are:
• Halibut and salmon fishing charters from Ninilchik and Deep Creek (see p110)
• Walking Creek Street in Ketchikan (see pp128–9)
• Visiting Saxman Totem Park near Ketchikan (see p129)
• Flightseeing in Misty Fiords National Monument (see p130)
• Riding the Mount Roberts tramway above Juneau (see pp142–3)
• Helicopter tours to the Juneau Icefield (see p145)
• Riding the White Pass and Yukon Route Railroad in Skagway (see pp150–53)
• Brown bear watching in Denali National Park (see pp166–9)
• Alaska Railroad trips to Denali (see pp166–9) or Seward (see pp102–3)

Helicopter readying for a flight at Skagway's heliport

Floatplane taking off from the serene waters of a lake

# OUTDOOR ACTIVITIES

Known around the world as a premier wilderness and adventure holiday destination, Alaska offers visitors a diverse range of outdoor activities. In the summer, visitors can go sportfishing *(see pp44–5)*, hiking, mountaineering, canoeing, and whitewater rafting, while the winter brings opportunities for snowmachining, dog sledding *(see pp42–3)*, and skiing. The daring can even try heli-skiing. Operators usually organize transport, food, and equipment, and even provide guides. For those with the proper equipment, camping, hiking, backpacking, canoeing, and Nordic skiing can be inexpensive and spectacular. However, anything that involves bush travel or motorized vehicles such as snowmachines and ATVs will require extensive planning and cost considerably more. For a price, operators will provide equipment and handle all the logistics.

Hikers on a trail in Girdwood on the outskirts of Anchorage

## Hiking

Alaska is a hiker's paradise, and Southcentral, Southeast, and Interior Alaska boast numerous picturesque hiking and trekking trails. The possibilities range from short 2-mile (3-km) strolls to all-day hikes, multi-day backpacking trips, and cross-country wilderness expeditions.

In Southeast Alaska, nearly every city and town lies within easy reach of scenic hiking trails that lead up through lush forest and muskeg to points offering great views. The most popular long-distance route here is the historic Chilkoot Trail *(see pp152–3)*, which requires stamina as well as preparation. **Gastineau Guiding** offers the best excursions around the Juneau area.

Most of the popular trails in Interior Alaska, such as those in Denali State Park *(see p164)* and Wrangell-St. Elias National Park *(see pp192–3)*, are longer, often unmarked routes that demand at least some hiking experience. Even in popular Denali National Park *(see pp166–9)*, there are few marked trails. Here, most hiking is cross-country, and needs backcountry permits, orientation skills, and the ability to ford unbridged rivers. **Denali Trekking Company** organizes customized trips for visitors.

Even on the outskirts of Anchorage, it is possible to hike one of the many trails in Chugach State Park or around Girdwood. On the Kenai Peninsula, many routes through the spectacular state parks and the Chugach National Forest, including the popular Resurrection Pass Trail *(see p105)*, make excellent introductions to multi-day hiking. **Arctic Wild** adventure guide service offers a range of specialty ecotours.

In Southwest, Arctic, and Western Alaska, hiking is limited to cross-country wilderness routes that can be accessed only by bush plane. **Kodiak Treks** conducts low-impact bear-viewing trips.

## Bush Travel

Due to Alaska's limited road and ferry systems, transport around the state is quite different from other parts of the US. Access to the bush – any place off the highway or Marine Highway systems – requires a helicopter, a boat or water taxi, or a bush plane on wheels, floats, or skis.

Bush flights, which carry residents and supplies to remote homesteads and fly anglers and rafters to uncrowded streams also provide access to rural villages and bush lodges. **Rust's Flying Service**, **Wrangell Mountain Air** and **Brooks Range Aviation** are some of the better operators that arrange trips for tourists. Clients must pay not only for the flight out, but also for the pilot's return trip. The rates differ according to the type of plane, the number of passengers, and the duration of the flight. Client luggage is always limited to the amount of gear that the plane can safely carry. Anyone who wants to haul a boat or camping gear

Floatplane taking off for the bush, Lake Hood, Anchorage

Cross-country skiing in an Anchorage park, against the backdrop of the Chugach Mountains

and supplies for the length of the trip may have to pay for more than one run to the drop-off location.

Usually, a pre-arranged pick-up is scheduled, but travelers need to be flexible, and it is always necessary to carry extra supplies. Note that once the water taxi or bush plane has dropped off its passengers and is out of view, people are on their own until the pick-up date. Remote areas are ruled by the weather, and clouds, wildfires, storms, snow, and wind can make travel impossible, so it is important not to embark on a bush trip without a fair amount of cushion time.

## Snowmachining

In the winter, rivers and lakes in the Interior freeze, becoming transport routes and opening up much of the state to relatively easy access. These routes were historically nego-tiated by dog sled, but today, sleds have been replaced by snowmachines (or snowmo-biles). They not only provide access to places off the road system, but also serve as rec-reational vehicles that allow adrenaline-pumping runs. Snowmachines range from 550cc to 700cc models, and only those who are confident of their riding and navigation skills should consider renting one. Rentals require a hefty security

deposit, and tax and fuel may be extra. **Alaska Snow Safaris** and **Glacier City Snowmobile Tours** offer rentals and a range of guided trips, including short introductory runs, half-day backcountry trips, and full- and multi-day tours.

## Mountaineering

Mountaineering is extremely popular in Alaska and Denali is the destination of most climbers. While it can be scaled without a guide, guided expeditions must use one of the six accredited outfits listed on the **Denali National Park** website, including the recommended **Alaska Mountaineering School**. All climbers, guided or not, must register with the **Walter Harper Talkeetna Ranger Station** *(see p162)* 60 days before the trip and pay a Mountaineering Special Use Fee of $200.

Alaska is one of the few places in the world that still offers summits that are as yet unclimbed and even unnamed. Most serious climbers arrive either with a pre-organized expedition or come months in advance to seek out appealing peaks and prepare for the ascent. Guiding companies such as **St. Elias Alpine Guides**, **Alaska Mountain Guides and Climbing School**, and **Kennicott Wilderness Guides** accept prospective mountaineers of all levels.

## Skiing

Alaska's only world class downhill ski resort is Alyeska, at Girdwood, 40 miles (60 km) south of Anchorage. There are also smaller resorts at Alpenglow and Hilltop in Anchorage, Eaglecrest in Juneau, Cleary Summit near Fairbanks, and Mount Eyak near Cordova.

Heli-skiing – downhill skiing on mountains and glaciers accessed by helicopter – is rapidly gaining in popularity, especially around Valdez and Haines. **Valdez Heli-Ski Guides** offers coaching and individual packages, and **Tordrillo North** runs trips in the remote Tordrillo Mountains. In the summer, Ruth Glacier, in Denali National Park, and the Juneau and Harding Icefields become ski fields. Note, however, that glacier skiing is only for experienced skiers with safety training and equipment.

Nordic or cross-country skiing is widely available, and snowmachine tracks all over the state double as ski trails. Cross-country skiing and noisy snowmachines are not fully compatible, but the fine groomed trails around Anchorage and Fairbanks are reserved for skiing. In the Mat-Su, Hatcher Pass *(see p91)* offers excellent wilderness trails. The Fairbanks area has good trails both in town and at Chena Hot Springs *(see p177)*.

## Cycling and Mountain Biking

In the summer, cycling and mountain biking are popular activities, but cyclists must be prepared to encounter animals, traffic, and narrow shoulders on most paved highways. The Copper River Highway *(see p123)*, the Denali Highway *(see p165)*, the extensive routes on Prince of Wales Island *(see pp132–3)*, and the Edgerton Highway/ McCarthy Road *(see p187)* are among the best, most scenic routes. Biking is allowed on most trails in the Chugach and Tongass National Forests and on limited routes in the state parks. **Alaskabike, Alaska Backcountry Bike Tours,** and **Backroads** offer guided cycling tours all over Alaska. Anchorage's **Downtown Bicycle Rentals** and **Pablo's Bicycle Rentals** hire out bicycles. The **Arctic Bicycle Club** offers information on cycling, mountain biking, and organized rides.

## Rafting and Canoeing

For most people, the appeal of a whitewater trip lies in running the rapids. Rapids are graded Class I to V, but anything above Class III will need good whitewater skills, while Class V will need an expert guide. The most popular rivers, and the easiest to access, include the Nenana River *(see p172)* and the Chulitna River near Denali National Park, the upper Kenai River *(see p100)*, the Matanuska River, the Eagle River near Anchorage, and Six Mile Creek south of Anchorage. **Nova River Rafters** and **Chilkat**

Rafting on the Chilkoot River near Skagway

**Guides** are among Alaska's oldest adventure companies, offering statewide packages. **Talkeetna River Guides** rafts rivers in the Interior. **Arctic Wild** runs rivers in the Brooks Range.

For a more contemplative, secluded experience, canoe trips of a day or more are possible on many of Alaska's lake and river systems, such as the Lynx Lake Loop *(see p160)* north of Anchorage and the Kenai Peninsula's Swan Lakes Loop *(see p109)*.

## Ocean Kayaking

One of the best ways to see Alaska's sheltered coastal areas is by kayak, providing easy access to remote beaches in Southeast Alaska, Prince William Sound, the Kenai Fjords, and other well-sheltered waterways. On fine days, the scenery is spectacular, and there is a chance of spotting marine wildlife. Thorough preparation is essential, and a number of companies hire out gear and offer instruction, kayak

transport, and guides. **Anadyr Adventures** and **Prince William Sound Kayak Center** offer trips around Prince William Sound, while **Alaska Canoe and Campground** and **True North Kayak Adventures** operate on the Kenai Peninsula, with **Sunny Cove Sea Kayaking** specializing in Kenai Fjords National Park. Good Southeast Alaska specialists include **Glacier Bay Sea Kayaks** in Gustavus, **Sitka Sound Ocean Adventures**, and **Southeast Sea Kayaks** in Ketchikan.

## Tours

Visitors who prefer organized activities can select from a range of operators. In the Southeast, **Alaska Waters** organizes a variety of tours, **Breakaway Adventures** offers jet boat rides, **Allen Marine Tours, Juneau Whale Watch,** and **Kenai Fjords Tours** arrange whale-watching tours, **Coastal Helicopters** sets up glacier tours, and **Chilkoot Charters and Tours** runs fishing trips. **Phillips Cruises and Tours** *(see p118)* and **Glacier Wildlife Cruises** offer tours in Prince William Sound, while **Glacier Bay Tours** explores Glacier Bay National Park. **Katmailand** runs freshwater sportfishing trips and **Kenai Fjords Tours** offers wildlife cruises. **K2 Aviation** has flightseeing tours over Denali, and the **Northern Alaska Tour Company** offers visits to the Arctic. **St. Paul Island Tours** and **Wilderness Birding Adventures** lead birdwatching trips in western Alaska.

Kayakers preparing to set off, Whittier

# DIRECTORY

## Hiking

### Arctic Wild
Fairbanks. **Tel** 577-8203, (888) 577-8203.
[w] arcticwild.com

### Denali Trekking Company
PO Box 93, Talkeetna.
**Tel** 733-2566.
[w] alaskahiking.com

### Gastineau Guiding
Juneau. **Tel** 586-8231.
[w] stepintoalaska.com

### Kodiak Treks
11754 S Russian Creek Rd, Kodiak. **Tel** 487-2122.
[w] kodiaktreks.com

## Bush Travel

### Brooks Range Aviation
PO Box 10, Bettles. **Tel** 692-5444, (800) 692-5443.
[w] brooksrange.com

### Rust's Flying Service
Anchorage. **Tel** 243-1595, (800) 544-2299.
[w] flyrusts.com

### Wrangell Mountain Air
McCarthy. **Tel** 554-4411, (800) 478-1160.
[w] wrangellmountain air.com

## Snowmachining

### Alaska Snow Safaris
Palmer. **Tel** (907) 745-2505. [w] snowmobile-alaska.com

### Glacier City Snowmobile Tours
Box 1018, Girdwood.
**Tel** (877) 783-5566.
[w] snowtours.net

## Mountaineering

### Alaska Mountain Guides and Climbing School
PO Box 1081, Haines.
**Tel** 766-3396. [w] alaska mountainguides.com

### Alaska Mountaineering School
PO Box 566, 3rd St, Talkeetna. **Tel** (800) 733-1016. [w] climbalaska.org

### Denali National Park
[w] nps.gov/dena

### Kennicott Wilderness Guides
PO Box MXY #1, Glennallen. **Tel** (800) 664-4537, 554-4444 (summer), 554-1070 (winter).
[w] kennicottguides.com

### National Outdoor Leadership School (N.O.L.S)
**Tel** 745-4047, (800) 710-6657. [w] nols.edu

### St. Elias Alpine Guides
**Tel** 554-4445, (888 )933-5427. [w] steliasguides.com

## Skiing

### Tordrillo North
**Tel** 230-7112.
[w] tordrillonorth.com

### Valdez Heli-Ski Guides
Valdez. **Tel** 835-4528.
[w] valdezheliskiguides.com

## Cycling and Mountain Biking

### Alaska Backcountry Bike Tours
132 W Arctic Ave, Box 4260, Palmer.
**Tel** 746-5018.
[w] mountainbike alaska.com

### Alaskabike
8511 E 84th Ave, Anchorage. **Tel** 245-2175.
[w] alaskabike.com

### Arctic Bicycle Club
[w] arcticbike.org

### Backroads
Berkeley, CA.
**Tel** (800) 462-2848.
[w] backroads.com

### Downtown Bicycle Rentals
333 W 4th Ave, Anchorage. **Tel** 279-5293.
[w] alaska-bike-rentals.com

### Pablo's Bicycle Rentals
501 L St, Anchorage.
**Tel** 272-1600.
[w] pablobicycle rentals.com

## Rafting and Canoeing

### Arctic Wild
See Hiking.

### Chilkat Guides
PO Box 170, Haines.
**Tel** 766-2491.
[w] raftalaska.com

### Nova River Rafters
38100 Glenn Hwy, Chickaloon. **Tel** 746-5753.
[w] novalaska.com

### Talkeetna River Guides
Main St, Talkeetna.
**Tel** (800) 353-2677.
[w] talkeetnariver guides.com

## Ocean Kayaking

### Alaska Canoe and Campground
Sterling. **Tel** 262-2331.
[w] alaskacanoetrips.com

### Anadyr Adventures
Valdez. **Tel** 835-2814.
[w] anadyradventures.com

### Glacier Bay Sea Kayaks
PO Box 26, Gustavus.
**Tel** 697-2257.
[w] glacierbaysea kayaks.com

### Prince William Sound Kayak Center
PO Box 622, Whittier.
**Tel** 472-2452.
[w] pwskayakcenter.com

### Sitka Sound Ocean Adventures
112 Tovio Circle, Sitka.
**Tel** 752-0660.
[w] kayaksitka.com

### Southeast Sea Kayaks
1007 Water St, Ketchikan.
**Tel** 225-1258, (800) 287-1607.
[w] kayakketchikan.com

### Sunny Cove Sea Kayaking
Seward. **Tel** 225-4426.
[w] sunnycove.com

### True North Kayak Adventures
Homer Spit, Homer.
**Tel** 235-0708.
[w] truenorthkayak.com

## Tours

### Alaska Waters
PO Box 1978, Wrangell.
**Tel** (800) 347-4462, 874-2378.
[w] alaskawaters.com

### Allen Marine Tours
Juneau. **Tel** (888) 289-0081; Ketchikan. **Tel** (877) 686-8100; Sitka **Tel** (888) 747-8101. [w] allen marinetours.com

### Breakaway Adventures
PO Box 2107, Wrangell.
**Tel** 874-2488.
[w] breakawayadven tures.com

### Chilkoot Charters and Tours
PO Box 1336, Skagway.
**Tel** (877) 983-3400.
[w] chilkootcharters.com

### Coastal Helicopters
8995 Yandukin Dr, Juneau Airport, Juneau. **Tel** (800) 789-5610. [w] coastal helicopters.com

### Glacier Bay Tours
179 Bartlett Cove, Gustavus.
**Tel** (888) 229-8687.
[w] visitglacierbay.com

### Glacier Wildlife Cruises
Valdez. **Tel** (800) 411-0090.
[w] lulubelletours.com

### K2 Aviation
Box 545B, Talkeetna.
**Tel** (800) 764-2291.
[w] flyk2.com

### Katmailand
4125 Aircraft Dr, Anchorage.
**Tel** (800) 544-0551, 254-5448. [w] katmailand.com

### Kenai Fjords Tours
Seward Waterfront, Seward. **Tel** (877) 777-4051.
[w] kenaifjords.com

### Northern Alaska Tour Company
PO Box 82991, Fairbanks.
**Tel** (800) 474-1986, 474-8600.
[w] northernalaska.com

### Juneau Whale Watch
76 Egan Dr, Juneau.
**Tel** 723-9209.
[w] juneauwhalewatch.com

### St. Paul Island Tours
**Tel** (877) 424-5637, 278-2316.
[w] alaskabirding.com

### Wilderness Birding Adventures
40208 Alpenglow Circle, Homer. **Tel** (907) 299-3937.
[w] wildernessbirding.com

# SURVIVAL GUIDE

# PRACTICAL INFORMATION

Thanks to its unparalleled natural beauty, abundant wildlife, and rich cultural history, Alaska attracts a growing number of visitors from all over the world each year. The state's tourist infrastructure is fairly well developed, offering a range of accommodation and restaurant options. A large number of local tour operators can also organize just about any sort of adventure a visitor may want to undertake. Road and rail systems link numerous sites of interest, but even places away from the highways can be readily accessed via the extensive air transport and ferry routes. Visitor information centers, even in small towns, are plentiful and go out of their way to provide information and assistance. The following pages include tips on a range of practical matters that will assist visitors in getting the most out of their visit to this sprawling, majestic state.

## When to Go

The finest weather in Alaska usually occurs from mid-May to mid-July, when most of the state, except for the Southeast and the Aleutians, experiences almost perpetual daylight. This is the time when all parks and services are open.

Rainfall is common all year round in Southeast Alaska, while the Arctic receives little rain. In most parts of Alaska, the annual "rainy season" begins in mid-July, ending in early September, when most national park facilities close. However, there many reasons to visit in the off-season. As nights become darker, the chances of seeing the aurora borealis increase. From December to April, there are outdoor activities (*see pp264–7*) and winter festivals (*see pp48–9*) to enjoy. The May and September shoulder seasons are pleasant, avoiding the bad weather and minimal facilities of the off-season, and the prices and crowds of the high season.

## Visa Regulations

Citizens of Canada, Australia, New Zealand, the UK, and most European Union nations can visit the US without a visa, but need a passport that is valid for at least six months after their trip, an onward or return ticket, and a completed Electronic System for Travel Authorization (ESTA) form, available online at https://esta.cbp.dhs.gov/esta. Canadians need to show their passport to enter the US. Visitors from nations that require visas must apply to a US embassy and may be asked for proof of financial solvency and intention to return home.

## Travel Safety Advice

Visitors can get up-to-date travel safety information from the **Foreign and Commonwealth Office** in the UK, the **State Department** in the US and the **Department of Foreign Affairs and Trade** in Australia.

## Visitor Information

Most tourist offices in Alaska are known for the quality of their information. All offer free maps, brochures, and hotel and restaurant listings, and local staff can answer most travel-related queries. The **Alaska Public Lands Information Centers** and the **Alaska Travel Industry Association** are also good information sources. National parks have their own visitors' centers, with rangers and volunteer staff who help with planning and organizing the necessary permits. The **Alaska Department of Fish and Game** issues hunting and fishing licenses. Most visitor centers are open long hours in the summer, but winter hours are limited. Throughout this guide, details of visitor information centers in major towns are provided.

Rainforest around Ward Lake, Ketchikan

◀ Challenging driving conditions near Nome, just south of the Arctic Circle

## Taxes and Tipping

While Alaska does not have a state sales tax, most cities and boroughs impose local sales taxes. These can be up to 8 percent of the purchase price, added to the total at the checkout. A host of taxes are imposed on goods and services that apply mainly to tourists. A bed tax applies to B&Bs, hotels, hostels, lodges, and some campsites. A statewide $40 per head tax is applied to all cruise ship passengers. Rental cars are also subject to tax, and drivers renting vehicles from airport rental desks may have to pay up to 29 percent extra to cover airport maintenance.

Service is not included on restaurant checks, and the tip is usually 15 percent *(see pp246–7)*. Taxi drivers will expect around $5, depending on the fare. At hotels, tip $2 per bag and $1 per day or more for the room cleaner. In wilderness lodges, the tip is given to the desk clerk, to be divided among the staff. While tour guides get about $10 per day, depending on the service, fishing guides often get a sum commensurate with the success of the trip.

## Smoking

As in the rest of America, Alaska's attitude toward smoking has changed dramatically and towns are moving to restrict where smoking is permitted. Smoking is banned in all public buildings, shops, and public transport vehicles. Most accommodation options are also smoke-free, although a few may offer specific rooms where smoking is allowed.

In Anchorage, Barrow, Haines, Juneau, Petersburg, Sitka, and Unalaska, all restaurants and bars are smoke-free by local ordinance.

# DIRECTORY

## Travel Safety Advice

### Australia
Department of Foreign Affairs and Trade
**W** dfat.gov.au
**W** smarttraveller.gov.uk

### UK
Foreign and Commonwealth Office
**W** gov.uk/foreign-travel-advice

### US
US Department of State.
**W** travel.state.gov

## Visitor Information

### Alaska Department of Fish and Game
**Tel** 465-4100.
**W** adfg.alaska.gov

### Alaska Public Lands Information Centers
605 W 4th Ave, Anchorage.
**Tel** 644-3661.
**W** alaskacenters.gov

### Alaska Travel Industry Association
2600 Cordova St, Suite 201, Anchorage. **Tel** 929-2200.
**W** travelalaska.com

## Anchorage

### Anchorage Convention and Visitors' Bureau
524 W 4th Ave, Anchorage.
**Tel** 257-2363.
**W** anchorage.net

### Chugach State Park Eagle River Nature Center
**Tel** 694-2108. **W** ernc.org

### Mat-Su Convention and Visitors' Bureau
**Tel** 746-5000.
**W** alaskavisit.com

### Palmer Chamber of Commerce
**Tel** 745-2880.
**W** palmerchamber.org

## The Kenai Peninsula

### Alaska Maritime National Wildlife Refuge
95 Sterling Hwy, Homer.
**Tel** 235-6961.
**W** islandsandocean.org

### Homer Chamber of Commerce Visitors' Center
**Tel** 235-7740.
**W** homeralaska.org

### Kenai Fjords National Park Visitors' Center
**Tel** 422-0500.
**W** nps.gov/kefj

### Seward Convention and Visitors Bureau
**Tel** 224-8051.
**W** seward.com

## Prince William Sound

### Cordova Chamber of Commerce
**Tel** 424-7260.
**W** cordovachamber.com

### Valdez Convention and Visitors' Bureau
**Tel** 835-2984.
**W** valdezalaska.org

## Southeast Alaska

### Haines Convention and Visitors' Bureau
**Tel** 766-2234.
**W** visithaines.com

### Juneau Convention and Visitors' Bureau
**Tel** 586-2201.
**W** traveljuneau.com

### Ketchikan Visitor Information Center
**Tel** 225-6166.
**W** visit-ketchikan.com

### Petersburg Visitor Information Center
**Tel** 772-4636.
**W** petersburg.org

### Sitka Convention and Visitors' Bureau
**Tel** 747-8604. **W** sitka.org

### Skagway Convention and Visitors' Bureau
**Tel** 983-2854.
**W** skagway.com

## Western Interior Alaska

### Denali National Park Visitor Access Center
**Tel** 683-2294.
**W** nps.gov/dena

### Fairbanks Convention and Visitors' Bureau
**Tel** 456-5774.
**W** explorefairbanks.com

## Eastern Interior Alaska

### Copper Valley Chamber of Commerce
**Tel** 822-5555.
**W** traveltoalaska.com

### Dawson City Visitors' Center
**Tel** (867) 993-5566 (summer), (867) 993-5575 (winter).
**W** dawsoncity.ca

### Wrangell-St. Elias National Park Visitors' Center
**Tel** 822-5234.
**W** nps.gov/wrst

## Southwest Alaska

### Kodiak Island Convention and Visitors' Bureau
**Tel** 486-4782.
**W** kodiak.org

### Unalaska/Dutch Harbor Convention and Visitors' Bureau
**Tel** 581-2612.
**W** unalaska.info

## Arctic and Western Alaska

### Inupiat Heritage Center
Barrow. **Tel** 852-0422.
**W** nps.gov/inup

### Nome Visitors' Center
**Tel** 443-6555.
**W** visitnomealaska.com

### Northwest Arctic Heritage Center
Kotzebue. **Tel** 442-3890.
**W** nps.gov/kova/parknews/nwahc.htm

Strolling down Anchorage's 4th Avenue

## Traveling with Children

With its great opportunities to see wildlife and get outdoors, Alaska is excellent for children. Many towns, especially Anchorage, have attractions that were built with children in mind, such as the H2Oasis water park and the Alaska Zoo. Most museums offer free or discounted admission for children, with the cut-off age ranging from 3 to 17 years. Many Alaska National Parks offer **Junior Ranger programs** for kids, and the majority of hotels and restaurants are child-friendly. Some hotels offer parents discounted or free accommodation for children in their booking.

Many tour companies welcome children, but some wilderness lodges, upscale restaurants, and adventure tours, such as helicopter tours or kayaking, have a minimum age limit.

Anyone organizing a family driving trip through Alaska should bear in mind that distances are long, especially if the trip starts in the Lower 48. Renting an RV (see pp288–9) can make the journey easier. There are plenty of parks and highway pull-offs where families can stop for picnics or where kids can take a short walk with a field guide to identify plants, birds, and animals. The show, **Travel With Kids**, is a useful resource for general information about traveling with children.

## Senior Travelers

Although the age defining a senior citizen is usually 65, discounts are sometimes accessible to those over 55 or 60 as well. While many senior travelers in Alaska opt for all-inclusive cruises and package tours, many prefer to travel independently in private vehicles, especially RVs. However, it is worth noting that most car and RV rental firms have an upper age limit.

Several national institutions give senior concessions. The

**National Park Service** offers Senior Passes that reduce the cost of entry, camping, and services in national parks. **Road Scholar** (formerly Elderhostel) has educational trips for travelers over 55, which may include inexpensive accommodation, lectures, and meals. For around $16, seniors can join the **American Association of Retired Persons (AARP)**, which issues cards that make available a host of travel discounts.

## Student Travelers

Students receive few special considerations in Alaska apart from discounts on some cultural programs and museum admissions. However, it never hurts to ask. Proof of student status will be needed, such as a current student body card from a specific school or university or an **International Student Identification Card** (ISIC). Inexpensive tickets can be arranged by **Student Travel Association** (STA) branches.

## Travelers with Disabilities

While the Alaskan back-country can be quite challenging for travelers with limited mobility or other disabilities or health problems, the state does offer a large number of accessible

Travelers aboard a tour boat in Rudyard Bay in Misty Fiords National Monument

options. As in the rest of the country, Alaska has regulations requiring government offices, businesses, public transport, and taxis to be designed to accommodate wheelchairs, while road crossings in cities have dropped curbs to enable easier access. In addition, most car parks, public toilets, hotels, and supermarkets offer special arrangements for the wheelchair-bound. Service animals, such as guide dogs, are allowed on public transport and in public buildings.

Frontcountry areas of most national and state parks often have paved or graded trails and viewing platforms that are wheelchair accessible. The National Park Service also offers an America the Beautiful Access Pass, which grants disabled individuals free entry to all national parks.

Cruise ships, tour buses, and railway cars all cater to disabled travelers, and many adventure tour companies do their best to accommodate clients with disabilities. **Access Alaska** can assist in finding accommodations and services for disabled travelers.

In the winter, the challenges can be greater, as snow renders streets and sidewalks difficult for wheelchair users and absorbs many of the acoustics that assist navigation for the blind. More information, from how to rent a specially adapted car to qualifying for parking permits, is offered by the **Access-Able Travel Source** and the **Society for Accessible Travel and Hospitality**, who promote awareness and accessibility for travelers with special needs.

## Etiquette

In general, Alaskans are polite, friendly, and helpful, although they may appear to be a bit more outspoken than other Americans. Visitors from across the world are welcomed, but are also expected to respect local ways, especially when visiting Native villages. It is illegal to bring alcohol into some areas and it is always wise to ask before taking photographs, especially of ceremonies, homes, or dances. Dress-wise, Alaska is one of the most relaxed states in the US. Attire tends to be informal, climate-dependent, and practical. Casual clothes such as jeans, T-shirts, flip-flops, and light woolens can be worn even for public performances or in upscale restaurants. Many Alaskans do not allow smoking in their homes or cars and it is considered courteous to check with your hosts if you may smoke (see p271).

## Electricity

Across the US, the electrical current is 110 volts at 60 hertz. Visitors from abroad need an adaptor plug for the two-prong sockets and a voltage converter to operate 220-volt appliances, such as hairdryers and rechargers for cell phones and laptop computers (unless they have a built-in adaptor). However, bear in mind that most hotel rooms have hairdryers and dedicated sockets for electric shavers.

## Conversion Chart

One US pint (0.5 liter) is smaller than one UK pint (0.6 liter). One Imperial gallon is the equivalent of five US quarts. To convert from degrees Celsius to degrees Fahrenheit, multiply by 1.8 and then add 32. From degrees Fahrenheit to degrees Celsius, subtract 32 and divide by 1.8.

**US Standard to Metric**
1 inch = 2.54 centimeters
1 foot = 30 centimeters
1 yard = 0.91 meters
1 mile = 1.6 kilometers
1 ounce = 28 grams
1 pound = 454 grams
1 US quart = 0.947 liters
1 US gallon = 3.79 liters

**Metric to US Standard**
1 centimeter = 0.4 inches
1 meter = 3 feet 3 inches
1 kilometer = 0.6 miles
1 gram = 0.04 ounces
1 kilogram = 2.2 pounds
1 liter = 1.1 US quarts

## DIRECTORY

### Traveling with Children

**Junior Ranger Program**
w nps.gov/kids/jrRangers.cfm

**Travel With Kids**
w travelwithkids.tv

### Senior Travelers

**American Association of Retired Persons (AARP)**
601 E St NW, Washington, DC 20049. **Tel** (888) 687-2277.
w aarp.org

**National Park Service**
**Tel** (888) 275-8747.
w nps.gov/fees_passes.htm

**Road Scholar**
11 Avenue de Lafayette, Boston, MA 02111-1746.
**Tel** (800) 454-5768.
w roadscholar.org

### Student Travelers

**International Student Identification Card**
w isic.org

**Student Travel Association**
w statravel.com

### Travelers with Disabilities

**Access-Able Travel Source**
PO Box 1796, Wheat Ridge, CO 80034.
**Tel** (303) 232-2979.
w access-able.com

**Access Alaska**
1217 East 10th Ave, Anchorage.
**Tel** 248-4777.
w accessalaska.org

**Society for Accessible Travel and Hospitality (SATH)**
347 5th Ave, Suite 610, New York, NY 10016. **Tel** (212) 447-7284.
w sath.org

# Personal Security and Health

In contrast to much of the US, Alaska has no really large cities, and while Anchorage has some gang and drug-related violence, it is not usually directed at visitors. On the whole, Alaska is a relatively safe place to visit, but even in small towns, it is wise to be alert and learn which areas are unsafe, especially at night. For visitors on adventure holidays *(see pp264–7)*, safety is paramount in the wilds of Alaska. Carry maps and follow the advice of rangers or visitors' centers – they can offer invaluable information on wilderness survival and basic safety procedures. Those on organized tours or cruises should follow the instructions provided by crew or tour leaders. Before setting out, it is a good idea to check local newspapers and television and radio channels for weather reports.

Police patrol car

## Personal Safety

Surprisingly, Alaska possesses one of the country's higher crime rates, although most tourist hubs are relatively non-threatening. Nevertheless, visitors should observe a few basic rules. Never carry large amounts of cash. Wallets kept in back pockets will tempt pickpockets. It is best to wear handbags and cameras over the shoulder, strapped firmly across the chest, and to keep passports separate from cash and traveler's checks. Drivers should try to keep valuables locked in the trunk of their car when parked at trailheads, especially those around Anchorage – they are known for break-ins. Large towns can be unsafe at night, so avoid walking around alone and try to stay away from areas that are known to be risky. Avoid panhandlers or anyone visibly intoxicated.

In Alaska, law enforcement in cities, towns, and certain boroughs is handled by local police departments. The **Alaska State Troopers** cover the rest of the state. In national parks, some park rangers are additionally in charge of law enforcement.

## Lost Property

It is necessary to report all lost and stolen property to the police in order to make an insurance claim, even though it is unlikely that small items will be recovered. Victims should telephone the **Police Non-Emergency Line** and report the incident. They will subsequently be issued a police report, which can be used to file the claim.

Stolen and lost credit and debit cards should be reported to the issuer immediately to avoid misuse. US law requires cardholders to be indemnified if loss or theft is reported immediately. Most card companies have toll-free numbers *(see p277)*.

Foreign visitors who have lost their passport should contact their nearest embassy or consulate, which will probably be in San Francisco or Seattle. Normally, the consulate will issue a temporary replacement. In order to speed up the replacement process, visitors might find it useful to keep photocopies of their driver's license, birth certificate, and passport.

## Medical Concerns

Hospitals in Alaska's largest cities are very well-equipped, but small towns usually only have health clinics, while rural villages often have just a public health nurse. Bear in mind that a range of drugs, such as codeine-based painkillers, may need prescriptions in the US. Prescription medication in the US is expensive, so those with prescriptions should carry extra supplies and a **Pharmacy Discount Card**, available online, which will provide significant discounts. All pharmacies sell prescription drugs, but only a couple of hospital pharmacies are open 24 hours. Be sure to keep a list of the generic names of drugs you may need and seek assistance in a drugstore if you are having difficulty finding the drug. Most supermarkets such as Fred Meyer and Walmart stock over-the-counter remedies.

Denali National Park ranger guiding visitors, Toklat Ranger Station

Medical care in the US can be expensive. Even with medical insurance, you may still have to pay upfront and claim reimbursement from your insurance company later, so ask for all forms and receipts.

## Travel Insurance

Partly due to the high cost of medical care in the US, visitors are urged to purchase travel health insurance for the duration of their stay. The package should cover death or dismemberment, dental and medical care, flight delays and cancellations, and lost or stolen baggage.

## Emergencies

For emergencies that require medical, fire, or police services, dial 911. Contact numbers of ambulance services, the Coast Guard, Rescue Services for stranded hikers or campers, Fire Departments, and the Poison Control Center are listed in telephone directory Blue Pages.

All hospitals in Alaska are equipped with emergency rooms, and their numbers are listed in the telephone book. Although critical emergency cases cannot be turned away by hospitals, evidence of the ability to pay may be required before treatment in non-emergency cases.

Hotel personnel will usually be able to call a doctor or a dentist and recommend a hospital on request. **Fairbanks Memorial Hospital** in Fairbanks and Anchorage's **Providence Alaska Medical Center** offer general medical care and critical care services. **Alaska Regional Hospital** also offers a Physician Referral Service. **Bartlett Regional Hospital** in Juneau has an acute care and emergency department, while **Central Peninsula General Hospital** in Soldotna has a shock trauma center.

## Outdoor Hazards

Alaska's weather can be extreme and volatile, and without proper clothing and shelter, even in the summer, hypothermia is a risk on wet, windy days. The layering method works best, and must include layers for warmth and insulation, as well as an outer waterproof shell.

At higher elevations, the summer sun can be surprisingly strong. It is wise to use an effective sunscreen, wear a hat, and carry sufficient water. Filtering any water taken from natural sources is vital, as Alaskan streams and lakes harbor the giardia parasite.

In the summer, wildfires and thunderstorms are perpetual risks, especially in the Interior.

Classic Smokey Bear fire prevention sign, Dawson City, Canada

It is important to watch campfires closely and to extinguish cigarettes carefully. Visitors who see a developing forest fire, especially near populated areas, should move away and report it to the authorities. During lightning storms, avoid ridges or open areas, and do not stand or camp beneath tall trees.

Earthquake and tsunami warnings are issued by the **Alaska Tsunami Warning Center**, but the chances of these occuring during a visit are remote. While most people are concerned about bear encounters, following a few simple guidelines (see p111) will almost eliminate the possibility of harm.

# DIRECTORY

## Emergency Services

### All Emergencies
**Tel** 911.

### Alaska State Troopers
Anchorage **Tel** 269-5511.
Fairbanks **Tel** 451-5100.
Juneau **Tel** 465-4000.
Ketchikan **Tel** 225-5118.
Kodiak **Tel** 486-4121.
Mat-Su **Tel** 373-8300.
Sitka **Tel** 747-3254.
Soldotna **Tel** 262-4453.

### Alaska Tsunami Warning Center
**Tel** 745-4212.
W wcatwc.arh.noaa.gov

## Hospitals

### Alaska Regional Hospital
2801 DeBarr Rd, Anchorage.
**Tel** 276-1131, (888) 254-7884 (physician referral).
W alaskaregional.com

### Bartlett Regional Hospital
3260 Hospital Drive, Juneau. **Tel** 796-8900.
W bartletthospital.org

### Central Peninsula General Hospital
250 Hospital Place, Soldotna. **Tel** 714-4404.
W cpgh.org

### Fairbanks Memorial Hospital
1650 Cowles St, Fairbanks.
**Tel** 452-8181.

### Providence Alaska Medical Center
3200 Providence Dr, Anchorage. **Tel** 562-2211.
W providence.org

### Pharmacy Discount Card
W goorx.com

### Police Non-Emergency Line
Anchorage **Tel** 786-8500.
Fairbanks **Tel** 459-6500.
Juneau **Tel** 586-0600.
Ketchikan **Tel** 225-6631.
Kodiak **Tel** 486-8000.
Sitka **Tel** 747-3245.
Soldotna **Tel** 262-4455.
Wasilla **Tel** 352-5401.

## Consulates

### Australia
575 Market St, Suite 1800, San Francisco, CA 94105.
**Tel** (415) 644-3630.

### Canada
1501 4th Ave, Suite 600, Seattle, WA 98101.
**Tel** (206) 443-1777.

### New Zealand
10649 N Beach Rd, Bow, WA 98232. **Tel** (360) 766-8002.

### UK
1 Sansome St, Suite 850, San Francisco, CA 94104.
**Tel** (415) 617-1300.

# Banking and Currency

Visitors will generally not encounter any problems with financial transactions in Alaska. Banks are plentiful and foreign currency exchanges are available in larger cities, but it is best to verify opening hours before visiting banks or exchange bureaus. Automated teller machines (ATMs), which enable visitors to make cash withdrawals with debit or credit cards, are available all over Alaska, even in small towns and some villages. Found in most banks, supermarkets, and general stores, these are open 24 hours a day. Some banks even have drive-up ATMs. Credit cards are commonly used for making payments, especially at hotels and car rental companies.

ATMs can dispense cash, enact account transfers, and show bank balances

## Banks and Foreign Currency Exchange

Alaskan banks are generally open from 9 or 10am to 4:30, 5, or 6pm on weekdays, and often on Saturdays from 10am to 2 or 3pm, but these hours can vary across the state. Banks will convert traveler's checks to US dollars, and for a substantial commission, some **Wells Fargo** banks in Anchorage, Fairbanks, and Juneau will also change foreign currency traveler's checks and cash.

## Traveler's Checks

Traveler's checks, while rarely used in the age of ATMs, are safer than cash as they can be replaced if lost or stolen. It is important to keep the checks separate from the list of check numbers, which are required if checks have to be replaced in case of loss or theft. Foreign currency traveler's checks may be cashed at Wells Fargo banks in Juneau, Anchorage, and Fairbanks, but they are otherwise of little use in Alaska. To avoid extra charges, it is best to carry **American Express** or **VISA** traveler's checks in US dollars. These are always accepted as cash, without fees, in hotels, restaurants, shops, gas stations, and other businesses across Alaska, except in some of the smallest rural villages. Often, some form of photo ID, such as a passport or driver's license, is required as identification when using traveler's checks.

## Credit, Debit, and Charge Cards

Credit and charge cards are practically essential when traveling in the US. The cards are usually required as a guarantee when renting a car or RV (see pp288–9), and are used to book tours, airline tickets, and tickets for most forms of entertainment. The most widely used cards are **VISA** and **MasterCard**, but most places also accept American Express, **Diner's Club**, and **Discover Card**.

ATMs offer better foreign exchange rates than banks, and all credit, charge, and debit cards can be used to withdraw cash from ATMs, with a bank transaction fee of $2 to $3, in addition to the credit card company's charges. The most common international systems are Cirrus and Plus. Before you leave home, it is best to ask your bank or credit card company which ATM system your card can access.

## Wiring Money

Money can be wired to Alaska from more than 100 countries. Money transfers can usually be sent and received within 15 minutes, but in some cases, it may take as much as a full day or even up to a week. The fastest and most popular service is **Western Union**, which is found all over Alaska, but banks also offer wire services, albeit slower. Thanks to the number of foreign crew members on cruise ships, other businesses offering wire services can usually be found near the cruise ship docks.

## Currency

US currency is based on the decimal system, and the standard unit is the US dollar, divided into 100 cents. Bills, or bank notes, are all of similar size and greenish in color (newer bills have subtle color backgrounds), so it is wise to always check the denomination and count change carefully. In villages and remote areas, smaller bills are preferred, and in some places, $50 and $100 bills are not accepted at night. Similarly, some liquor stores will not change $50 or $100 bills unless the purchase is over half the amount of the bill. The quarter (25-cent piece) is useful for the now rare public telephones. It is also best to carry cash for small transactions and tips, and for use on public transport and in taxis.

## Coins

*US coins come in $1, 50-, 25-, 10-, 5-, and 1-cent pieces. Each coin has a popular name: 1-cent coins are pennies, 5-cent coins are nickels, 10-cent coins are dimes, and 25-cent coins are quarters. State quarters are in circulation, as are goldtone Sacagawea dollars. The Susan B. Anthony and Eisenhower dollars are uncommon, as is the John F. Kennedy 50-cent coin, which is now a collector's item.*

25-cent coin (a quarter)

10-cent coin
(a dime)

5-cent coin (a nickel)

1-cent coin (a penny)

1-dollar coin (a buck)

## Banknotes

*US bank notes come in denominations of $1, $2, $5, $10, $20, $50, and $100, but the $2 bill is rare. Paper bills were first issued in 1862 to finance the Civil War, when metal for coins was in short supply. The size and design of the notes was decided in 1929, and in the 1990s, the artwork for all but the $1 bill was re-engraved with anti-counterfeit markings.*

1-dollar bill ($1)

5-dollar bill ($5)

10-dollar bill ($10)

20-dollar bill ($20)

50-dollar bill ($50)

100-dollar bill ($100)

# Communications and Media

The United States has some of the most sophisticated communications systems in the world. Postal, telephone, and Internet services are all widely available, providing fast and efficient services to destinations both in-state and worldwide. In these days of widespread cell phone usage, public card phones and pay phones are found in decreasing numbers around the state, and in smaller towns and villages, cell phone coverage is usually quite limited.

## Telephones

All local telephone numbers have seven digits. The cost of a local call is 25 to 35 cents, which is usually good for any length of call. Alaska's area code is 907, though the village of Hyder uses 250. This is required when calling long-distance, even in-state. Long-distance calls to any number outside the local area (especially in-state calls) cost considerably more, but are cheaper when dialled direct or at off-peak times, usually in the evenings and on weekends. Calls made on hotel phones will usually be charged at much higher rates.

**Phone cards for long-distance calls**

Pay phones are becoming increasingly rare as cell phones replace landlines. They can be used for international calls, but callers will need a stack of change to dial direct and will be interrupted by an operator when more money is needed. A phone card is easier, but it is advisable to use only reputable companies such as AT&T. Cards can be purchased at supermarkets, convenience stores, and hotels for values between $5 and $50, and operate by providing a series of numbers to punch into the phone, which then accesses the account and announces how much time remains on that card. Each card has clear usage instructions printed on it.

Toll-free numbers are widely used in the US for contacting hotels, car rental companies, tour operators, and even some tourist offices. While most toll-free numbers are not accessible when calling from outside the US, in some cases they may occasionally be connected through an operator and charged at the regular toll rate.

## Cell Phones, Internet, and Fax Services

Many travelers bring their own cell (mobile) phones, but service varies among operators, so check if your service provider provides coverage in Alaska. Coverage is usually good in towns, and even, surprisingly, in many remote areas, but may be erratic outside towns. International travelers can purchase a prepaid SIM card, a **TracFone**, or a temporary cell phone, available at larger retail outlets, for a few dollars.

An increasing number of box stores, shops, and restaurants offer Wi-Fi access to patrons. Most hotels offer Internet access to their guests. Virtually all libraries also have free Internet access. Faxes can often be sent from larger hotels and copy centers. Many places in rural Alaska have only limited Internet access.

## Mail Services

In the US, all domestic mail is First Class unless otherwise requested, and generally takes between three and five days to arrive. First Class mail costs only about 20 percent more than parcel post (surface mail), which is also available. International mail sent by air takes between five and ten days to arrive, but surface parcels may take over four weeks. Special parcel services are also offered by the **US Postal Service**. Priority Mail delivers faster than normal First Class and costs only marginally more. Express Mail guarantees next day delivery within the Lower 48 states, and a day or two more to Hawaii. International Express

**Typical US mailbox**

## Useful Dialing Codes

- To make a direct-dial long-distance call within Alaska, the rest of the US, or Canada, dial **1** (the country code) followed by the area code and local number. Useful area codes: Alaska **907**, Yukon Territory **867**, British Columbia (and Hyder in Alaska) **250**.
- For international direct-dial calls, dial **011** followed by the desired country code. Then dial the area or town code (omitting the first 0 or 1), and the local number.
- To make an international call via the operator, dial **01** and follow the same procedure as detailed above.

- For international operator assistance, dial **01**.
- For local operator assistance, dial **0**.
- For international directory inquiries, dial **00**.
- For local directory inquiries, dial **411**.
- For inquiries in another US or Canadian area code, dial **1** followed by the desired area code and **555-1212**.
- For emergency police, fire, and ambulance services, dial **911**.
- Dial **844** for temperature, weather, and time.
- **1-800**, **866**, **877**, and **888** indicate toll-free numbers.

Newspaper vending machines on 4th Avenue, downtown Anchorage

Mail guarantees to deliver in five working days. Several private international couriers offer next-day delivery for foreign mail, the best known being **DHL**, **Federal Express**, and **UPS**.

All Alaskan towns have at least one post office. Small packages and letters may be dropped into mailboxes, but all parcels will need to be inspected at the post office counter. Contract post offices in shops and small towns often have shorter queues, but don't accept international parcels.

## Newspapers, Radio, and Television

The major daily newspaper in Alaska is the *Alaska Dispatch News*. Other major papers are the daily *Fairbanks New-Miner* and *Juneau Empire*, and the weekly *Mat-Su Frontiersman*. Bestselling national daily papers such as the *Wall Street Journal*, the *New York Times*, and *USA Today* are also available, although a few days late, at large bookshops and newsstands in major airports. Some visitors' centers and shops offer free papers listing local weather, events, and news. The most popular of these is the *Anchorage Press*.

The Alaska Public Radio Network has stations in all major cities and towns. Anchorage's 91.1 FM is the most popular; 650 and 700 AM have news and talk. In Fairbanks, 970 AM has the news, while 104.7 FM plays rock. 630 AM in Juneau has the news. Most hotels offer a range of cable and satellite TV channels.

## DIRECTORY

### Mail services

**DHL**
Tel (800) 225-5345. W dhl.com

**Federal Express (FedEx)**
Tel (800) 463-3339. W fedex.com

**UPS**
Tel (800) 742-5877. W ups.com

**US Postal Service**
Tel (800) 275-8777. W usps.com

### Phones

**TracFone**
Tel (800) 867-7183.
W tracfone.com

## Alaskan Lexicon

**Baleen** – strips of fibrous tissue from the mouths of baleen whales, used to filter plankton from the sea.

**Breakup** – wet and muddy period when the ice melts in April.

**Bush** – the part of Alaska that is off the highway and ferry systems.

**Cache** – hut built on stilts and used to store items out of reach of animals.

**Camai** – an Athabaskan greeting (pronounced "cha-MAI") that is the Alaskan equivalent of "Aloha."

**Cheechako** – a newcomer who has been in Alaska less than about 20 years.

**Chinook** – warm wind from the Southeast that can melt the snow, even in midwinter.

**Igloo** – a variation of the Inupiat word *illu*, which means "house." The ice block variety is used only as an emergency shelter.

**Lower 48** – all US states except Alaska and Hawaii.

**Mukluks** – moosehide or sealskin boots.

**Muktuk** – whale or seal blubber favored by Native Alaskans.

**Mushing** – driving a dog sled, also Alaska's state sport.

**Native** – spelled with an uppercase "N," it refers to an indigenous Alaskan. Spelled with a lowercase "n," it refers to anyone born in Alaska.

**Outhouse** – outdoor toilet consisting of a hole in the ground covered by a shelter.

**Permafrost** – permanently frozen ground overlain by topsoil or muskeg.

**Potlatch** – Southeast Alaska Native feast in which the host distributes numerous possessions.

**Scrimshaw** – Native designs etched onto walrus ivory.

**Skookum** – anything that's strong, great, or wonderful.

**Slough** – stagnant backwater formed by old river channels (pronounced "slew").

**Snowbirds** – older people who summer in Alaska but winter in the Lower 48.

**Snowmachine** – what other North Americans would call a snowmobile or ski-doo.

**Sourdough** – an old-time prospector or any long-time Alaskan, usually those who have been in Alaska for at least two decades. The word is derived from the bread made with sourdough starter *(see p248)*.

**Taiga** – Russian for "little sticks," referring to black spruce. Much of Alaska's muskeg and boreal forest consists of taiga vegetation.

**Tundra** – derived from the Finnish word for "treeless plain," it refers to areas of miniature plants in Alaska's northern and alpine areas.

**Ulu** – a crescent-shaped knife used by Natives for cleaning and skinning animal skins and cutting meat.

**Xtra Tufs** – high-top rubber boots used throughout Alaska.

# TRAVEL INFORMATION

The majority of overseas visitors to Alaska land in Anchorage, the state's main gateway. Those coming from the Lower 48 can fly from Seattle directly to Ketchikan or Juneau. Bus services link the Lower 48 and Canada with Anchorage and Fairbanks, but many visitors journey overland by car on the Alaska or Cassiar highways, or sail on an Alaska Marine Highway vehicle ferry from Bellingham, Washington, through the Inside Passage to Southeast Alaska. There, travelers can transfer to ferries bound for the Kenai Peninsula, Southwest Alaska, and Prince William Sound, where it is possible to connect to the Alaska Railroad. Within Alaska, rental vehicles are a good alternative to the limited public transport systems and provide maximum freedom. Sites off the highways can be accessed by an extensive network of scheduled or chartered flights.

## Arriving by Air

All major cities and towns in Alaska have an airport, while remote towns and villages have airstrips for transport planes and bush traffic. The state's biggest airport – and the one most visitors are likely to see first – is Ted Stevens International Airport in Anchorage, which receives all international flights from Europe and Asia and the greatest number of flights from the Lower 48.

As the only non-stop intercontinental flights to Alaska are from Frankfurt and Reykjavik, most overseas visitors arrive via Seattle. There are also non-stop flights from select US cities, including Minneapolis, Salt Lake City, Maui, Honolulu, Los Angeles, Dallas, Portland, Phoenix, Chicago, and Denver.

Alaska's major airline, **Alaska Airlines**, is based in Seattle and connects a host of cities across the US, Cuba, and Mexico to a wide variety of Alaskan destinations such as Anchorage and Fairbanks, several towns in the Southeast including Juneau, Sitka, and Ketchikan, Cordova in Prince William Sound, Nome, Kotzebue, and Barrow in the north, and Kodak and Dutch Harbor in Southwest Alaska.

Scheduled flights into Anchorage are also offered by **Condor**, **American Airlines**, **Iceland Air**, **Delta**, **Jet Blue**, and **United Airlines**. They connect Alaska with the US and international destinations.

## International Arrivals

Overseas visitors arriving in the US must present a passport and, if necessary, a visa to immigration officials before claiming their baggage. Those catching connecting flights must collect their luggage at the first point of entry into the US and take it through US Customs before checking it on to their final destination.

Non-resident adults are allowed to bring in a limited amount of duty-free items. These include 0.2 gallons (1 liter) of alcohol, 50 cigars, 200 cigarettes, and up to $100 worth of gifts. There is no legal limit on the amount of money that can be brought into the US, but cash amounts over $10,000 should be declared to US Customs. Completed customs declaration forms must be submitted to a US Customs officer while exiting the Customs hall.

Most major airports offer a wide range of services such as newsstands, car rental companies, shuttle buses, and taxi services.

Specially painted Alaska Airlines aircraft underscoring the carrier's role in transporting Alaskan seafood

Floatplane taking off to tour remote corners of Alaska

## Internal Flights

In addition to the numerous Alaska Airlines services, several domestic airlines offer convenient, if occasionally somewhat expensive, services. **Ravn Alaska** (formed by a merger between Era Alaska and Arctic Circle Air) flies throughout the state, including from Anchorage and Fairbanks to Prince William Sound, Kenai, Peninsula, Kodiak, and Western Alaska. **PenAir** flies to a host of destinations on the Alaska Peninsula and the Aleutian Islands, including the Pribilof Islands. **Bering Air** accesses tiny places in Western Alaska from Nome and Kotzebue, and also operates charter flights to the Russian Far East. **Grant Aviation** does daily runs between Southwest Alaska, Anchorage, Homer, and Bethel. **Wings of Alaska** serves the Southeast, and **Warbelow's Air Ventures** links the northern outposts of the state.

Alaska also has a host of charter airlines which can take passengers to just about any airport or airstrip in the state, as well as bush airlines (see p264) that land fly-in hunters, anglers, river runners, or hikers on remote lakes, rivers, glaciers, or gravel bars.

## Air Fares

There is a vast array of fare types and prices available for travel to and around Alaska. Airlines compete with each other, and it pays to compare and book early to get the cheapest fares, especially during the busy summer season. Although several websites do offer bargains on last-minute bookings, direct flights to the US and Alaska usually need to be booked in advance.

Online agents such as **Kayak**, **Orbitz**, and **Travelzoo** usually provide the most economical tickets. They offer a choice of flights and itineraries for a range of fares, including bargain options. These flights can prove expensive to exchange. Therefore, it is advisable to provide for trip changes or cancellations with a travel insurance policy, usually purchased at the time of booking. These can be clubbed with bargain car rentals and hotel bookings.

Travel agents may also be able to offer special deals to visitors who book rental cars, accommodation, and domestic flights in addition to their international ticket.

## Baggage Restrictions

Most airlines now charge for checked bags, but allow carry-ons consisting of one piece of hand luggage and a small handbag. On smaller domestic airlines, flightseeing trips, and bush flights, only one piece of hand luggage is accepted and the weight of checked baggage may be limited to as little as 20 lb (9 kg) per person.

# DIRECTORY

## Airline Carriers

**Alaska Airlines**
Tel (800) 252-7522.
W alaskaair.com

**American Airlines**
Tel (800) 433-7300.
W aa.com

**Bering Air**
Tel (800) 478-5422.
W beringair.com

**Condor**
Tel (866) 960-7915.
W condor.com

**Delta**
Tel (800) 221-1212.
W delta.com

**Frontier**
Tel (800) 432-1359.
W frontierairlines.com

**Grant Aviation**
Tel (888) 359-4726.
W flygrant.com

**Iceland Air**
Tel (800) 223-5500.
W icelandair.com

**Jet Blue**
Tel (800) 538-2583.
W jetblue.com

**PenAir**
Tel (800) 448-4226.
W penair.com

**Ravn Alaska**
Tel 248-4422, (800) 866-8394.
W flyravn.com

**United Airlines**
Tel (800) 864-8331.
W united.com

**Warbelow's Air Ventures**
Tel 474-0518, (888) 459-6250.
W warbelows.com

**Wings of Alaska**
Tel 697-2201, (800) 789-9464.
W wingsofalaska.com

## Online Agencies

**Kayak**
W kayak.com

**Orbitz**
W orbitz.com

**Travelzoo**
W travelzoo.com

Most terminals also offer facilities for the disabled.

# Alaska Marine Highway

Often called the "Blue Canoe," the state-run Alaska Marine Highway provides year-round access from Bellingham in Washington state and Prince Rupert in British Columbia, Canada. It also connects the mostly roadless areas of the Southeast, Southwest, and Prince William Sound. The route is so beautiful that it has been officially designated a National Scenic Byway, a term usually reserved for highways. The Marine Highway is also an easy, if expensive, way to transport a vehicle to Alaska, and with advance planning, it is possible to stop off in any of the ports of call along the way. Schedules, however, can often go awry, so it is wise to allow a bit of buffer time.

## Routes

The Alaska Marine Highway has three main routes: Southeast, Southcentral, and Southwest. The Southeast route is the longest one, following the spectacular Inside Passage up the west coast of North America from Bellingham in Washington state to Prince Rupert in Canada, and then northward through Southeast Alaska's islands and channels to Haines and Skagway. Ports of call along the way usually include Ketchikan, Wrangell, Petersburg, and Juneau, with some sailings calling in at Sitka. The MV *Kennicott* does the cross-Gulf run, from Juneau in the Southeast to Whittier in Prince

William Sound via Yakutat, Cordova, and Valdez. The Southcentral route connects Whittier to Cordova, Valdez, and Chenega Bay, and also to Kodiak, Port Lions, Homer, and Seldovia. On the Southwestern route, the MV *Tustumena (see p215)* sails between April and September from Homer to Seldovia, Kodiak, and Port Lions, and down the Alaska Peninsula and the Aleutians to Chignik, Sand Point, King Cove, Cold Bay, and Dutch Harbor.

Access to Prince of Wales Island from Ketchikan is provided by **Inter-Island Ferries**, while **British Columbia Ferries** sails from Port Hardy, near the northern tip of Vancouver Island, to Prince Rupert.

Marine Highway ferry sailing away from Valdez in Prince William Sound

## Ferries

Eleven different ferries of various sizes regularly ply the Southeast, Southcentral, and Southwest Alaska routes. Traditionally and legally, the vessels in the fleet are named after Alaskan glaciers. The largest of the ferries, the flagship MV *Columbia* holds 625 passengers and is usually used on runs between Bellingham, WA, and Haines, as is the MV *Malaspina*. Both ships boast a dining room, gift shop, cocktail lounge, solarium, and observation lounge.

The MV *Aurora* and the catamaran MV *Chenega* run shorter routes in the Southeast and also serve Prince William Sound. MVs *Kennicott, Taku, Matanuska, LeConte, Lituya* and the catamaran MV *Fairweather* do a variety of runs in the Southeast. The fleet's oldest, sturdiest ship, the MV *Tustumena*, popularly known as the "Trusty Tusty," does the turbulent Aleutian Island run.

## Facilities

In general, the long-haul ferries are better equipped than the ones doing day runs. Except for the fast catamarans MV *Fairweather* and MV *Chenega*, which have only snack bars, the larger vessels have cafeterias that serve snacks, hot meals, and beverages. The MV *Columbia* and MV *Tustumena* also have full-service dining rooms, where both American and Continental breakfasts are available, and lunch and dinner menus usually offer a daily special or choice of main dishes, featuring seafood, salad, and vegetable dishes. Sandwiches and snacks are always available. Mixed drinks are sold only on the MV *Columbia* and MV *Tustumena*, but beer and wine are available in the snack bars on the fast ferries.

MVs *Columbia, Malaspina, Matanuska, Tustumena*, and *Taku* offer cabins with private bathroom facilities, while the MV *Kennicott* has a few two-berth unserviced rooms without facilities. The five short-haul ferries do not have cabins. All ferries have public showers.

Under the solarium on the upper deck of a Marine Highway ferry

## DIRECTORY
**Ferries**

### Alaska Marine Highway
6858 Glacier Hwy, Juneau, 99811.
**Tel** 465-3941, (800) 642-0066.
**w** dot.state.ak.us/amhs/pubs

### Inter-Island Ferries
PO Box 470, Klawock.
**Tel** 530-4848, (866) 308-4848.
**w** interislandferry.com

### British Columbia Ferries
**Tel** (250) 386-3431, (888) 223-3779.
**w** bcferries.com

Deck passengers on overnight trips can sleep in the indoor recliners, or on reclining plastic deck chairs in the heated solariums on the top decks of the ferries. On all overnight sailings, travelers are allowed to pitch tents on the top deck and fix them with waterproof duct tape. These are usually quite close to the smokestack and noisy engines, so it may be useful to carry some earplugs. All ferries have elevators and wheelchair-accessible facilities, and the larger vessels also offer cabins suitable for disabled passengers.

## Life on Board

There are few things more relaxing than sitting in the observation lounge or warm solarium of a ferry and watching the passing scene. While onboard amenities are spartan by most standards, there's always plenty to fill up the time. In addition to watching the undeniably spectacular landscapes along most routes, passengers find they have plenty of time to lean back with a book, take a hot shower, sleep or lounge in the fresh air, and meet people from across the world.

## Taking a Vehicle

Book as far in advance as possible in order to transport a vehicle on the Marine Highway, especially between Bellingham, WA, and Haines in the peak season from June to August. Tariffs depend on the size of the vehicle, measured from the front bumper to the end of the back bumper or trailer. Most vessels on the Southeast and Southcentral routes can take vehicles up to 70-ft (20-m) long, but the maximum length on the MV *Tustumena* is 40 ft (12 m). Except in some small ports,

drivers will usually be required to check in two hours before sailing. The crew will direct them to their parking location, where they must set their hand brake, take any possessions needed onboard, and lock the vehicle. The vehicle deck will not be accessible while sailing. However, escorted trips to the vehicle deck are periodically announced by the purser, and there is vehicle access while the vessel is in port. RV propane tanks and fire-arms must be reported to the purser upon boarding, so they can be sealed by the crew. Boats under 100 lb (45 kg), bicycles, and kayaks incur an extra charge, while larger boats will be charged as vehicles. Except for guide dogs, transporting pets also incurs an extra charge.

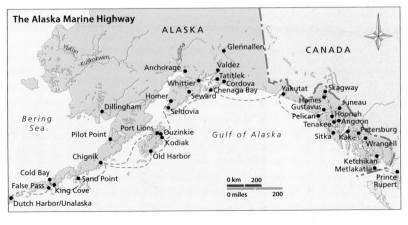

The Alaska Marine Highway

# Traveling by Bus and Train

Although slower than car and plane travel, taking a bus or train in Alaska can be an enjoyable way of exploring the region. Long-distance bus services, however limited, are the least expensive way to travel, although some places are served only by costly tour buses. Within the larger cities, local buses are the only form of public transport. Although these tend to focus on daytime services for local commuters, they are also useful to visitors since most centrally placed attractions lie along or near main bus routes. The best way to cover long distance journeys within Alaska is through the several private bus lines, as well as the Alaska Railroad, Alaska Marine Highway, White Pass and Yukon Route Railroad (WP&YR), and Gray Line buses in Alaska.

Alaska Railroad train pulling into Denali National Park station

Gray Line tour bus

Skagway's popular yellow tourist bus

## Traveling by Bus

In Alaska, only a handful of popular routes are served by long-distance buses, and those services that do exist are generally infrequent. Many services are operated only during the summer.

The best-served routes are those between Anchorage, Fairbanks, and the Kenai Peninsula, and points in between. **Park Connection Motorcoach** runs from Seward to Denali National Park via Talkeetna, Anchorage, and Whittier. **Seward Bus Lines** connects Anchorage with Seward while the **Homer Stage Line** runs between Anchorage, Homer, and Seward. **Alaska-Yukon Trails** has a year-round service between Anchorage and Fairbanks, as well as summer services to Dawson City and Whitehorse in Canada. **Interior Alaska Bus Lines** operates services between Anchorage, Fairbanks, and Tok.

**Kennicott Shuttle** buses run between Glennallen and McCarthy in Wrangell-St. Elias National Park. **Gray Line Alaska** runs tours to places of interest throughout the state.

To reach Alaska by bus from the Lower 48 states, it is best to take **Greyhound Canada** to Whitehorse, and connect to the Alaska Direct Bus or Alaska/Yukon trails to Anchorage or Fairbanks. **Green Tortoise** is a unique bus touring company with several 10- or 14-day trips each summer. It's an especially popular option with young international travelers.

## Traveling by Train

Traveling by train in Alaska means riding the **Alaska Railroad** (*see pp286–7*) between Seward and Fairbanks or taking the tourist route on the **White Pass and Yukon Route Railroad** (*see pp152–3*) from Skagway. While rail services are limited and relatively expensive, they're both relaxing and scenic, and most visitors will want to experience at least one rail trip during their stay.

The Alaska Railroad is an extremely popular and convenient way to reach Denali National Park. While there are no overnight trains and, therefore, no sleeper services, all visitor-oriented trains on the main line between Seward and Fairbanks offer onboard dining services. Because so many cruise ships and tour companies use the Alaska Railroad to transport their passengers from Seward

Park shuttle buses lining up for passengers, Denali National Park

White Pass and Yukon Route Railroad depot, Skagway

and Whittier to Anchorage, Denali National Park, and Fairbanks, many trains have special double-decker domed observation cars owned by Princess Cruise Line and Holland America Line *(see pp256–9)*. Accessible only to tour members, these offer onboard guides and other amenities. In addition, the railroad has its own luxurious "Goldstar" railcars with open-air viewing platforms. A number of seasonal day trips are also offered by the **Alaska Railroad** from Anchorage and other cities. Especially popular is the all-day Spencer Glacier float

trip. This includes a rail ride to the glacier on the Kenai Peninsula with a gentle raft trip past icebergs on the lake and then down the Placer River.

## City Public Transport

Only Anchorage, Juneau, the Mat-Su, Fairbanks, and Ketchikan have regular public bus services, but Barrow, Kodiak, Sitka, and Skagway have limited services or shuttles. In Anchorage, **People Mover** covers most parts of the city from the Downtown Transit Center. Services run from 6am to 10pm from Monday to Friday, with limited routes on

weekends. People Mover will take passengers as far north as Eagle River. Within the Mat-Su Borough, **Mat-Su Community Transit** (MASCOT) operates buses around Wasilla and Palmer. **Valley Mover** runs services between Wasilla and Anchorage. With a day's notice, **Anchor Rides** provides door-to-door transport for disabled or elderly passengers. **Metropolitan Area Commuter System** (MACS) covers the Fairbanks area. **Capital Transit** in Juneau links the downtown area with the Mendenhall Valley and Douglas Island. **The Bus** in Ketchikan connects the downtown area, the North Tongass Highway, and Saxman village.

## Tickets and Bookings

For trains and buses, it is advisable to book tickets well in advance as this ensures availability, confirms the place to meet the bus, and provides assurance that the service is operating – bus lines cancel trips if there is insufficient interest. Buses leave from the bus company's offices or from a centrally located landmark.

# DIRECTORY

## Bus Companies

**Alaska-Yukon Trails**
PO Box 84608, Fairbanks.
**Tel** (800) 770-7275.
W alaskashuttle.com

**Green Tortoise**
**Tel** (415) 956-7500, (800) 867-8647.
W greentortoise.com

**Gray Line Alaska**
800 5th Ave, Suite 2600, Seattle, WA 98104.
**Tel** (888) 425-1737.
W graylinealaska.com

**Greyhound Canada**
877 Greyhound Way SW, Calgary AB T3C 3V8.
**Tel** (800) 661-8747.
W greyhound.ca

**Homer Stage Line**
Homer. **Tel** 235-2252, 868-3914. W stageline inhomer.com

**Interior Alaska Bus Lines**
PO Box 501, Anchorage.
**Tel** (800) 770-6652 (Anchorage).
W alaskadirectbusline.com

**Kennicott Shuttle**
PO Box 65, Glennallen.
**Tel** 822-5292.
W kennicottshuttle.com

**Park Connection Motorcoach**
PO Box 22–1011, Anchorage. **Tel** (800) 266-8625.
W alaskacoach.com

**Seward Bus Lines**
3333 Fairbanks St, Anchorage. **Tel** (888) 420-7788, 224-3608.
W sewardbuslines.net

## Rail Companies

**Alaska Railroad**
PO Box 107500, Anchorage. **Tel** 265-2494, (800) 544-0522.
W alaskarailroad.com

**White Pass and Yukon Route Railroad**
231 2nd Ave, Skagway.
**Tel** (800) 343-7373.
W wpyr.com

## City Public Transport

**Anchor Rides**
Anchorage. **Tel** 343-7433.
W muni.org/departments/transit/anchorrides

**Capital Transit**
Juneau. **Tel** 789-6901.
W juneau.org/capitaltransit

**Mat-Su Community Transit**
**Tel** 864-5000.
W matsutransit.com

**Metropolitan Area Commuter System**
Fairbanks. **Tel** 459-1011.
W co.fairbanks.ak.us/transportation

**People Mover**
**Tel** 343-6543.
W peoplemover.org

**The Bus**
Ketchikan. **Tel** 225-8726.
W borough.ketchikan.ak.us /145/Transit

**Valley Mover**
**Tel** 892-8800.
W valleymover.org

# The Alaska Railroad

The Alaska Railroad may not be that far off the mark when it claims to offer the best rail trips in the world. Few journeys in the country cross such beautiful and wild terrain as this ribbon of steel that stretches across the landscape between Seward and Fairbanks. The trains allow passengers the best views possible, with all seats facing forward in the 1950s railcars. Travelers on the *Denali Star* can book seats in the domed viewing cars and access outdoor viewing areas from where the best photographs can be taken. Some trains also carry viewing cars owned by cruise companies and reserved exclusively for their clients.

### History of the Railroad

The Alaska Railroad had its beginnings in 1903 when the Alaska Central Railway was built northward from Seward. In 1907, after 50 miles (80 km) of track were laid, the company went bankrupt. After the firm was reorganized as the Alaska Northern Railway, another 21 miles (34 km) of track were laid. In 1914, the US Congress sanctioned $35 million for the construction of a complete line between Seward and Fairbanks, and the tent city of Anchorage was designated as a railroad construction camp. The entire 470-mile (756-km) Alaska Railroad line was finally completed in 1917, and was inaugurated by President Warren G. Harding in Nenana in 1923 (*see p173*).

A branch line to Whittier was laid during World War II by blasting tunnels through the Chugach Range, and the railroad began making a profit by transporting military and civilian supplies. In addition to the $30 million damage caused by the 1964 Good Friday earthquake, the railroad has overcome landslides, heavy snowfalls, derailments, and even chemical spills. The rolling stock was upgraded between 1999 and 2005, and today the scenic lines of the Alaska Railroad rank among the state's most popular tourist attractions.

**Baggage tickets issued by the Alaska Railroad**

### Regular Services

While some regular commuter services on the railroad double as tourist services, other trains cater specially to tourists while also accommodating local passengers. Most of the visitor-oriented trains carry a dining car and railway gift shop, and each summer, guides on the trains interpret the history and wildlife seen along the route.

Between mid-May and mid-September, the daily Coastal Classic runs between Anchorage and Seward. During the same period, the regularly scheduled Glacier Discovery connects Anchorage to Whittier, followed by an optional trip to Spencer Glacier. From the glacier, passengers can either take a raft trip or continue to Grandview Pass for spectacular glacier viewing. The most popular route, however, is the Denali Star, which does the incredibly scenic run between Anchorage and Fairbanks, stopping en route at Denali National Park. The summer Hurricane Turn has Thursday to Sunday services, with extra runs on certain holidays, to serve bush passengers between Talkeetna and Hurricane. This 60-mile (97-km) local route has no food services.

In the winter, the Aurora does a weekend run between Anchorage and Fairbanks, with flag-stop services. From October to May, on the first Thursday of each month, the winter Hurricane Turn does the return day trip between Anchorage and Hurricane, offering wonderful views of the Susitna Valley and the Alaska Range.

The Hurricane Turn rolling across Hurricane Gulch, between Talkeetna and Denali National Park

Flag-stop passengers boarding the Alaska Railroad

## Flag-Stop Service

The Alaska Railroad proudly boasts that its summer Hurricane Turn train between Talkeetna and Hurricane is one of the last rail journeys in the world to offer a flag-stop service. Passengers can flag down the train – also called the "Bug Car" due to a profusion of onboard mosquitos in the summer – anywhere along the route, and it will stop to let them board. In the winter, all Alaska Railroad trains offer a flag-stop service. This is important for bush residents who live in remote areas without ready access to the road system. Similarly, travelers can disembark anywhere for a few days of hiking or fishing, and then board the train again wherever they would like to

continue with their journey. Note that stove fuel cannot be carried on the train.

## Event Trains

During the off-season, the railroad runs many special services between Anchorage and Portage or Seward. Known as Event Trains, these are, in effect, rolling festivities with specific themes. The Alaska Railroad Blues Train runs in September and features local blues bands, a blues concert, a barbecue, and an overnight stay in Seward. In October, the Great Alaska Beer Train offers Alaskan appetizers and microbrews from Anchorage's Glacier Brewhouse *(see p250)* while traveling between Anchorage and Portage. During the Alaska State Fair between late August and early September, the popular Fair Train provides a great way to visit the state fair in Palmer. Trains leave Anchorage in the morning, returning in the evening. For Halloween, the Alyeska Mystery Trail includes a rail trip to "Girdwoodvania" for a haunted murder mystery. The railroad's website has detailed information on tours.

## Special Tours

The railroad has teamed up with local operators to offer visitors unique rail-based itineraries and peripheral tours. These include a fabulous ten-day trip covering the entire railbelt, taking in Anchorage, Seward, Denali, Fairbanks, and Whittier. Other options take in sections of these routes, including a Prince William Sound cruise with

### DIRECTORY

## Alaska Railroad

**Main Office**
PO Box 107500, Anchorage.
**Tel** (800) 554-0552, 265-2494.
W alaskarailroad.com

**Anchorage Depot**
411 W 1st Ave, Anchorage.
**Tel** 265-2494.

**Denali Park Depot**
Mile 1.25, Denali National
Park Road.

**Fairbanks Depot**
1745 Johannsen Expressway,
Fairbanks. **Tel** 458-6025.

**Seward Depot**
410 Port Ave, Seward.
**Tel** 224-2268.

**Talkeetna Depot**
Mile 13.5, Talkeetna Spur Road,
Talkeetna.

## Tour Operators

**Mahay's Riverboat Service**
**Tel** 733-2223, (800) 736-2210.
W mahaysriverboat.com

**Phillips Cruises and Tours**
**Tel** 276-8023, (800) 544-0529.
W phillipscruises.com

**Phillips Cruises and Tours**, a flight to the Arctic Circle offering magnificent views, river trips in Talkeetna with **Mahay's Riverboat Service**, and a Glacier Bay cruise with glacier landings by helicopters. The railroad's website provides timetables and details on special tours.

## Tickets and Booking

In the summer, cruise lines and organized tour companies book up large blocks of seats on the Glacier Discovery, Coastal Classic, and Denali Star. While many clients are accommodated on the companies' special private rail cars, other seats get booked up quickly – especially the Alaska Railroad's own domed cars – so it pays to reserve online, or call or mail the railroad as far in advance as possible. For the smaller local trains, such as the summer Hurricane Turn, tickets are available onboard or from railroad reservation counters.

### The Alaska Railroad

Fairbanks
Nenana
*Tanana*
Clear
Healy
Denali National
Park
*Denali National Park*
Cantwell
*Susitna*
Talkeetna
Willow
Palmer
Wasilla
Matanuska
Eklutna
Anchorage
Valdez
Portage
Girdwood
Grandview
Whittier
Kenai
Moose Pass
Ninilchik
Seward
Homer
*GULF OF ALASKA*

0 km        100
0 miles        100

# Traveling by Car and RV

Although it is possible, with some effort, to travel around Alaska on public transport, nothing compares to the freedom of the open road that comes with using a private or rental vehicle. For both residents and visitors, driving is a necessary part of life and will also be the only means of reaching many sites of interest. The road system may be limited, but where it is possible to drive, few will be disappointed with what is on offer, as the scenery is spectacular throughout the state. In addition, some fabulously scenic routes, such as the Denali Highway, the Elliott Highway, the Steese Highway, and the back roads of Southeast Alaska are accessible only by car.

### Renting a Car

Anyone over 20 years of age can rent a vehicle, but some agencies impose a surcharge on people under 25. Overseas visitors need an International Driving License if their home license is not in Roman script. It is also essential to have a credit card to pay rental deposits, as few agencies accept cash. Child seats or cars for disabled drivers must be arranged in advance.

Visitors who rent a car in one city and leave it in another have to pay hefty drop-off fees. Cars must be returned with a full tank of gas.

Collision Damage Waiver (CDW) insurance, covering the car for any visible damage, and state and local taxes can increase the final total by 20 to 30 percent. Discounts may be available for members of the **American Automobile Association** (AAA) or the American Association of Retired Persons (*see p273*). Most national agencies, such as **Alamo**, **Avis**, **Budget**, **Hertz**, **Thrifty**, and **Enterprise**, have outlets at airports, but charge more than local agencies and may add airport taxes. For inexpensive rentals, try the local **Cheap-wheels Rent-a-Car**.

The biggest issue drivers will face is that rental agencies do not allow their non-4WD (four-wheel drive) cars to be taken on unpaved roads or to be driven off-road, and some of Alaska's finest routes are gravelled, including the McCarthy Road and the Taylor, Denali, Elliott, Steese, Dalton, and Top of the World Highways. Driving any of them in a rental vehicle will invalidate any insurance or maintenance agreements, which means an accident or breakdown could wind up being very costly. However, be aware that renting a 4WD vehicle will typically double the charge. Only **Denali Car Rental** allows gravel road travel (except on the Dalton Highway north of the Yukon River) in a non-4WD. They require advance booking, especially in the summer peak season.

Kodiak Island license plate

### Renting an RV

Renting a Recreational Vehicle (RV) can be an excellent, if expensive, way of getting around. Rates are lowest before mid-May and after mid-September. Smaller vehicles start around $185 per day in mid-summer with unlimited miles. Fully equipped motor homes usually include a bathroom, a kitchen, and hideaway beds, sleeping four to eight people and costing as much as $240 per day. National RV rental agencies such as **Cruise America** and local ones such as **ABC Motorhome Rentals**, **Alaska Motorhome Rentals**, and **Clippership Motorhome Rentals** offer a wide range of RVs. **Great Alaskan Holidays** also rents larger RVs with expanding "pop-out" living rooms. Private RV campsites usually provide dump stations and water and electricity hookups. Some rental agreements, especially those for over a week, include unlimited mileage, while others may limit drivers to 50 or 100 miles (80 or 160 km) per day, after which an additional per mile charge applies.

### Rules of the Road

Alaska's road systems are not as developed as those in the Lower 48, and there are less than 60 miles (96 km) of freeways. Highway speed limits range from 50 mph (80 kmph) on frost-heaved roads to 65 mph (105 kmph) for open stretches on main roads. The limit on some highways is 65 mph (105 kmph) but most roads are 55 mph (90 kmph). On gravel roads, the limit varies from 30 mph (50 kmph) to 50 mph (80 kmph). Posted

Traffic on Tudor Road, one of Anchorage's main thoroughfares

Recreational vehicle in Alaska

## The Great American RV

Every summer, people from the Lower 48 head north in motor homes equipped with every imaginable amenity, including televisions, satellite dishes, microwaves, gas cans, showers, bicycles, and row-boats. Many pull trailers carrying the family car or a pair of ATVs (all-terrain vehicle). The snail analogy is enhanced by the fact that the slow, heavily loaded RVs cannot reach speeds acceptable to drivers of smaller cars, and winding or busy roads can rapidly become jammed as traffic backs up behind a string of RVs. RV drivers should note that in Alaska, drivers must pull over by law if more than five vehicles are being held up behind their vehicle.

limits vary in towns, and during school hours, limits in school zones drop to 20 mph (30 kmph). Local police and the Alaska State Troopers enforce speed limits with particular vigilance in and around Anchorage, Fairbanks, and Juneau, and in road construction zones and 'safety corridors' (Anchorage–Girdwood, Sterling–Soldotna, Wasilla–Knik, and Wasilla–Big Lake), traffic fines are doubled.

The blood alcohol content limit in Alaska is 0.08 percent and there are heavy penalties for driving while drunk.

### Gas Stations

Fuel is much cheaper in the US than in Europe, but prices do vary, and gas is sold by the gallon, not by the liter. In remote areas, drivers may pay a third more than they would in major cities, and prices may double along the Dalton Highway and other gravel roads. All stations are self-service, and take most major credit cards at the pump. At non-automated stations, drivers may have to pay in advance. The cheapest gas is found at stores such as Fred Meyer, Carrs, and Costco. Those traveling on remote routes should carry extra gas as stations can be few and far between. The longest stretch without fuel is the 244-mile (390-km) leg between Coldfoot and Deadhorse on the Dalton Highway.

### Off-Road Driving

While traveling in remote parts of Alaska, it is important to have the latest maps, check the route in advance, and be aware of seasonal dangers. If there is a chance of snowfall, it may be best to change plans, as snow could make an otherwise viable route impassable and few minor roads are main-tained in the winter. A 4WD is essential in many areas, especially in the winter and during the spring thaw. Minor routes may have unbridged river crossings that become impassable to low-clearance vehicles after rain, and many forestry roads are little more than parallel ruts meant for logging trucks. Avoid driving off-track, as it damages vegetation and increases the risk of the vehicle bogging.

While information about the weather and routes will be available at tourist offices, local residents should also be able to help. It is wise to inform local tourist offices of your route and return date, and report back to them upon returning. Carry extra water, food, and gas for emergencies.

# The Alaska Highway

For many drivers, the Alaska Highway – formerly called the Alcan, short for the Alaska-Canada Highway – is the adventure of a lifetime. Crossing some of the wildest territory in the world, every stretch of this 1,390-mile (2,224-km) road offers breathtaking sights and experiences. Starting in Dawson Creek in Canada's British Columbia, it crosses remote ranges, running through taiga forests and past crystalline lakes into the Yukon Territory. At Haines Junction, drivers can take the Haines Cut-Off *(see p154)* to Southeast Alaska, or continue northwest through Canada's strikingly lovely Kluane National Park. For the next 200 miles (320 km), it crosses scenic mountain country to the US-Canada border, and continues northwest past the Alaskan gateway town of Tok for its final stretch to Fairbanks.

Truck hauling freight over Tok River Bridge east of Tok

## History of the Highway

Although an overland route to Alaska was being considered as early as 1930, it was not until the December 7, 1941, attack on Pearl Harbor that it became clear how militarily strategic this route would be. In February 1942, President Franklin D Roosevelt authorized the construction of the Alaska Highway, and soon, an agreement with Canada granted the US right of way and waived taxes, import duties, and immigration requirements.

The first surveyors who marched across the wilderness to locate a route roughly followed a chain of airstrips known as the Northwest Staging Route. Wherever possible, they used existing winter roads, pack trails, and trap lines, often having to divert to avoid muskeg and rough terrain. Construction began in March 1942, with temperatures of -40° C (-40° F), while in the summer, the workers battled mosquitoes, black flies, and the blazing sun.

In June 1942, the Aleutian Islands were invaded by the Japanese army and a sense of urgency arose to complete the road. More than 10,000 troops worked feverishly 16 hours a day, seven days a week, cutting trees, mashing out a road surface, and bridging rivers and streams. The final construction work ended on October 25, 1942. While the military road officially opened in November, civilian traffic was restricted until 1948.

Welcome sign, Alaska Highway

## Driving the Alaska Highway

The Alaska Highway has long had a reputation for challenging road conditions, but over time, the conditions have improved. The entire two-lane highway is now paved or chip-sealed, and is also shorter than it originally was, with at least 35 miles (56 km) of the historical route having been cut off due to rerouting and straightening. It is still a long trip, however, and the roadside scenery is so fabulous that it is worth allowing extra time for sightseeing.

Despite these improvements, some parts of the highway still suffer from serious cracks, frost heaves, and potholes, and every summer, long stretches of the road undergo extensive construction and repair, which can significantly slow drivers' progress. The roughest, most frost-heaved portion is between Canada's Kluane Lake and the Alaskan border, while the most serious grades and turns are found between Dawson Creek and Watson Lake in Canada. Information on highway conditions can be obtained from **Drive British Columbia**, **Yukon Daily Road Report**, and the **Alaska Road Traveler Information Service**.

As far as safety regulations go, drivers in Canada are required to use their headlights at all times and this is also required on some Alaska highways. Drivers should watch out for wildlife on the road. Moose are common everywhere and a collision can destroy both the animal and the vehicle. There are bison in northern British Columbia and the Yukon Territory, in the winter, caribou stand on the road to lick salt off the surface.

At the US-Canada border, US and Canadian citizens must present a passport. International visitors must show their passports and, if necessary, their visas *(see p270)*.

Alaska Highway passing through the Yukon Territory, Canada

## Alaska Highway Services

Between the 1940s and the early 1980s, fuel was available only every 250 miles (400 km) or so, but as the road became more traveled, more businesses sprang up along the route, and now there are gas stations approximately every 50 miles (80 km). There are also plenty of roadhouses and lodges along the way, where drivers can stop for a meal or a night's rest. The towns of Fort Nelson, Watson Lake, Whitehorse, Haines Junction, Beaver Creek, and Tok all have breakdown services and shops selling groceries and other supplies. Whitehorse, which is the capital of the Yukon Territory, has the most amenities and services.

## The Cassiar Highway

Coming from the US or the Canadian west coast, many drivers opt to take the Cassiar Highway, which is a shorter but equally beautiful and more rugged alternative to the Alaska Highway. The Cassiar Highway is entirely asphalt surfaced, but the stretch between Iskut and Dease Lake in Canada contains several steep and winding sections.

Beginning at the Skeena River Bridge at Kitwanga in the Canadian province of British Columbia, the Cassiar Highway runs north for 450 miles (720 km) before connecting with the Alaska Highway 13 miles (21 km) west of Watson Lake in the Yukon Territory.

The Cassiar is also the access route to Hyder, Alaska (see p130), 40 miles (64 km) west of Meziadin Junction, and to Telegraph Creek on the upper Stikine River (see p135), 70 miles (112 km) on a gravel road west of Canada's Dease Lake.

There are several highlights along the way. The Kitwanga Fort National Historic Site located at Mile 2 is the site of an 18th-century indigenous fortified village and offers excellent views of the Kitwanga River valley. The beautiful Kinaskan Lake Provincial Park at Mile 227 is good for trout fishing. Drivers can see huge jade boulders being cut at Jade City at Mile 375. Boya Lake at Mile 397 is known for its clear aquamarine waters and excellent camping and fishing.

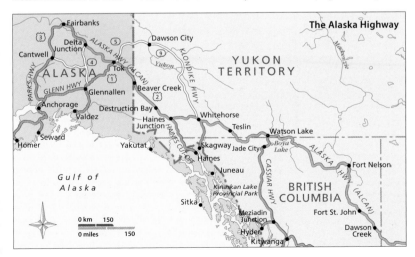

# General Index

# Acknowledgments

Dorling Kindersley would like to thank the following people whose contributions and assistance have made the preparation of this book possible.

## Main Contributor

After graduating from university, Deanna Swaney cast around in search of a career befitting a hopeless travel addict and eventually – following a bout of financial systems programming – she stumbled across travel writing and photography. As a result, over the past 20 years, she has researched and written eight first edition Lonely Planet titles, covering Bolivia; Tonga; Samoa; Iceland, Greenland, and the Faroe Islands; Zimbabwe, Botswana, and Namibia; Norway; The Arctic; and Namibia. She has also collaborated on dozens of Lonely Planet updates on six continents and has contributed text and photographs to numerous newspaper, magazine, and web features. Between trips, she finds time to work on construction projects around Big Lake, Alaska, and seeks out additions to her increasingly burdensome collections of rocks and frogs.

## Additional Contributor

Eric Amrine is a freelance writer, photographer, and musician living with his wife and two children in Seattle's Fremont district. His favorite travel assignments include hiking, kayaking, and wildlife, and have taken him through Alaska's Inside Passage via luxury yacht, white-water rafting in Oregon's Rogue River wilderness, and expedition cruising to the pristine beaches and remote islands of the Sea of Cortez in Mexico. Eric is passionate about the Caribbean, having reviewed the cruise ships that regularly sail there.

**Fact Checkers** Don Pitcher, Claus Vogel
**Proofreader** Vandana Bhagra
**Indexe**r Jyoti Dhar

## Design and Editorial

*Publisher* Douglas Amrine
*Publishing Managers* Jane Ewart, Scarlett O'Hara
*Senior Editor* Kathryn Lane
*Senior Designer* Paul Jackson
*Senior Cartographic Editor* Casper Morris
*Senior DTP Designer* Jason Little
*DTP Designer* Natasha Lu
*Picture Researcher* Ellen Root

## Editorial and Design Revisions

Louise Abbott, Claire Baranowski, Mariana Evmolpidou, Emer FitzGerald, Anna Freiberger, Camilla Gersh, Julia Harris-Voss, Mohammad Hassan, Christine Heilman, McKibben Jackinsky, Cincy Jose, Bharti Karakoti, Sumita Khatwani, Priyanka Kumar, Phoebe Lowndes, Hayley Maher, Alison McGill, Sonal Modha, George Nimmo, Carolyn Patten, Helen Peters, Marianne Petrou, Don Pitcher, Rada Radojicic, Ellen Root, Ankita Sharma, Neil Simpson, Susana Smith, Joanna Stenlake, Rachel Thompson, Conrad Van Dyk

**DK Picture Library** Romaine Werblow
**Production Controller** Linda Dare

## Additional Photography

Geoff Brightling, Eric Crichton, Peter Gathercole, Frank Greenaway, Andrew Holligan, Ellen Howdon, Dave King, Ian O'Leary, Kim Taylor.

**Cartography** DK Cartography, London

## Special Assistance

Dorling Kindersley would like to thank the following for their kind permission to photograph at their establishments: Alaska Aviation Heritage Museum, Alaska Native Heritage Center, Jason Wettstein and the Alaska SeaLife Center, Alaska State Museum, Janet Asaro and the Anchorage Museum of History and Art, Baranov Museum, FOAST Law Enforcement Museum, Hammer Museum, Isabel Miller Museum, Petroglyph Beach State Historic Site, Pioneer Park Air Museum, Pratt Museum, Saxman Totem Park, Sheldon Jackson Museum, Sheldon Museum, Sitka National Historical Park, Soldotna Historical Society Museum, Southeast Alaska Discovery Center, Totem Heritage Center, Town Docks Museum, Hull, Valdez Museum, Wrangell Museum.

## Picture Credits

Key: a-above; b-below/bottom; c-centre; f-far; l-left; r-right; t-top

Works of art have been reproduced with the permission of the following copyright holders: *Crystal Lattice* © Robert Pfitzenmeier Front Endpaper Ltl, 66; *Raven the Creator* © John Hoover 76tr.

The publisher would like to thank the following for their kind permission to reproduce their photographs:

**123RF.com:** Alberto Loyo 222tr.

**Alamy Images:** Accent Alaska.com 10cl, 13tl, 180; Ace Stock Limited 85br; Alaska Stock LLC 24tr, 24bl, 44cl, 44br, 45tl, 45cr, 84tr, 82tr, 82bl, 118bl, 182cl 184t, 231br, 262b; Alaska Stock LLC/Design Pics Inc 237-236; Alaska Stock/Design Pics Inc/Patrick Endres 218; Wally Bauman 161c; Walter Bibikow 38br; Steve Bly 23tr, 44tr; blickwinkel 45br; David Boag 119br; Bill Brooks 41tl, 154bl; Bryan & Cherry Alexander Photography 51tr, 60b, 224tl; Loetscher Chlaus 179cl, 189tl, 219b, 220tr, 224br, 225crb; Gary Cook 183tr, 199cra, 199crb, 199bl; Danita Delimont 48t, 139cl, 166cl, 204cl, 261tl; Danita Delimont Agent/Dave Bartruff 254bc; David Sanger Photography 22t, 27bl, 36-37c; Design Pics Inc 11tr, 116tr; Design Pics Inc / Mike Criss 86-87; Design Pics Inc / Michael DeYoung 2-3; Design Pics Inc /Matt Hage 250br; Robert Destefano 38tr; Douglas Peebles Photography 240tc; DY Riess MD 41cr; Dennis Frates 248tr; Lee Foster 66; Jeff

Greenberg 248cl; Blaine Harrington III 62-63; Bill Heinsohn 15tl; Imagebroker 90cl, 91c, 150cr, 153tl; Jon Arnold Images 57bl, 57br, 79cr, 90tr, 188cl, 193bl; Jon Arnold Images/Walter Bibikow 40cl; Steven J. Kazlowski 137br; Terrance Klassen 21b; Dennis MacDonald 74tl; Medioimages 30tr, 136t; Ron Niebrugge 20t, 21tr, 22bl, 23b, 31tl, 38clb, 47bc, 48br, 65tr, 106cla, 106clb, 165bc, 183cr, 188tr, 193tl, 198cl, 220cl, 222cl, 223b, 252bc; Luc Novovitch 37tr; Purcell Team 36clb; RGB Ventures/SuperStock 10bc, 36br; Kevin Schafer 203b, 214bc; John Schwieder 147tl, 158cl, 194br; Steve Bloom Images 210cl; Allen Thornton 165cl; Daniel Tycholiz 251tr; Mireille Vautier 230tc; Visions of America, LLC 109cb; Westend61 GmbH /Erich Kuchling 207crb; Doug Wilson 44bl; Richard Wong 11br; WorldFoto 39bl.

**Alaska Airlines**: Alaska Airlines 280b.

**Alaska Photographics.com**: 89bl, 156; Patrick J. Endres 20bl, 25tl, 33crb, 37cr, 40tr, 40br, 41bl, 42-43c, 43ca, 43bl, 47tc, 49cc, 49br, 88, 115b, 163b, 173bl, 176cr, 188bl, 189cr, 193cr, 197bl, 198bl, 199tl, 210tr, 210bl, 222br, 223tl, 226b.

**Alaska Public Lands Information Centers/NPS**: 70cla.

**Courtesy of the Alaska Railroad Corporation**: Calvin Hall 286b, 287tl.

**Alaska SeaLife Center**: Clark James 104cl; Jason Wettstein 104clb, 105tl, 105cra.

**Alaska Volcano Observatory**: Alaska Division of Geological and Geophysical Surveys/C Nye 29tl, 211cr, C.Neal 211br; U.S. Park Service/ B Cella 192cl; Image Analysis Laboratory, NASA Johnson Space Center 28cl, 28cr; Bill Stahl 29bl; Game McGimsey 29tr.

**Alaska Wild Berry Products**: 80tl.

**Photos courtesy of Anchorage Museum of History and Art**: 71cr, 73cb.

**Autographs and Ogden Photography**: © 2005 Doug Ogden 185tr.

**Bridgeman Art Library**: Jamestown-Yorktown Educational Trust, VA, USA Alaska, Purchased from Russia in 1867 (tapestry), Mabelle Linnea Holmes (1894-1987) 8-9.

**Corbis**: 56br, 58bc, 151br; Dave Bartruff 25tr; Tom Bean 26crb, 31cra, 207t, 209tl; Peter Beck 44-45c; Joel Bennett 26cl, 208bc; Bettmann 52, 55br, 57tr, 58cb, 59tr, 60tl; Gary Braasch 121br; Tom Brakefield 33b; Brandon D. Cole 84br, 131bl; Richard A. Cooke 205b; Roy Corral 211tl; Richard Cummins 257tl; Design Pics/Michael DeYoung 13br; Michael DeYoung 157b, 265t; Kevin Fleming 46cl, 133br, 159b; Natalie Fobes 61tl, 202, 214cl; Werner Forman 25bl; D. Robert/Lorri Franz 34br; H.S. Graves 58t; Gunter Marx Photography 59br, 290cl; Peter Guttman 27crb; Historical

Picture Archive 54t; Eric and David Hosking 113tr, 240br; Rob Howard 155bl; JAI / Walter Bibikow 135-134; Ann Johansson 24br, 235b; Mark A. Johnson 146bl; Wolfgang Kaehler 39cra; Karen Kasmauski 186cl; Steve Kaufman 35cr, 169tr, 195cr, 209b; Blake Kent 197tr; Kit Kittle 139tr; Bob Krist 81br, 91tr 126; Dan Lamont 26bl, 133tl; Jacques Langevin 36tr; Danny Lehman 166bl; George D. Lepp 232cl; W. Wayne Lockwood, M.D 32cr; Michael Maslan Historic Photographs 36cla; Arthur Morris 233tc; David Muench 30cla; Museum of History and Industry 56cl; Pat O'Hara 24-5c, 33cl, 42cla, 231tl, 235tl; Charles O'Rear 36bl; Papilio /Bjorn Backe 195cb; Douglas Peebles 39tl, 43cb; PEMCO - Webster & Stevens Collection/ Museum of History and Industry, Seattle 42tr; Greg Probst 31bl, 129tr; Progressive Image/Bob Rowan 25cra, 27tr; Lynda Richardson 84cl; David Samuel Robbins 249bl; Joel W. Rogers 34tr, 107tl; Galen Rowell 34-35c, 64tr, 88br, 226tl, 227cr; Galen Rowell 221t; Kevin Smith 12bl; Richard Hamilton Smith 169br; Scott T. Smith 33cr; Paul A. Souders 32bc, 33bl, 42bl, 64bl, 75tl, 89t, 131br, 162bl, 186bl, 233bl; Vince Streano 39crb, 151tl, 174cl, 187br; Tim Thompson 132cl, 147cr, 151cr, 216cl; Visuals Unlimited/Hugh Rose 225cra; Kennan Ward 35br, 111cr; Karl Weatherly 137tr; Stuart Westmorland 167tl, 217br; Staffan Widstrand 27cla, 225bl; Yogi, Inc. 168b; Zefa/Frank Krahmer 225br, /Elisabeth Sauer 164bc; Zuma /US Airforce/Joshua Strang 176b.

**Dreamstime.com**: Aivoges 14tc; Galyna Andrushko 170-171, 190-191; Hasan Can Balcioglu 15br; Bennymarty 127t; Cecoffman 114; Chamey 175br; Sorin Colac 4c, Tom Dowd 181b; Eddydegroot 288c; Jeanninebryan 5cr; Karrapavan 14bc; Jeffrey Kreulen 100tl; Roman Krochuk 187tl; Paul Lemke 100br; Marchello74 99br; Kenneth Mellott 18; Raymona Pooler 223cr; Cenk Unver 4tc; Lawrence Weslowski Jr 98cl, 99tr, 253tr.

**Ben Moeller-Gaa**: 246bl.

**Getty Images**: Michael Cogliantry 268-9; Design Pics / Patrick Endres 196t; Digital Vision 176cl; John Elk 246cra; Gerry Ellis 225cl; Kim Heacox 30-1c; David Madison 228-9; National Geographic Image Collection/Joseph Baylor Roberts 213t; Lucas Payne 101cl; Photographer's Choice 230b.

**The Granger Collection, New York**: 53bl, 54bl, 56-7c.

**Historic Anchorage Hotel**: 238br, 239br, 242bc.

**Holland America Line**: 33clb, 258tr, 258br, 259tr; Andy Newman 260bc.

**House on the Rock B&B**: 241tr.

**iStockphoto.com**: ad_foto 130b

**Juneau Convention and Visitors Bureau**: 32tr.

Mary Evans Picture Library: 55tc, 56bl, 57cr.

Masterfile: Andrew Wenzel 42br.

Mount Aurora Lodge: 244tc.

Courtesy of National Park Service Digital Image Archives: 212tl, 212b.

National Oceanic and Atmospheric Administration: Central Library 29crb.

North Wind Picture Archives: 55clb.

Photolibrary: Index Stock Imagery, Inc /Mark Gibson 46bc.

Silverbow Inn Bakery and Catering: 243tr.

Deanna Swaney: 82clb, 83cr, 101br, 161c, 245br.

Kevin Turinsky: 255tr.

University of Washington Libraries, Special Collections: Negative Nummber UW9069 57tl.

US Fish and Wildlife Service, Alaska Image Library: 33tc, 33br, 161bc, 213br, 232tr; Steve Amstrup 111br; Bob Angell 217bl; Kate Banish 32br; Connie Barclay 227tl; Vernon Byrd 216br; David Cline 33tr; Donna Dewhurst 161cl, 161crb 217tc; Steve Hillebrand 32bl, 111cl; Dean Kildaw 217cl; John Sarvis 161br; Art Sowls 217tr, 217cr.

USDA Forest Service, Tongass National Forest: 31crb

Harry M Walker: 70br, 234b.

Front Endpapers: Alamy Images: Accent Alaska Rtr, Alaska Stock/Design Pics Inc / Patrick Endres Rtl; Lee Foster Lcla; Alaska Photographics.com: Patrick J. Endres Rcr; Corbis: Bob Krist Lcra; Natalie Fobes Rbc; Dreamstime.com: Cecoffman Lcrb.

Cover images: Front and Spine: Alamy Stock Photo: Dennis Frates; Back: Dreamstime.com: Eugene Everett.

All other images © Dorling Kindersley
For further information see: www.dkimages.com

# Transport Map of Alaska

ALASKA
CANADA

*Kenai Peninsula*

*SE Alaska*

RUSSIA

*Bering Sea*

*Arctic Ocean*

*Chukchi Sea*

Point Lay

Point Hope

Kivalina
*Noatak*
Cape Krusenstern NM
Noatak

Kotzebue

Shishmaref

Deering

Wales

*Bering Land Bridge National Preserve*

Teller
Kougarok

Council
Ha

Nome

Shaktoolik

Gambell
Savoonga

*St. Lawrence Island*

Stebbins

Kotlik

Sheldon Point

Anvik

Mountain Village
Holy Cross

Hooper Bay

Newtok

Kasigluk
Bethel

Kipnuk
Kwigillingok
Quinhagak
*Wood Sta*

*Kuskokwim Bay*

Platinum
Togiak
Alek

*Walrus Islands State Game Sanctuary*

Dilling

*Bristo Bay*

## The Kenai Peninsula

Anchorage
*Chugach State Park*

*College Fjord*

Hope
Whittier
Blackstone Bay

*Captain Cook State Recreation Area*

*Resurrection Pass Trail*

Moose Pass

Kenai
Sterling
*Kenai*

Cooper Landing

Soldotna

*Chugach National Forest*

Chenega

Clam Gulch

Seward

Ninilchik

Nikolaevsk

Anchor Point
Homer

Halibut Cove

Seldovia

*Kenai National Wildlife Refuge*

*Kenai Fjords National Park*

| 0 km | 50 |
| 0 miles | 50 |

St. Paul
*Pribilof Islands*

St. George

Po
Heide

Port Moller
Ch

Cold Bay
*Izembek NWR*
Sand Point

False Pass
King Cove

Dutch Harbor
Akutan
Unalaska

*Aleutian* B *Islands*

*Pac*

## Key

- ✈ International airport
- ✈ Domestic airport/airstrip
- ⛴ Ferry port
- — Alaska Highway
- — Major road
- ⋯ Minor road
- — Alaska Railroad
- ⋯ Alaska Marine Highway
- ▬ International border

31901060970193